REV NICK MERCER
Director of Training
LONDON BIBLE COLLEGE
GREEN LANE
NORTHWOOD HA6 2UW
(09274) 26064 (Home & Office)

ANY OLD IRON

ANY OLD IRON

ANTHONY BURGESS

HUTCHINSON
London Sydney Auckland Johannesburg

This edition first published in Great Britain by
Hutchinson, an imprint of Century Hutchinson Ltd,
Brookmount House, 62–65 Chandos Place London WC2N 4NW

Century Hutchinson Australia Pty Ltd
89–91 Albion Street, Surry Hills, NSW 2010

Century Hutchinson New Zealand Ltd
PO Box 40–086, Glenfield, Auckland 10, New Zealand

Century Hutchinson South Africa (Pty) Ltd
PO Box 337, Bergvlei, 2012 South Africa

Phototypeset by Input Typesetting Ltd, London
Printed and bound in Great Britain by
Butler & Tanner Ltd, Frome, Somerset

British Library Cataloguing in Publication Data

Burgess, Anthony, *1917–*
  Any old iron.
  I. Title
  823'.914 [F]

  ISBN 0–09–173842–3

In Memory of
Richard Ellmann
1918–1987

Eisen, Lumpen, Papier!

Arab street cry in Tel Aviv

This madness has come on us for our sins.

Tennyson: *The Idylls of the King*

A gentleman in the street: 'Mr Jones, I believe?'
The Duke of Wellington: 'If you believe that you
  will believe anything.'

UN

STEEL, as you probably don't have to be reminded, is an alloy based on iron. It contains anything from 0.1 to 1.7 per cent of carbon, as well as traces of sulphur, phosphorus, manganese, nickel and chromium. It is tough and yet malleable, so you can make swords out of it. It is Mars's own alloy. Its only trouble is that it deteriorates in air. The layman assumes that this has something to do with acids. But the deterioration is caused by electrolytic attack, and electrolytes do not have to be acid. Natural salts like sodium chloride and sal ammoniac can eat into steel and devastate it. I'm no metallurgist, merely a retired terrorist and teacher of philosophy, but I can see how metallurgists have to reject the claim that the sword Excalibur survived into the twentieth century. All those salts resident in air and soil and water, eating steadily at what was itself called the eater. For the name Excalibur comes from the Welsh Caledvwlch, which is tied up with the Irish Caladbolg, and Caladbolg means hard belly or capable of eating anything.

Some ignoramuses in Cardiff and elsewhere called for radiocarbon dating to confirm that the rather moth-eaten sword they handled with reverence and wonder belonged to the Arthurian age. But radiocarbon dating won't work on an inorganic substance like steel. It can give you the age of a chunk of wood, because the radioisotope ^{14}C gets into wood from the atmosphere when the wood is still a living plant, and it decays into the nitrogen isotope ^{14}N with a half life of 5730 years. The wooden scabbard of the alleged Caledvwlch, allegedly deposited with that genuine chunk of metal in the cellars of Monte Cassino, has, I believe, been dated back to the sixth century after the death of

1

Christ by use of the carbon fourteen technique, but there is no device which can give the age of metal.

I never saw the sword, but I understand that it was of the broad variety, with a sharp point and two cutting edges: an offensive weapon, then, no mere symbolic ornament. Hilt and guard were both long gone and point and edges blunted, but the blade shone with a memory of defiance, and on the blade had been stippled a capital A or alpha. It was shallow close pitting, presumably done with a nail and a hammer. This was clearly an initial of ownership. The A, I understand, was serifed with stylized beechleaves, and a leafy flourish grew an inch and a half out of the apex of the A, on its left side. The A did not primarily denote the ownership of King Arthur, who may or may not have existed, but that of a more formidable personage who certainly existed: I mean Attila the Hun. The legend of Attila's lieutenant general Scotta finding the sword on the Hungarian plain is, I think, well known. Aware of bleeding in his ankle, Scotta looked down to find a swordpoint sticking out of the earth. He disinterred the whole weapon and had no doubt that this was the legendary Sword of Mars, which conferred victory on all who owned it. He gave it to Attila, who ordered the stippling of his initial (A or alpha: he knew both Latin and Greek). The Sword of Mars did not bestow victory on Attila in his northern Italian campaign, and, before he limped back to the Danube, he bequeathed the weapon to Aetius, the Roman general who had been both his friend and his enemy. After the assassination of Aetius on imperial orders from Ravenna, the sword passed to Ambrosius Aurelanius, king of Britain.

You will find this story in Giraldus Cambrensis, who got it from Christianus Piger, who got it from a document called *Notitia Dignitatum*. Or so I understand: I have little taste for light reading. The continuity of alphaic ownership was, I should think, a matter of sheer coincidence. I reject the notion of divine ordination that the sword of the Scourge of God should pass to a British defender of the faith through a literal irony resolved in God's own designation of himself as Alpha (though also Omega), destroyer and preserver as in Hindu theology. It is all superstition and a highly implausible story.

To return to this matter of the sword's preservation. One of the early biographers of Attila the Hun, Achthophoros of Constantinople, states that the great conqueror tried to fix the eastern limits of his plan of conquest of the Eurasian landmass by visiting the Emperor of China and concluding a nonaggression pact with him. On his journey across what would now be the steppes of Russia, he observed what Marco Polo was to observe centuries later – the gushing of mineral oil from the earth. The sages of China, who recorded that Chinese deep level mining for mineral oil went back as far as what we would call 330 BC, taught Attila that mineral oil was a sovereign preservative of metals. It was possible then that, during periods of truce and the renewal of a childhood friendship, Attila taught Aetius the secret of prolongation of the life of weapons. The Sword of Mars, or Excalibur, was perhaps laid in a sealed bath of oil rich in Russian naphthenes. I do not believe Ambrosius Aurelanius brought a quantity of this specific back from Rome, or Ravenna, but I think it possible that olive or walnut oil was used, even in Britain, for the conservation of Excalibur, since any oil will ward off electrolytic attack. But I cannot accept that the sword waved by the Sons of Arthur, as they called themselves, was Excalibur at all: at the earliest it dated from the late middle ages and was probably an Irish *claidheamh mor* of no greatly noble provenance. To hell with them anyway. I have had my fill of terrorism.

THE implausibility of this Excalibur story attaches to the man who, by his own account, brought the sword back from Soviet Russia at great personal risk. This was Reginald Morrow Jones, an implausible name for a Welshman, but his father was implausible too. I knew Reg Jones very well, and I met his father, and also his Russian mother. Of these two I must say something.

David, properly Dafydd, Jones was so christened in Calvinistic Methodist ritual in a chapel in Tredegar in the county then known as Monmouthshire. His father Elis Wyn Jones was not much given to religion, though there was a strong element of Calvinistic determinism in the brand of socialism he picked up during breaks for snap. He had worked for many years as an anthracite miner and been morally shaken by two pit explosions and morally unmanned by a third. His wife, Florence Mary née Evans, had a cardiac weakness aggravated by the bearing of their one child.

3

She was from Caernarvon in North Wales and was considered a foreigner in the south. A malicious false report of her husband's being brained by a falling pitprop in that third explosion induced a terminal infarctus. Elis Wyn Jones wept bitterly and cursed God.

He then yielded nightly to the volume intoxication of weak Welsh bitter beer. One night he brutally clouted young David when he caught him onanizing to a steel engraving of Belshazzar's Feast in the family Bible. David Jones ran away to sea, joining a coastal vessel at Cardiff as a deckhand. He was put to work in the galley as peeler and chopper and brewer of tea. But when the cook, who had a fine line in the rhetoric of revivalism, succumbed to delirium tremens off Newcastle, the boy of fifteen took over his simple crafts without notable complaint from the crew. He was blessed with a powerful stomach, and in the roughest seas he never blenched even at the frying of fish with onions.

Shortly after the son left home, the father had a dream in which his own father leaped like a wallaby while trying to light an end of candle stuck in a gold sconce. He had not heard from the old man for some time, but he understood that he was doing well in Australia though now, so the dream said, he might not be doing so well. There was nothing for Elis Wyn Jones in Old South Wales, so he took his small savings to a shipping agency in Cardiff and bought a ticket for New. He was not surprised, on arrival in Sydney, to find the old man terminally ill. The old man, Haydn Mozart Jones (tone deaf, unlike the choirmaster who had begotten him on one of his contraltos), had deserted his wife in Bangor and gone gold prospecting in Ballarat, Victoria. In old age he was said to bear a lively resemblance to Karl Marx, but so did many Victorians. He had lived as full a life as the colony offered and died in moderate affluence. Elis Wyn Jones returned to Monmouthshire with his inheritance and lived in sin with a girl from Ebbw Vale in a semidetached house on Sunnybank Road, Blackwood. There, in the names, you see the English inheritance of the county. It was never considered quite to be South Wales until its ancient name of Gwent was restored to it.

David, the son, was later to tell tales of the seafarer's life which

4

did not necessarily have to be believed, Wales and the spirit of romance going well together. For instance, he swore he had served as cook on a freighter called the *Bluebell*, whose first mate was a thick-spoken Pole named Korzeniowski. This foreigner was a fiercely intolerant seadog born, as for some reason he was always saying, in the eighty-fifth year of the Muscovite oppression of his country. This same Korzeniowski wrote foolishly, under the name Conrad, about the loss of the ship called the *Titanic*:

> You build a 45 000 ton hotel of thin steel plates to secure the patronage of, say, a couple of thousand rich people, you decorate it in the style of the Pharaohs or in Louis Quinze style – I don't know which – and to please the aforesaid fatuous handful of individuals, who have more money than they know what to do with, and to the applause of two continents, you launch that mass with 2000 people on board at twenty-one knots across the seas – a perfect exhibition of the modern blind trust in mere material and appearances . . .

David Jones kept that newspaper clipping until it fell to pieces. 46 000 tons, to be accurate, he used to say. If Korzeniowski had had his way, he said, there would have been no *Titanic*, or else its master would have been named Korzeniowski, a mariner whose experience in the southern seas had taught him to steer clear of growlers. He regarded the disaster as a judgment on the rich, leaving out of account the huddled masses in steerage seeking a new life, as well as the intrepid captain and mates and those who went down doing their duty. David Jones, who had once in extreme youth heard a performance of Vaughan Williams's Sea Symphony in Newport, used to sing that bit, though inaccurately.

David Jones sailed from Southampton on the SS *Titanic* at noon on 10 April 1912. That was certainly when the ship sailed, but posterity has only his word that he was on it. 'Bloody lucky they said, boy,' he said to me more than thirty years after, 'to get that bloody berth, me not having got much higher in the trade than banana boats carrying a baker's dozen of passengers and one eastern run very low down in the scale with the P and O line, assistant to the vegetable cook. But the bloody *Titanic* was bad news almost before she was laid down, among them that knew, meaning common seafaring folk that had read their bloody Bibles. Not even God Almighty himself will be able to sink this bloody ship was the blasphemous boast that was started off by Bruce Ismay of the White Star line. That was asking for bloody trouble, boy bach. Greatest liner afloat, eleven storeys high and a sixth of a mile long and so unsinkable there was a shortage of bloody lifeboats to prove it.

'Well, there was me overboiling cabbage for the steerage, Micks most of them and they liked their cabbage overdone, getting the odd glimpse from a long way off of the swells and the nobs, the Astors and the Morgans and for all I know, I never checked on it, the bloody Rothschilds, and there was a loudmouthed common Yankee bitch that got herself called the Unsinkable Molly Brown, all got up to kill in their feathers and finery, while me and three others was crammed in a bloody rathole stinking of oil and vomit, boy bach. It was what you might call a microcosmopolitan capitalist society, those being the words of Ianto Pritchard who was educated.

'Then in the middle of the night, five days out, there was a smell of green ice, like a slap in the bloody jaw it was, coming through the open porthole, and we knew something was wrong, and Ianto, from Newport he was, said to me *It's the smell of the judgment come upon us, boyo.* So we dress and up to the deck and the first thing we see is these Irish comeallyes with their flat caps on but no overcoats, they not having any see, playing football with chunks of the green ice that had broke off the mother berg. Then it was something nobody could believe, believe you me, and little Ianto kept crying on the great white Jesus, it was like in a fairy story, this bloody great tower of a green growler flashing and sizzling in the little bit of a moon there was, longer than a street, bloody beautiful she was, sort of singing a great bloody Hallelujah Chorus in praise of the Lord God Destroyer of the Works of bloody Man, and she sort of sidles alongside without so much as a by your leave and slices two hundred bloody feet out of the side of the poor bloody ship below the waterline. Everybody laughed at first, it was done so bloody neat, bachgen. And those that were playing poker for high stakes in first class were going haw haw, make us a couple of hours late at New York what I guess and calculate, we being thirty-six hours away by what they called the estimated sailing time.

'Then capitalism started to show its green fangs when they found out we were going down and not enough lifeboats. Women and children first, and nobody questioned that, asking why women and kids, and looking back I think it should have been bloody questioned. Whether I dreamed it or not I can't be sure, but there was one man to my imagination or recollection who went down with that ship, a very poor man in steerage that looked a bit like a lascar, I thought at first he was Welsh because of his voice, and he had read all the books of wisdom and he had the gift of healing, because he cured headaches and tooth-aches with the touch of his long dirty brown fingers, and he went down very dignified with the ship, while useless high society women were saved and lived to give posh dinner parties and talk about their terrible experiences my dear, boy bach.

'And I have a nightmare still sometimes, and I see a lifeboat being lowered full of useless foulmouthed common sluts, what you might call a floating knocking shop with no customers, the customers all being at the taffrail looking gravely down at their watery grave which needs no bloody digging. And yet these would never be customers, being all serious labour leaders and great musicians and thinkers and engineers and big revivalist ministers, and all with beards waving in the song of mockery sung by the sea wind and all useful to the world, and a voice cries over the wind's song and the organ of the storm and the bursting of the boilers and the screams of the scalded *Where's the bloody justice?*

'But where was the justice with the rich capitalists and their brazen ladies bribing the ship's officers and the leading seamen in charge of the lifeboats, let us all go off to safety as one happy everliving family, Rothschilds and bloody Rothschildren, here is a cheque for two pounds no make it guineas made out on the back of last night's dinner menu, twopenny stamp stuck on to make it legal, lower away, stand back you scum, one last load of gentry, lower away there? And the Irish scum in steerage, swelled with my overboiled cabbage, shot at by this bastard of an officer Murdoch, Scotchman he was, loading up on the starboard side, listening to "Nearer My God to Thee", song of the Church of England and the ruling class, played by the ship's band while the scum had to sing "Faith of Our Fathers" with Father Byles I believe his name was, waiting to go down with no bloody orchestra, boy bach.

'I got off in Boat C, one of the Englehardt collapsibles, with three fireman and the steerage barber and twenty-seven women and kids, and four Limehouse Chinese huddling under the seats that thought Murdoch could see and shoot them for being Chinks, but Murdoch couldn't see, the murdering Scotch bastard. Then he let Ismay on, and Ismay stood in the boat shivering with all the steerage women there, a toff and the boss that should rightly have gone down with the skipper. So it was lower away, and a few yards out we saw her start to go down, and then a lot more yards away, more like a half mile, we saw her sucked into the sea, people clinging like woodlice to rails and capstans and winches, and the last hundred and fifty feet of her stood up straight like a bloody monument against the eternal stars, and then it was all over. Everybody wailed and wept, even some of these Chinks. She went down at 2.20 ack emma by the watch of one of these Chinks, an Ingersoll he was proud of, triumph of Western science, less than three hours after the collision, and the *Carpathia* sighted Englehardt C about four o'clock and we were dithering up that ladder ready for a hot mug of tea nearly all rum.'

WHEN David Jones landed at New York, according to his story, he was very voluble to the press and he was asked how he felt about being safe and sound when so many had perished in the deep. It was then that he was struck dumb and had to wrestle like a Jacob with the God of himself, this God asking him what were his special qualifications for continuing his life, what of outstanding value had he to contribute to the world. David Jones was later convinced that he had seen, in the *New York Universal Record*, a journal that appears never to have existed, a cartoon fantasizing the perils of contemporary trust in technology. A ship called the SS *Colossus* was shown going down with King George V and Queen Mary, Shaw, Kipling, Arnold Bennett, Wells, Korzeniowski, Asquith, Lloyd George, Sir Edward Elgar and Sir

8

Hubert Parry on board. Thumbing his nose at the foundering was a nondescript vulgar little man on a raft. In his guilty nightmares, David Jones identified this figure with himself, the mediocre Welsh seacook.

He now became a landcook, and he got a job in a short-order eatery on West 35th Street, his being a *Titanic* survivor granting him a certain cachet. What, you don't like the way these eggs is scrambled, don't you know he was chef on the *Titanic*? To which the expected response was: Well, I guess he should have gone down with it, eggs and all.

He lodged in a decrepit lodging house on 12th Street. It was recommended to him by another expatriate Welshman, also a David or Dafydd or Dai, a Williams however, with a locker full of mildewed books on the history of the principality. Dai Williams was given to a kind of Welsh nationalism, not at that time a popular movement and virtually unknown in the United States, a great country of fresh starts where, unlike Fenianism, it seemed to have no relevance. It was not, though equally irrelevant, unheard of in the Argentine, some of whose snub-nosed Indian women had been taught Welsh by their common-law husbands and even forgotten their own uncouth dialects. Money was eventually to trickle from Latin America to help the cause of an independent Wales. It was Dai Williams who taught Dai Jones something of the long troubled history of Cymru, which the English or Saeson called Wales or the Land of the Foreigner.

'The Celts, boy,' he would say, 'were bloody Christians two hundred years after the death of the Big White Jesus, God give his bones rest, and they kept their hot breath blowing on the faith when the whole of the island called Britain which was their rightful property worshipped false gods, Odin and Thor and other bloody deaf and wooden idols. Roman Christianity it was, with hot baths and white woollen togas and marble temples dedicated to the one true God until the murdering bloody Saxons came in and drove us into Cornwall and Cumberland and the stronghold of what we call our native mountains, smashing up Roman Christian Britain as they'd smashed up the holy mother of the Empire itself, them or their filthy hairy brothers and uncles and cousins. But the princes arose like a flame in Cymru – Cadwallon the Long Handed and his son Maelgwyn Gwynedd and the other Cadwallon that was the great-grandson of the first one. And they strove gainst the brutal bastards under the swine with the uncomely name of Ethelfrith, king of the Angles in Northumbria, till by brutality and treachery we lost Strathclyde and the whole of Northern Britain and got smashed and butchered at the infamous battle of Chester. And Cadwallon died in his last noble and frustrated effort to break the evil power and win back the British crown and left to his son Cadwaladr a country plagued and broken and stricken, God curse the foreign bastards that had the bloody nerve to call the Welsh foreign bastards on their own soil. Aye, Cadwaladr, king of Gwynedd and dead in rage and misery six hundred and thirty-five bloodstained years after the bloody death of the great white redeemer of human souls.'

This Dai Williams was a man from Pembroke. He was sixty years old and worked as a tailor in the New York clothing district, traditionally (not that the tradition went back very far) a preserve of Jews forced to a new diaspora by murderous bastards of Christian Russians. Dai Williams knew neither Welsh nor Hebrew, but he had been told by some drunken false scholar that the two tongues were cognate, and that the Welsh were originally a lost tribe of Israel that miraculously, or through some quirk of climate, became pale, tall and fair-haired. So he regarded the Ashkenazim as cousins and brothers and sisters when he tried to encourage the sweated tailors and seamstresses to fight for their rights, but this proclamation of kinship was not reciprocated. He himself was small, stooped, blackeyed and greybearded, with what the Welsh term a biblical face, and he had picked up Jewish gestures and vocal inflections of dismay. He was unmarried and lived mostly on the one pan of mutton broth which, with sporadic additions and constant simmering, had nourished him, he claimed, for the near thirty years of his expatriation. He would never go back to Wales, he swore, a stinking place full of corruption and hypocrisy and lechery, but he would keep alive for ever in his heart the record of the foul wrongs done to the land of his fathers and try to spread the word that a new generation might some day arise ruthlessly to right those wrongs.

'And with his bitter death, boy, the hope of the recovery of

10

the north of Britain was for ever lost, aye. Six hundred years of struggle between the princes of the tribes and the kings who swore they wore the crown bestowed by the Caesars of Constantinople. And there was Rhodri the Great that fought back against the invading pagan Danes but was slain brutally by the brutish bloody Mercians. And Howel Dda, that made himself master of the land but bowed down in homage and kissed the filthy toenails of the bloody usurper Athelstan.'

Dai Williams got Dai Jones very drunk on the night of St David's Day on whisky Scotch and Irish, complaining bitterly at one point during the long carousal that the hypocritical drunken Saxons reeling out of their meadhalls had smashed the pipes and vats and the whole tradition of a native Cymric firewater or water of life. But then he extolled the Brythonic Celts for their sobriety and lechery, qualities unknown among their Scots and Irish cousins.

'Owen of the Red Beard, boy, and his son Dafydd, our bloody name, that lorded it over the chiefs of Gwynedd, never a drop of wine defiling their gullets, the pure water of the mountains to quench their thirst after the fire of battle, and their eyes bright with the health of lust as they sought the couches of their concubines. And then Henry II of England, enemy of all Celts, tried to quench the Welsh princes for ever, as also likewise the princes of Ireland, but he had to reckon with Rhys ap Griffith, Lord of the Vale of Towy. Well now, it's shame to say it but honest to admit it, there's a weak strain in the Celtic blood, or some say it's a sense of bloody reality, knowing which side your bread is buttered on, and Rhys ap Griffith passed on to Llewelyn ap Iorwerth the Great the secret knowledge that the English could not be beaten in a fair fight. So the thing was to get into the ruling family of the enemy, which Llewelyn did, for he married the illfavoured daughter of King John Lackland, hump on her back and warts on her chin, and the filthy rot of alliance and feudal dependence began. It all ended up in the Act of Union when Welsh kings inherited the English throne but they called themselves English now, with the treacherous bastard Thomas Cromwell in charge of the Act and the banishing of the Welsh language from the law courts and the conversion of the marcher lordships into shire ground, Brecknock and Denbigh and

11

Monmouth and Montgomery and Radnor, curses on the evil of the wrongdoers and God help those that are left to the infinite sorrow and shame of it all.'

At this point David Jones, with seven slugs of whisky inside him said: 'Ah, shut up.' Dai Williams swayed at the bar of the Fulton Street tavern in astonishment at hearing this from a whippersnapper not long past the age of sucking loshins, ungrateful little bastard that he'd tried to educate in the wrongs of his native country and the perils of the vast city of towers for a mere *plentyn* still adither from a frightful adventure on the frothing and bucking Atlantic.

'You're bloody drunk, boy bach.'

'Ah no, not yet. I'm just sick of hearing of all the wrongs and evils done in the old days. It's all gone under the water and what we have to do is like make a fresh start.'

Dai Williams nodded with some show of indulgence. 'Ay, ay, there is your youth that is talking. The future all before you, not like me, and you bloody lucky to be alive. But you won't be rid of the wrongs of history all that quick, boy bach. When you step into the future you will always have the mud and filth of the past stuck to your boots and no iron scraper will ever be able to clean it all off.'

'I'm washed clean of it. And I'll not put to sea again.' He knew from the newspapers about the publication of the Mersey Report and the rigour of the new maritime regulations, and had read an article by a certain W. P. Doomster about never again would the sea worm crawl over mirrors meant to glass the opulent, whatever that could conceivably mean, but he thought he was sincere in what he now said.

'Staying here then, is it?'

That was the question, nor did he know its answer. He was a *Titanic* survivor, a seaman who had, and it was reasonable enough, forsaken his trade, and the immigration authorities were not yet harassing him, but he would have to decide soon whether to make formal application for United States residence or go north to rejoin the British Empire or else trust the sea one more time for a voyage back to the land of his fathers. The sea, like the land, was ruled by capitalists and Saxons, and he was no more for it. But he had to remind himself that a lot of Saxons

12

and capitalists had gone down while he, a Celt of radical tendency, had been saved.

The barman was named Art, and Dai Williams, hearing a drinker call for 'five more Art', burst again into his song of injustice. 'There's a bloody mockery and a twisting of the noblest name of the lot, meaning Arthur, Arcturus the Bear, the red giant, that being his known and holy and royal name but his Welsh one a great secret till the end of time. He's waiting there with the sword Caledvwlch sheathed but ready to be drawn again in the fight. A fight I'm too old for, bachgen, but you not. Back to it with your youth and your vigour and it is your shout now.'

LET us now come to the Russian connection. David Jones had been at work five days in a German hash joint called Steiner's, this being his fourth job, and after the St David's Day carouse he was unable to report for work until late in the afternoon. In the kitchen he found a wall-eyed Calabrian, his evident replacement, frying hamburgers in tepid fat, and, after hard words with the proprietor, he now had to search for his fifth job on land.

He travelled to the borough of Brooklyn and at length found work in the Flatbush area. There was a restaurant there called the Nevsky Prospect, owned by a certain Pete or Piotr Likhutin. This man was a Russian atheist who had been a professional thief but was now reformed. He had fled St Petersburg in 1907, not for reasons of political persecution or poverty but because he had been forced, in self-defence, to batter a pawnbroker near to death when entering her shop late at night. He had been seen by somebody who looked like an informer and so had to get away. He hopped a Finnish timber freighter with his wife and daughter and got to London by way of Tilbury.

In London he bought himself a share in a restaurant run by his second cousin Gregor Petrovich Prishvin, the *Sutky* (so called because it was open day and night), situated not far from St Giles Circus. It was in their lodgings in Clipstone Street that Piotr Likhutin's wife Sonya, a woman proud of her clean tombstone teeth, in trying to shatter a brazil nut with her molars choked on a shard, she being alone in the house at the time and nobody to smite her back for her. She was buried with genuine tears in

Highgate Cemetery, not far from the known lecher and eccentric Dr Marx. The widower, not at all badly off, what with fenced loot and legitimate earnings, one day clanked a bag of sovereigns aboard the SS *Empress* with his daughter, a girl as golden as the sovereigns, and after a smooth crossing disembarked in Brooklyn.

In this great borough he had Russian anarchist connections through his wife's mother's second husband, though he was not himself a political man, being, in the cultural and activist spheres, merely mildly interested in, for the general betterment of mankind, the dissemination of atheism. His heart and soul had never really been in crime: he had undertaken the thief's trade out of a fundamental laziness. In 1910 he opened the restaurant and catered to East European exiles like himself, leaving most of the work to his daughter and to paid staff. The food was not kosher, but local Ashkenazim buried ritual pedantry or, in their chauvinistic conviction that the Russian and Polish cuisines were their own invention, assumed the orthodoxy of its preparation in their relish of the borshch and blini and salmon caviar. Pete Likhutin did well and, in 1913, needed a second cook. For this post David Jones applied.

The Likhutins were of Viking stock, big-boned and blond. David Jones found the proprietor drinking Brooklyn vodka behind the bar – Sholokov's, the real McCoy – and felt small and dark and Silurian in the presence of this greying golden mountain of a man. For though the big blond Celts had, in prehistoric times, robbed the dark and dwarfish incumbents of their agricultural land, leaving them to grouse and plot revenge over their metal mining and forging of swords and sickles, to steal blond babies and leave dark changelings in their stead, to sail to Ireland as leprechauns and, eventually, to man the bicycle factories of the English Midlands, intermarriage with them revealed them to be of a tougher physical stock than the Celts, destined for long survival. David Jones was properly one of them. He was small, dark and wiry, but the Viking's colour was too high, his belly enormous, he had to sit on a stool day long to ease the monstrous pains in his calves. He smoked imported papirosi at the rate of four packs daily. One mad fit of rage would do for him.

The daughter, Ludmila Petrovna, came in to finish the laying of the luncheon tables. David Jones was heavily smitten. Breasts as round and high, as the poet Ubitiy might put it, as duplicate domes of St Isaac's, corn hair like an overabundant Ukraine harvest, green eyes like twin winter Baltics. 'You from England?' Pete Likhutin asked. From Wales. 'You make funny, *chelovyek*? I seen whales. Whales big fish.' I will show you Wales on a map. 'I not want maps. I go no place. Here stay, die here. America one fine country,' meaning Brooklyn. 'I see you look with big eyes at my daughter. Ah no, you not look. I fire men look like you look but hit hard on head before I fire. You look at work only. You got job.' He had been too busy to learn English properly.

And so David Jones learned the Russian cuisine under a dour cook named Ivan (a name easily Welshified into Ifan), who had himself served on merchant ships plying the Baltic, had then scorched steaks in a low Paris brasserie, setting the kitchen on fire on an occasion of depressive drunkenness, had sobered up after a medical assessment of the state of his liver, had ended up in Brooklyn sober and competent, though in a depression no longer tempered by mania. He taught David Jones classic Russian dishes in French transliteration – *borshch is riba; stschigreschenevai-kache; Smolenski kache; rossolnick ç'agourtzami; filet po Neapolitanski ç'izoume.*

David Jones was intermittently on fire for the daughter Ludmila, but she was unmoved by his Welsh sheep's eyes and remained haughty and untouchable. Her English was better than her father's, but it was limited to commands and complaints. Ivan remained dour and his assistant frustrated, but, life being always full of surprises, it was Ivan who one day tried to breach the casemates of her officious coldness by taking her in his arms. It was lunchtime and the restaurant was full of customers with hats and beards, Pete Likhutin sloshing out measures of Sholokov's behind the bar. It was a summer's day, early July 1914, and with neither a growl of lust nor a dourness melting to frank concupiscence, Ivan grabbed her in the kitchen as she stood beautiful and barking that they should hurry up with the *Smolenski kache*, and tried to tear her thin muslin dress from her shoulders. David Jones intervened, introducing the Esperanto of an iron potling cracking against male bone while she railed in Russian. Ivan desisted; she looked gorgeous with her flush of

15

rage and her outraged green eyes and the flash of pink flesh where the tear was. Ivan, stricken hard and tottering, moaned. The father at the bar was not told, not yet. The luncheon service continued, with David Jones doing all the work. Ivan sat on a kitchen stool and moaned but seemed to bear his assistant no ill will. His assistant made him some hot strong black caravan tea with a spoonful of apricot jam in it.

But the old man was told later and he approached apoplexy. He fired Ivan while trying to swipe at him from a distance, breathed deeply and dangerously after, swigged Sholokov's vodka straight from the spout, then crashed like a house, making the entire stock of crockery and glassware clang and rattle like a gamelan. 'Vratch! Vratch!' called Ludmila, so David Jones ran off for the vratch round the corner. This medical Jew, luncheon bib still on him, ordered an ambulance, and Pete Likhutin was whipped off to the hospital in Flatbush, snoring from the depths but still living. Then, life being still full of surprises, Ludmila said to David Jones: 'You now come home with me.' Home? With you? What for? But his heart raced. 'You see when we home. The sign that speaks CLOSED. This up, then we lock. We open not tonight.'

Home was the two top floors of a four-storey brownstone on Brooklyn Heights, with a distant view of the Statue of Liberty. The whole house was owned by Pete Likhutin, the two lower floors being let to decent regular paying tenants, Jews of course. Ludmila opened up with her kliuch to disclose a bourgeois Russian living room, well stuffed chairs in crimson plush, tarnished gilt, a scent of aniseed and subdued cabbage, the reek ineradicable of the papirosi of Pete Likhutin. She led him up a single brief flight of faded purple and orange carpeted stairs and into her bedroom. 'Now,' she said in her brusque kitchen tone, 'you take off all your clothes.'

David Jones, though small, had inherited from his father a tidy musculature and a flat belly. He was brown and salted. He had never worked in the mines and so there was no disfigurement of subcutaneous coaldust. He was ashamed to undress before those great Baltic eyes only because he had an erection ascending higher than his navel. Naked, he at once tried to hide this erection by advancing on the wholly clothed, save for that shoulder

16

rip, Ludmila and taking her in his arms. But she pushed him back and ordered him to turn about, appraising him as though commercially, buttocks, nape, clavicles, and finally saying in satisfaction: 'Khoroshcho'. Then she kicked her shoes off and got into bed clothed. She undressed between the sheets in the manner of a nun or servant girl, nakedness not to be exposed to the all-seeing God who fashioned it. There were no ikons or holy pictures in the room, but there was a very bad framed reproduction of an animal painting of the American school founded by Landseer's pupil Tisch, a herd of deer with liquid innocent eyes looking at the looker. 'In now you come,' she ordered, 'and we make love.' That seemed supererogatory to David Jones, who, under the gaze of the painted deer, got in there and did as he was told.

It was a long and wholly animal session, interrupted only by Ludmila's getting up twice to make strong tea served in glasses with tarnished *zarfim*, a dollop therein from a preserved peach jar, and later cold blinis spread with smoked salmon and red caviar. Later, as though it were, which it probably was, an after-thought, she telephoned the hospital to find out how her father did. She went *da da* at the information given, then clipped David Jones in a powerful embrace. How is he? He is not good. It is the heart. He will die before breakfast. She meant *zavtra*, tomorrow, not *zavtrak*. How can you, how can we, how can you think of, I mean it's not decent. But in a sense it was. Life opposed death. More, the gestures of the making of life opposed it. For this was the anticipatory consummation of a marriage unproposed in any words. No condoms or interrupted coition. David Jones had had small experience of women, but he knew a virgin when he met one, and this Ludmila, whose father was now dying on behalf of her chastity, was not one. Never mind. The restaurant would, before breakfast, belong to her, and she needed a husband to run it. Ludmila Jones, which in Russian was Ivanovich, no true surname.

So David Jones and she were married under state law with no benefit of clergy at the beginning of August 1914. He proposed broadening the cuisine of the restaurant to embrace Welsh leg of mutton, miner's brandy broth, swedes and potatoes mashed to the mixture called potch, buck rarebit. No, she said, no foreign muck in the way of dishes. David Jones, though he worked hard enough in the kitchen with an ageing Pole well past concupiscence as assistant, felt somewhat like a kept man. The capital was all hers, she gave too many orders, though fewer now in bed. Like many Welshmen, David Jones knew how to please a woman. The biggest complaint made by Welshwomen against the men of non-Cymric provenance, with the exception of Tiger Bay blacks, is that they are *not loving*.

On 4 August the Great War burst like a boil on sick Europe, and the New York newspapers reported patriotic headlines in the British ones. David Jones felt guilt at not at once rushing across the Atlantic to join in it. He was a citizen of the British Empire, though the Empire had done nothing for him, his father had frequently reported that it was called by some of his politically minded butties a machine of capitalist oppression, boy bach, and he still did not consider seriously the taking of United States citizenship. He did not think of bashing the Huns to avenge the violation of Belgium; he thought rather, though vaguely, of his having escaped whole and not even too uncomfortable from the wreck of the *Titanic* and a sort of duty to death of giving it another chance to have at him. Besides, America was being too bloody smug, boy bach, about not being wartorn bloody Europe, and he knew, without being able to articulate it, that he was a European. His wife was European too, and Brooklyn, though it was full of Europeans, was not Europe. White nights over the Neva. Miners singing four-part harmony on the way back from the shift. Eating with a knife and fork.

David Jones had not kept in touch with his father, though he wrote a letter to an aunt in Tredegar saying that he had married a Russian girl, real lovely she is, and was doing all right in the States and please to pass the information to dad, whom he now forgave for clouting him when drunk and hoped forgave him in his turn for running away to sea, wherever dad was. There was no reply. Never mind.

There was no reply until the end of April 1915. By that time the restaurant was flourishing, David Jones could speak some Russian and, with difficulty, read a little, Ludmila's English had improved and had a marked Welsh lilt. Despite the vigour of their nightly lovemaking the vital spermatozoon was not striking home. Never mind. There was time for building a family. He was only twenty-one and his wife, she thought, she was not sure, something over nineteen. The letter that came from Tredegar was from his cousin Iris, not his aunt Gertie who was a good pastry hand but poor with the pen. It said that his father was very ill with a growth in his chest, and the doctor said that if he lived another three months he would be doing nicely. His father had not been apprised of his true trouble and thought he was suffering from bronchitis. He, young Dai, had better get to No 2 Sunnybank Road in Blackwood quick, Russian wife and all, a thing not heard of in the family ever before.

'Yes,' Ludmila Jones said, 'I come too because I not trust you with women.' This was his reward for being so good in bed, a man so fervent in the act would naturally be after women. 'But who is to look after the restoran?' If you think I'm coming back to America, David Jones said, you're mistaken. We're not coming back, no argument about it, time I was boss, sell the place and the house too and put the money by as a nestegg. I'll be joining the army, not the navy, no bloody fear, had enough of the sea, and we'll think about the future when the war's over. There was a long argument, but Ludmila, having one day just missed being scalded by an overturning pan of borshch, consented to sell the Nevsky Prospect to a shifty man from the Bronx named Keller. She got twenty-five thousand dollars for premises, stock and goodwill, a fair amount in those days. She would not sell the brownstone but let the top floors furnished and arranged for the rents to be collected and banked by the legal firm of Peyser, Reich, Koenig and Sharp. She wanted to see St Petersburg again. There were too many foreigners in New York.

David Jones went to a shipping agency in Manhattan and booked second class passages on the SS *Lusitania*, due to sail early in May. But the evening before they were due to embark Ludmila went down with a stabbing pain in the lower abdomen. This was diagnosed as appendicitis. The operation was successful and her recovery was swift, Ludmila being as strong as a mare, but they were not now able to sail until early June. Meanwhile the news of the sinking of the *Lusitania* on 7 May came through, at least 1200 lives lost. David Jones was awed. There was something evil about his good luck. They sailed from 42nd Street to

Southampton on the SS *Monroe*, a ship equipped with an abundance of lifeboats and no cache of illegal ammunition, safe from Hun torpedoes after the strong warning words of President Wilson.

'We stay a little time in Angliya till your father die. Then we got to Petersburg, no place is like home,' We'll think about Russia when the war's over, girl, and we're not going to Anglia East West or North but to South Wales. But they were not really, since Monmouthshire was administratively, except for education, a part of England, and it would have been difficult to find a more English address than No 2 Sunnybank Road, Blackwood.

The bedroom of Elis Wyn Jones was full of the smells of medicaments and the noise of his agonized breathing. He was only fifty-two but he looked eighty, all skin and bone and white prophetic hair though no beard. The woman from Ebbw Vale with whom he had lived in sin was long gone, but there was a hired nurse from Cefn Fforest downstairs drinking her fill of a golden Russian woman brewing strong tea and looking for apricot jam. The father asked his son for a cigarette, and he was given a Gold Flake. After the preliminary paroxysm it seemed to ease his breathing. He said:

'Kept myself alive waiting for you to come and now you're here I can go peaceful. Lungs always weak with the anthracite. I'm done for but never mind, had my life, fair play. Lots of young lads at the front being done for that have had no life worth talking about, poor young buggers.' Save your breath, dad, don't talk so fast. 'Pretty girl you have down there, a bit bossy, never mind. Things happening in Russia, country of the future, you'll see. Give me another of those, son, they help a bit, clear the pipes like, fair play.' Young David gave him another Gold Flake, but his father handed it back trembling after a couple of bedshaking draws. 'Not such a good idea, then.' He retched a rusty gob into the pudding basin by the bed. 'Better up than down, as they say, look at the size of it. Listen, bachgen, go now to the bottom of the wardrobe and you'll see a brown paper parcel with string round it. Heavy it is, so don't be surprised when you lift it. Bring it here to the bed, boy.'

David brought it over, surprised enough, using both hands. His father said:

20

'You ever hear of the Welcome nugget, son? Mined in Ballarat
in 1858 I think it was, and your grandad could never stop talking
about it. It weighed near two hundred bloody pounds if it
weighed an ounce and was worth near nine thousand quid in
those days, think what the bugger would be worth now. Now
what you have there is yours, and it weighs thirty-eight pounds
which is getting on for three stone, saw it tip the scale with my
own peepers.'

What the hell did you, how did you?

'Easy, bach, no call for excitement. Your grandad gave me that
on his deathbed as I'm giving it to you on mine. In Wellengong,
where he's dead and buried, queer sort of name you'll be saying,
just outside Sydney. Set up nice there he was, though everything
very simple. Very guilty he seemed always to be about it, but he
said it was rightly his though he couldn't prove it, a bit of a long
story you might say.'

David fingered the rocky lump that rested just below his
father's blanketed feet, shedding metallic flakes on the coverlet.
It was impure in that it was embedded in lead, copper, iron, but
the authentic glow was there, discreet and lordly in the rainy
Welsh summer afternoon light.

'That'll be your problem, Dai boy, selling the bugger. I didn't
dare, too many questions asked. Kept putting it off and no
wonder. And there has been more than enough for my needs,
fair play, never trusted the banks, you'll find a bag of three
hundred and twenty-five sovereigns, jimmyogoblins as they do
call them, tucked nice and safe under the watertank in the cockloft. So there is your legal legacy, boy bach, all fair and square
with the lawyers, bought this house outright and a good investment too the way things are. You ran away from home, not
proper in some ways, but guts you have had and got away safe
from the *Titanic* when the other poor buggers went under. Not
like your aunt Gertie and the rest of them, the only life they are
seeing is from behind lace curtains, and that Jack Probert is, I
am telling no lie, the stupidest bugger that ever walked on two
legs. And another thing is . . .'He now started coughing desperately, turning puce, and the hired nurse from Cefn Fforest took
her time coming upstairs, chewing too with her mouth open.

The next day the old man, not so old really, had an accession of unseemly appetite and told his son that before he died he would like a boiled leg of Welsh mutton with port and brandy in the sauce. He would have it that evening, posh, dinner like the nobs, do the bloody thing properly. He said: 'Funny how a thing will stick in your mind, bachgen. Up in the loft there you will find the encyclo, I forget the rest of the bloody word, that I got from your grandad. Bought it off a barrow at King's Cross Sydney he did, may be valuable. Well, there's a big thing it has in it on Wales, and it says Welsh lamb and mutton are EXQUISITE. Never forgot the word, though I don't know if I pronounce it right. So I will have it before I go to Abram's bosom, not much of a prospect that is when you come to think of it.'

David Jones did not dare allow himself to be bewildered by the promise of his continuing luck, all of which could be cancelled by a Hun bullet. He had made up his mind to join the army, only fair to death to give it another chance. But one thing at a time, get his poor dad underground first, in the family plot in Bedwellty. For his poor dad he simmered a fine leg of Welsh mutton with turnips, leeks, carrots and onions, a tumbler of port wine to be added five minutes before the end of the cooking, a small glass of Martell's Three Star at the last minute. Typical miner's dinner at weekend with six or seven sons down the mine also, plenty of money coming in. Poor old bugger, Abram's bosom indeed. During the simmering some of the relatives came by stopping train from Tredegar – aunt Gertie, her husband Jack Probert, her daughter Iris and Iris's husband Owen Davies, called by his mates in the steelmill where he was a roller 'Golly', short for *golygus* or handsome because he was so bloody ugly. They all lived in the one house on Chwefrer Street behind very clean lace curtains.

Expecting their cut, David Jones said to himself, sitting with them in the front room and regarding the insufficiently subdued rapacity in their dark mean eyes. They had surveyed with satisfaction the wasting sleeping form of Elis Wyn and now sat waiting for Ludmila, funny sort of a name, foreign, to wait on them with tea and welshcakes. Tea she served in the barbarous British fashion and also a plate of the heavy pastries the Russians, without irony, called zephyrs. Ludmila gazed at them with her Baltic green eyes, weird foreigners, fascinated.

22

'There's funny her English is,' aunt Gertie said. 'Not had foreigners in the family before except for your mam that was a
Northwalian. There's hard these cake things are. Jack do need
to eat soft things because of his teeth. Big jobs going now what
with the war, but Jack's not fit to work.'

'What's the matter with him, then?' her nephew asked.

'Art.'

'What she mean, art?' Ludmila asked. Her husband explained.
'Oh, gart,' said Ludmila. Aunt Gertie sniffed and detailed her
ailments, she ought to be the one that was stretched out not her
brother upstairs sleeping peaceful. 'And there was that Mrs
Evans Number 3 going on about her back, and Dr Cronin that is
Scotch says to her: What about that poor little Mrs Probert, she
do have the pink pills, you do only have the white.' She removed
with finicking delicacy an unbitten morsel of zephyr from her
ceg, saying: 'Iris here had done the baking, and Dr Cronin says
before he left: Well, who have baked these tarts? My daughter,
doctor. Well, there's nice they do look. Well, stay and have a
slice, doctor. No, no, I haven't time now, but I'll say this: We
don't get tart like that in *our* ouse.' And she smirked, pleased as
bloody puss. David Jones felt very weary: bugger the lot of them,
bloody Wales, narrow lot of stupid bastards, don't know the
bloody world exists. His father called down feebly. Aunt Gertie
gleamed dully: near the end now he is, fair play.

'Get that lot out of my house, bloody vultures gnawing the
bones of the dead while they're still alive. Get them out and get
me my dinner. I'm starved, bach.' So the relatives were cleared
out for a long rainy wait at Blackwood Station, and dinner was
served to Elis Wyn on a tray with a bunch of sweet william in a
jam jar, Ludmila's idea. The dying man ate with vigour. 'Not
enough pepper, boy bach.' But pepper will start you off coughing
again, dad. It did too. And then something seemed to crack
inside him. The coughing stopped and he had to give what
energy he had to breathing. The son watched the night long and
heard the miners coming off shift singing *Cwm Rhondda*:

Bread from Evan's
Tea from Thomas's
Beer from the Colliers Arms . . .

The old man woke from dyspnoeal coma, smacked his lips, said firmly: 'A pint would be bloody nice, boy.' Then he died. The nurse came from Cefn Fforest at half past eight, shut the dead man's dreaming eyes, pulled the sheet over his head, and then went to look for Mrs Cadwallader on Caerdydd Avenue, layer-out for the community.

David Jones had seen death on a vast and public scale but never before domestically and at close quarters. This domestic death revolted him. He had never before realized that death in a bed was a dirty business, not the angelic transit of Little Eva in the film of *Uncle Tom's Cabin* he had seen in New York. The bowels and bladder collapsed, sheets and mattress had to be burnt at the bottom of the back garden. The body, having vulgarly shed its ordures, now turned into an ordure itself. That was because the soul had deserted it. So there was such a thing as a soul then, the preachers were right. This chunk of decaying matter being got ready for the coffin was not his dad. His dad had buggered off somewhere where there was no beer or Welsh mutton, he was a freed soul, but what was he doing now, who could tell? There were a lot of freed souls now rising out of chunks of ordure in the muddy fields of France, and perhaps he, the living son and comfortable inheritor, might soon be joining them. It seemed to him that it was a good deal healthier, meaning cleaner, to die like that than in a bed promptly defiled by the soul's losing hold of the muscles. To die at sea was clean too, but to give your ordures to the soil was good for it, whereas a drowned corpse only gave food to the fishes, which probably had enough already. Soul and soil: it seemed a fair antithesis.

'WELL, girl,' he said to Ludmila, the morning after the funeral, 'I'll be off to Newport tomorrow to join up. You'll be all right here. A bit lonely, but there's always the neighbours, bloody narrow lot they are from the look of them at their front doors as the hearse went by. You'll get the pay of a soldier's wife, and there's all the dollars in the bank here, each one turned into just over four bob.' He did not mention the raw gold and the bag of sovereigns he had shoved in an old gladstone of his dad's into the bank vault: he was entitled to his secret hoard, every man was. 'The war won't last for ever, and there's leave too that they give you now and again.'

'I go,' she said, 'to Petersburg.'

'Oh Christ, girl,' he cried in distress, 'you can't do that. There's a bloody war on there too, the Germans are fighting every bugger, and you'll only add to my worries. I want you here in this house, keeping the home fires burning.'

'The weather too hot for a fire.'

'That's only a manner of speaking, as they say. And, look here, we have the word *is* in English. *Is is is*. You'd better start using it or the neighbours will laugh fit to bust.'

'In Russian is not *is*. Here they say *do be*.'

'Let it go,' he sighed. 'Why should you want to go to St Petersburg anyway?' And he looked at her, the other side of the empty fireplace in the dining and living room which looked out on to the bit of untended garden, the front room preserved in its mustiness only for special occasions, like Christmas and death. She was only a girl really, a girl wife as they put it. Did he love her? What was love? Did she love him? What was (what was it now?) *liubof?* He knew well enough why she had pulled him into the proleptic bed of marriage, but that cause, male muscle and authority in a Flatbush restaurant, clearly no longer applied. No good going into all that, they were man and wife, one flesh though two souls (you died alone: that had been made very clear to him), prospective parents though the biological engine, like that steam one of Crawshay-Bailey famous in Welsh legend, seemed reluctant to go. 'There's nobody you know now there, girl.'

'My auntie Anya and my uncle Boris in the prison. We write to each other letters. You have seen.'

'Jesus, you are a criminal lot. You never said about the prison.'

'He say kill the Czar, they laugh at him, but they put him in the prison just the same.'

'Wait,' he counselled after sighing very profoundly. 'One thing at a time. Time, there's plenty of that. St Petersburg will not vanish over bloody night.' She shook her lovely head, gleaming in the dull light of summer morning like that ingot no longer in the cockloft. The other treasure there cached was now ranged in the otherwise near empty glass-fronted bookcase: the encyclo-

25

paedia, Kelly's, in twelve volumes. She could improve her English with it, the only other literature available in the house being the family Bible over which he had once onanized, a bit too old fashioned to be any good to her. Shook her lovely head as though she knew better, just like history.

So he took the train to Newport and applied to join the Royal Gwent Regiment. It proved more difficult to get into the war than he had imagined, trying to do his king and country a favour but it looked like the other way round. Trade? No trade really, just odds and ends of labouring like. But that blue tattoo on his left forearm, an anchor and a crown above it, as well as the marine squint and salted brown complexion, would have given the game away to anybody who looked closely. Nobody did. Next of kin? Ludmila Jones, née Petrovna Likhutin. Yes, Russian. They weren't too happy about that, though Imperial Russia was gallantly pushing back the Hun in Galicia. He was not summoned to the training depot at Chepstow until the late summer of 1915, where, A1 category, 73386, a tradeless man, first class foot-slogging cannon fodder, he joined other Joneses, as well as Williamses, Evanses, Morgans and the odd Pritchard. He had to have his surname dogtagged with his final digits: Jones 86. There was one lone Cadwallader in his intake and, instead of rejoicing in the easy identifiability of that uniqueness, the company sergeant major, a foreigner from Cadbury, said what sort of a bloody monicker is this? Cadwallader did not understand the CSM's accent, so Jones 86 said, remembering the instruction he had received in Manhattan, 'One of the kings of Gwynedd.' Where's that, bloody Mesopotamia? Who asked you to shove your bloody oar in anyway, and what's more you'll say sir. Sir. But the second in command of A Company said: 'Cadwallader and his goats, eh what, haw haw.' There were a lot of foreigners in the Royal Gwent Regiment, especially among the officers, none of whom spoke with a proper Welshy accent. The hierarchy reminded Jones 86 of the *Titanic*, the barracks like a becalmed ship with quartering segregations ranging from first class to steerage, OUT OF BOUNDS notices everywhere. No women, though, except in the inflamed glands of the lonely men. The captain of the ship was the colonel, a remote numen except to serious defaulters, and captain was a fairly lowly commissioned rank. Pte Jones was in steerage, but the slop served up by the cookhouse would not have been tolerated even by the Irish immigrants for whom he had overboiled cabbage. Yet he forbore to say that he could do the job better than the corporal cook (the sergeant cook being a drunken and cursing figurehead) who snivelled snot and blew fag-ash into the porridge cauldron.

So he formed fours and did squad drill, keeping his bleeding head high, for all them tanners had been picked up already on first parade. In the grey morning he and the others of his platoon were told loudly to get out of them wanking pits and get fell in on the road. Rise and shine rise and shine, hands off your cocks, pull on your socks, orderly room's at nine. When, weary and dirty, for there was but a lone cold tap to wash from, they got into their blankets and obeyed the bugle that sang its tonic and dominant lights out ('Tonic and dominant those two notes are called, boy,' Evans 73 the choirmaster told him nightly), the swarthy Morgan 02 would, from his corner palliasse, enlighten the barrackroom as to the faded glory of the Brythonic Celts.

'Christians two hundred years after the death of the Big White Jesus, God give his bones rest, and they held to the faith when the whole of the island called Britain which was their rightful property worshipped false gods, Odin and Thor and other bloody deaf wooden idols.' Jones 86 felt homesick, hearing all this, for the ease and fleshpots of New York. So, some objected through the dark, why were we fighting for the bloody English and not on the side of the bloody Germans who shouted the odds about Gott strafe England? A grave lay preacher's voice reviled from near the door as always the dirty language, but he was told to get his bloody duff down. 'Well now, that is what many would be saying is a fair objection, but the time will come, boys. What are the Germans but first cousins to the English?' Cousins german, the weary voice of Williams 39 the lawyer's clerk said unheeded. 'See them out of the way first, and then what is to prevent the armed Welsh from rising up to give what for to their oppressors? Already they say that the ghost of Arthur the King has been seen galloping over the hills on his charger, the sword Caledvwlch brandished high. The glorious days will be coming soon and the Welsh ready for them, trained in the use of weapons by the English who are too soft to see the bloody portents.' There were some members of the platoon who understood little of this, too many long hard words, man. 'It will be like it was before, when the princes arose like a flame in Cymru, Cadwallon the Long Handed and his son Maelgwyn Gwynedd and the other Cadwallon who was the great-grandson of the first. And they strove against the brutal bastards under the swine with the uncomely name of Ethelfrith, king of the Angles in Northumbria, till by brutality and treachery we lost Strathclyde and the whole of Northern Britain and got smashed and butchered at the infamous battle of Chester.'

But there was a man in the opposed corner, Evans 12, who cried out against this outworn nationalism and maintained that the true struggle was between the workers and the capitalists, and that out of this war, which would produce industrial breakdown on a large scale, the revolution would be generated. But another socialist maintained from a third corner that no working man should be fighting this war anyway, what was it but worker killing worker while the armaments manufacturers made fat profits, he would not have joined up himself if he had not thought he could do some good in the ranks of the fighting proletariat by spreading the workers' gospel. Then the three-cornered wrangle, with the lay preacher's bourdon against filthy language, would be overborne by song from the nonpolitical:

> Crawshay-Bailey built an engine
>   And the engine 'ouldn't go,
> So they pulled it by a string
>   All the way to Nantyglo.

The platoon corporal who slept in his own little *cwb* or kennel at the end of the barrackroom came in late and beery from the corporals' mess to yell at them in the tones of Irish Liverpool: 'Crash them swedes, you bloody Taffs.' There was silence except for mutters against the overbearing foreign bastard, then snores and groans till reveille: tonic and dominant again, boy, begin the day and end with it, over your grave in Flanders field too.

Pte Jones was, at the end of his training, to be posted to the First Battalion of the Royal Gwent Regiment outside Monmouth, but he got leave first. He was greeted by his wife at the front

door with *'Bore da. Dewch i mewn.'* He knew this was not Russian.
He said:

'What in the name of God, girl – '

'Mrs Jones Number 7 do be my *athrawes.*'

'Oh Jesus Christ almighty.'

'There is fatter you are, *nghariad.*'

'Porridge, slops, spuds, beer. *You are*, you said. Better that is.'

'I read the books. I am now reading the second letter. Bendigo
name under which the British pugilist William Thompson was
known. Also town in Victoria, Australia. Eighteen fifty-one
alluvial gold was found and there was a rush. I have been to
Cardiff. There is a Russian church there with a pope. His name
is Father Kiril. He sold me a dictionary, English and Russian. He
makes my Russian better too. And now we go to bed.' They
went to bed and afterwards, singing something Russian from her
childhood, she prepared a high tea in the British fashion: ham
and eggs, bread and butter cut thin, plum cake and fancies, a
full steaming brown pot, She no longer used the samovar she
had brought from Brooklyn. Waiting for his tea in that mixture
of content and guilt that follows the making of successful love,
Pte Jones found the first volume of Kelly's Encyclopaedia on the
little table beside one of the armchairs beside the fireplace. It was
open at Benedictines, The, whoever they were. The term he
knew only in the singular: a liqueur in the bar of the officers'
mess, which he had twice had the honour to clean up after a
party, and a proper filthy mess it had been. He read with
complete lack of curiosity:

. . . founded by St Benedict (480–547) at Subiaco, where he set
up twelve or more monasteries. At Monte Cassino, which
became the central seat of the order, Benedict wrote out his
rule for the monastic life. He was visited there shortly before
his death by the Ostrogothic king Totila, whom he converted
to the Christian faith. The commonly held view that the
Benedictine order owed its introduction in England to the
missionary St Augustine was contradicted in 1889 by the
discovery of a manuscript attributed to the monk Roderigo and
at present in private hands. This document presents a brief
account of the evacuation of a Benedictine house in the West

of England in 577 shortly after the battle of Deorham and the
resumption of the West Saxon advance. The fleeing monks, to
whom had been committed for safety several treasures of the
British royal house, proceeded to Italy and Monte Cassino
where, according to Roderigo, these treasures were deposited.
No trace of them has yet been reported . . .

His tea was ready, and he was ready for it. At the end of his
leave he was, though well fed, somewhat thinner and rather
gelatinous in his limbs. She cried at the station as she saw him
off. She was lonely, poor little Russian girl, despite her occasional
visits to Cardiff and the pope who ran the small Russian
Orthodox church near the docks. She read in the Russian newspapers this pope received by mail about the terrible atrocities
wreaked by the Hun on Russian territory. She did not now wish
to go to St Petersburg because of the danger. She wanted only
her husband. The atheism inculcated by her father was now dead
with the sharper memories of the man himself, who was, when
she came to think of it, not really a person of virtue. Now she
prayed to the God of the Russians for the end of the war and
the return of her husband, safe and ready for bed. Amen to that,
Pte Jones 86 said.

At Monmouth, just before Christmas, he learned that the
battalion was being broken up for drafts, and that he was to be
one of a draft ordered to proceed overseas on active service. In
full marching order, greatcoat with buttons newly polished but
no rifle or sidearms, he was paraded in the dark and answered
his name and number as, by a hurricane lantern, the roll was
called. Then they were marched off to the railway station with
the band in the vaward playing 'Have you ever caught your
ballocks in a rat trap?' In the train compartments he and his
companions became disorganized, foulmouthed with too many
gaspers, suspended in a sordid emptiness of elliptical motion (for
the train did not run straight to Paddington via Newport but
picked up other cursing and coughing drafts at Ross, Northleach,
Hungerford) and a very little light. Unbuttoned and tooth-
sucking, their unlaced boots apaddle in dirty fag packets and
sandwich wrappers and copies of *John Bull*, each withdrew into
an ill-furnished room of private meditation.

Why, Pte Jones wondered, had he volunteered? Be called up sometime anyway, losses on Western Front, *Western Mail* said, not being made good by volunteer system, Lord Derby at work on manpower comb-out, separating the dispensable conscribable from the overpaid munition workers lapped in union protection. But the real reason was to do with big public death being permitted to have another go at him, otherwise he might be kicked to little private death by a drayhorse or choke on a mackerel bone. Seaman's superstition, sort of. Too much good luck so far.

And then: what was the bloody war about, anyway? They were off to France to fight the Huns, who, according to *John Bull*, made bully beef out of Belgian babies and had to be stopped. Why were they called the Huns when they called themselves Germans or the German equivalent of Germans which turned them into Dutch or something like? Pte Jones began to conceive a vague sense of a great square battlefield luridly lighted in the middle, the light becoming dusk and then dark as it flowed to the perimeter, gridded, sort of, like a map, with European time and European space. Moustached roarers with pointed helmets raged over the double field, brochetting howling naked babes as in pigsticking or some such ruling class sport. The grown-up population fled into the darkness in a variety of fancy costumes. He saw monks heaving cases of benedictine liqueur out of a kind of ascetic cosiness and the wrath to come. There was always the wrath to come to have gone to come again. The train was circuitously lurching him towards an appointment with history, which he knew nothing about. History was all luridly lighted darkness and roaring and points of swords or bayonets in the guts, and it went back a long way. Maelgwyn Gwynedd and Cadwallon the Long Handed and the king called Brothelbreath or some such bloody name. But they were all really the one big bearded roarer quelling and grabbing. It was all grab.

It went back a long way. All one piece, a train so long you couldn't see the engine, new coaches added at every stop, and you had to get into one already crowded, come on me lucky lads and what's your bleeding religion they'll want to know what you are when they stick a fucking wooden cross on top of you in the dark field of European history where the poppies grow. Why did poppies mean sleep? It was because of the opium. There had been that Chink scullion on the *Bluebell* who puffed his regular three pipes off watch, slept like a baby sometimes, sometimes whimpered, sometimes screamed that the Polish first mate was turning into a dragon to eat him alive. Pte Jones escaped from his confusion into the confusion of uncomfortable sleep, holding his backpack like a great square baby on his lap, sinking his cheek on to the blancoed straps and the metal fittings smelling of Bluebell. Bluebells I'll gather, take them and be true. Someone had played that on the concertina for all to sing to in steerage. The concertina did not sink right away: the waves squeezed it gently and it whimpered a little dirge for itself before going under. He and the rest were wakened in the middle of the night at Paddington, shouts and steam and steamy breath and the whole station stinking of rotten eggs.

They formed fours in the icy station road under an unknown RSM and, squad after squad, marched on slippery cobbles, fuck it, down the Edgware Road, the Welsh singing quietly in deference to the slumbering munition workers:

Crawshay-Bailey he play football,
He play football for Llanelly,
But the efty Swansea forward
Went and kicked him in the belly.

The goose hiss of the double L sprinkled Oxford Street as they crossed it. Park Lane, Grosvenor Place, Buckingham Palace Road. 'Easy lies the head that wears a crown,' Powell the bloodyminded said. 'Bloody German himself, cousin to Kaiser Bill, Family feuds and we do the fucking fighting for the bastards.' Victoria Station and the boat trains ready for a trip to the Continong. A Salvation Army tea wagon served tea, but there was not enough to go round. Crammed in again, they dozed till Folkestone. It was full winter morning over the Channel. A troopship was waiting for them, one of the old regular packets stripped and converted and smelling of a ghost of passengers' vomit, and a pack of torpedo boats sniffing for U-boats. Pte Jones, strong in the stomach while some of his mates gargoyled into the foamy green, stood steady in his boots on the pitching deck and snuffed his old friend and

32

enemy with relish, letting the wind welshcomb his black wiry cropped nob. And then he shivered and felt claws in his throat. Caught a bloody cold. There was also the promise of a sharp pain in his side.

At the rest camp looking on the sick sea of Boulogne, they were shoved into bell tents, half a platoon for each, and Pte Jones lay down coughing on three filthy kapok biscuits over bare boards rich in splinters, seven filthy grey blankets over him. The dinner bugle called them to stewed bully, but he could not fancy food. He got up while the rest scoffed and staggered to the wooden hut that sold fags and boot polish and there he found Owbridge's Lung Tonic. A big call for it, he was told as he shook out money to pay, and no wonder, that sky looks like snow all right. He downed the black syrupy contents of a large bottle in one. Then he slept a laudanum sleep for twenty-four hours, missing parade but unnoticed. He woke, very shaky and empty, for the drawing of tin hats, rifles, bayonets and gasmasks. Then he drank sugary tea by the quart, shivering. He would not report sick, they would think he was dodging the column. Christmas Day was like any other, except that the cook had prepared a watery sludge of plum duff. The cough came back, very dry, and his head span. He cracked ice and tried to shave. He bled from the chin, but the blood froze. There was this pain in his side, bugger it.

The day after Boxing Day they were told by the orderly sergeant that they were going up the line, and that the train, a French bugger, proper run down, was already ready for their trip to the railhead, chrysanths in lovely silver vases and snowy tablecloths in the dining car, a pity about the broken windows. Get fell in after dinner to draw unexpired portion of the day's rations. And the best of luck, you lucky fuckers.

On parade, in the rear rank, Pte Jones 86 fell and made fall by falling the man in front. He awoke in the base clearing station in sad winter twilight. His inner monitor had told him to wake in order to vomit, a thing he had never in his life done before. A nurse heard urgent retching and brought a kidney bowl. She took his axillary temperature: 102°. When the MO came round he told Pte Jones 86 that he had acute lobar pneumonia. Hot water bottles, ice packs to the side where the pain was, there was a pain there, don't tell me, I know. Pte Jones 86 looked painfully all over the ward and saw genuine wounded soldiers. He felt ashamed. The MO, Captain Ferguson, RAMC, looked closely at him and said: 'I noticed that tattoo on your arm. Navy, were you? You were moaning about an open boat.'

And then Jones was out with it: '*Titanic.*'

'Ah.' It made up for not having his face blown away like the moaning patient three beds down. And then: 'Survivor, eh? You were lucky. You're lucky again. One more day and I wouldn't have given a brass bawbee for your chances.' And he moved on to the next bed, half an arm and a whole leg missing. David Jones felt terrible. It did not seem right that a soldier should be suffering from what any bloody fool could pick up in civvy street. He felt worse when, eight days later, Evans 23 and Williams 68 from his draft were wheeled in. Reinforcements for the Second Battalion of the Glamorganshires. Spewed back from the front, what was bloody left of them. Evans 23 had lost his right eye, Williams 68 had had the left side of his face opened up from cheekbone to chin. The Hun began to bomb the base now. Those that could be evacuated would be. That meant Blighty for some, Pte Jones 86 among them.

When he got home on convalescent leave, his uniform too big for him, Ludmila was on Breakspear, Nicholas. 'The only Englishman to become the pope that is in Rome, the Catholics have only one pope. See Adrian IV. But I had already seen it,' she said. She watched her husband clean his dinner plate with a chunk of bread and his horny thumb, saying: '*Ydych chi eisiau rhagor?*'

'Yes, I'd like a bit more, if that's what that mouthful means.'

'You a bloody Welshman and not to speak bloody Welsh.'

'You're coming on, girl.'

Ludmila's feeding him up but then taking it out of him in bed meant that, at the end of his leave, his uniform was still too big. He reported to X Battalion of the Royal Gwent Regiment, all odds and sods, stationed at Towyn, wooden huts for the men, HQ in a country house that belonged to the Earl of Barmouth. The war went on behind his back while he fed the incinerator. On 2 March 1916 the second phase of the battle of Verdun began, the French fell back behind the Goose's Crest, the Huns failed at Vaux, won a few furlongs near the Béthincourt-Cumières road, leaving Mort Homme still in French hands. Meanwhile the Irish discomfited the British already sufficiently discomfited. But the Sinn Feiners failed to meet Sir Roger Casement's U-boat. On Good Friday morning he was arrested and taken to England. On Easter Monday the rebellion went ahead without him. Padraic Perse spoke against the backcloth of the flapping tricolour of 1848: 'Irishmen and Irishwomen – In the name of God and of the dead generations from which she receives her ancient tradition of nationhood, Ireland, through us, summons her children to her flag and strikes for her freedom.'

Lieutenant-Colonel Boyce, commanding officer of X Battalion, suffered from a neurasthenic speech impediment and left it to Major Feather, his second in command, to announce on parade that men in medical categories A and B would be at once formed into a fighting draft to restore peace in Dublin, along with troops brought in from the Curragh, wherever or whatever that was. Pte Jones 86, downgraded to B1, was once more issued with a tin hat and a rifle but, the Irish possessing little known chemical talent, no gasmask. That evening in the troops' canteen Pte Pritchard 05, a heavy gloomy man with the ghost of lost stripes on his arms, spoke inflammatory words:

'Make no mistake about it, comrades, brothers, fellow Welshmen, this is not the war we signed on freely to fight. They take advantage of our desire to serve the cause of liberation and convert us into a force of tyranny and oppression. For the Irish want no more than what we wanted till the power of the great weakness seized our spirits and paralysed the bones and muscles that else should have put down the English tyrant. They want liberation from the unjust rule of the Saxon, and the Saxon in arms is supposed to step in there terrible in his bloody wrath and put down a just insurrection. Well, we are not Saxons but bloody Welshmen and brother Celts, and we will not do the bidding of an oppressive power whatever the consequences. Shame on the kilted Scots, who are already shooting Irish children on the cobblestones of Dublin and are a disgrace to the Celtic heritage. Better to face the firing squad. Yes, brothers, I know the word is mutiny, but have no fear of that word. Tomorrow we parade as ordered with our arms. At the given word that shall come from my mouth we drop our arms and stand in the cold wind of spring and obey no further order. I have done.'

Another soldier, less eloquent, stood to say: 'What I am saying is to bloody hell with the bloody Micks. They do come over as July barbers to reap the harvest at half pay, and they do bring bugs and lice and drunkenness and priests into our clean bloody country. So if they do want a bullet in the guts what I say is they can bloody have it.' There was then some fighting.

Pte Pritchard 05 was nowhere to be seen when the draft paraded. He had gone sick, it was said, with a pain in the balls, proper doubled up, couldn't stand upright. So the draft travelled north, passing majestic Cader Idris to the east, through Gwynedd where Cadwallader was king (his poor bloody namesake was now all mashed guts), and on to the Isle of Anglesey and the port of Holyhead. Then there were groans and vomiting, though not from Pte Jones 86, all the way over the bucking sea to Kingstown. In a godown of the harbour that had been converted into a military depot, many of the prostrate men had to be revived with beer and sal volatile before they could undertake the night march into the city.

In Boland's Mill Volunteer guns under an arithmetic teacher with a Spanish name, dregs of a lost Armada, were trained on the approach to the torn but beating heart of a wronged nation. The sick British troops marched, while a gunboat shelled Sackville Street. That blaze over there was the Post Office. Some of the rebels were couched in the shrubbery of Stephen's Green. British rifles poked from the shattered bay windows of the Shelbourne Hotel. A mad old woman in tatters cursed the curse of Cromwell from the glass-strewn gutter. Out of the way, ma. Light infantry came running from Grafton Street. Rifle cracks primed echo after echo after echo in the soft air. Mallard rose in alarm from the park lake. Half a platoon, with Lieutenant Hoskins in the lead waving a pistol, entered the park over corpses that had just done cursing bloody Jesus. Pte Jones 86 to the accompaniment of excessive dry noise felt his collarbone disintegrate and watched crimson flood the left upper segment of his tunic. He sat down stupidly on a park bench seeing captured Micks in need of haircuts led, dragged, carried.

Ludmila had arrived at Chatham, William Pitt, First Earl of, 1708–78. Pte Jones tried, difficult with the plaster, to help her set the tea table. She said: '*Ewch chi allan i'r ardd i ddarllen neu ewch yn ôl i'r gwely i gysgu. Gadewch y cyfan i fi.*' White bloody Jesus Christ. So he went into the summer back garden, which she had got into some sort óf order, sweet william thriving, to read the *Star of Gwent*, which listed local boys who had fallen on the Somme. The *Daily Mail* congratulated the Australians on capturing Pozières. Well, here he was in his own garden, still alive, the shattered collarbone reconstructed and coming along nicely. And Ludmila pregnant with Welsh and English and useless information from a secondhand encyclowhatsit from a Sydney hand barrow but not with progeny. Time enough perhaps if his luck held. He was curious to know what kind of children might spring out of their coupling. But anyway, perhaps, bugger it, begetting fruit of your loins. That butterfly there with a chocolaty fur coat, lime and orange specks, didn't worry about progeny and he would be dead by day's end without malefit of Hun guns. As for the Huns, he had in his kitbag a book on the Huns given to him in hospital by the author, an educated man who had never wanted a commission because he believed there was more chance of staying alive in the ranks. An acting unpaid corporal now reduced to private.

He was to be discharged now, having lost his left hand and wrist on the Somme and had his right eardrum burst to buggery, a meagre sacrifice as he put it to the gods of death and money. He could still hear music with his left ear and he was a right-handed writer. Discharged with his measly pension, already a mature man of thirty-six, he would write to show up the infamy of the world. He was the first man David Jones had met whom he sincerely admired. He would read his book sometime. His name was Reginald Morrow, but the ward had called him Vegetable Marrow. 'I'm not married,' he said, 'and I don't think I will be now. What woman wants a one-handed fumbler? I'll have no children, but my children will be my books. You're married, Taff, and you'll have kids, and if you've any sense of duty to humanity you'll bring up those kids to spit in the eye of government and piss in the mouth of all authority. And not to

37

be taken in by the big words. We don't want this lot to happen again.'

PTE JONES 86 returned to the depot of the Royal Gwents when his leave was up, then was sent to the military hospital at Risca to have his plaster chipped off. He was pronounced fit though not enough yet for sustaining the shoulder-kick of a rifle. Light duties only. He was baffled to find himself crossing the sea again, but only as far as Osborne on the Isle of Wight. There was an officers' convalescent home there, and in its kitchen he was set to the scrubbing of pans. The sergeant cook despised his own trade as well as the officers he fed. He spat in the stew. He thickened the gravy with cigarette ash. Pte Jones protested less on behalf of the consumers than his own hidden avocation. 'Stripes or no stripes,' he said, 'I take the liberty of saying you're a disgrace to the cook's profession, and if this was a restaurant and me in charge I'd have you out on your thick dirty ear, *wus.*' The assistant cook, a corporal who guffawed at his master's infamies, and the other kitchen hand, a silent though sometimes sobbing case of shellshock from the Marne, looked at Pte Jones with incredulity and awe. The sergeant adopted no pose of rank offended. He said instead:

'Taffy boy, I'd put you on a charge if it was worth it. But there's no guardroom here and this isn't a barracks where they have jankers.' He gobbed distractedly into the stewpot. 'There's many a one like you who's a case of nerves, look at that bugger there, he screams out things he shouldn't, this war having gone on already a bit too long. So if you think you can do the job better, and if you think this lot here that scoffs the muck gives a bugger about good cooking or bad, you can take it over all day tomorrow while me and Corporal Borrowdale looks on. We could do with a bit of a rest.'

Pte Jones threw down the wire brush with which he had been cleaning a thickly encrusted porridge pot and walked out blazing, ignoring the sergeant's yell to come back you bastard. He walked out of the hospital grounds and down to the monastery of the Benedictines, not knowing why they were there, not knowing that they had been driven out of their house at Solesmes by the anticlerical laws of 1906. He liked sometimes to sit on a grass mound outside their chapel and listen to the plainchant, which he found elevating and soothing. It suggested the better part of history, which the worse side was forced by devilry to expunge if it could. At this time of day there was no song. A monk strolled by reading from a little book and nodded. Pte Jones nodded back and said, to his own surprise:

'The fleeing monks, to whom had been committed for safety several treasures of the British royal house . . . Sorry, I forget the rest.'

'Where did you learn that?' the monk asked in a thickish foreign accent. He closed his book, which was a breviary.

'Something my wife was reading.'

'You do not speak like an Englishman.'

'Welsh. Sorry, I shouldn't have spoke. You have a big place, you lot, somewhere in somewhere or other. They're there, these things the book tells about.'

'Monte Cassino? In Italy?'

'It might be that.' He added: 'Sir.'

'There is no need to call me sir. I am not one of your officers. You say there are great British treasures at Monte Cassino?'

'British meaning Welsh, I think. What they call the British now are the English. It would be Welsh royalty then. Sorry I spoke. It's nothing really. It just came out like. As things will. I'd better be going back.'

'Yes,' the monk said, shaking his head, recognizing the war's unhingement. 'Monte Cassino is very big and very old. It is full of cellars with stones instead of doors. Nobody knows everything that may be in Monte Cassino.' And he blessed Pte Jones 86 with two fingers.

Calmer, as if a quick bathe in history had done him good, Pte Jones walked back to the convalescent home, while the monk finished shaking his head and returned to his breviary.

The next day Pte Jones cooked unlumpy oatmeal and made fishcakes out of canned mackerel and sardines while the corporal cook looked on grinning and then not grinning. Stupid as he was, he recognized what looked like, you know, the professional touch. The sergeant cook appeared while Pte Jones was preparing luncheon – a light soup in which canned unsweetened milk and garden parsley were ingredients, *boeuf Stroganof* with fluffed mashed potatoes, a feathery queen of puddings. 'I'll get you for this,' the sergeant swore. 'By suffering Jesus Christ I'll have you out of this kitchen.' And he spat in the soup. Pte Jones, enraged, hit out at him with an iron frying pan. The orderly officer came in to make his inspection while the sergeant lay kicked and drenched in ruined soup. He did not put Pte Jones on a charge, for RAMC officers were rarely pedantic about regimental procedure, but he assigned him the post of ward fatigueman and recommended that he be posted away. And so Pte Jones 86 went back to his depot.

By the end of the year he had been regraded A2. The Second Battalion of the Royal Gwent Regiment had been reformed and was now up to strength, and he was posted to A Company in it, still a private but bearing a wound stripe. He had no embarkation leave before marching off yet again to the front; the band in the vaward playing 'Don't throw the lamp at father, it's a shame to waste the oil'. At the base camp at Harfleur they were informed of the general situation. The Hun had been taken by surprise at Verdun. Positions between Fleury and Fort Douament had been recovered, and the latest news was that the Frogs had captured Vacherauville, Poivre Hill, Haudromont Wood, Chambrettes Farm and Bezonvaux. The Hun was retreating to what he called the Siegfried Line but the allies, rejecting mythic fancy, the Hindenburg one. He had to be pinned there for the time being in a wholly defensive posture until breath could be taken for what was hoped would be the final Allied push. All clear, men? From his fortress the Hun would be unleashing new and frightful weapons in his desperation, including toxic gases of an unprecedented foulness.

The battalion, section by section of platoon, had to submit to being enclosed in a sealed hut with a gas corporal who released a canned effluvium that smelt of human faeces, rotten duck eggs, decayed hay, and a boiled sweet factory. They had to take a lungful of this raw in order to recognize it as G12 before being permitted to fumble on their respirators. Some of the respirators were old and perished and they leaked. Pte Jones felt the lung formerly stricken but now officially healed howl loud in memory of its old affliction. Gasmasked but taking in gas, he fought coughing to get out of the hut and was not the only one. The gas corporal opposed monstrous talc eyes and a corrugated snout and curses that seemed to come from down a long padded corridor while he wrestled with these mutinous.

Outside the hut Pte Jones vomited the breakfast tea and porridge and fried bread. Then blood. He was scared by the sight of that blood. He went, despite the threats of the platoon sergeant calling him to a fresh parade, to the MI room. He was not standing any more bloody nonsense about bloody scrimshanking and dodging the bloody column. There was the bloody blood, *wus*, bright as paint on a white bloody snotrag, bugger it. He was put into the base hospital. Thus he failed to entrain with the battalion for Arras. When, a month later, he was pronounced healthy enough to be slaughtered, he was made to join a draft of inadequate replacements for the Royal Gwent Regiment, which had been reduced to some two hundred and fifty fighting men.

Paraded at battalion headquarters, some two miles behind the line in the ruined village of Mazentin, he was ordered to act as runner between the company and Batt. HQ. The company was A Company, and its acting second in command was Lieutenant Griffiths, a young pared and trembling bank clerk from Swansea: his toothbrush moustache was already grey. As for the operation that immediately faced them, the Hun had set himself up on a hill from which he could survey the whole of the British line, what was left of it, and this hill had, for the third time, to be assailed and, this time, taken. Lieutenant Griffiths led the replacements, which amounted to a platoon and a half with a neurasthenic acting sergeant and a newly appointed lancejack rustically gormless, along the shelled road that led from Mazentin to the line. It was February, the rains had been heavy, the mud was a skating rink where it was not flats that sucked in boots with succulent relish. 'There,' Lieutenant Griffiths pointed. 'We don't know the local name but we call it Shit Slope.' It was about half a mile off, a beechwooded crown to be reached through scrambling up a steep slushy marl in the enemy's full view, sheer bloody suicide.

That it was to be sheer bloody suicide was the message, gorblimied into military phraseology, which Pte Jones 86 bore from Acting Captain Perry, the company commander, to Battalion HQ.

The return message was that what was left of the Royal Gwents was to assume a supporting role. The Midlothians and the Third Caledonian Rifles were to attack first and the Gwents to hold themselves in readiness. It would be easier to scramble up that hill over a paving of corpses. They had it cushy.

Pte Jones 86's company waited in a churchyard among graves, disinterred bones and fragments of ruined steeple. The fallen weathercock was rusty but entire, and the acting sergeant claimed it as a souvenir. Bit too heavy to carry, sarge, that is. It was eleven of the clock of a drizzly February morning. The Huns knew they were there and started to shell. Pte Jones 86 heard noise unbelievable and saw an apocalyptical rain of shattering metal and bodies taking to the lower air before they subsided as corpses. The living needed no order to retreat to the ruined church under a wheeling of crows protesting. Pte Jones started to run. He heard an eight-inch shell crack behind him and saw the headstone of a grave in front disintegrate. His brain imploded and he became one with the flying stone fragments.

LUDMILA learned that she was a widow in a brief letter signed by a squiggle Major RGR. The War Office notification would follow later. The letter was in purple ink, peeled off a hectograph of gelatine and glycerine, and save for the pencilled Jones after the duplicate Mrs was quite impersonal. Very much regret. One of very many heavy casualties. Recent advance taken terrible toll. Good soldier and fine comrade.

She did not weep, not at first. After all, she had lived for some time now in the expectation of being widowed. There was a great deal of empty future in front of her, but such past as she had had with her late husband had been satisfactory and sometimes, specifically when they had been in bed together, rather more than satisfactory. She had been a faithful wife. That she had not come to marriage a virgin had not, as it might have some men, disconcerted him greatly. Her defloration, which she had been too young to recognize as such, had occurred on the evening of an outing to Coney Island, a noisy resort of coarse pleasures where she and a girl named Sandra, a probationary waitress too insolent to be confirmed in the post, had drunk Coca-Cola spiked with something from a metal flask plied by one of the two young

men they had met. The lovemaking under the American moon
had been rough at first but later more tender. It had meant little
enough. It had meant something more with a young French
Canadian who had briefly delivered meat to the restaurant while
her father, with a chill on his liver, had kept to his bed. They
had kissed and wrestled on the floor of the kitchen, the cook
Ivan not yet having arrived. It had meant a good deal with her
poor dead husband. She started to cry.

She ceased crying to lunch off a stringy beefsteak. Food was
becoming a problem now because of the U-boat attacks on
merchant shipping. She drank two cups of strong black tea and
started crying again. But crying was of no use. She must act. The
house was hers. Sell it, go home to St Petersburg, which was
now called Petrograd? But that was not quite home, except
ancestrally. She spoke Welsh now and had, shopping on the
High Street, spoken Welsh with women widowed earlier than
herself and in black to prove it. She also spoke English with
those who spoke no Welsh, and her English was no worse than
theirs. The thing to do was to go to her relatives in Petrograd, if
there were any ships going that way these terrible days, and
think there what to do with the future. She would have those
ravening relatives of her late husband round if she did not get
away. They had been round twice before, all four of them, hoping
he might be dead, sniffing at the furniture and saying, when she
had made the hospitable offer 'Ydych chil eisiau te?', that they
spoke no Russian, girl. Lock up the house and leave it as it was
and get away for a time. Perhaps for ever. She did not know yet.

She bravely dried her tears, laved her eyes, powdered her face
with Poudre Tokalon, put on a plain black narrow-brimmed hat
and the worn sable coat that had been her mother's, and then
walked upright through the light Welsh drizzle to the railway
station, smiling at Mrs Evans's youngest, making no outward
show of grief. A return ticket to Cardiff, change at Newport. She
had, seated in the train, a sudden ignoble sensation of total
liberty: money in the bank in her name and a cheque book in
her handbag, a British passport there too, promising that the
king of England would protect her on whatever travels she
undertook. The Czar of all the Russias looked very like the king
of England, but he would probably protect her less efficiently.

She knew the Russians, young as she was. Young as she was, she was herself Russian.

The Cardiff pope, Father Kiril, commiserated from behind his black beard and said she was probably wise to wish to blow away her grief on a voyage to Petrograd, whether to go for good he could not be sure. There were big winds blowing in the motherland and the people were opening their mouths wide to howl for bread and against the misconduct of the war, both at the same time. For himself, he had found South Wales a safe and humane place and the Welsh not unlike the Russians, meaning manic depressive and liars. He directed her to a Norwegian shipping agency near the docks, with tattered posters of ships long out of commission on the buff walls with chocolate dadoes. A Norwegian who had married into South Wales found buried under the bills of lading on his desk various shipping schedules. He had a tic on his left cheek as regular as a metronome. There was, he said, while the cheek ticked, a freighter named the SS *Hellige Gral* due out of Newcastle in one week's time with a variety of lading for Copenhagen, Stockholm and Petrograd. There was passenger accommodation for twelve, not much of it normally taken up, and he could cable for a reservation at once and make out her ticket. She paid by cheque, signing in careful Romic her name – L. Jones. Nothing Russian there, and the surname a kind of tombstone.

Back in Blackwood, she went to the post office and arranged for mail to be forwarded to her care of her aunt, Anya Gregorovna Likhutina at Number 32 Ulitsa Mizinchikova, Petrograd, Russia. There's funny, the postmistress said, hard to spell it is too. Ludmila wrote it for her on one big envelope in Romic and also in Cyrillic print script. What mail was she expecting, then? A farewell letter saying: As I go into battle your love and beauty make heavy my heart? His will and testament made out in his paybook? An official note saying that the report of his death was all a mistake? Compensatory money from a government that had sent out her man to be slaughtered?

She travelled by slow dirty train to Newcastle, crammed in a carriage with soldiers too tired to ogle her, though one tooth-sucking sailor with HMS *Hero* on his cap clucked at her as if she were poultry. In Newcastle she did not understand the English spoken, but she found the docks late at night and was shown to her cabin on the SS *Hellige Gral* by a steward so blond as to seem bleached. It was a slow and bucking voyage with what seemed to be game stews, salted fish, and much *akvavit*. There were two mournful Russian men, one of them with a crying, probably newly motherless, son, but they said nothing to her. The captain had a forked yellow beard and ate mostly with his fingers. Late one night he could be heard roaring outside her cabin. They arrived at the port of Petrograd at the point of a cold dawn on 6 March 1917.

She took a battered cab to Ulitsa Mizinchikova, which was off the Fontanka Canal near Nevsky Prospect. She remembered the city of her early girlhood as being either under snow or endless daylight. There was thin snow under a late winter sun, and there were people muffled against the cold tramping round in it, weaving brief codas of smoky breath. There were also people lining up to buy bread, but there seemed to be no bread. There was little smoke from the chimneys. Shortage of fuel, she was told by her thickly moustached driver. In South Wales there had always been plenty of coal. 'There's going to be big trouble, lady,' the driver said. 'We can put up with so much and no more, as the donkey said. They've turned Peter into a military district under this General Khabalof, and he has a face like a duck's arse, pardon the expression, and he says he'll hang any like Christmas geese that make disorder. My wife spends all day queueing for bread, sits on a soapbox and does her knitting. If this is a military district there ought by rights to be a ration, and there's no ration. You've come home at the wrong time, little lady.'

Her aunt Anya, who lived on the top floor of the apartment block at Number 32, swamped her in Russian love and sympathetic tears. The apartment was cold, and she was feeding the stove with old copies of *Den* and the *Russkaya Volya*. Never throw anything away, poor Boris always said, you never know when it will come in useful. Poor Boris was still in the Kresti. Ludmila showed the roubles in her purse and took tins of corned beef from her one suitcase. The little mother of the blessed baby Jesus shower kisses on your feet, sweet angel, slobbering gratitude all over her face. We've not known how to manage. We? Yes, she had Boris's sister's son Yurochka staying with her, the poor widowed girl being wounded after serving as a sister of mercy or *sestra miloserdiya* with the Sanitar. Aunt Anya put the samovar on with Lyon's tea in it. The tea we get here is all dust nowadays, the heavens crown you with glory, sweet girl.

On Thursday, 8 March, Ludmila and her aunt were walking down Nevsky Prospect after looking for bread. A company of Cossacks appeared and they were surprised to see it gallop at speed, hoofing up snow dust, towards the Admiralty Quay. A man with a deep chest and broad shoulders under a ragged overcoat said to them: 'Trouble over there, ladies, I've no doubt, as the dogfox said when it smelt the hounds. Workers causing it and quite right, I'm a worker. And what's the Duma been doing this past week? That Rittich that's the Minister of Agriculture saying it's all right to let the people starve. Starve like motherless leverets while they spend fifty million roubles to put on that thing of Lermontov's at the Alexander, that's where I used to work as a sceneshifter till the stage manager and your humble serf here rubbed each other up the wrong way. I tell you it can't go on. Stormclouds, ladies, thunder and lightning to follow.' And he bowed with rough courtesy before striding east. When Ludmila and her aunt got home, little Yurochka told them that he had seen looting going on in a baker's shop just by the nuns' school and he'd grabbed this black loaf, see, out of a fat and quarrelsome lady's basket. Good little Yurka, heaven bless the child. They tore at the loaf and spread it thinly with Swift's corned beef, sending weak tea after it.

The next day there were no newspapers, but word came through about the fistfight in the Duma when the government disclaimed responsibility for Petrograd's food supplies and said that had been handed over to the City Department for Public Affairs. Cossacks patrolled the streets, cheered by the people. It was a glorious late winter day, the air the only champagne the people would ever get. 'Listen, dear friends,' a Cossack said, while his horse performed a confined step dance, 'don't think for one minute we're going to fire on you lot. We're in this together, as the eggs in the basket said. We've disobeyed orders before and we'll do it again. The police are altogether a different pot of cold borshch.' With a tight white cabbage, damnably expensive, in her aunt's shopping basket, Ludmila passed Kazan

Cathedral to see stone, bottles, and loosely wrapped balls of kitchen garbage thrown at the police. A mounted officer raised his revolver to the blessed weak winter sun and cracked out four shots as a warning. The police were arresting a couple of protesting workmen in blue and kicking them off to a lockup on the Kazanskaya. The crowd, not all men, growled and rushed. A squad of soldiers held them off from the outer yard of the police building, rifles poised but aimed groundwards, their officer with his hand shakily raised in warning of the signal to fire. When the Cossacks came thumping up, the footsoldiers broke ranks and ran. The Cossacks grabbed the two arrested workers and delivered them courteously to the crowd. The crowd nearly tore off the blue workclothes with rejoicing. Ludmila saw all this.

'What it is,' her aunt said later that day, 'is the *levorutsia*.' She nodded in satisfaction at knowing the hard word, all three chins squashing into the high collar of her rusty black dress. Little Yurochka, poor boy, his father dead at Tarnopol and his mother in an orthopaedic ward, a thin ragged lad reading the serial story in an old copy of *Den* before feeding it to the stove, looked up and said:

'It's *revolutsia*.'

'And what sort of a word would that be? The Czar's on the right and the workers are on the left, and that's *levo*, so it's *levorutsia*, which means Russia is turning left, don't contradict your elders.'

'Yureshche,' Ludmila said, 'you need a new coat. I think I saw one in that window round the corner from the Astoria. Let you and me go to look at it while it's still light.'

But the coat was too small and too expensive, and, anyway, the shopkeeper was anxious to shut up his shop. Streetfighting nearby, and the crowd gawping as though it were Tscharlie Tschaplin. In the middle of the Prospect, Ludmila and Yurochka saw a workman standing on an upturned tub crying to the crowd: 'Out with the Stürmers and the Golitzins and the Protopopofs, God curse them. We need bread, and what I say is: no work without bread.' The crowd yelled against the war: stop it, bleeding us dry, it's the Czar's quarrel not ours. 'Ah yes,' the workman cried, a superior workman with the ends of his moustache twisted, 'but don't forget that the blood of our sons

47

and brothers must not be spilt to no end. Get rid of this government and then conclude an honourable peace so the Russians can hold their heads high. And as for us here, let's have no rioting. There are what they call provocative agents around, and they want the people to riot so the government can bring out the big stick and beat them. Calm is what we want. Go home now and I'll go too, and we'll all go singing songs.' There were about a hundred Cossacks on the verge of the crowd, their horses mildly restive. They did not interrupt. They watched benignly as the crowd dispersed, some singing 'In a wood there stood a firtree' and others a distorted and Slav version of 'Tipperary'.

The next day was Saturday, payday. Workers, paid but with little to buy, were an orderly sea on the Neva's bank. No sleighs, no trams. Motor cars tried to come steaming through but the crowd gently shoved them back. At nightfall some shots were fired by, it looked like, soldiers, but the crowd was convinced that these were police who had put on military uniform. Workmen's meetings took place in cinema queues. There was much talk of a day's strike, which meant nursing weekend crapula all day Monday. 'The Duma,' a coarse fat boilermaker said, 'is defiling its pants with apprehension. Tomorrow may be the big day.' And he handed over his ten kopeks at the paydesk to see an Amerikansky film about the French *levorutsia*.

Bells clanged in an icecold blindingly bright Sunday. Notices had been stuck up before dawn, signed by Khabalof, the military governor: any worker who did not go back to work on Monday would be sent at once to the front; people must not collect in crowds; police and military had received orders to effect dispersal of unlawful gatherings with all the force at their disposal. Nevertheless crowds collected, bigger than before, children in worn Sabbath best clinging stickily to well-wrapped mothers as they hurried, like at a Shrovetide fair, from one exhibit of the possibility of riot to another. 'All we want,' a workman cried from the uneasy crest of three beer crates, 'is food. The government's got it and the government's hanging on to it, letting it go bad.' Then the Instructional Detachment of the Pavlovsk Regiment fired over the heads of the crowds and the crowds scattered. A company of the Pavlovsk Regiment mutinied and was at once disarmed by the Preobrazhensky Regiment. Or so the report went. At sundown there was firing near the Evropa Hotel and in front of the Anichkof Palace. Nevsky Prospect was cleared of crowds and guards were posted. Ludmila, hearing of this and of the massacre of two thousand which turned out to be two hundred, wished she was back in Monmouthshire.

Rumours came through of a telegram to the Czar sent by Rodzianko, President of the Duma. Anarchy in capital, it said, transport and food and fuel supplies disorganized, general discontent, disorderly firing in public places, troops raising rifles at each other, absolutely necessary to invest someone who enjoys the people's confidence with powers to form new government, no time must be lost, pray God that at this perilous hour the responsibility may not fall on the wearer of the crown, signed Rodzianko. Stories of the Duma prorogued, some members refusing to be prorogued and forming provisional government or rump.

But on Monday, 12 March, troops of the Preobrazhensky Regiment refused to fire on dissident workers; they turned and shot their officers instead. Companies of the Volynsky Regiment were rushed down to quell the mutiny, only to join the mutiny themselves. Workmen and revolutionary schoolmasters and failed journalists appeared to bring civilian order to military aimlessness, crying 'Storm the arsenal!' Workers soon had rifles and grenades in their unhandy paws, clicking bolts uncertainly. More regiments were despatched to put down the mutineers, but all joined them – the Litovsky, the Keksholmsky, the sappers, about twenty-five thousand troops in all.

But Ludmila and her aunt and little Yurochka saw nothing of this. From their window they looked down on skaters on the Fontanka Canal. The aunt had an old friend in the fish market who panted up the stairs with some stinking mackerel and a battered beetroot, and from her they learned that the Law Courts had been set on fire and a barricade erected. But, more important, soldiers and workmen and students were opening up the prisons. She had heard that a big crowd was rushing to Viborg ready to set fire to the Kresti. Setting fire to the prisoners? screamed the aunt. No, getting the prisoners out first and then burning the place down. 'Come on, Ludmila,' shrieked her aunt, 'we're going. Oh, my dear Boris.'

They had difficulty in pushing through the crowds. A Cossack who was rocking in his stirrups, a red handkerchief in his cap, waving his sword to the crystal heavens, cried: 'Citizens, don't leave all the work to the troops. This is France all over again. Long live the glorious revolution.' A machine-gun spat and chattered. 'Run, run,' Ludmila panted. Then she went down into dirty snow, pushed by a great lewd fist of metal that hammered her right buttock. She realized she had been shot. So that was what it was like to be shot. She heard her aunt howling to the sky. Shot, she was shot. She lay there, smelling the dirty tang of the trodden snow. There were hoofs all about her. She felt for blood, but felt nothing. She smelt also the smoked bacon zest of rifle fire. Then she was lifted by strong arms, smelling sweat and the reek of papirosi. Yells and yells, get the women and children out of the way. The clang of a horsedrawn ambulance, two snorting piebalds. She was lifted in to join other maimed moaners. She was trotted off to the Rievskaya Bolitsa.

There, with a swift injection of cocaine and a sharp probe, the injured buttock was treated by a Doctor Karaulof. He tossed bits of bright metal up and down gently in his hairy right hand. Cannot get them all out, he regretted to have to say. Till your dying day you will have fragments nestling in the fat to commemorate the failed revolution. No offence, but the female buttock being fatter than the male, the male leaner and stringier and more muscular, damage is minimal, *gospozha*. Rest on the other buttock while this one heals. You will be out of here soon. Then he said: 'Soon no one will be called *gospozh* or *gospodin*. The great word will be *tovarishch*.' This was to show which side he was on.

Aunt Anya and released uncle Boris came to see her. He was a check weigher not yet back at work, fierce, small, energetic, not unlike her poor dead husband, though of course much older. He embraced Ludmila till she winced. He gave her news. The garrison of the fortress of SS Peter and Paul had mutinied, police stations were being burned and police records destroyed. 'But,' he gloated, 'the big thing was the breaking into the building of the political police and consigning all the documents to the big bonfire. That was what you should have seen, niece, like the taking of the Bastille, and the only documents that have been burnt were the dossiers of what used to be called the enemies of the state, the others have been kept to show the filth and corruption and tyranny going on in the government.'

'And what has the Czar done, *dyadya*?'

'Threatened, the stupid fool, not knowing a thing about what it was really all about away there with the Stafka, saying that the troops had broken their oath to the Emperor and had got to be punished. But Kerensky and Cheeidze got troops to stand guard over the Duma and they got rid of the regular Duma guard. And now there's an executive government being formed, and that bastard, forgive my bad language, that bastard Sheglovitof that was Minister of so called Justice is under lock and key expecting the worst. Oh, and poor little Yurek has lost a thumb.'

'Poor little Yurochka,' her aunt cried. 'He was told not to play with other people's rifles.'

'Oh no,' Ludmila cried. 'Poor little Yureshche. Is he in the hospital too?'

'Not this one. The one for measles near Peter and Paul, he doesn't have measles but they've taken him in. He'll be all right. Well, to tell the truth, it was only the top piece of the thumb, the left one, from the nail to the knuckle. Are they feeding you well in here?'

'It's mostly soup. But there's enough bread.' She fancied a slice of Welsh mutton with swedes and potatoes mashed. When her uncle and aunt left on the ringing of the handbell dismissive of visitors, the lean limping man who rang the bell started selling copies of a gazette for ten kopeks. Ludmila bought one, paying from her purse that was under her pillow. It was ill-printed and a single folded sheet, put out by the workers and called *Russkaya Pekhota*, Russia's battleline. Not many in this women's ward could read, so Ludmila had to bawl out the news, lying on her left buttock and receiving complaints from those on the side of her injured one that they could not hear. Protopopof, Minister of the Interior, had given himself up. Troops had come in from Oranienbaum, Strelna, other places, and joined the revolutionaries. Red flag flying over the Duma building. Division between Duma Executive Committee and Workmen's Social Democratic Association. Guchkof, Strube and Prince Lvof leading the Duma executive. 'God bless the prince,' a toothless crone with a broken shoulder cried, and 'Amen' others. The news made little sense

51

to them and not much to Ludmila, who had become a kind of foreigner. Regiments pouring into Petrograd, waving red flags easily contrived – an old shirt dipped in somebody's blood. Plethora of committees, including committee for the laying down of rules for procedure in committees. Colonel Englehart appointed President of the Duma Military Committee, which had already begun quarrelling about procedure laid down by committee for deciding on procedures. Czar reported to be on his way at the head of royalist troops from Finland. 'God bless the Czar,' cried the crone, 'our little father.' Others added 'Amen'.

This last news was contradicted in the *Russkaya Pekhota* of 15 March. Czar states willingness to abdicate, on his own behalf and that of the heir apparent. The Czarina at Tsarkoe Selo gives herself up to revolutionary troops, saying: I am Empress no more, I am just a sister of mercy looking after my sick children. 'God bless the poor dear, our sainted mother,' the crone prayed, 'Amen' others. Words of Kerensky: Comrades, I have been appointed Minister of Justice. No one is a more ardent republican than I, but we must bide our time. We shall have our republic, but we must win the war first. Loyalty to Prince Lvof as Premier and Minister of the Interior. Democrats to support Provisional Government until end of war. Measure carried one thousand to fifteen.

Ludmila read all this aloud. The revolution seemed to be over. It was twilight. The electric lights came on in the ward. This was a great moment for some of the patients, who crossed themselves as at a miracle. '*Liktrichestvo*,' breathed the crone. Ludmila sighed but said nothing. The old women meant *elektrichestvo*, but *lik* was a religious image, like of the Virgin Mary who was sometimes confused with the Czarina. This same crone thought the ward was the *bublik* one not the *publik* one, and every day would ask where was the *bublik* or bagel to go with her tea. There was another woman, a gross one with an eyepatch, who thought that *kommunist* was really *kumanist*, which was something to do with the *kumanika*, a wild raspberry. She saw the dream era which was not to come as cornucopial with fruit for the masses. Ignorant old dears. Never been given a chance to learn.

On 16 March aunt Anya came alone. The streets were calm, she said, some shops open, but the trams not yet running. And oh here was a letter. If that was England's Czar Yuri on the stamp, then he had a great likeness to the Czar of all the Russias that was that no more. Ludmila's heart jumped into her pharynx and then back into its proper cavity, where it turned itself into a tenor drum. It was her own writing on the big envelope. Inside there was a small envelope and she did not recognize the writing at all: some comrade of poor dead David sending his condolences. Then she opened up and read:

> No 17 Military Hospital
> Blackpool, Lancs

My dearest wife,
   I am not writing this but a friend Dan Tetlow is taking down my words because I have a bandage on my eyes. But dont worry I am not going blind. I was hit about a good deal by bits of stone and metal and dead people's bones and was left for dead till they saw that I was breathing. The major was a bit too quick in sending out letters, it was as if he wanted us all to be dead, less trouble for him. I have had most of the bits removed and have to stay here for a bit. It looks like my fighting days are over. I am aloud visiters so please come and see me kariad if thats how you spell it. All love from your loving husband.

And then, in his private dark, he had scrawled his name and added crosses for kisses. Ludmila wept. 'He's alive,' she sobbed. 'They made a mistake. He's not dead.'
   'So that's how they write in Angliya,' her aunt said, looking at the letter. 'Funny sort of an alphabet it is they have. Well, this is good news for you. You won't be staying with us much longer.'
   In two days Ludmila had herself discharged. The buttock was sore and one big purple bruise; she limped, a wounded soldier. From the general post office she sent a cable in Romic: I IN PETROGRAD BUT NOW I COME. Then she went to see little Yura Petrovich Shulgin in the children's hospital, proud of his lost thumb joint, kissed him goodbye and said they would meet again sometime, fellow wounded soldiers. Back with her aunt and uncle, she suddenly realized that she did not have enough

roubles to buy a passage home, yes home. Her cheque book was useless here. Her uncle Boris said:

'You've got this here Anglisky passport, never seen such a thing before, a little book that says you are who you are, which you know anyway, so I reckon it's the Anglisky government that's responsible for you, little sweet rose of all the world. Supposed to be friends of the Russians but a fat lot they did during the great days, skulking like bears in their offices. There's this place on the Admiralty Quay called the Anglisky Russky Bureau. It's their job to get you on to a ship. Not that we want to see the back of you, little one, though a dear little back it is, straight and clean as your poor mother's. Get this war over and you'd be living in a free and glorious republican Russia.' Ludmila went round to the Admiralty Quay and up in a lift. The office she entered was full of clacking typewriters and pictures of rural England; there was also a great map of the London Underground. A cheerful red-faced official in tweeds puffed a cork-tipped cigarette at her and said:

'Cashing a cheque? A British one? Really? We're not a bank, you know, but I tell you what, you go in there and see our Mr Walpole. Very kind man, pockets dripping with roubles, drops them all over the floor. Shouldn't be any trouble for him, the fool.' Ludmila sniffed the air, not at all Russian: Gold Flakes and lavender floor polish. Mr Walpole was a vague young man with a big head and pinchnose spectacles. He said:

'Russian, are you, married to one of ours? That's nice. I say, this letter here's from a Russian, he's tired of his six kids and wants to swap them for six English ones. At least that's what I *think* he says.' Ludmila confirmed this. 'Thanks awfully. I say, you're an awfully pretty girl. Want to go back to the UK? Can't say I blame you. Want a cheque cashed? Let's see what we can do.'

The way back was not out of Petrograd, whose port was congested with shipping made idle by a strike of loafers or stevedores. It had to be from Romanof, which meant a week's train journey past Lake Ladoga and Lake Onaga through Karelia up to Onega Gulf and Onega Bay to the White Sea. Ludmila travelled painfully up on one buttock to a region of log huts and plank walkways and wolves and ptarmigans. Then she boarded a

54

freighter which had not yet changed its name from SS *Czar*. She sailed off into the Arctic, rounding the Kola Peninsula along the Murman Coast, seeing a sea all glassy with, inlaid, an infinite squashed rainbow. Varanger Fiord and Njarg and Varjag. Upper fanged edge of Norway, that was. She picked at the rough stews the ship's officers scoffed, leering at her until she hissed: 'Where were you during the revolution, comrades?' The U-boats were, she heard, too busy on the Atlantic and in the English Channel to bother then up here, end of the world, and she slept soundly on her sound buttock, her cabin door locked against the urgencies of the woman-starved crew. They slid down into the North Atlantic, hugging the Norwegian coast. They took on some anonymous bales at Stavanger, and then sailed west to the Orkneys. Then Western Scotland was on the port side, and the air felt like South Wales. She landed with a suitcase full of dirty underclothes at Liverpool.

She discovered there to her delight that Blackpool was not far, a workers' pleasure city on the Irish Sea. It was breezy and full of troops, mocked by a great Luna Park wheel whose revolutions had been suspended for the duration, topped by a sort of Eiffel Tower. Here she got herself a room in the Imperial Hotel on the sea front and then went to see her husband, whose hospital was inland but not far behind the South Shore pleasure park. The air was gritty with flung sand, and sea holly grew on the sparse grass banks.

The two wounded soldiers fell on each other, wincing. David Jones was fierce in the eyes but no longer bandaged there. 'What happened, girl, was this gravestone sort of exploded all over me and bits of granite got lodged in me everywhere, and a chunk of shrapnel shot right through the ribcage and out at the back, clean as a whistle, and a great shower of gritty stuff went into my buttocks.'

'Into mine too. One buttock.'

'Here's not the place to talk about him because he's just gone to the sluice,' David Jones said with a lowered voice, 'But he was the one that saw I was alive and got me carted quick to the dressing station. Dan Tetlow, that wrote the letter. He lost his manhood just one day later, poor bugger. Never had any kids, end of the line for the poor bastard. I'll not forget in a hurry.

Cheerful as a lark, lost his manhood. Walking about in his blue, whistling. Clean as a whistle they were off.' Then he said, fierce sore eyes on the future, 'I'm applying for a cook's course when I get out. Officers' mess cooking, the posh stuff. This bloody war looks like it's going to go on for ever. I've done my bit, I think, and it's time I got back to the trade and thought about the future. What was it like in St Petersburg? Couldn't make much sense of what they read to me out of *John Bull*, bloody rag as it is.' He listened as she told him (Petrograd) and then nodded. 'Yes, the light that failed but they'll have another try before the year's out. A kind of a rehearsal call it. Nobody ever thought things would be as they are. Shooting at both of us. Mixed up in bloody history, which ought to be none of our business. I've got this book here by the man they called Vegetable Marrow, best man I ever met, and I've had the time to have it read out to me by Dan Tetlow, second-best man that's lost his manhood. A big flaming sword with A written on it. The A's for Attila the Hun, though he doesn't seem to have been a German, and also for Arthur, who was king of Wales. Different, but both the same, as the sword shows, for what is history but slashing the innocent with a sword? What we have to do is get out of it and down to the things that matter. I mean food mostly. Food's what matters, people will always eat and always have done when history's kindly permitted them to. Melt the sword down and make knives and forks out of it. You get home, girl, I don't want you stuck up here spending money in hotels. We'll need every penny we've got before we finish. And look after that buttock.'

It was on 3 March 1918, the day of the signing of the Treaty of Brest-Litovsk, that the first child of Sergeant and Mrs Jones was born, a girl they named Beatrix, though without benefit of Christian baptism. It seemed to them that the name came from nowhere. There was nobody in either family of that name, nor had it lodged in either of their minds from the reading of a poem or newspaper. Ludmila had merely said, holding the scowling baby in her lovely white arms: 'We call her Beatrix.' But there is, we are told, such a thing as subliminal penetration. There had been a literary display in the Anglo-Russian Bureau, glorification of one or other of the glories of British letters, changed every week, and, that particular day of her visit, seventeen-year-old

Peter Rabbit had been celebrated, a big floppy fubsy toy with a photograph of his creatrix solemnly weeding an English garden. Sergeant Jones nodded, saying: 'Just as you say, love. It sounds a nice name. I like the tricks bit at the end.'

As a sergeant cook in charge of officers' mess catering at the regimental depot, he found it easy to get home at weekends, having a good corporal under him with a mania for showing he was as good as his superior. He was able to see his wife often and his child grow, more than could be said of the poor muddy bastards in trenches waiting for the big Hun drive on the Somme. Lucky. They both were. Gold from that cobwebbed cockloft glowed in the bank vault, a sign of it. He already had fears for this bonny quietened babe at her lovely mother's lovely blue-veined breast. Luck was not a thing that was passed on.

The generative engine, so long unaccountably idle, was at work now, and on 18 January 1919, while the delegates of the Peace Conference knocked hell out of each other in Paris, Reginald Morrow Jones was born. His father was still waiting to be demobbed but, on furlough and in the Miner's Arms in Blackwood, he was able to justify the aggressive Anglo-Norman Reginald and the stressing of the Morrow to make the surname sound doublebarrelled by telling the conservative socialist drinkers that he, and his family, were about to walk into a new dispensation. Dai Jones and Ianto Pritchard and Ifan Evans were ingrown names of the insular and downtrodden. The children of this particular Dai Jones were to inherit a freer and wider world. Dr A. J. Cronin, visiting Blackwood from Tredegar where his practice was, drank to that and spoke of his own ambition to become a popular novelist. The future at that time seemed bright for some. David Jones and his wife and son and daughter were to settle in the country the Welsh called Lloegr, in the city of Manchester, birthplace of the great if devious Welshman David Lloyd George.

A visiting catering officer with a General List badge (Crosse and Blackwell's regiment) had expressed appreciation of the lightness of Sgt Jones's lemon soufflé. His name was Captain Zimmerman but the freemasonry of the culinary vocation expunged rank as he drank Grand Marnier in the officers' mess kitchen. 'And what do you propose to do when you get out of

57

uniform?' he asked in the slightly adenoidal tones of Jewish Manchester. My tones, by the way, my birthplace. The name, not that it matters, is Harry Wolfson.

'Never to say sir again, sir, except in the way of ordinary politeness. That means being my own boss and that means running a little restaurant. Sir.'

'Got money, have you?'

'A bit tucked away in the bank. Some rent money coming in from a brownstone in New York.'

'Hm, a travelled man. Cosmopolitan. Listen. My brother and I run a well thought of restaurant on Deansgate, Manchester. The Trianon, a bit pretentious but never mind. My brother's exempt from military service because of his asthma, he runs it alone at the moment but he says the damp air's killing him. When I get back he'll want to get out and go south. You know where the money is? The restaurant side's only a front. The money's in home catering, Masonic catering. Hayboxes and thermos containers, seven-course dinners sent out. Weddings, funerals, bar mitzvahs. Of course, it's been a bad time lately, rationing and rationing likely to go on so we can feed the starving Germans, but things will get better. Besides, it's not the rationed stuff the well-off worry about. Oysters, lobsters, smoked trout, Morecambe Bay shrimps. The luxuries never get rationed except by price.'

'Are you offering me a job? Sir?'

'More than a job really if you could put some money in. There's a big future there, and that isn't sales talk. You married? Right, talk it over with your wife.'

'My wife,' Sgt Jones said, 'is Russian. She was the daughter of the man who ran the Nevsky Prospect restaurant in Brooklyn, NY.'

'My God, we've got a lot of Russians in Manchester. Jews and the other sort, goys, Russian Orthodox. And there are more coming in, what with this Revolution. I see great things ahead. Talk it over with the missis.'

The third and last child, a son, was born on 22 February 1920 at Number 231 Dickinson Road, Rusholme, Manchester. They named him Daniel Tetlow Jones. He was not the brightest of the three, nor the most handsome. The daughter and the elder son inherited the Viking properties of the Slav side and grew tall and blond. Dan was dark and small, like his father. He seemed sometimes to be not quite right in the head, which was a perverse comfort to David Jones, who saw in him a mitigant of the luck that otherwise continued. What Daniel Tetlow Jones seemed mostly to care for in his life was fish.

DAU

'IT'S a pity you never knew it,' said Reginald Morrow Jones. 'After all, you Jews are supposed to be addicted to refined feeding.' We were taking tea in the Kardomah teashop on Deansgate which had, till quite recently, been the Trianon restaurant. 'It was good. And the clientèle was good too. Actors and musicians mostly. Noël Coward, John Gielgud, Artur Schnabel. They had their signed photographs all over the walls. And look at the walls now.' The walls now were all grossly enlarged willow pattern. 'The real trouble was not my mother's coughing because of the Manchester air. It was the police getting nasty about the renewal of the drinking licence. Anyway, they'd made their little pile and now they have this nice little pub outside Abergavenny. But it's a pity really. It was the best restaurant in Manchester.' And then: 'I'm sorry about what I said then. About the Jews, I mean.'

'Worse things are said about us. And it's true about the refined feeding. Refined but heavy.'

I did not know the Trianon because I hardly knew Manchester at all, though I was born in Cheetham Hill. I spent a great deal of my youth outside Manchester and indeed outside England. I was outside England because my father was an engineer engaged on overseas contracts. Engineering was an unusual vocation for a Jew at that time. A Jew could create art but not build bridges. My father's studies at the Manchester Technical College had been encouraged by no less a personage than Dr Chaim Weizmann. He, a son of the pale of Motol in Grodno, a graduate of Berlin and Freiburg, had in 1904 become a reader in biochemistry at Manchester University and a friend of my grandfather, at one time a fairly distinguished Jewish atheist. Weizmann was to become first President of the Jewish state of Israel in 1949, but he had been working for the foundation of this state all his life. He was also working for the British War Office during David Jones's war, and his discovery of a process for the manufacture of acetone, essential to high explosives, gained him the reward of the foundation of the Colony of David in Palestine. He became the chief voice in world Zionism. He believed that the Jews of the diaspora should prepare themselves for the literal construction of the Jewish state – meaning its roads, cities and bridges, its warships and heavy weapons – by cultivating the applied sciences. As there was no money in my grandfather's atheism, Weizmann assisted my father to pursue his studies in civil engineering. My father became a very good, if somewhat bad-tempered, civil engineer.

From 1917 until 1920, the year I was born, the British military administration of Palestine disbursed British money on needful amenities in the territory, including the throwing of a steel bridge over the river Jordan, and on this work my father was engaged. A good deal of Zionist money came in for other projects, mostly from America, but the peaceful development of a modern Palestine was, as always, hindered by the Arabs: my boyhood in Jaffa was loud and dusty with riots and terrorism. My father's firm, based in Trafford Park, had him out of dangerous Palestine and at constructional work in Argentina and Peru (railways mostly), but we were back in Palestine in 1928, when the failed Schofin Letsipren project was initiated: this was to be a triumph of metallic tension, the thinnest building in the world. I remember in 1929 the eruption of the riot over the Wailing Wall, and, young as I was, realizing that the future lay in terrorism.

As you probably know, the Wailing Wall is so called, by goyim if not by Jews, because it is the site for the loud recital of the Book of Lamentations. Jews call it the Kotel Ma'arabi or Western Wall and claim it as the most ancient shrine of the faith, erected long before Mohamed drove his first camel. The Muslims contest this, asserting that the wall and the pavement which skirts it are holy monuments of their own upstart religion. Hence the riots. I saw fists and howling mouths and then Weizmann's own acetone at work, and I was visited by a philosophical speculation rather mature for a boy of nine: that religious and political causes were only pretexts for smashing things and people; it was the smashing that mattered. Human beings were balls of energy, masses of fleshly acetone, and the energy could best be fired to a destructive end, creation being so difficult and requiring brains and imagination. But since man is a creature of mind as well as nerve and muscle, some spurious cause has to justify destruction. Destruction, best expressed in this age in which I write as terrorism, is truly there for its own sake, but the pretence of religious or secular patriotism converts the destructive into the speciously creative.

Reg paid the bill for tea, which was a very Manchester meal with fried egg and chips as the main course. He had more money than I. Then we walked down Deansgate towards Piccadilly. We were, I suppose, well-set-up young Englishmen of the period, though neither of us was English, whatever the term means. I think it ought to mean having English as a first language. Reg was a Viking and I was a Jew, whatever a Jew is. True, I was circumcised, but so were many Gentiles. There had been no religion in the family since my atheistic grandfather. I was of the Mediterranean and Reg of the Baltic. He had a high forehead and the thinness of blond hair on his scalp promised early baldness. I ran strongly to dark hair and had to shave twice daily. I resented my hirsuteness. Indeed, I had a neurotic horror of all kinds of plethora. We were passing a gramophone shop on Piccadilly that cried its wares with a record of 'Underneath the Spreading Chestnut Tree', a song made popular by King George VI in his capacity as scoutmaster. I thought of Roquentin and said:

'Have you read *La Nausée*?'

'Never heard of it. French?'

'A Frenchman called Sartre. Not long out. Not yet translated into English. Colin Smith is mad about it. He brought it back from Paris and he dictates chunks of it to us. It's about a man who is appalled by the fecundity of a chestnut tree. All that excess, that teeming ghastly life contradicting the human desire for refrigerated simplicity. I see his point. Look at this blossoming plenum of the world all about us,' meaning Piccadilly with its shoppers and red buses. 'I know what he means by nausea.'

'Who means?'

'The hero of the book, Roquentin. It's in us as well as outside us. A damnable complexity of guts and glands, the confusion of the psyche with its contention of identities.'

'Dear dear dear,' Reg said. 'You want a bomb should drop on it all?' He sometimes used Yiddish syntax when speaking to me, though my family knew no Yiddish. He meant no harm. We caught a Number 44 bus. He was going to Fallowfield to see Jorge Lewis, his lecturer in Catalan. I had had tea, but I was going to a tea party in the Philosophy seminar. The party was one of the regular get-togethers organized by Professor Pears. It was, I suppose, no wonder that I was studying Philosophy, with French and German on the side, despite my father's exhorting me to do good in the world and learn something practical. In my course in metaphysics with Profesor Nussbaumer I could comfort myself with the reality of monads and the vision of a final state which, after the restless flurry of life's perpetuating itself, would show the timeless simplicity of a true perpetuum which might as well be called God, uncreative and not even self-regarding. But I had to attend classes in moral and political philosophy as well and meet the bewildering mess of man's trying to impose order on himself. And at Professor Pears's tea parties there would be an informal discussion about the ideal state or the ethics of polygamy on a shipwreck island where there were ten female survivors and one man. Attendance at these bun fights was not compulsory, but it made a difference to one's term marks. I was really going because Reg's sister was usually there.

I was attracted to her as I had not been to many women. The women I had seen in the hot places of the world resembled my mother and sister in being like Roquentin's chestnut tree, created by the gods of biology to add to the existing plethora – fleshly rich, hippy, bosomy, all too excessive, earth-motherish, ready to smother all except the progenitive urge of a man in a forest of midnight hair. They had the faint smell of a cow. Beatrix Jones was fair and Baltic-eyed like her brother, her skin the thinnest of envelopes over prominent Slavic cheekbones. Her body was exquisitely shaped but very spare. She wore straight simple dresses, pastel and unpatterned; she disdained bangles and earrings. She was far from cold, but her sexual heat was governed as by some intellectual thermostatic device. I discovered later that her cool sexual approach to me reproduced that of her mother to her father, though she did not have marriage in mind. She had a career before her.

On the upper deck of the bus Reg opened a new packet of Player's but did not offer me one. He was not so much ungenerous as thoughtless. I lit up my last Gold Flake and said: 'This meeting with your Mr or Señor Lewis will, I take it, have something to do with the Spanish Civil War?'

'If we fight for Catalonia we're assured of a pass in Catalan. Even if we get killed.'

'A lot of bloody Welshmen fighting for republican Spain. It's mad.' For the Hispanic department had mostly Welsh students, Spanish being a substitute for Welsh, the same vowel system and so on. But this Jorge Lewis was from Chile, where there were a lot of Welsh surnames. He had fallen in love with Catalonia and ran the subsidiary course in Catalan, which apparently had a rich literature.

'Mad, is it?' Reg said. 'It's everybody's war. It's yours too, if you had the sense to see it. The Jews have a stake in killing the fascists.'

'That'll come later,' I said, 'despite the bloody betrayal at Munich.' It was October 1938, and the university term had just begun. That lunchtime we had had the first of the Men's Union debates. Reg and I had opposed each other on the motion that this house prefers Groucho to Karl. It had been carried, but only just. Reg had spoken for Karl, far more wittily than I for Groucho. I had praised him as a linguistic philosopher; Reg had extolled Karl as a purveyor of boisterous fun, having invented the great game of dialectical materialism. He had ended with lines sung to Mendelssohn's Wedding March, from Auden's *Dance of Death:*

Oh Mr Marx we've gathered all the essential facts.
We know the economic reasons for our acts.

Then he had put on a false beard like a bird's nest and stomped off to cheers while Jack Pickford played Chopin's Funeral March on the piano. Then we had gone together to Steuermann's on Deansgate so that he could buy a very thin brandy flask. The rest of his fighting equipment would be issued when he and the others of Jorge Lewis's band of volunteers landed at Barcelona.

I said: 'And what does Professor Pulga think about this temporary
or permanent desertion of his department?' It was well known that
Pulga was a fascist.

'He thinks we're fighting for the Catholic Church. Even Lewis.
Pulga's a fool. He has to be, being what he is. He thinks we'll be
fighting in Castilian. A legitimate part of our education. Mad.'

'As I said. Mad.'

'It's mother and dad I worry about,' Reg said. 'Dad's always
been going on about his luck. He has been lucky too, very lucky.
He thinks a compensatory flood of disaster will overtake his
children. Welsh superstition. A load of nonsense. We've all been
cosseted. Too well fed, too much pocket money.'

'If,' I said, 'you could spare me one of your Player's – '

'Take two. Three. Take the lot.' He handed me the packet,
not, as I have said, ungenerous. I would now have cigarettes to
offer his sister at the bun fight. The bus was nearing Lime Grove
and I ran down the stairs. He travelled on to Fallowfield.

Beatrix or Trixie was pouring tea and one of her pimply adorers
was handing round biscuits. She was twenty but, it seemed to
me, very mature with her upswept gold hair and her green
simple dress and her gunmetal stockings and high heels. So
many girls of her age slouched and had awkward gestures and
smelt of the sweat and ink of the sixth form. Beatrix was in total
control of her bodily movements and could not lift the lid of the
big red teapot without grace. She had, in respect of her erotic life,
a reputation probably without precedent. She was unwooable,
unflirtatious, and yet was known to sleep with men. The medical
students, whose response to the revelations of the dissecting
room was a coarse guffawing attitude to sexuality, never
mentioned her name with a leer. When she entered the university
cafeteria she provoked no theatrical groans or wolf howls. She
was not seducible; it was she who seduced. Men who had been
seduced by her evinced not the silly tropes of sexual triumph:
they kept quiet about it, as though a goddess had descended
and enjoined silence about an inexpressible ecstasy.

She was in her final year in the History department, but one
of her subsidiary subjects was Political Philosophy. Her specialization was the brief annals of Soviet diplomacy. Having Russian
as a mother tongue, she could read with total ease such docu-

ments as got to the West from Moscow, and she could translate them into an English as spare and elegant as her body. Professor L. B. Namier thought highly of her. He was probably in love with her. She had not, it was generally believed, attempted his seduction. That would not have been playing the game. She seduced to no advantage except her own erotic gratification.

Professor Pears beamed all around, his pipe bubbling nicely, and the ten or twelve of us sat while he proposed a theme for discussion. The theme was the relation between the reality of the state and the philosophy of nationalism. I sat near to Beatrix and ofered her one of her brother's cigarettes. I lit it for her with a tubed chemical device which produced a glow on inspiration. She examined it with curiosity. She looked at me with curiosity, as though she had never noticed me before. But I had been at the university a whole year. The chemical lighter, just on the market, was not to last: it imparted a sour taste to the first draw. Sooner or later the discussion got on to the racialism of the Nazis, and one youth with smeary glasses and an unclean collar unwisely spoke up for the maintenance of pure stock. Hitler was wrong in many ways but was right, the youth asserted, to insist on a national homogeneity which miscegenation must not be permitted to sully. 'You mean,' I said, 'kick the Jews out?' In our ignorance at that time we believed that that was all the Nazis wanted.

'Not just the Jews. Niggers and Chinks and Japs. A nation should not be a whatsit stew.'

'By whatsit,' Professor Pears said, 'I take it you mean hetero-geneous. By those opprobrious terms you used I take it you mean the Negroes and the Chinese and the Japanese. This is not a street corner meeting of the British Fascist Party.'

'I,' Beatrix said, 'as many of you know, am a product of miscegenation. Russian mother, Welsh father.' There was no need for her to say more. Her sharp brain and exquisite body exalted the mixing of bloods. I said:

'All bloods are the same. What makes one race different from another is language and culture. But history shows that both language and culture are transmitted. What I mean is, they're not chthonic.' The word earned me, I could tell, the respect of Beatrix. 'What I mean is, they don't spring out of one's native

66

earth. Call me a Jew, and what do you mean by it?' It was the first time my Jewishness had ever entered a philosophical discussion. I could feel Beatrix's eyes going over me, looking for Jewishness. 'My distant background is Mediterranean, as for the Arabs, Spaniards, Maltese, Italians. I do not hold to the Hebraic faith. Nor do my parents. In a fit of recidivism my mother insisted I be circumcised. As for diet – '

'What's circumcised?' asked a first-year girl.

Professor Pears lowered his pipe from his lips and opened his mouth in wonder, showing a tooth coating of fresh brown juice. 'You have,' he said in wonder, 'never read the Bible?'

'Dad wouldn't let us. He wouldn't let us go to church either. He calls himself a freethinker.'

'Meaning,' Professor Pears said, 'unwilling to grant the right of free thought to his offspring. You must bring him along to one of our tea parties.'

'He doesn't drink tea.'

'Circumcision,' I said, 'is the cutting off of the foreskin.' I indicated roughly where that was. 'A hygienic measure but mythicized into the sign of a covenant between Jehovah and his chosen people. The Muslims, who have something of Hitler's racism in them and, like him, loathe the Jews, are also circumcised.'

'I'm a Presbyterian,' a lad who smoked halves of Woodbines said, 'and I've had it lopped off too. Our doctor believed in it.'

'There you are then,' I said, for no clear reason. Or perhaps I meant that circumcision was as close to this ignorant girl as was the fast-filling ashtray. I gave Beatrix another cigarette and told her she could keep the chemical lighter if she wished. She did not wish. At the end of the session we were all more or less agreed that a nation was all the better for being multiracial, and then Beatrix invited me to tea in her digs in Rusholme. A week that day. I was one of the chosen people, and my circumcised penis shrank in prospect.

My sister and I lived with our aunt Bérénice in her modern detached house on Dickinson Road. She was, though Jewish, no blood relation, being the widow of our uncle Ben and also French. Uncle Ben had made his money out of the export of British-made Escoffier sauces to France, and had met his bride in Paris. Aunt

Bérénice had helped to Gallicize the cuisine of the Mancunians by writing a weekly food column in the *Manchester Evening News*. She had known the Trianon restaurant but said that it was too Eastern European for her taste. She spent much of her time now with her stockbroker, organizing her portfolio against what, like all Jews, she knew to be the day of coming wrath. She was thin, chic, and economical, and doled out sparse pocket money to us. Our parents were still abroad, though not in Palestine. My father was working in Venezuela, throwing a steel bridge over the Orinoco. He sent adequate money home for our keep and small pleasures, but aunt Bérénice considered that it was sinful not to invest money and much of our allowances slid into her portfolio. She fed us elegantly but sparsely, so that we were always wiping the dark French sauces off our plates with bread. Half-starved, we lunched off student's stodge. My sister was at the Manchester Royal College of Music. She was a year older than I, straight-nosed and creamy skinned. I will come to her later. I had some difficulty in coaxing from our aunt an advance on next month's allowance. I needed to buy condoms. There was a shop on Oxford Road that had the Works of Aristotle in the window. The greyhaired woman there, wrapping my Durex, said that it looked like being a wet weekend.

The tea that Beatrix Jones fed me would have suited my aunt if she had been in the habit of consuming *le five o'clock*. It was austere – brown bread and butter, very thin, very plain biscuits, and Earl Grey strong and sugarless. After the meal she ordered me to take off all my clothes. I was shocked but I obeyed, trembling of course. She surveyed my Jewish hairiness and was interested to meet circumcision as a surgical fact, not just a feast of the Church or a bit of Semitic folklore. She satisfied herself that no blot other than a dateshaped birthmark on my left clavicle marred my skin. She nodded and then took off her own clothes, meaning a single garment of red silk. Her body was, of course, superb, and her pubic mane was rich gold leaf. We made love on a plain russet rug before the gas-fire, which glowed at half strength because of the slight autumn chill. I was tremulous but, experienced despite my youth, which had after all been spent in lands where the sexual flashpoint was low, I made satisfactory love, or rather she made it to me. She lay upon me, Mars observed, and procured her own orgasms. I sweated though she did not. She raised herself at climax and briefly sang at the ceiling. 'I love you,' I said, as a man will in easy payment for high pleasure, but she said, 'Nonsense'. But I did love, while I was caressing it, that spare silken body, the pert breasts, the mane like gold foil. I said: 'I did not. I should have. I didn't expect,' lying. For I had been granted no opportunity to unroll and don a Durex. But she: 'All right. I did.' She was always in charge and there was no dangerous impulse in it. How many other men? I did not ask. She was two years older than I, a mature woman.

So we rested naked on the rug while the few leaves that were left on the chestnut tree in the garden shushed at the window. I surveyed her bare room, with its books in English and Russian and the framed photograph of L. B. Namier, signed. He had a frog's face, and he pouted. She was to follow Namier to the Foreign Office as, officially, an assistant principal, actually as his right-hand woman. I said: 'This is terrible, but I have to go.'

'Why terrible?'

A big word, *terrible*, descriptive of what terrorists do. 'I mean, I don't want to go, the last thing in the world I want to do is to go, but there's this concert–'

'What concert?'

'My sister. At the College of Music. She's singing in *Flos Campi*.'

'What's *Flos Campi*?'

'It means Flower of the Field. It's a sort of – '

'I know what it means, stupid. What is it?'

'I was trying to tell you. It's by Vaughan Williams and it's supposed to be about the Song that is Solomon's. There's a chorus but it just goes oo and ah. You're supposed to know it's all about Jewish sensuality from the titles of the movements. The solo viola does most of the work. The music sounds all too English and folky to me.'

'And your sister's going oo and ah in it?'

'Yes. And she's also playing in one of the other things they're doing – Constant Lambert's *Rio Grande*. She's one of the percussion players. There are five altogether, I think.'

'Are all Jewish families musical?'

'There's usually one who takes to it. Some Jews carry jewels

69

round the world, others fiddles. Now Zip proposes carting a whole percussion section round with her. Very un-Jewish.'

'What did you call her then?'

'Zip. Short for Zipporah. The wife of Moses, you know.'

'I didn't know. We're not a Bible family. Though I did know about circumcision. Theoretically.' The humorous tenderness of a cool hand on my groin would have done well there, but she implied merely that she knew more than before and I was a sort of book. I said:

'Her name and my trip to the moyl or mohel are not really typical of our family. My mother used to have recidivist fits.'

'You have this large vocabulary, don't you? And Hebrew as well I take it to be. And you can't be all that old.'

'Eighteen.'

'Oh, my God, I'm baby snatching.'

'I'm older than my years. An education in the barbarous regions of the world. And Zip too.'

'The promise of Jewish sensuality,' she said. 'Your term, remember. I didn't find anything out of the Manchester ordinary, if you don't mind my saying so.'

'Perhaps next time,' I said with a certain male insolence.

'Don't be too sure about that.' A French sexologist had written that men always look ridiculous at any stage of dressing or undressing, women always charming. Men wore too much in those days. I had a tie to knot, braces, suspenders. I dressed as quickly as I could, so as not to look ridiculous. But she was already dressed, watching me. 'I think I'll come with you,' she said. 'I'd like to see your Zip ooing and ahing and doing the other thing.'

'Many other things,' lacing my shoes. 'Xylophone, marimba, Turkish crash, sidedrum. It's by invitation, but be my vicarious guest.'

'And then there's Reg's farewell party.'

'I didn't know. I thought he'd already left.' I looked hurt.

'You're invited. He's only just back from South Wales. He asked me to pass the invitation on.'

'He knew you were inviting me?' I said, and added: 'To tea.'

'To tea, yes.' And then she said: 'Dad thought he was studying something nice and safe. Trade with the Argentine and the value

70

of commercial Spanish. Now he'll blame himself. Reg has always been the coddled one. Keep him safe so you don't have to worry about his being lucky or unlucky. Luck isn't a thing that's passed on.' She was glossing what Reg had told me himself a week before. 'What time does this thing start?'

We took a bus to the Royal College of Music. First there was Walton's Overture *Portsmouth Point,* played with rough intonation by the student orchestra stiffened with professors, but it was a rough work anyway. Zip was not in the percussion section, not as big as in the Lambert piece and manned only by men. Then came Stanford's *Songs of the Sea,* with a professorial singer and a male chorus. 'That's her,' I said, when the girls came on in white for *Flos Campi.* The scent of Beatrix's skin was maddening in that crammed hot hall. I had derided the music as all too English and folky, but something of the Solomonic sensuality got across, primed by the close presence of this cool Welsh Russian girl.

'She's pretty.' Zip was too, I supposed, intensely blackhaired, bare arms aglow, in virginal white. When Lambert's work began with the side-drum crescendo under pizzicato strings I was proud of my sister, making all that noise. The pianist professor who played the solo had a fine jazz touch. The chorus sang:

By the Rio Grande
They dance no sarabande
On level banks like lawns above the glassy lolling tide . . .

The concert, which was entirely of British music, ended with Parry's *Jerusalem,* and we all stood to join in. When it was over and Beatrix and I went round the back to pick up Zip to congratulate her, I said:

'The dark Satanic mills are really churches, you know, and Jerusalem signifies the unfettered imagination and an abundance of free sensual pleasure.'

'Who told you that?'

'The words are by William Blake. I've read Blake. I read him in the holy city itself, where there's as much fettering as there is here. I understood Blake. The only true world is the world of symbols.' She had had my body; I wanted her to have it again. Then for some reason I said: '*Guf*', which is Hebrew for the body.

71

'It is guff too.' Zip had appeared in black skirt and emerald sweater, her virginal dress in brown paper. I introduced girl to girl and they surveyed each other, woman to woman. 'Of course you're coming to the party,' Beatrix said. 'You deserve a party after all that hard work with sticks and things. And you looked lovely when you were going oo and ah. Really you did.' Zip looked at me with new eyes: I had picked myself a peach and no error. There had to be more in me than she had ever suspected. She clung to my right arm possessively as we walked to the bus. Reg's digs were not far from the university; they were -- I had been there before – two big rooms in a Georgian house on Ducie Grove, a town mansion brought low and all peeling stucco and decay, something, when you came to think of it, that was more Dublin than Manchester. But we went first to a fish and chip shop on a side street. I did not know it, but Beatrix did. It was full of people, greasy steam and the stench of malt vinegar. To my surprise she went up to one of the two servers behind the zinc counter and kissed him with warmth. Zip looked startled, wondering what she had been let in for. When a goddess kissed a low dark ugly chipshoveller anything could happen. But Beatrix said: 'This is Dan. My brother.'

This was something to be thought over. Two tall golden handsome intellectuals had a troglodyte of a brother who fished out fried fish from a seething vat and shovelled chips into bags. Dan, whose full name I was to discover was Daniel Tetlow Jones, named for the emasculated saviour of his father's life, said: 'He was in, Trixie. We're having a busy night, but I'll be there at closing time. He's already took.'

'Took, has he?'

'Ten bob, all told. Warming up in the oven.' It was an honest Manchester accent with a Welsh tinge. But then he said: '*Do zvidaniya*' and Beatrix spoke the same formula in reply. Now Zip wondered what the hell really was going on. But Beatrix explained. Some people, after all, did have Russian mothers.

When we got to Reg's digs the eating of fish and chips and the drinking of bottled Threlfall's ale was well in progress. Reg's landlady had done the warming up. She, a greyheaded retired tart, was lamenting the stupidity of war and the waste of high blood and fine bodies. 'I don't know what gets into men,' she said. 'There's that Chamberlain saying it's peace in our time, but you're not satisfied, oh no. Geared yourselves up for a war like, and anybody's will do. Not that I don't think them Spaniards as has stripped nuns naked and set fire to churches don't deserve what they're going to get. Even though both was RC.' Zip and Reg took to each other, I could see that. Physical thesis and antithesis. Reg, going off to war, was in a mood to foresee himself slain and lamented by beautiful women. I had lain with Reg's sister that afternoon; it would, I thought fuzzily over my third bottle, be an apt completion of a quatrain to have Zip spending the night with him. And then I shook the abominable image away, dark and golden hair commingled, the uncircumcised with a daughter of Israel. No, no, an unfraternal fancy. But for some reason I started singing about the dark Satanic mills and explaining what they were.

There were no other women present, only the old whore and these two young beauties. My transport of the afternoon, and the matter of physical contrast, made me endue the tactile apparatus of another man, any man but me, and imagine the beauty of Zip in his caressing arms. But then I saw his burial under that midnight hair and those moons of breasts and felt Roquentin's sickness. And this made me want to grab the damnably cool Beatrix and embrace her roughly under the reproduction Gauguins on the dark landing that smelt of old cabbage. It was best to listen to what Reg's reader in Catalan, Dr Jorge Lewis, was saying. He was saying, an indiscreet thing from member of faculty to student, that Professor Pulga had foolishly given him the farewell gift of a small golden cross that had long been in the Pulga family and told him he was one of Christ's soldiers, the stupid old idiot. One of Reg's guests and prospective fighting comrades looked green, whether from fish and chips and beer or last minute misgivings about the whole mission was not clear. He began to sing quaveringly the Welsh national anthem and others, for nearly all were Welsh, joined in:

Gwlad, gwlad, pleidiol wyf i'm gwlad.
Tra môr yn fur i'r bur hoff bau
O bydded i'r hen iaith barhau.

73

Dr Lewis, despite his name and ancestry, knew no Welsh. He tried to overcome the irrelevant patriotism with something in Catalan. Reg said, when the anthem was over: 'Not so impertinent as you think, *wus*. We're fighting for the rights of all oppressed minorities.'

'With the help of the Soviet Union,' his sister said, 'which has done its own fair share of oppression.'

'You know better than that, Trix,' Reg said, though with little confidence.

Nearly all were Welsh, I say, but only six of the fifteen or so at the party were off to the war. The others were mostly fellow students of the Hispanic languages but more prudent, less idealistic. One of them, not Welsh, his name Higgins, was prudently idealistic in that he was waiting for the red revolution to come without doing much to assist it. He was sitting sipping beer from the bottle, under a poster which showed Spain as a bleeding bull bristling with fascist banderillas and he said:

'It's the only hope. Russia is our only hope.'

'You don't mean Russia,' Beatrix said. 'You mean an unrealistic and totally outmoded ideology imposed on a long-suffering people. As for Spain, do you honestly think' (she was addressing Reg) 'that there's a desire on the part of Tovarishch Stalin to save Catalonian anarchism and syndicalism and liberal socialism? I shouldn't be surprised if Moscow gold isn't helping to finance Franco.' There were outraged howls at that, then a boy named Glendower Owen, or it may have been the other way round, said:

'Well, there's some Welsh gold going in on the right side, anyway.' Reg turned on him in quiet fury and a gagging gesture, and Beatrix was quick to hiss:

'What's this?' And then, sharp strong nails, as I knew, ready for her brother: 'You bloody liar and thief and traitor, where is it?' Then she was striding into Reg's bedroom, which opened off the big untidy studio we were in. Reg was after her, unbrotherly fists bunched, and I had to be, assuming lover's rights rightly or not, after Reg. But Beatrix could, I discovered, be a wildcat. She was swinging a heavy gladstone bag at Reg and Reg was going 'ow' and retreating. He performed a brief rollerskate act by treading on a beer bottle that lay on its side, and he ended

74

tousled and blazing at the feet of Zip. Beatrix had dragged the gladstone bag in and opened it. 'There,' she said. She half lifted from it a thing I have described earlier: the rocky lump from Wellengong. Reg's landlady, not seeing clearly and assuming a severed head or a dead baby, came over for a close look.

'It's like a bit of old stone,' she said, disappointed.

'It's gold,' Beatrix announced, 'and it's not going to be sold to buy ammunition for the republicans. You're a bloody thief, Reg Jones, even if you think it's in a good cause, and I knew you'd try this on when dad had the bloody innocence to get it out of the bank and put it in a glass case.'

'It's been doing nothing,' Reg said from Zip's feet. 'It's been a waste. You could get a couple of machine-guns with it. You could feed a hundred starving Spanish families. I'm taking it.'

'Oh no, you're not,' fiery Beatrix cried. '*I'm* taking the train for Abergavenny first thing in the morning and putting it back where it belongs. You just don't understand, do you? This gold is absolute pitch.' Nobody understood except Zip. 'This is an absolute, a solidity, the real thing, not like bloody paper money. They made dad convert his sovereigns into paper pounds against his will, but he had the sense to hang on to this lot. This will be wealth when a pound note's the price of a newspaper. Gold is gold is gold and it stays gold, you stupid thieving bastard.'

At this moment Dan Tetlow Jones came in, bringing another absolute with him – the eternal stench of frying. 'Ah,' he said, seeing the gold, 'dad's thing. What's it doing here?'

'Take your big brother's head,' said Beatrix, 'and shove it in one of your chip vats, making sure the oil's bubbling nicely. He's done something he shouldn't, but he's not getting away with it.' Dan now showed not merely strength but vindictiveness. He thumped his brother's head with a big fist all scored with knife marks, then he dragged him to his feet. Dan came up to Reg's chest: it is the small not the tall who have to learn fistwork in the hard education of the school yard. He belaboured Reg until Beatrix told him to stop. Reg's landlady said:

'I know the rent's paid regular and all, but I don't like these goings on on my lawful premises, so I'll have to ask you all to stop before worse happens. But give Danny boy here a beer, he works harder than any of you lot, and then off home, there's some lodged here as has to get up early.' Dan, a frothing glass in his hand, now made a speech:

'I don't say I work harder, like what Emmie here says. I work different. Like my and his and her dad worked different. Feeding the five thousand, as dad used to say. I'm sorry I had to bash him here like the way I did, but he asked for it. I never yet knew of a time when he didn't ask for it. He carries on sometimes like he's not all there. Too much book learning.' Reg took all this without demur, so I assumed a regular pattern of family behviour. He was more concerned with getting his arm round Zip. 'Fish,' Dan then said, in a process of thought less illogical than it appeared, since fish are perhaps the last creatures one could imagine reading books, even the waterproof ones D'Annunzio read in his bath, 'fish have been brought low where I am. Bits of white stuff smothered in batter and then fried till golden brown. Where is the head and where is the tail? But it'll be different. I'm not staying there for ever, and Grimshaw's little lass keeps trying to get into bed with me. Sleeping over the shop's no good. Don't try it. I want to see fish nicely laid out on the slab. And that'll happen soon.'

'All right, Dan,' Beatrix said soothingly. 'Drain that nut brown and then to beddibyes. You,' she ordered me, 'pick up that bag and phone for a taxi and take me home.'

'I have,' I said primly, 'a prior duty to my sister.'

'I'll take her home,' Reg said, 'if she'll grant me the honour of so doing. As for you,' he said to his brother, 'it'll be you that'll be nicely laid on the slab. That hurt, sod you.'

'Meant to,' Dan said, his lower lip out. 'Meant to bloody hurt.'

'Language, language,' I said, still prim. 'My sister isn't used to this ready obscenity.' I went to the telephone on the landing and ordered two Luxicabs. I took Beatrix and the family gold to her digs but she did not ask me in for cocoa or other comfort. When I arrived at our aunt's house Zip and Reg had not yet arrived. I prowled the laurel bushes until they had and, well hidden, listened to their kisses and his whispers. Took to each other, as I said.

BEATRIX invited me no more to tea but I did not greatly repine. I was haunted by her smell for a week or so and felt rage when she ignored me in the cafeteria or on the corridors of the Arts Building. But then I got over it though I sought no other woman in my spare time. I was playing rugby football that autumn and winter and I was boxing and occasionally leaping horses in the gymnasium. Those activities took care of my body while my mind floated free in the contemplation of universals and monads and the swirling time-space points of Professor Alexander. As for Reg, nobody at the university had word of him: it was my sister Zipporah who received the odd letter with a Barcelona date stamp. The letters were heavily censored with black crayon, so she did not know where he was. But he talked of love and the bliss of her body in his arms, so I was constrained to ask her: 'How far did this business go?'

'Whatever you mean by business, it's none of yours.'

'I don't like this pert tone. I have a brotherly right to ask.'

'What you like is neither here nor there. If you must know, I spent two days with him before he went off, but it was all chaste and above board except for the usual thing.'

'What do you mean by the usual thing?'

'Kisses. Embraces. Sweet nothings. Now shut up and leave me alone.' She was trying out a complicated rhythm in a work of Bela Bartok with two drumsticks on the edge of the kitchen table. Our father was learning that Zip's vocation cost money. She needed drums and a glockenspiel and cymbals and a Chinese gong. It looked as if she would also need a plain van to cart her instruments around in.

'Do you love him?' I asked. 'Did he talk about marriage?'

'Oh, leave me alone and don't talk stupid. We're too young.'

'There'll be a lot of youthful marriages before long, you'll see. There's a war coming, you know.'

Zip put down her sticks and said: 'We've been told there's not going to be a war. This Spanish thing is supposed to be a lesson to everybody. Futility and so on. Now please get out of the kitchen and let me work.' I went to my own work in my bedroom. I had to write an essay on Spinoza. ' "Good and evil are relative to finite and particular interests, but in the absolute the distinction is transcended." Discuss.'

Reg returned from Spain after Christmas. His nose had been broken and badly mended; the septum was twisted and his nasal

77

consonants were denasalized, as if he had a bad cold. A bullet had grazed the upper tip of his right ear. He limped. At least he was alive, which was more than could be said of Jorge Lewis and Morgan Philips; they had been caught by the same sniper outside Tortosa. Alive, but a little mad: I did not like the look in his smoke-blue eyes. After only two weeks of infantry training with other POUM volunteers at Sitges, the Manchester University contingent had joined a platoon sent to reinforce a company, very ill-equipped, trying to hold a segment of the line that stretched from Reus to Caspe, just south of the Ebro. There was not much activity; it seemed to be a stalemate. But in early December the German Kondor air detachment and the Italian Legionary Aviation supported a massive artillery barrage and the rebels began to attack on a hundred-mile front. The Negrin government was already talking of leaving Barcelona to its fate and taking to the mountains of northern Catalonia. There was immense demoralization in the government forces, and Reg and his companions joined the ragged retreat towards Gerona. It was in Sabadell that he had been traumatized, but not by the Italian bombs that were falling. He, and a lad named Llewelyn Probert, were arrested. Arrested by the Russians. Reg still could not believe it. But it happened all right.

'There was a kind of sub-headquarters of the Soviet Military Mission at Sabadell. It was housed in a convent of the Sisters of the Nativity that the republicans had blasted – but that's another story. Probert and I had had some thick red wine in a bodega and tottered a bit as we came out. We were the only ones on the street. It was pretty late and we didn't know there was a curfew, though God knows who imposed it, there didn't seem to be a town commandant or even any police. We were picked up by a couple of men in the same sort of non-uniform as ourselves – you know, boots and leggings but the rest sort of tramp civilian. Then we were taken to this place and brought before an officer, a major I think he was, in what I took to be a very correct and clean Soviet army uniform. He wanted to see our passports, so we handed them over. The sort of lieutenant with him spoke some English but not much. I had the feeling that it might be dangerous to speak Russian, so I said in English that we were university students, volunteers in the fight against fascism and so on, but they didn't seem to be greatly impressed. The lieutenant said "Reghinald Morrov Zhonis", which wasn't too bad, and a man with a typewriter at a little table apart typed the name, in Cyrillic I suppose. There was evidently going to be a report on Probert and myself, God knows why. When they came to Probert's first name they had trouble. The lieutenant had never met a double L at the beginning of a name before, and he didn't know what it meant. So he asked Probert to say his name, and Probert came out with *Llewelyn* as he should, the unvoiced L like a goose hissing, and the two officers thought this was very droll and kept making Probert do it again and again. It was then that I got mad and gave them a mouthful of dirty Russian. That shook them pretty badly, I can tell you.'

He was telling a number of us all about it in the cafeteria. Beatrix was there. She had started the spring term by being coolly friendly to me, and I wondered if this meant that, with the coming of the daffodils after the snowdrops, I might be invited once more for Earl Grey and ordered to strip. She said: 'You bloody fool.'

'Easy for you to say that,' Reg went hotly. 'You weren't in my blasted position. And if you do any told-you-soing I'll hit out, I can tell you.'

'Go on,' I said.

'Well, my knowing Russian got them very suspicious. They let Probert go after they found out he was a member of the British Communist Party, though they had a good sneer at it. Then they started on me. Why did I know Russian? I told them. What was my mother's maiden name? I made a name up. What was I doing there, who was I working for, what were my political affiliations? I said I had none but I was attracted to cooperatism. I was fighting for negative reasons – getting rid of something rather than promoting something. They seemed to believe nothing I said. Then they brought in a real bruiser in a dirty undershirt and he began to bash me about. The truth, they kept saying, we want the truth. I've told you the bloody truth, I said, and I got bashed again. Then they shoved me in a cell for the night. I still can't believe it,' he said, shaking his head too fast. 'In the morning they started on me again. God knows what would have happened if they hadn't received a move order. They opened the cell door and I found them ready to go north in trucks. No good asking for a lift. I went to my billet and got my gear and rifle. I didn't know where Probert was, I didn't know where anybody was. I was on my own. I got lifts in army trucks as far as Figueras. Then I sort of smartened myself up by stealing a civilian overcoat in a bar there and I got across the border without too much trouble. Snow everywhere, though. And so it was right up through France by train to the Channel. I had fifty quid in fivers in my back pocket. I was a bloody fool.'

'As I said,' said Beatrix.

'But,' Reg cried, 'what do we do about the injustice in the world? Do we just sit on our arses and read the *Daily Worker* like those buggers over there?' He meant some members of the University Communist Party, who sat in conspiracy smoking Player's from a twenty packet and drinking coffee. 'The trouble with the damned Russians was that they didn't feel like the enemy. I mean, they spoke mother's language. They just felt like a lot of suspicious bastards who thought everybody was against them. I don't know where the hell I am.'

'Where you are,' I said, 'is back to being a student of Spanish again, though not, presumably, of Catalan.'

'It's going to taste of blood,' Reg said in gloom. 'Lope de Vega dripping with the blood of the slain.'

'Oh, cut it out.' That was, of course, Beatrix.

'I haven't seen Zip yet,' Reg said. 'I've got to see Zip. Your sister,' he added to me, as though that identification was necessary.

'She's around,' I said. 'Banging hell out of drums and tubular bells.' So: he wanted to see Zip; he seemed to be in love with Zip. Why was he in love with Zip? It was pointless, I supposed, trying to attach a physiological or metaphysical formula to it. Drawn to the Mediterranean, for if anyone looked as if she was soaked in that sea, Zip did. Antithetical to his sister and, I supposed, his mother. The Welsh were one of the lost tribes of Israel, equipped with biblical faces. Nothing biblical about Reg's face, with its nose mending awry and its Baltic stare. All this was nonsense; stick, as it were, to fish. Dan had left the fish and chip shop and was working with cold wet fish, headed and tailed, in Tussock's on Princess Road, Moss Side. He was a good hand at carving smoked salmon. He wore a blue and white striped apron stained with fish guts. He wore a straw hat or cady. Stick to solidities: fish and gold. Nobody, by the way, ever saw Probert again.

'The gold?' I asked Beatrix. I had not properly spoken to her since bowing her out of the Luxicab last autumn. She looked at me as if it were none of my business, which it wasn't. But, of course, she had not been in communication with Reg since then either. It was to Reg she spoke, saying:

'Dad knew it was you. That's why he didn't call the police. Dad said you know what you deserve. Wait till Dan gets on to you again. First he'll hit you with an ungutted flounder.'

'Leave Dan out of it,' Reg whined. 'I've suffered enough.'

'Welcome back,' I said, rising. 'I have a lecture on the Kantian categories. I'll tell Zip you're home and wounded. But watch it.'

'Watch what?'

'Zip's a very romantic type of girl. She can easily get carried away. So watch it.' And I left.

Father and mother came back from Venezuela in the early summer. Despite what the British politicians were saying, it was evident that war was on its way. My parents wanted to be home in the island fortress. They were brown and thin, looking all of their fifty-odd years. The attempt to bridge the Orinoco had been, as my father had foretold, an expensive failure. The government in Caracas had decided to default on its contract. That the Nazis were going to take over the whole of Europe was generally believed all over Latin America. Nazi propaganda was powerful, in Venezuela as elsewhere. There was little respect for the British, and Jews had stones thrown at them. My parents were glad to be home, but they had no intention of settling. They stayed with their children at aunt Bérénice's until they found a flat not far from Trafford Park. There was no room for Zipporah and myself in it. The habit of separation persisted; they might as well have still been abroad, though they telephoned us more and even came to tea on occasional Sundays. Zip said nothing to anybody about a scare she had, though I could tell from her pallor and the smell of gin on her breath what the nature of the scare was. She came down from breakfast one morning looking relieved though still pale. Love was going too far.

It was my idea to take her to Eastbourne for what we all felt would be the last of the summer vacations. It was not my idea that Reg should follow her. He turned up at the Ormond Hotel on the esplanade while Zip and I were sitting in the lounge digesting breakfast – eggs, pork sausages and bacon and strong English tea. Not a kosher breakfast, but we felt not even a twinge of ancestral guilt. I was reading the *Daily Mail*, which said there would be no war: America was our real enemy. Reg was dressed for a summer resort in white flannel trousers and a University blazer. His speech was no longer denasalized and his ill-mended nose enhanced rather than impaired his handsomeness. He was very brown. 'Thought I'd come down,' he said. 'Life at home's rather difficult. Dad's locked his gold away.' He sat in one of the biscuit-coloured chunky armchairs. 'Nicer than my place,' he said, looking round. 'A tatty little place just off the prom. I think I'll move in here if they have room.' Zip was blushing: she might have had the grace to inform me that all this was at least half her idea. I said:

'Come off it. A put-up job. All worked out beforehand.' I began to see more clearly why I was resenting this love affair. If Beatrix had fallen into my arms demanding endless sex with me and me only I would have felt very differently. It was the lack of symmetry that was annoying. 'Come out with me,' I said. 'We'll take a walk.'

'A blow along the prom,' Reg nodded. 'Right.' But he kissed Zip before leaving.

It was a wet British summer's morning, the sky coldly boiling and the sea leaden. We did not walk far. We went to a teashop and drank weak coffee. 'I want to know your intentions,' I said.

'In loco parentis.' He sipped and grimaced: he had recently become used to stronger coffee. 'Not up to you, is it? Up to her dad. I've already drafted a letter. Not sent it to him yet, but I will.'

'You mean marriage? That's nonsense and you know it. Students don't marry.'

'Soldiers do. It won't be long now.'

'You've already been sleeping with her, haven't you? And sleeping rather carelessly, if I may put it that way.'

'Oh, we still haven't spent the night together, if that's what you mean. Listen, you silly bugger. I love her.'

'What the hell do you know about love?'

'You want a nice neat philosophical definition? I love her, you damned idiot. My heart races when I see her. I have to bite my nails to stop myself rushing to embrace her in public places. I dream about her and wake up wet.'

'That's filthy. That's just sex.'

'Oh, sex comes into it all right, but the soul's there as well. Both our souls. She feels as I do. She wants us to spend our lives together. One unitary life for ever and ever. Or till the Hun blows us all to pieces. That's love. That means marriage.'

'How about her career? Being a professional fiddler's one thing. Doing her kind of thing is another. All that equipment, the cost of it. Xylophones and timpani in the attic gathering dust.'

'I won't interfere with her art. We're both agreed that it's a sin to bring babies into the kind of world we're living in. I don't expect her to turn into a good little *Hausfrau*. I've great respect for art, even when it's just banging things with hammers. Anyway,' he said, 'we're engaged.'

'I haven't seen any ring.'

'She keeps it in her handbag. Nice little thing with three diamond chips. Platinum. Got it at Remington's. Five quid it cost. Perhaps you'd permit her to bring it into the open, wear it here. Not that she needs your permission or anybody else's. Where's your authority, blast you? You're not even older than she is. You're her little brother, you idiot. Zip's a good girl. She didn't want you shouting the odds. It's up to her dad whether we marry under age. I'm going to send that letter.'

I wished the pubs were open. I said nothing. Then I said: 'Have you thought about, er, nomenclature? Zipporah Jones isn't a very plausible name.'

'Nor was Ludmila Petrovna Jones. Zipporah Morrow Jones sounds like a comity of nations. I agree that the abbreviation Zip sounds more appropriate for a striptease performer. Zip – another garment removed. Seriously, though, no more rabbinical growls and minor prophetic thunderings, right? A daughter of Israel, flower of the field, is to marry a Russian Welshman. It needs a poem, a whatyoucallit, an epi-something.'

'Not an epithalamion, not yet. Prothalamion is the word.' And then: 'Looking to the future, if we have one, what do you propose to do? What career, I mean?'

'Something to do with Spanish, I'd say,' he said vaguely. 'Teaching it or something. But we shan't be poor,' he added in eager haste. 'Dad made a pile out of catering. We'll do all right.'

'Did you do all right in Part One?' Part One was the examination taken by honours candidates after their second year; if you failed it you were thrown out of the honours school and made to take the degree that was called ordinary. I had achieved a top second.

'I got a first. Had to, hadn't I? Fighting for the honour of a language now to be defiled by fascism. Trix got a first in finals.'

'I know. That was to be expected. Where is she now?'

'Looking for digs in London. She's going into the Foreign Ofice, assistant to Namier. Any day now the balloon's going to go up.'

Any day was right. Three weeks from that Sunday, to be exact. We reported back for the continuation of our honours courses in October, not knowing properly whether we were doing the right thing. Lope de Vega and Kant seemed irrelevant. Both Reg and I were among the first for callup. We could go before a sort of tribunal and request deferral until the completion of our studies. But, the university authorities said, if we decided to do the patriotic thing we could have our Part One successes commuted into ordinary baccalaureates. A thesis, of no great length or depth, was obligatory for the honours final qualification: we could come back, if we survived, and lengthen and deepen it into a master's thesis. That seemed reasonable. Neither Reg nor I waited to be called up; we volunteered. He went to South Wales and enlisted in his father's old regiment. I went to a recruiting office in Manchester and asked to be put down for the Army Physical Training Corps. Before he left for his basic infantry training, Reg married Zip in a register office. His parents did not attend; ours did. My father groused about having to continue the financing of Zip's studies, meaning the purchase of a glockenspiel and tubular bells: that was surely the husband's responsibility. Reg compromised by buying his bride a slapstick and a tambourine. He was only a private soldier, he told this prosperous engineer: come off it, be reasonable, there's a war on, *wus*, dad I should say, *av* I believe in Hebrew, *em* for mother even in the Aryan languages. And then, at the Trocadero restaurant in Piccadilly, we had a dinner of hors d'oeuvres, chicken soup, poached turbot, beef Stroganof, roast chicken with bread sauce, peach Melba, devils or angels on horseback, and several bottles of the house Médoc. There was a war on, but you would not have thought it. Nor in Scarborough, where Reg and Zip spent an exhausting three-day honeymoon.

Why, I asked Reg after the ceremony, had not his father and mother made the trip to Manchester for the occasion? 'Well, they run this pub outside Abergavenny and the licensing laws forbid even a day's closure, except for Sunday, which, in antinomian Wales, is the busiest day of the week, though all the drinking is done in the back parlour.' Why not get a locum tenens in? 'No, dad doesn't trust the Welsh, being one himself, too many fights and bugger closing time and the loss of the licence.' We all, even Beatrix, felt that was no real excuse. There was a certain antisemitism in Ludmila Jones, typical of Christian Russians. David Jones was disgusted with his elder son, who, after all the care and cosseting, was showing symptoms of self-destructive delinquency. He could have opposed the marriage on the grounds of Reg's minority (not twenty-one until January 1940), but he wearily let it go through. There was no wedding present, which was disapproval enough. The marriage, David Jones said, could only lead to trouble. There was something in that, as time would show.

By late 1939 Reg was an acting unpaid lancecorporal in the Second Battalion of the Royal Gwent Regiment. Why, I wondered, had he chosen his father's outfit? A remnant of filial piety perhaps. Even a kind of patriotism (*Gwlad, gwlad, pleidiol wyf i'm gwlad* and so on). Why infantry anyway? Reg had fought, literally, and failed. Fascism had won in Spain and had better not win in Europe. Germany and Soviet Russia were in cautious alliance: Reg thought himself engaged in opposing tyrannies which, theoretically antithetical, were really much the same. In the infantry you really fought – with a rifle and bayonet and automatic weapons which, in the manner of touch typists, wrote death fast and modern. Reg was a romantic.

I was not. I did not want to fight, but I did not want to be an orderly room clerk either. My war work was rendering men fit enough to go out there and be seen off by the enemy. I became a sergeant instructor, with three stripes and crossed swords above, misread by cruel civilians as the insignia of a regimental tailor. I did rehabilitative work in hospitals, persuading orthopaedic cases to kick footballs with the foot that was healing, and I was promoted to quartermaster sergeant instructor in an infantry training centre. I went to Aldershot on unarmed combat courses and, later, on more rigorous courses that involved knives, trip-wires, and other devices of barbarous execution. Metaphysics and moral philosophy were far away. I sowed the seeds of my later occupation as a trainer of terrorists.

The summer of 1940 was glorious, even in Manchester, and it mocked the men returning shattered from Dunkirk. Reg was among them. He needed the comfort of Zip's arms, but Zip's arms were greatly busy beating the drums of the Hallé Orchestra. That body had formerly been a male preserve, but its reorganiz-ation under Sir John Barbirolli, known to his players as Bob O'Reilly, let women in. A woman played first trombone. Zip was deputy timpanist. It was considered in order for her to clang bells and triangles, but Manchester's audiences found it hard to accept the white arms of a personable young woman thundering away in Wagnerian climaxes. So she played the subsidiary percussion in works which required it (not Beethoven except in the Ninth, not Brahms except in the third movement of the Fourth, not Haydn or Mozart ever), but, when Alfred Repton was sick, which he was often and increasingly, she took over the kettledrums. Her arms grew strong, apt for the protection of her broken soldier from his nightmares, but she was not always available for marital comfort in the bedroom set aside in our aunt's house: the orchestra toured and discoursed beauty in northern town halls. England, home and. It was part of the patriotic trinity.

I was on leave myself when Reg was spewed home from Dunkirk. The madness I had suspected in him, a product of the shock of Spain but perhaps also a genetic trait, a magnification of the manic depression which the Welsh are supposed to share with the Russians, seemed to be burgeoning dangerously. Neurasthenia call it, perhaps. We were at breakfast one morning, aunt, Zip, he, I, when he squinted evilly at his wife, not much more than a bride really, and said: 'I know what it is you're smiling about.' Zip said:

'You can't. You've not read it yet.' She meant that morning's *Manchester Guardian*, which carried a report of the previous evening's Hallé concert. She was reading this and smirking a little at 'her shapely arms smote smartly and accurately'. He said:

'Surrounded by men, isn't it?' That was very Welsh and unwonted. 'Take your choice, can't you, isn't it? Beery trumpeters and drunken fiddlers and lecherous clarinettists. Don't think I don't know because I do. Half the men in my unit were worried about their wives as well as the bloody Luftwaffe knocking hell out of them. *Semper infidelis*. The war's bringing it all out. Cuckoldry issued with the rations.'

'Look, idiot,' I said, 'if you're accusing my sister of infidelity I'm going to take you outside and slap you around the back garden.'

'Don't pull your three stripes and your muscle and your bloody sibhood on me,' Reg said. 'What God has put together let no bastard pull asunder.' Aunt Bérénice said:

'This is monstrous,' with her Parisian r. 'I will not have such language and such accusations in my house.'

Reg grinned sillily and said: 'You could write a whole book about r. Probably done already. The rhotic and the arhotic. *Perro* and *pero*. They're quite different. Opposition between a double trill and a single. Only occurs once in the whole language. You're looking very very beautiful, darling,' he smiled at Zip. 'Sorry I said what I said. I don't quite know where I am. Jealousy, natural enough. Has it ever struck any of you that this war's based on jealousy? Jealousy of the empireless for the empired. Jealousy within the service structure – rank, privilege, pay. That's what *Othello* is about. Military jealousy promotes marital jealousy. I must go and shave.' He got up, toast just buttered not eaten, and embraced his wife openly in a manner that should have been reserved to the bedroom. Zip looked disturbed, rightly. Concerned. Pitying. Also loving. He went upstairs to shave. We looked at each other. Our aunt began to sob, taking from her dressing gown sleeve a lacy inadequate cologned handkerchief to sob into. She sobbed:

'Poor France. Poor, poor France.'

There then came the double knock of the parcel post. Zip went. She came back puzzled and weighed down by a vast brown-papered package though grasped in both strong hands. The postmark was Abergavenny and it was addressed to L/Cpl (wrongly, since the appointment had been an acting and local one revoked after Dunkirk) and Mrs Jones. Zip opened it and found the Jones family Bible. There was no covering letter, no inscription on the flyleaf. Our aunt was shocked by the illustrations. 'Pornography in the manner of Alma-Tadema,' she said. 'See this – the feast of Belshazzar. The *goyim* vulgarize the holy, stain it too - see, there is a kind of snailtrail on this engraving. Why do they send it? A strange present. Perhaps to symbolize the union of Jew and Christian embraced under covers. Perhaps – see here at the front – that the Christian baptism of the offspring be duly recorded. All these Joneses, and all with good Hebrew first names. There is something insulting about it, but one cannot be sure. Zipporah, place it in that low cupboard there and lock it with this key.' Like a *châtelaine* she wore a bunch at her waist. 'We hardly need it.' I began to suspect madness in the whole damned family. Beatrix's sexual electism was hardly sane, was it? Dan, who had somehow been shovelled into the First Battalion of the Royal Lancaster Regiment, was, to coin a term, ichthyocentric and clearly not quite the round shilling. Reg was upstairs shaving, having forgotten that he had already shaved before breakfast. But who was I to talk, having felt nausea at the plethora of bare biblical limbs just exhibited? Perhaps everybody was mad and war the great sanitizer.

In July 1940 the War Office belatedly decided on the formation of an Intelligence Corps, and Reg got himself into it. He was not dodging his duty of killing the enemy. He had left his weapons behind on two failed fields of battle and discovered that wars could be fought with the brain. Razorblades in pigswill. Bombardment of the innocent. Intelligence. Damn it, I was fighting a war with knees bend and arms stretch on chilly parade grounds. Zip was the only one of our lot who was bashing things. She bashed Beethoven and Wagner, though those had probably been good Germans. Up to a point.

MY readers will approve now of my activating the fast forward button. You know all about that remote war, having seen it enacted by pacifist actors on television. I have to come quickly to the Sons of Arthur or, if my Welsh is right, *Meibion Arthur*, and the peripheral roles played by the Jones family in granting that nationalistic body a fighting symbol. It was a body first formed on the Rock of Gibraltar.

Reg was posted there in 1943, not specifically because of his knowledge of Spanish: the other lancecorporals who sailed with him (lancecorporal was the lowest rank in the Corps, as in the Military Police) were professors of French, German and even Lithuanian, though there was the son of an operatic impresario who spoke most European languages and even had a smattering of Arabic. They had all been promoted to sergeant for the voyage – it was not clear why – and they were stripped of two stripes immediately on arrival, but Reg achieved war substantive sergeant's rank in 1944.

The duties of the Intelligence Corps in Gibraltar were for the most part ludicrous. Its members should properly have wandered in civilian clothes through southern Spain, listening for evidence of the infraction of Franco's neutrality, but for the most part they had to sit at Four Corners and inspect the food bags of Spanish dayworkers entering and leaving the Rock to see what they were bringing in or taking out. Nobody was told quite what to look for. They also had to visit La Linea, in mufti and posing as ordinary soldiers on pass seeking a whore, to see if British money was changing hands for too many pesetas. Troops being sent home, on leave, on courses, on discharge, were usually paid pound notes of the United Kingdom not the Gibraltar variety, and, going to La Linea for a last fleshly fling before sailing home to their wives, they could often be persuaded to exchange their banknotes for twice the number of pesetas they got at the official rate. It was believed that Nazi spies were buying these notes. The Intelligence Corps was told to do no more than rebuke the troops involved in these transactions and report them to their units. This was neutral territory and it was not permitted to beat up German agents in lavatories and then, dragging them over the frontier as befuddled companions, deliver them to the British authorities. Reg, as you will see, grew tired of the blandness of his duties and exceeded his orders.

In Gibraltar, in two rooms above a fruiterer's store on Main Street, a Welsh Club met nightly. Members could read the *Western Mail* there, or the *Merthyr Tydfil Chronicle* or the *Star of Gwent*, though in two-month-old issues. They could drink spirits though not beer. The importation of British beer was in the control of the Q branch and its issue was limited to the NAAFI and the naval and military messes. The Welsh, unlike the Irish and Scots, are not much given to spirits, and a solitary dram was enough to make them aggressive. Province would sneer at province and town at town, and sneers would be followed by blows. Sometimes there would be regional unification so that South and North could go for each other. The club premises were small and unsuited for fighting. Aled Rhys, the club president, deplored all this. He was a warrant officer class one in the Army Educational Corps, a teacher of mathematics in Glamorgan in civilian life, a Welsh speaker and, though bespectacled, paunched, and nearly bald, a man of authority. 'The Welsh are Welsh,' he would cry, 'and this internecine warring is bloody unseemly. The Welsh must be united and prepare for the future that is almost bloody well upon us.' The mild obscenity was, as always in Welsh English speech, a substitute for the stress element it lacked.

The Welsh love oratory and the Gibraltar Welsh would listen with pleasure and rising fire to Aled Rhys's almost nightly orations. He spoke in English because his brand of Welsh was not greatly liked outside of Glamorgan and some of the club members had never learned their native tongue. 'Why are we fighting this bloody war?' he would ask. 'It is for the liberty of subject peoples. The Welsh are a subject people. Driven into the mountains by the invading bloody Anglo-Saxons, they survey from their fastnesses a rich land which was once bloody well their bloody property. The Anglo-Saxons and the Vikings and the Normans claimed the right of conquest and the Welsh have in bloody feebleness bowed down to their claims. There is much talk of Welsh nationalism these days, and the heart's desire of any true bloody Welshman is to see his land liberated from the rule of bloody Lloegr. But I take it further. I speak for the recovery of the whole island that is Britain and its renewed rule by the bloody Welsh. When Arthur reigned he looked out on rich fields and fair towns united in language and in faith. It was in the south of Scotland that the bards Taliesin and Aneirin sang in deathless bloody verse of the iniquities of the invading Saxons and of the bravery of the Britons who fought them. That was in the sixth century, when the Germanic hordes grunted a speech that was uncivilized and bowed their bloody heads to stocks and stones. We have forgotten the extent of our bloody heritage and the time has come to recall it and to recover it.'

Reginald Morrow Jones, still a lancecorporal in 1943, spoke up in protest. 'My father heard the same talk in the first war and it got nowhere. You cannot rewind history as if it was a film. The Wales you talk of was not free. It was under the rule of Rome. What was Arthur but a *dux Romanus* taking his orders from Ravenna? You will never see a Welshified Britain again, and you will not see even an independent Wales. The Welsh and the English are intermixed, and the Welsh have turned themselves into functionaries of a united kingdom, with the Paddington area full of Welsh milkmen. You have had Welsh kings on the British throne and even a Welsh dictator in Oliver Cromwell. Then the time of the Welsh passed away. The Tudors are long finished. Lloyd George was a Manchester man with the gift of the *hwyl*. Such talk as yours is acceptable turned into verse for an Eisteddfod, but there is no political reality in it.'

A dark corporal with fierce black eyes, not unlike Reg's father, stood to say: 'You have been talking enough of your fighting for a free Catalonia when you have done us the bloody kindness of taking time off from Spanish women to visit the club here. You bow down now to Franco's villainous extirpation of Catalonian freedom, calling it the process of history or some such bloody thing. But Wales is not Catalonia and our only enemy is an enfeebled *Sais* that has kindly taught us how to handle bloody weapons. What Aled Rhys here has said may be too bloody visionary if that is the right word, but when this war is finished it will be the only time to strike, and I do not use the word in its union sense of downing tools but of picking up the tools of freeing Wales from the tyranny of England. So there you have it, boy.' This corporal, who was in the Army Service Corps and named Ben Griffiths, then sat down. Reg said:

'I don't like what you said then about me going after Spanish women. When I go over to Spain it is in the line of bloody duty, as the Yanks say, and I resent your filthy insinuation. And now I ask this question: where do you get the money from? Are you going to beg for Moscow gold to free yourselves from the English? Because if you are you will not be given even a wooden rouble. The Russians will have their work cut out getting back on their own shoeless feet without helping Wales to do down the English capitalists. A fat lot the Russians did for Catalonia. You'll be on your own, *wus.*'

A scholarly private stood to say: 'There are always ways and means, brothers. You have to begin with a subversion of conventional morality. To a people seeking to free itself from tyranny it is no crime to kidnap, blackmail, or rob banks. It would be a great and virtuous act to kidnap Hitler or annexe Goering's bank account. What is right in this war will be right in whatever war is fought for a liberated Wales. Now, there are some who want to see a republican Wales and even a communist Wales, but to be communist means bowing down to the Soviet Union, which is godless, materialistic and doesn't give a damn about the Welsh people, even if it knows who they are. Wales was glorious under the Welsh kings and chieftains. Wales is, under the English, a principality. I would say promote Wales to a kingdom. We are the sons of King Arthur and scorn to join the tinpot republics of the world. *Meibion Arthur.* It has a ring nobler than *Plaid Cymru* or any other of the upstart nomenclatures.'

There was then the expected squabble. Welsh union members and card-carrying communists from Little Moscow (variously identified as Tonypandy, Pontypridd and Ebbw Vale) spoke up as unrealistically as the nationalist dreamers, and the evening was brought to an end only by the former choirmaster Owen Pritchard's sitting at the wretched Spanish upright (a gift from the Gibraltarian Chris Hogado, who had once slept with a Welsh girl) and banging out *Mae hen wlad fy nhadau yn annwyl i mi.*

It was about this time that a squadron of Luftwaffe bombers – was sent out to destroy Ebbw Vale but was mostly foiled by

British fighter planes. This was one of the so called 'scalded cat' raids, which, because the German air strength was being concentrated on the Russian front, were rare, usually light, and directed at fringe targets. The decision to bomb the Welsh coalfields may have been an astrological one. Or perhaps the Spirit of History was directing Germany's bomber command, for the outcome of the raid was historically of extreme interest. One of the Nazi aircraft was badly bruised by its attackers and, limping towards the Bristol Channel, rid itself of its load. Bomb after bomb was loosed on to farming country between the rivers Usk and Gavenny. The pub of David and Ludmila Jones, the Black Lion, which stood in the village of Gilwern, was a mile or so from the nearest explosion, but all its front windows were shattered. Two bombs struck the town of Abergavenny. One failed to explode and was gingerly defused by a disposal squad; the other made more ruinous the ruins of the ancient Benedictine priory. Sheep had flown high over the fields and landed in disjected members. Farmers complained in the public bar of the Black Lion. One brought in a bit of potsherd and a jagged piece of stone with an eye carved on it. Dr Lewis looked at this with interest. He said:

'Well, as we all should know if we don't, the ancient name of Abergavenny was Gobanium. It was a famous Roman settlement.'

'Is that so, doctor?'

'Yes. Perhaps here you have the remains of some temple to Mithras or even the god Jupiter himself.'

'There's interesting,' said a commercial traveller, not much interested.

'Yes. It is strange that the Germans, in trying to destroy this island, have sometimes added to the evidence of its ancient civilization. They dig up the land without spades. The cities too. For ancient temples have come to light in London itself and part of the stone wall that surrounded Londinium.'

'There's bloody fascinating.'

'Well,' and Dr Lewis downed his halfpint of Rhymney ale, 'we leave all that to the Cardiff archaeologists. My immediate concern is Mrs Pritchard's youngest's whooping cough. So I will say good day to you.'

93

'*Bore da, meddyg,*' Ludmila Jones said from behind the bar.

'Knows it all then?'

'Has to, him being a doctor.'

It was about three months after these efforts at destruction which destroyed only windows and sheep that I sat at breakfast on leave in my sister's flat on Wilmslow Road. It was a miserable breakfast of reconstituted dried egg. I read a letter to Zip from my father: 'Portsmouth is in a bad way but the Luftwaffe will leave it alone now, being busy elsewhere. God knows when the Mark III you-know-what will be off the drawing board. Your mother and I are well enough. Love to Harry when you see him.' Zip was reading the *Manchester Guardian*. 'So,' she said, 'it seems he was no myth then.' She had moved out of our aunt's house because our aunt had leased it to a trade union official working in liaison with the Manchester branch of the Board of Trade. It was termed liaison but it was really obstruction. Our aunt was in charge of the Free French *haute cuisine* in London. She did not intend to return to Manchester. I said:

'Who?'

'There's a team of archaeologists working at this place where those bombs fell. I shouldn't have thought archaeology's a reserved occupation. No. It's an old professor from Cardiff and a gang of boys and girls from a grammar school. They've come across bits of carved stone and Latin inscriptions. GLAD ART REG is one of them. It's on what they call here a kind of stone plinth with a slit in it. A sort of nonportable scabbard. GLAD means GLADIUM means a sword. ART REG is Arthur the king. The man here says that Professor Rhys Jones had better not jump to hasty conclusions. It's not Camelot they've discovered. Camelot, this man says, was at Cadbury. Some professor of Welsh literature is burbling on about the sword in the stone. The Mabinogion. Have you ever heard of that?'

'I don't think so.'

'This is the stone, he says. Fill the slit with hot wax or something and wait till it hardens, then they can tell what the sword looked like. Bit of a waste of time, I'd say. After all, there's a war on.'

'Life has to continue. That means archaeology. Also music, I suppose.' I went on grimacing over the reconstituted egg and the margarined toast and the weak tea.

She looked at me suspiciously with her fine black eyes. She was in a torn rainbow dressing gown of her aunt's, her lovely white neck and a segment of her left breast on show. Being her brother, I was not supposed to be moved. 'What do you mean, suppose?'

'That concert last night was wretched. No wonder you had no audience. Who wants to hear bloody Bruckner?'

'The rough with the smooth,' she said obscurely. 'Sad art, glad art. And then Reg. Curious that, very. Reg wrote me a very queer letter. Got it here,' meaning her dressing gown pocket. 'Read it.'

I took the blue airmail letter form doubtfully. 'I don't like coming between husband and wife.'

'Read it.'

I read it. Oh my God. 'I believe in total honesty, dearest Zip,' it said. 'Perhaps you're able to sublimate sex into bashing drums and gongs and things. I not. I was over in La Linea and I fell. Call it infidelity, but I had to do it. You see, she was so much like you. Not your intelligence, not your talent, not your beauty, but a half-hearted attempt at you in a mantilla, and I fell. Then I felt terrible about it. Don't worry about the you-know-what angle, because I took every precaution. Now I writhe on my bed longing for the real you, not some imitation reeking of garlic.' Oh my God. 'There's a big neat square hole then, as though he cut something out with a razorblade,' I said, flushing.

'That would be the censor. What man in his right senses would send a letter like that to his wife?'

'At least it's original. Most husbands would keep quiet about it.'

'He should have kept quiet. What the eye doesn't see. A massive lack of discretion. It's disgusting.'

'The war's making us all a bit abnormal. We'll have to write some things off when it's over. For people like Churchill it's life, the fulfillment of his bloody career. For the rest of us it's a parenthesis. A mad life in brackets. Start again and pray for a return of sanity.'

'We'll never be the same again, none of us. Whatever the same was. I mean, youth's the formative part of our lives. We're being formed in the wrong way.' And then: 'I got married too young. He did too, I suppose. Not much time to look around.'

'Are you,' I said carefully, 'looking around now?'

'If you really want to know,' she said, 'not that you've any real right to know, he drove me to it. It was the first time, and it happened the day he finished his embarkation leave. After the concert at the Gaumont. And that's a stupid thing to say to a woman – looking around. It's the men who do that. It was with Geoff Thurston – you wouldn't know him, he plays second oboe. That evening he'd played the cor anglais solo in *The Swan of Tuonela*. He bought me a couple of gins and I went back to his place.'

'Now you can write back to Reg and reciprocate his total honesty.'

'Are you mad? I shouldn't really have told *you*. But he drove me to it.'

'In what way?'

'You're not going to believe this.'

'The army has widened the sights of my credulity.'

'That damned Bible. It got itself packed with my things and brought here. I was in the kitchen making him a sandwich and a cup of tea. I came in here and found him scattering seed over one of the pictures in it. He looked up quite unembarrassed and said he'd have to learn, his words, irregular modes of release. And he said that his wife was his right hand but now his right hand must be his wife. I told him to get out, but he said he was going anyway or he'd miss his train. And he tried to kiss me, you know, lovingly.'

'I see. What do we call this – madness, sincerity, lack of discretion?'

'I don't know what the hell to call it. I think he ought to see a doctor.'

'He sees those all the time. Regular medical inspections and so on. In the Bible, eh? Just like his father. His father's father caught him firing on to Belshazzar's Feast. That's why he ran away to sea. Bashed for ungodly behaviour. Reg told me about it.'

'It *was* Belshazzar's Feast. I had to wipe it with a dishcloth. Men can be filthy.'

'Talking of missing trains,' I said, getting up from the table. 'Don't take it too hard,' I said. 'Reg is eccentric, that's all. I dare say some people think that you're eccentric, beating drums and clashing cymbals. Instead of building tanks for the Russians to pretend they've built for themselves. Never mind. Where did I leave my cap FS?' I found it stuck in a corner under a gaudy cushion on Zip's landlady's worn sofa where I had slept, and then I kissed her cheek goodbye. I hauled my kit to the 44 bus that took me to London Road station. I was catching a train to Euston. I was fully loaded with packs and kitbag. The Infantry Training Centre where I had been working had closed down to coincide with the start of my privilege leave, and I was, if another eventuality did not occur, to report back to the Depot at Aldershot.

In London I reported to an office at 62–64 Baker Street, where an organization called the SOE or Special Operations Executive was headed by the famous Brigadier Colin Gubbins MC. A Captain Soames with a long thin face interviewed me, addressing me familiarly as 'Q'. He said: 'It's instructors we need, but first we have to instruct the instructors, don't we? Physical fitness and alertness are obvious prerequisites and so is the level of intelligence indicated by your BA.' He frowned at my dossier. 'But why philosophy, for God's sake? If it hadn't been for Kant and Hegel we might not have been in this mess, but never mind. Your instructors will be civilians and very few of them British. The course will comprise efficient techniques of interrogation, terrorization, sheer simple murder and so on. This, as you'll have guessed, is to do with the invasion of Europe.'

'Terrorization, sir?'

'We've not been tough enough. We tried to fight this war like bloody gentlemen, which is not the way of the jerries and the Reds. You won't have gentlemen instructing you, I can tell you that. May I take it your application is a serious one?'

'Serious, sir?'

'I mean, you can withdraw it and go back to arms bend knees stretch and no hard feelings. Otherwise you report right away to

Number 6 Transit Depot and await further instructions. Serious, then?'

'Oh yes, sir. Damnably serious.'

'Good show.'

Number 6 Transit Depot was a kind of army limbo where dim lights burned all night long to accommodate mysterious arrivals and departures. It had an extraterritorial smell to it, to be recalled much later in international airports, though there was no equivalent to a VIP's lounge. Indeed, the army hierarchy was ruthlessly mocked. A lancecorporal in carpet slippers pushed a master gunner and myself into line at the service hatches of the dining hall, where a kind of timeless meal in the manner of international flights was being served. The stew that was shovelled into my messtin was cold and abominable, so I emptied some of it on to the lancecorporal's carpet slippers. As I hurried out to catch a meal in Soho, the RSM bawled at me to be back in by 23.59.

I dined on horsesteak and chips in a restaurant opposite the Fitzroy Tavern run by the Maltese Mafia. In the Fitzroy Tavern afterwards I saw, with no surprise, Beatrix Jones drinking beer with a prototypical private soldier, squat, neckless, baggy as to battledress, coarse of feature, totally unpromotable. They were speaking fluent Russian to each other. Surprisingly, she recognized me. Her brother Dan did not. I said:

'I had the pleasure of seeing him bash your brother Reg at that farewell party. And the later pleasure of having him cut me half a pound of smoked salmon for my aunt.' Dan scowled at me, looked at the pub clock and said:

'Now.'

'Are you sure you know where Tottenham Court Road tube is?' she asked solicitously. He thought he knew. He had been spending a forty-eight hour furlough with his sister and was taking the night train to Glasgow. His sister kissed him on the lips very warmly. 'A good sweet boy,' she said to me. She was smart in a wartime London manner, blond hair rolled, cinnamon two-piece suit square-shouldered, shoes utility and sensible. She fondly watched Dan lumber out through the swing doors into the blackout. Sweet was hardly the word I would have chosen for him, though he did not now smell either of frying grease or of fresh fish. He smelt rather of cheap fags and frowsty blankets.

'Devoted to him, are you?'

'He's my baby brother. He needs looking after. I don't think the army's doing that very well. But he'll survive. He's tough. He won't stand any nonsense.' He would certainly stand no nonsense from fish, attacking hake and flounder with the relish of Ahab's men harpooning.

'I've often wondered,' I said, when I had fought to get more beer from the bar. 'About him and you and my esteemed brother-in-law. No intellectual, I mean. To say the least of it, if I don't offend.'

'Oh, there's something missing there, but it's not important. Some of his Russian grandfather's alcohol got to his brain perhaps. He had trouble learning to talk, but only in English. Our mother tried him with Welsh, but dad said Welsh was not much good in Manchester. So none of us learned much. Mother fed Dan Russian, and that seemed to work. Fed us too while she was at it. Dan got his English from the Manchester streets. Russian's his true mother tongue. But he wouldn't let himself be mothered or cosseted by his father, not like Reg. Dan was always tough and always went his own way. That's why he needs looking after.'

'Why fish?'

'Oh,' she said vaguely, 'we all have to specialize in something.' And then: 'What are you doing in London, anyway?' I told her. 'Yes,' she said, 'we're getting ready. Uncle Joe doesn't believe it, of course. One part of him doesn't really want it to happen. The Red Army sweeping to the Channel.' She looked at me bright-eyed and said: 'It's a bit late to invite you to tea. But I have a case of genuine Russian vodka. A present from the Soviet Embassy. I seem to have a sort of cousin there.' So. I was to be given another order to strip. She would find now a more muscular browner body. But I had to be in at 23.59. To hell with orders, which I could always implausibly pretend I had not distinctly heard. It was a quarter past eleven already anyway, and to be late was a matter of essence not degree. If you got up before reveille you could be charged with being up after lights out. The pub was crowded with Free French and Québecois and a few Yanks as well as scrimshanking civilians, and it was smoky and reeked of beer slops with a tinge of distant piss and vomit: it was hard to reconcile total blackout with even minimal ventilation. I took her back to her flat in West Kensington. It was a slow crammed cramped tube journey, with drunken GIs ogling Beatrix and one saying: 'How's about joining the *real* army, beautiful?' Beatrix gave him a mouthful of Russian. At the inner stations blitz-haunted Londoners got ready for bed in the platform bunks: you never knew when the Luftwaffe would return. Beatrix's flat, a bedsitter really, was on the third floor of a Victorian merchant's mansion. Her bed was as narrow as the one in her Manchester digs; on the floor beside it were tumbled blankets where her brother had slept. She had a gas-ring, a shelf with a cocoa tin and a tea caddy, and a rickety chestnut-coloured chest of drawers. She gave me good raw vodka in a teacup. She did not order me to strip. I took her in my arms and gave her good raw kisses and fully clothed embraces. She returned them, though not with enthusiasm. Then I surprised myself by saying:

'I love you, you know.'

'I don't know. It sounds like the voice of tumescence.'

'I think we ought to be married.' I was even more surprised. 'I know it sounds like an itch for symmetry, but why not? A lot of people are doing it. An army wife's allowance might be useful. Oh, I don't mean that. I mean it's a sort of stability. In a terribly unstable world.' My sentences were brief and breathy.

'Absolute pitch. Only your sister understood when I said that. It was when I was talking of gold that time. I don't think marriage is all that absolute. I don't want to marry. Not while Dan has to be looked after.'

I was appalled. I didn't understand. Nor do I yet. I nearly said: 'But, Jesus Christ, that's unhealthy. It's in – '

'Incestuous? Don't be silly. Dan's an absolute.' I didn't understand, still don't. 'Anyway, he comes first. Now at least. If anything happened to Dan I wouldn't be able to give any attention to a mere husband. And mere husbands wouldn't understand, any more than you do. So forget it. Thanks for proposing. Now take off your clothes.'

I did, but it was as if for a medical inspection. I surveyed myself, limp as oiled lettuce. I said in shame: 'Blame the army. I should have been back before now. Guilt's a terrible detumescer, if that word exists. I love you, anyway,' more boldly now, not having to make the claim good. They wouldn't put me on a charge. It was too extraterritorial a place for paper discipline.

THE COURSE I was sent on was held at Ty Morgannwg on the borders of Glamorgan and Monmouthshire. It was a mansion leased to the army by one of the richer of the Rhys families, the one that controlled the Glamorgan Tea Company, and it had wide grounds and a beech plantation, both useful for outdoor antipersonnel exercises. The twenty or so students were all senior NCOs and warrant officers. The military staff was small, but the civilian instructors seemed to be more than one could count, chiefly because they all looked alike – dark, meagre, brooding, bitter, tough. They disclosed neither their names nor their origins, but they all seemed to be of Central European prov-enance and, whatever a Jew is, I guessed that a good quarter of them were Jews. They were known by single initials which, because they did not carry the colour of a genuine surname like Silbermann or Virag, were not easily registered and were often confused. They taught us to treat the enemy as, I presumed, they themselves had been treated. They knew about the pressure points of the body, the spot on the skull which, if pressed, could make the whole cranium shatter like a dropped vase, the relationship between the number of teeth or fingernails drawn and the information that would be gritted out by the victim before he fainted. We were shown rusty garden shears that had actually been used in the act of castration. The gouging out of eyes was demonstrated on a very lifelike model. We heard recorded screams and were taught to interpret them on a scale of *keevs* (I wondered and then ceased to wonder why a Hebrew term had been chosen instead of a Greek). It was important that we be milked of all human sympathy in confrontation with the enemy, and we were subjected to Nazi films of ghastly interrog-ation which were repeated until we yawned in protest. After the first week it was wisely recognized that we all needed a weekend break to recover from nausea. I did not go back to Manchester but booked a room in the Angel at Abergavenny. I hired a bicycle and rode out to see how the archaeological dig was getting on.

It was getting on well. The northern wall of a late Roman settlement had been uncovered and what, from various jigsaw

ikon pieces put together again, seemed to be a Christian chapel.
There was what I was told was an image of the Virgin Mary in
Byzantine mosaic, as well as the remains of a sculpted sandalled
foot stuck to its plinth, with the residue (CTVS) of the legend
SANCTUS somebody. A bald brown Welsh professor was organizing the transfer of the portable items to Cardiff on a cleaned-
up coal truck. The slitted stone with GLAD ART REG deeply
etched into it was in fact a buttress of the wall and quite immovable. The digging schoolboys and schoolgirls hearkened to the
professor's referee whistle and took a break for lunch of spam
and jam sandwiches. I got on my bicycle and wobbled over the
field then sped along the road towards the Black Lion. Of course,
that had been the real purpose of my excursion – to see my
sister's parents-in-law. Curiosity, concern (who were they to
reject Zip?), the need to know something of the frame out of
which Beatrix had stepped.

The Black Lion was a small old pub with a vegetable garden
behind it and the shelter of two elms for a couple of worn benches
at the front. I entered the one bar and found farm labourers
teaching how to play darts an intellectual-looking youth who had
probably, because of his conscientious objection to the war, been
directed to agriculture. A couple of ancient yokels sat silent over
their beerpots. A man wearing a fishing hat with a stethoscope
peering from his overcoat pocket was talking at the bar counter
with the landlord. 'I am not what you would be calling a reading
man,' the landlord said, 'but I know what I know.' This was
David Jones, survivor of the *Titanic* and the first war, a man with
gold and a healthy bank deposit, running a pub as a retired
hobby rather than a livelihood. He was dark, small, in hale early
middle age, with plentiful tar-coloured hair, unshaven for the
morning's trade, in a collarless dirty shirt with an open waistcoat.
When I ordered my pint, David Jones's sharp eyes caught the
crowns on my forearms, and he said: 'Yes sergeant major.'

'Quartermaster sergeant really,' I said. And, when the pint
was pulled and set before me, 'Thank you, Mr Jones.'

'You know my name then?'

'He thinks it safe to call any Welshman Jones,' the doctor
said. 'Well, I must see to Mrs Pritchard's youngest's croup.' He
downed the remains of his half and left with a general wave.

'Yes,' I said. 'I know your name. Your son married my sister.' I got the tribute of a long stare and a drop of the jaw. 'I've come on no mission. I just happen to be stationed near Newport. I hope you've no objection to my dropping in.'

David Jones called: 'Millie.' So that was what he had made of Ludmila. He called twice. His wife came in from the dark depths beyond the counter. She was a middle-aged Beatrix in a flowered apron, greying blond hair in curlers, plump, undeniably handsome but trying to subside into rural plainness. Her daughter would not so subside. 'This,' David Jones said, 'is the brother of the one that our Reg got married to.' And they both stared at me as though that were all my fault. Ludmila Jones spoke in English with more Welsh than Russian intonation. She said:

'He has not been a good boy.'

'Because,' I said, 'he married my sister? I have, besides brotherly love, great respect for my sister. She is a professional musician, skilled and hardworking. Your son fell in love with her. I warned them both that they were too young to marry, but I had no power to prevent them. My sister takes it hard that she does not seem to be accepted.' I gave it them bluntly. 'She thinks it is something to do with her being Jewish.' David Jones said, too quickly:

'No, it's not that. I worked with Jews. I ran a restaurant with a lot of Jewish customers. I've nothing against the Jews.' His wife said nothing but narrowed her Baltic eyes and pursed her full Slav lips. The intellectual landworker looked across from his darts and said:

'Nor has anybody except that they got us into this war.'

'That's bloody nonsense,' I said sharply.

'Read R. C. Crampton's *Jew War*,' said this youth. 'Read J. Clark's *Semitic Serpent*.'

'Go and hoe your bloody turnips,' I said.

'Closing time,' David Jones said. 'Let's have those glasses. You,' he said to me, 'had better have a bit of lunch with us. Tell my wife here all about it in the kitchen behind while I get shut up here.' He opened the counter-flap and ushered me through. I followed Ludmila Jones towards a heartening smell of something with a crust on. The kitchen was of a large farm kind with hanging onions. A fire blazed and there was a full coal scuttle

103

near it. A tabby dozed on top of a cardboard box that seemed to be full of old newspapers. There were two rocking chairs turned towards the hearth but no seat of greater comfort. Ludmila Jones took one rocking chair and thoughtfully rocked, scowling at me. The other must have been made sacred to her husband, for she motioned me towards one of the Windsor chairs by the table. A cuckoo clock gave out closing time. She scowled at me for a full rocking thirty seconds, then got up, went to a corner cupboard and brought out a bottle of *Molniya* vodka.

'Also,' I said while she filled three shot glasses, 'a gift from a relative in the Russian Embassy.' She looked sharply at me then.

'And so?'

'Your daughter Beatrix had the same brand from the same source.'

'*Dvayurni brat,*' she nodded, partially mollified. 'You would say a cousin.' She handed me a glass and raised her own. I gave the toast.

'*Mir miru.*'

'You are Russian Jew?'

'Manchester.' David Jones then came in, took the third glass and lifted it gloomily. He said:

'Let's get this bloody lot over.' And he downed the vodka as if it were that that he meant. His wife said:

'He says he a Manchester Jew.' David Jones sat, rocked, and said:

'Not your fault. Nobody can help what he is or where he comes from.'

'I've no particular call to be ashamed of what I am,' I said with some heat. 'The Manchester Jews helped to make Manchester what she is. More than Manchester. My father threw a bridge over the Jordan. My grandfather was an atheist of European distinction.'

'That's all right, then,' David Jones said. 'So long as you weren't in trade. Manchester Jews robbed me right left and centre. So there is plain speaking for you and you will know now the way I feel.'

'About Reg's marriage, you mean?'

'I did my best for all three of them,' David Jones said to his vodka. 'And it was not easy. There was never as much money as they thought, thanks to those Manchester Jews. They have been given a good education except for the youngest who did not take to it. I wanted one thing from their education and I did not get it.' He waited for me to ask what that one thing was. I asked. 'What I wanted was an explanation' – he stressed the syllables equally, in the Welsh manner – 'of the kind of world we are living in.' The aroma of the pie in the fire-fed oven was maddening: I was young, fit, of very good appetite, and had had dried eggs for breakfast. My belly must have rumbled, for David Jones said to his wife: 'We'll eat now, girl.'

'*Parod*,' she said, meaning ready.

It was a pie made of Welsh lamb, onions, carrots and potatoes, the crust flaky, and it was served with beetroot in vinegar, pickled walnuts, and a side dish of mashed swedes and spuds browned in the oven. David Jones served himself and me pints of draught bitter. Ludmila Jones drank water, which Russians call vodka without the k. I was busy eating for the first five minutes so I could not respond with any eloquence to David Jones's eccentric statement of need. They were a queer family all right. Both regarded my trencherwork with reluctant approval. 'There's famished you are,' David Jones said. 'It is the running about and the army half starves you, I know from personal experience. There is an apple tart and custard to follow.' His wife said, with renewed suspicion:

'How do you know Beatrix has the same?'

'The vodka, you mean? I met her in London. Old friends. Fellow students.'

'She's a mess of a girl,' David Jones said.

'How? The most intelligent girl I've ever met, as well as the most handsome. Doing good work at the Foreign Office. A great postwar career in front of her. A mess?'

'It was her life of love,' Ludmila Jones said.

'All right, girl,' and David Jones cut crust like an enemy. To me he said: 'New ideas. Flighty. A daughter of pleasure you might call her. It is not the way I was brought up. Talking about it too, open. Many's the slap she's been given. She has done well in the examination, but she cannot answer the big question. And Reg turned his back on it and started to study Spanish. See where it got him. Beaten up by some of his own mother's nationality. And it turned him into the ruffian he is. And thief too. But he was stopped there.'

'Look,' I said, while my second helping was being ladled out, 'I studied philosophy, and that's supposed to give you all the answers to the big questions, but it doesn't. It doesn't even begin to. What you learn is that there's no answer.' David Jones gave me the look of one who refuses to believe that the realization that he has been totally cheated is soon to dawn on him. He said:

'What's the good of it then?'

'The value is supposed to lie in the finding out.' He did not seem to understand that; he said:

'We paid in more ways than one. Four years of bloody hell and me in the big battles or very near, and their mother caught up in that bloody revolution in what they now call Leningrad. Lucky to get out alive, both of us, but some didn't have the luck. It's them we have to think about. I earned money and saved it and, yes I will be honest, inherited it too. Now what is money for? It is not for pleasure but for the buying of knowledge. And the knowledge has not been bought.'

'Nor ever will be,' I said. 'It's not on sale, not true knowledge. Meaning is there a God, and why are we here, and why are men always fighting each other. Education's there just to show you that the knowledge that you really want is unobtainable.' My pie plate was removed by the rather grimly silent Ludmila Jones and a deep flower-patterned dessert dish substituted. The apple tart had been made from their own windfalls, sweetened with a neighbour's honey (the Ministry of Food permitted a special sugar ration for beehives), and topped with a thick custard that tasted of cornflour but not eggs. I went on eating hungrily. David Jones said:

'On leave are you then?'

'Weekend only. I have to be back on a course on Monday morning.'

'And what kind of a course would that be?'

'New techniques of torture and murder.'

'It's a terrible bloody business,' he shuddered. Then, to his wife: 'There's no reason why he shouldn't stay here till Monday if he wants to. There's always the bed made up for either of the

106

single ones.' He said that bitterly. 'After all, he's like in the family.'

'He can stay,' Ludmila Jones said. '*Glân* he is,' meaning clean. 'He eats what he is given.'

'It was good,' I said. 'Thank you. I'd like to stay. I take it,' I added, 'that there are some who do not eat what they're given.'

'Our daughter picks,' David Jones said, 'and Dan always wants fish, and Reg will not eat fat.' It sounded terrible, that last accusation, because it was straight from Dotheboys Hall. Then Ludmila Jones asked me a terrible question. She said:

'You have been in bed with our daughter?'

I coughed on one of the cloves in the apple tart. I said: 'I asked her to marry me. Not much more than two weeks ago.'

'That is not what I want to know.' Ludmila had her Baltic eyes full on me while she poured boiling water into a big brown teapot. Her husband said:

'Ah, embarrassing thing to ask that is. You do not have to answer,' he said to me.

'If I don't answer it means yes. I'd say that it's very likely that I'm in love with her. And you know how that affects a man. She's a very lovely girl.'

'That is not what I want to know.'

'We know our own daughter,' David Jones sighed heavily. 'What she will do and what she won't. More men than hot dinners, as the saying goes. But she won't marry you.'

'I know that.'

'She'd marry her bloody halfwitted brother Dan if the law allowed it. He's the only man who is really in her bloody life.' The tone was of high anguish.

'I've been made aware of that,' I said. 'And I don't understand it.'

'Blood,' Ludmila Jones said, making it sound like *blad*.

'I beg your pardon?'

'She means that Dan saved her life by giving his blood,' David Jones explained. 'They didn't keep it in bottles at that time. At least not where we were they didn't. It was on holiday near Tenby. Dan's blood was the right group. It isn't always, though the whole family ought to have the same blood. Mine was no bloody good,' he said redundantly. 'It was a mad woman with a knife cutting cats' heads off. Then she went for Beatrix in the main street. She lost a lot of blood before they got her to the hospital. Like a stuck pig. In the stomach it was.'

'I've seen no mark.'

'Aaaaah,' Ludmila Jones cried in triumph. 'You give me my answer.'

'They took the stitches out and there was a scar and then there was no scar,' David Jones said. 'She was only eleven. Young flesh heals proper. Then the idea gets into her head that Dan has saved her life, which he did in a way, but it was his blood not him that had done it. Strange ideas they do get,' he pronounced, 'kids.'

'You give me my answer,' Ludmila Jones said yet again, putting before me a primrose yellow mug of very strong tea.

'There's the swimming baths,' I said tamely. 'Plenty of stomachs visible there. *Spasibo* or should I say *diolch*?' as she shoved milk and coarse beet sugar over. And then: 'What happened to the madwoman?'

'Dan strangled her,' David said, sang rather. I spluttered on hot tea. 'Well, not exactly. They found her in a wood outside Tenby, and Dan was in the lead of the party you could call it. They had to pull him off her. Always fierce he was. She was alive enough to be put away in a home somewhere.' The cuckoo jumped out of its little chalet four times and David Jones gravely confirmed the truth of its signal with his pocket watch. 'Seen the digging then, have you, that is going on in Bowen's field?'

'On the way here, yes.'

'Thought you might have. Many have seen it. I don't like it, as I may tell you honestly. It's things coming home to roost. The sword of Attila the Hun, there is no need to look at me like that. I am not what you would call a reading man, but I know what I know.' And then, very fiercely, 'Who would have thought it would follow us down the centuries? I fight in one war and Millie there is caught up in a revolution, and we thought we had earned like peace for everybody, but here we have two sons fighting in another war and a daughter baring her body to everybody while the Hun bombs come down over London.'

'Not now,' I said uneasily. 'The Luftwaffe is busy elsewhere.'

'It is best to forget,' he said, in sorrow, 'that we have children. Then if they do not come back the anguish is not so great.'

'They'll come back.'

'Some already have not come back. There are men who come drinking here, and when they have had a pint too many they weep over sons dead in Africa. There is no explanation.' Again the four syllables of equal stress. Ludmila Jones was already washing the dishes at the sink under the window, her back set, as it were, sternly to us both. The cat mewed round her ankles, and she spoke sternly to it in Welsh. 'It is only the cat that understands Welsh,' David Jones said. 'The past is dead and with it the children of the past,' obscurely. 'Come into the bar and we will drink another pint.'

We drank more than another pint. Ludmila Jones went up to bed for her afternoon rest, and David Jones told me about his long luck – the *Titanic* survival, the marriage, the money, a good peace after a war from which he emerged a winner, despite the treachery of certain Manchester Jews. 'We served the best, boy,' he said. 'Two lads in the kitchen I trained with my own hands, and the wife an attraction in herself, as you might say. We became famous among musicians and people of the theatre, being open late and with a drinking licence we lost, thanks to bloody police treachery, not enough handouts, see. There was the big singer Chaliapine, who would gorge ten helpings of borshch, none like it outside Moscow he would say, and the pianist Paderewski who ate like a bird but knew what he liked. Oh, it was not all the East European stuff, our French dishes were few but of the best, bachgen. Charles B. Cochran would come in with Evelyn Laye and Jessie Matthews, and there would be Noël Coward, very witty. Come into the back parlour now and I will show you my scrapbook.' We took newly drawn pints through the kitchen and across a dark corridor smelling of damp, and in the back parlour I saw in a locked bookcase his encyclopaedia and the nugget of gold I had already seen. I said:

'That surely was love, I mean, your daughter lugging it aboard a train and bringing it back.'

'Love, you say? Daughterly feeling, is it? Oh, she always had the idea that the gold was something special and had to be kept safe. Not because it was mine and my father's before me but

109

because it is, as she said, real value, not like money. Money ebbs and flows and goes down the drain, but gold is gold. I will never forgive Reginald for what he tried to do, sell it to give guns to stinking dagoes. Look at this now. Signed photographs and little rhymes and greetings and well wishing in all of the languages.' The scrapbook was, true, a fine record of the talented well fed and appreciative. Mark Hambourg, who had eaten one chicken before his Free Trade Hall concert 'to keep light' and another three after; Artur Schnabel, with a tribute to, I presumed, Ludmila Jones in a reference to *das Ewig-Weibliche*; Lorenz Hart and Richard Rodgers with a line from 'Mountain Greenery'; a scribbled bar of Chopin from Pachmann; a treble-chinned Tetrazzini, all jewels and smirk; Evelyn Laye with 'I'll see you again'; A. P. Herbert in self-caricature over the the lines 'Davy Jones may claim my bones/But my stomach David Jones'; the drunken scrawl 'Wholly admirable' from Winston S. Churchill. I said:

'You feel this to be a bit of a letdown?'

'Oh, it had to happen. The Manchester air was killing her. And then the Kardomah bought the premises, they belonging to those two Jewboys, see, I beg your pardon. And there'd been the trouble about the licence. Things had gone off a bit as they always do. Hard work is never enough, bachgen, and the luck you need can't last. So there it is then. I am not grumbling.'

I had had enough. I said: 'I must cycle back to Abergavenny and collect my things from the hotel there.' But I had no intention of returning. I fancied I would have to sleep in a haunted bedroom, full of the pong of decaying fish or the gurgles of strangulation. At best I would spurt on bedclothes that had once warmed Beatrix Jones and not be as *glân* as I looked. I had noticed a telephone in the kitchen on the Welsh dresser. I would ring up from the Angel and speak of urgent recall to the course that taught pain and murder.

TRI

PTE DANIEL JONES, of the third platoon of C Company, First Battalion of the Royal Lancaster Regiment, Third Infantry Brigade of the First Infantry Division, Sixth Corps, was permitted at dawn to fish in the lake called Albano for the local lake fish known as *coregone*. He fished with a borrowed crutch and a borrowed pair of artillery lanyards knotted, the hook a bent hussif needle and the bait a chunk of bully. He caught three by the time the sun was well up. His mate Wally Squire had lighted a fire for cooking, and they were able to eat breakfast of charred *coregone* before they were ordered to fall in for the march to Rome. The fish made a difference to Dan Jones: it seemed to relax his bowels and enable him to defecate behind a tree for the first time in a week. He had missed fish. Ever since the landing he had lived on bully straight from the can or stewed, varied with a bite from his iron ration, which was a cake of hard chocolate flavoured with meat extract. He had been taken prisoner near Campoleone, not far along the road to Rome that began at the bridgehead.

It had been a relief to drop his rifle and unhook his grenades. He had had enough of the campaign of liberation. There had been a smell of defeatism about it, at least among the other ranks, even before they'd embarked at Naples. Mr Hotchkiss, the platoon commander, had given a little talk about Peter Beach and showed them where it was on the map. He was a decent young man, an estate agent in civvy street, who believed falsely that his platoon laughed at him for having been beaten up and stripped and robbed in a Pozzuoli whorehouse. 'Scrub and sand and pine, chaps. Then we'll come across a river, it's called the Moletta if you're interested, but it's just wet like all rivers. There'll be plenty of wet without adding rivers to it. The weather forecast's about as bad as it can be, which is situation normal for this kind of caper. We'll have it bad but the Yank Rangers will have it worse on the Anzio main beach. It's not going to be a piece of cake for anybody.'

The convoy was so big that it had to push itself out into the Tyrrhenian Sea to have a good look at itself. They all had a good look at Capri and some sang:

> So she whispered It's best not to linger
> And as I kissed her hand I could see
> She had a plain golden ring on her finger.
> 'Twas goodbye on the isle of Capri.

'Right,' Lancecorporal Bates said, 'have a good shufti at it, cause you'll never see the bugger again.' When the sun sank on it the huge convoy creaked towards the mainland. Stars but no moon. No jerry planes either, why is that sir? 'Well,' Mr Hotchkiss said, 'they're all needed at Monte Cassino where our lads and the Americans are pounding away at the Gustav Line.' All felt cold and most felt seasick. Dan Jones felt dirty, useless, encumbered with packs and gasmask, desirous of sleeping for ever. 'Time for a kip,' Sergeant Reckett said. 'Get them swedes bashed if you can find room. Four hours before landing.'

The yawns of the waking got themselves frozen into gapes of disbelief when the racket started. Jesus Christ all fucking bleeding mighty. Never had they heard anything like it when the rocket ships started cracking at the landing beaches. Eight hundred rockets, each loaded with thirty pounds of TNT, cramming less than seven hundred seconds of time with day of judgment thunder filling the whole of space as they hammered blind at landmines, barbed wire, and whatever pillboxed jerries awaited the arrival of the landing force. And then the racket stopped except for wawawawawa echoes thudding back off what they were to find out were called the Alban Hills. Dan Jones knew he had gone deaf for ever. He looked at faces with silent gesticulating mouths descried very dimly in starlight.

When the Royal Lancasters disembarked, he found he could hear a bit with his left lug only. The assault craft ran on to a sand bar, and he was up to his neck with others in January sea water. He could hear Jesus buggering fucking Christ and then landmines going off. The rockets had not got rid of all the landmines. Bert Redway, by way of being a kind of mate, a thin-necked lad with respirator spectacles, had a foot blown off, and Jack Unwin was totally shattered, showering lavish blood and guts over Bill Ross, who was in his turn blown to buggery, meaning he gave limbs to all points of the compass. Dan Jones slithered over a lot of carnage to follow Sergeant Reckett's beckoning arm to what foredawn light showed to be dunes. They stood stamping and retching while the sappers laid pontoons from the sand bar to the shore, and the tiffies set up little lights with hoods on to mark a way through the mines. There were no jerries around, not one, not even in the concrete lookout posts. Loudspeakers started giving out instructions, as wawawa meaningless as railway terminus announcements. The platoon kept to itself as platoons do, huddling, frozen, fucking soaked, watching the vehicles of the Assault Brigade trundling ashore over runways of wire netting.

The roar of aircraft first scared then comforted: Spitfires and Kittyhawks, an umbrella over the umbrella pines. There was no sign now of Mr Hotchkiss: it was assumed that all the officers of the battalion were at a staff meeting somewhere in the cold wet dawn, having orders relayed down to them from Field Marshal Alexander in his fucking fur-collared coat or one of the Yank generals, the one with the corncob pipe who kept going lookee here. The beach was filling to overflow with troops, trucks, tanks, brengun carriers. The big square gobs of the landing craft gaped to disgorge Sherwood Foresters and Scottish Horse and KSLI and West Kents and London Irish and London Scottish, all stamping for the cold on the cold sand, sucking fags so that the dark was all glowworms. There was a hell of a report three miles out at sea as a minesweeper hit a mine and went down in three minutes flat. They were all cold and wet as fucking buggery and would have given anything for a fire and a brewup. An order went out to some somewhere that they had to start digging slit trenches. In this fucking sand? Have some fucking sense.

It was always like that. They never got dry. They coughed and they were costive and they wanted to vomit but there was

113

nothing to bring up. They were wet when they trudged in file through the southern segment of the Padiglione Wood, rain pounding on their helmets and their knees soaked below their caped groundsheets, wet cones crunching under boots that had let the wet in. Dan Jones was with the section sent on a recce to find out where the jerries were, trudging along the railway track that ran due north from Anzio harbour, whence the gun called Anzio Annie pounded. They halted at a place called Campo di Carne. 'This is Meat Field, chaps,' Mr Hotchkiss said, 'that's what the Eyetie means so we'd better take a bit of meat on board.' They ate bully and biscuit and drank water scooped from various shaly holes along the iron line. Then they were to march on to the little railway station at Carroceto. Dan Jones coughed and coughed and knew what misery was. The road they took was treelined, though the trees had lost their leaves, and on either side of the road were little farms. Pte 'Spag' Pirelli, whose dad before internment had run a little nosh shop in Stepney, called out: 'Ci sono tedeschi?' and the farmworkers paused in their hoeing to call back: 'Niente tedeschi.' Pirelli told Mr Hotchkiss that that meant there were no jerries around, but Aprilia just beyond Carroceto had three towers like factory chimneys, and Mr Hotchkiss said there had to be jerries there. The landing had to be opposed somewhere, and that looked as good a jerry stronghold as any. When they cautiously minced out of the little railway station into the main street of Carroceto, the jerries told them they were at Aprilia by firing shells that were not well aimed but were bloody deafening. They about turned and made across the road towards what the map called Buonriposo Ridge. With joy they met limestone caves, the first dry place since they had landed. Sergeant Reckett said they could gather twigs and make a fire and even have a brewup. Mr Hotchkiss got the battalion signaller who was with them to get through on his set to Battalion HQ. The men coughed and coughed. 'I'm getting this fucking clobber off,' Bob Solomon said, stripping. 'I'm having a fucking dry change whatever any fucker says.' They got a fire going and made tea with tea powder and sweetened condensed milk in five messtins. They sipped in gratitude. Mr Hotchkiss had rum in his waterbottle. They sipped in gratitude. The rain turned to sleet.

Most had a kip. 'Roll on death,' Joe Smedley said through fag-smoke, 'and let's have a go at the angels.'

The rest of the battalion found them at nightfall. C Company commander, Major Titterton, told Mr Hotchkiss that that cave would make a useful HQ for Lieutenantcolonel Mackintosh, and that the whole battalion had to bivouac in Campo di Carne. The battalion's role was to be supportive of the 24th Guards Brigade, which was to take Aprilia. Bivouacking meant digging in with spades and setting up groundsheets and gascapes to keep the sleet off. A ration truck had come up with the battalion vehicles, and cans of M and V could be broached cold. There was an issue of rum, and everybody breathed sweetly on everybody else. A battalion mess was set up in the cave that had belonged to Number 3 platoon's first section, and there were stories of wassailing and Mac singing rude songs to celebrate their triumphal landing in Italy.

They could all hear the noise of battle in Carroceto and Aprilia but there was a lot they couldn't hear, hand-to-hand fighting with bayonets and grenades. The Grenadiers were carved to buggery. Dan Jones, in costive pain behind a tree at the northern edge of the Padiglione Wood, heard sad feet shambling back along the railway line, jerry prisoners, a hundred he was later told, but a jock was to say it was all a total fuckup: brewing up among shit and corpses, and as for the fucking mud. He had seen three German Tiger tanks knocking hell out of the Grenadiers. They'd taken Aprilia but they'd lose it again: there was a hell of a lot of jerry stuff up beyond the three towers they called the Factory.

Major Titterton told C Company what Lieutenantcolonel Mackintosh had told the company commanders, namely that with Carroceto and Aprilia cleared of enemy it was the job of the British to push on along that road there, the Via Anziate, four miles up from Carroceto railway station to Campoleone, on the main railway line up from Naples to Rome, and that the Yanks would make for Cisterna, wherever that was. Southey, a bible-thumper in Number 2 platoon, told him it was the Three Taverns of the Acts of the Apostles, where St Paul met the Christians from Rome. Very interesting, the major said, not very interested. The First Battalion of the Royal Lancasters was to be held in reserve, the spear of the main attack being in the fists of the Irish and Scots Guards. Dan Jones heard them crunching up the railway line under cloud, frogs croaking and dogfoxes holding colloquies over a distance, then the moon came out big and full and the jerries started.

There was a medical post set up just south of the battalion lines of the Lancasters in the Padiglione Wood. It was from a Sherwood Forester with a leg blown off that some of them heard of the fucking shambles near Campoleone. There were these moaning minnies on railway trucks and tanks, and our lads had had no tank support because of the mud, and then the fucking rain started up again, and then there were the spandaus, some of our lot ran and you couldn't bloody blame them. But the Lancasters were ordered to march at nightfall in support of the Duke of Wellington's Regiment and the King's Shropshire Light Infantry, rum and M and V in their bellies but still cold. Hell broke out of earth and sky and the pitchblack flanks that led on one side to the Vallelata Ridge and on the other to the creek of Spaccomassi. Owls and frogs and the thrumming of the telegraph wires, and then hell hell and all hell. The jerries were there in full force, tanks, shells and machine-guns, and Dan Jones heard ahead of him with his one near-good ear the thud of rifles and grenades being dropped thud in the mud all along the line. He was glad to drop his. Great searchlights searched from trucks there to the left where they said the mud would swallow all vehicles, and there was a high class sort of voice from a loud-speaker telling them to do what they were already doing. Dan Jones's soaked boots followed the soaked boots of Eddie Cassell in front from the track on to the road that was called the french letter because it was straight and thin. Then they saw their own trucks with the div sign brightly illumined but with jerries guarding them, and a good number of their dead, mostly from A Company. Lights went out and it was all loud voices giving orders, but there were some ricks afire not many yards ahead and soon the moon came out bright as day to have a shufti before fresh clouds engulfed it. They were marched in the dark to the right and ended up in what seemed to be farm territory, what with pig grunts and the howls of cows surely not unmilked, not with the jerries there. A big new searchlight showed them each

116

other's scared faces and the stone walls of a yard. A voice spoke English and said to stay where they were and do nothing foolish, their war was over. It wasn't the voice of anyone anybody knew. It was all a fuckup and it had always been a fuckup, despite Alexander's 'You chaps are doing wonders' and Corncob Charlie Lucas's 'Lookee here, we'll be in Rome by payday.' Eddie Cassell said: 'We'll be all right, the jerries always do what's right, that's laid down, they won't shoot us nor nothing.'

Dan Jones felt something was wrong with his left trouserleg: the gaiter had worked its straps free and got away. He took off the other gaiter and let it lie in the farm mud. Soon they all lay in the farm mud on groundsheets and gascapes. The moon came out bright and lovely again and distant dogs bayed at it. In the far corner of the farmyard they got a glimpse of Major Cobbett, the second in command, and a huddle of officers. The colonel had had it then. Soon Mr Hotchkiss called through new dark: 'Number 3 platoon all present? Anybody missing?' Nobody said anything, not even 'We're out of it now, it's the jerries that gives the orders,' so Mr Hotchkiss called for Sergeant Reckett. Somebody said that Sergeant Reckett had scarpered, but Corporal Spencer shuffled up in the dark from somewhere to say that Sergeant Reckett had a bad attack of the squitters and was temporarily secluded. Other platoon commanders could be heard calling their flocks. A Company, in the vanguard, had fought back and been notably reduced: the gundropping and hands up had begun on Captain Street of B Company's example. Not much choice really. Not a chance really. A right fuckup as they all said.

Not many could lie down for long, it was so fucking cold. They were up and stamping and beating themselves, but were so confined, near a whole battalion in a farmyard, that they beat each other. It was a relief to see pale dawn and a bigger relief to see two jerries hauling in a sort of Soyer on wheels, with another two jerries pointing their rifles. They filled their messtins with hot soup – water with bits of spud and cabbage – and munched the jerries' black bread. The RSM, 'Mush' Knott, mush being Arabic for not, came round then and said: 'Get shaved and spruced up a bit, scrape that mud off, don't let the side down, we've got a long march ahead of us.' Where to, sir? 'To the infernal city, lads, with the pope all ready to give us a blessing.

Keep singing, don't be downhearted, show the fuckers what we are.'

It was Major Cobbett who got them lined up as a battalion on the road. There was what was left of the Guards and the KSLI up there ahead. Major Cobbett announced that the CO had bought it as well as the adjutant and various other officers but there was no need for anybody to feel ashamed that he'd joined the ranks of the defeated, that was what war was like. He gave a smashing salute to the jerry officer in charge, then they all right turned and were on the march. They sang 'Yours till the stars lose their glory' and 'There were rats rats big as fucking cats in the quartermaster's store' but without conviction. The jerries were winning and as a kind of earnest of this it was their song that rolled up from the vaward, though with Eighth Army words: 'Over the ether came that strain, that sweet refrain came back again: With you, Lilli Marlene, with you, Lilli Marlen'.' It was a dry chill day. Dan Jones found himself next to Pte Shawcross, a schoolmaster in civvy street who said unintelligible things about marching through history, this was the road the legions took when they returned in some triumph or other after disembarking at what they used to call Neapolis. One or two old peasants gawped from the roadside to see the long line of defeated, and some of the troops called 'Keep smiling, grandad' and 'Won't be long now'. They were given a meticulous five-minute break every hour to piss in the ditches, but they were not fed till they got to Castel Gandolfo. This, knowledgeable Shawcross said, was the pope's summer residence. A big lake and a hill road and build-ings behind an iron gate, but what Dan Jones gaped at was a mass of Yank prisoners disconsolate by the lake under German rifles and even a couple of machine-guns pointing from trucks. Captured at Cisterna and Velletri. One or two Yanks had tried to make it across Lago Albano but had been shot and went under. The jerries unloaded captured K rations, tins of bully and M and V and even cartons of Lucky Strike and Chesterfield and there them at the prisoners. They all tried to sleep huddled, but it was too fucking cold. There was a fight between the allies. You cocksuckers made a fuckup of it. Listen who's talking, get some in, Yank bastard. The jerry guards were faintly amused by confirmation of propaganda about Anglo-American dissension. This was at dawn when they got on the march again.

Just south of Rome they were joined by about four hundred other prisoners, British, Yank, even dark sullen bastards from Algeria, who had been caught trying to break the unbreakable Gustav Line. Night and the curfew were well under way as they were all marched past the Porta San Sebastiano and the Baths of Caracalla under a troubled Roman moon. 'Jesus,' a wit cried, 'they're going to throw us to the fucking lions.' For it was outside the Colosseum that they were halted and then prodded inside by bayonet points through the gates. The intellectual Shawcross was burbling something about Victorian heroines and death from Roman fever. Those that could shat among the mediaeval ruins that clogged the amphitheatre, but many were profoundly costive. A Yank lad cried for his mom and was comforted. Get some in, your fucking numbers aren't dry yet. In the morning, stiff and tousled, they were prodded out on to the road and made to march north to the Via Nazionale. All along the street Roman citizens observed them sadly. Both cheers and groans would have been wrongly interpreted. But some youngish men in black with parson's collars sort of sketched what could have been a blessing. A little jowly man who looked like a streetcleaner tried to give Fred Slade a cigarette. The guard marching near began to belabour him with his riflebutt. Dan Jones and Fred Slade and Jack Prothero broke ranks to have a go at the bastard, but they were snarled and riflebutted back into line. 'Sing up; lads,' somebody yelled, but they didn't know what to sing. Nobody had taught them any songs about beating the jerries and securing a great victory over the forces of evil and oppression. But a group started on 'Ballocks and the same to you' to the tune of Colonel Bogey. 'Ballocks, they make a damned fine stew. Ballocks, I'm singing ballocks, I'm singing ballocks, so ballocks to you.'

They were marched, ballocking away, to Termini, the name of a big railway station. A line of schoolkids in blue smocks led by a nun had a bit of a laugh at them. Prothero got his boots caked in horseshit and said: 'Horseshit from below and bullshit from above and always in the fucking dark, I might as well be a mushroom.' They were marched into the great dim entrance hall, where there were people actually buying railway tickets. A kiosk even sold copies of some lying rag or other. There were advertisements for *Acqua Sacra* and a brand of fag called *Nazionale,* and somebody had crossed out *Mussolini ha sempre ragione.* 'Going on our holidays then, are we?' the wit of the Colosseum quipped. 'Mum, I've lost me bucket and spade.' They were turned right through a kind of ornamental iron arch on to a great dirty endless platform. Along the platform a few blueclad miserable bastards of Romans swept up rubbish.

On this long dirty platform were a great number of packing cases with stencilled numbers on them. They were guarded by two young jerries with rifles. Nevertheless a Yank officer with two silver bars on his shoulders and square-framed spectacles on his nose came close to these and looked at them with interest. 'Loot,' he said, as though announcing his demotion. He did more. He prised up a loose slat with his gloved fingers and felt inside. One of the guards rapped him with his butt, whereupon the officer let off what sounded like very good harsh German at him in officerly rebuke. A jerry officer in lovely polished boots and a field-gray greatcoat came up to add his own gentler rebuke for treatment impermissible to a prisoner officer and then said in lovely English:

'Allow me to gratify your curiosity. Those boxes contain treasures taken from the Benedictine monastery at Monte Cassino. They are being transported at the insistence of the Abbot into the Reich for safekeeping. You will have the privilege of accompanying them. It is an ironic privilege, since the barbarous intention of international Bolshevist Jewry in its Anglo-American disguise to destroy the centuries-old centre of the Christian faith is all too well known. You will be in good company then on your passage east. I wish you all *Gute Reise.*' Then he stalked off with a Feldwebel after. The Yank officer said to his field-gray back something about Adolf Hitler's *Arsch.* Then the train started to come in. It was a long goods train, Italian rolling stock of many wagons. As soon as it came to a stop and sighed out its steam, a Yank corporal cried: 'Okay, fellers.' He and four or five others made a leap for it, down on to the rails among the couplings. They were on the other side before the guards could aim their rifles. But rifles got them on the other side. 'We'll go quietly,' the Yank officer said. 'The Chattanooga choochoo.' If he came from Chattanooga, in a way he was right. 'All aboard.'

WITH the news of the Normandy landings the political sense of the Gibraltar garrison grew sharper. The war was nearly over, it was thought, and now they had to think of the future. In the Engineers' Hall there was a political debate nearly every evening, organized by the Gibraltar Literary and Debating Society, and the Cymric separatists or Sons of Arthur had as much right to air their views as the communists or liberals or the oldwomanish zealots of the Commonwealth Party. There were no conservatives, except among officers of field rank.

WO First Class Aled Rhys waved what looked like a wooden sword at the assembly, which was very far from being all Welsh. 'Look at this,' he cried, 'and do not laugh at what has the insubstantiality of stage bloody property. For from the Breconshire excavations we at last know that the sword of Arthur existed, and that it was of this shape and size. So take it as the symbol of an ancient kingdom which lost its rights and is now in a fair way to recover them.' There was goodnatured heckling. What do you Taffs want then? Who made that wooden sword, John Player? (John Player was the name, derived from the sailor on the cigarette packet, given in joke to the pioneer sergeant of the First Herts, who had been ordered by his colonel to wear a beard in fulfilment of an ancient regimental tradition long in desuetude.) 'What we Taffs, as you call us, want is freedom from the overbearing rule of the Saxon, and that means our own parliament and our own ruler, elected and hence a president to start with, hereditary and hence a constitutional monarch, control of our own natural bloody resources, Welsh law and Welsh education, a Welsh army and a Welsh navy and a Welsh foreign policy, Welsh self-determination and Welsh passports, Welsh border guards and to hell with the *Sais* just walking in as if it was his own bloody property.' There were the hoots and jeers appropriate to an inferior comic turn, but Ben Griffiths, lean, dark and flashing, stood to quieten them. He said:

'Laugh, but you will laugh on the other side of your collective *Sais* face, you scorners and doubters, when the great day comes. They laughed at Hitler and his handful of thugs, but there's no

121

laughter now. They laughed at Lenin and Stalin but they'll never be laughed at again. Consider what we've been fighting for these last long years, if you can consider sucking oranges to be fighting, and you'll see it's all been about liberating nations from the tyrant's yoke. We needn't expect any of the parties that seek power in the election that's going to come after victory in Europe to give a bugger about Welsh independence, for what's in it for them? If there's to be Welsh freedom it must come from the Welsh themselves, but we ask the English and Scots and the Irish among you to remember that we are asking only for our rights and we want these rights to be clearly understood by the foreigner. Because they are basic human rights that all thinking men and women must out of a sheer sense of reason support. A free Welsh nation will shake hands with the nation on its borders, as with the nation across the Irish Sea and the Caledonia in whose own desire for self-determination we join in fraternal enthusiasm. For it is the age of the small free nations that is dawning. The world has been fighting these long years for freedom, but the fight belongs to the future. The wooden sword we raise is a pale symbol of the shining weapon which will cut the Saxon cancer from the living body of Wales. The land of our fathers will be restored to its sons and daughters.'

Sgt Reginald Morrow Jones should have been present at this meeting, but he was on duty, clad in sports jacket and flannels, in La Linea. The morning after, in tropical khaki, he reported to Captain Woodruff. Woodruff was a small public-school man whose only foreign language was public-school French. He could not, despite his Intelligence Corps commission, quite subdue a conviction that a mastery of tongues was for headwaiters and Port Said dragomans. He returned Reg's salute surlily and asked what there was to report. Reg said:

'Sir, last night I killed a German.'

'If you have nothing to report, sergeant, kindly say so. One of these days you'll go too far with your facetiousness. Have you or have you not anything to report?'

'Sir, last night I killed a German.' Captain Woodruff had on his desk a small wirehaired Scotch terrier that he called Pooh. He stroked the animal's chin; the animal raised its chin the better for him to do so. Woodruff said:

122

'So. Last night you killed a German. You went into La Linea and you met a German and you killed him. Perhaps you would put the whole story into writing and submit it to the editor of the *Rock Magazine*. "Last night I killed a German," by Sergeant R. A. Jones.'

'R. M. Jones, sir. Sir, you accuse me of facetiousness but it's you who are being facetious. If you want the report in writing you shall have it in writing. I thought it my duty to inform you orally first.'

The small dog looked at Reg. 'You're telling me,' the captain said, 'that you killed a German? A German civilian? In La Linea?'

'Yes, sir. He was wearing civilian clothes, as you divine, but that doesn't mean he was a German civilian. I was wearing civilian clothes too. I'm not a civilian.'

'You killed a bloody German?'

'Sir. I struck him down with a commando knife in an alleyway behind a bar called the Baraja. That word means a playing card. The bar is decorated with large crude representations of playing cards. Well, Tarot cards really. The Hanged Man and the Falling Tower and so on. The commando knife was not an issue weapon, by the way. I bought it off a Spaniard. I met this German inside the bar. He admitted he was a German. I guessed he was a German from the intonation of his Spanish and the kind of r he used. When I asked him he said yes he was a German and there we both were on neutral territory, both sick of the bloody war and let's have a drink together.'

'So you drank with the enemy?'

'How did you guess, sir?'

'Sergeant Jones, you're a bloody liar.'

'Captain Woodruff, sir, you're a bloody fool.'

Woodruff's tightening hand made his dog growl. Woodruff growled and the dog squirmed out of his grasp. It jumped off the desk and scampered to a basket in the corner. There it lay and yawned, showing a clean tongue and a pink ribbed palate. 'Do you want to be put on a 252?' Woodruff growled.

'Do that by all means, sir. My defence will be that I attempted to make in all duty a serious report about an act of hostile import and lethal effect towards one of the king's enemies and that you, my commanding officer, expressed incredulity in highly deleterious terms. Sir.'

'How,' Woodruff asked with a tightening larynx, 'do I know you are telling me the bloody truth?'

'Lancecorporal Whitcombe was with me, sir. He witnessed the act and then he vomited. He had advised against it. He also said it was unsporting to stab a man in the back. When the German, whose personal papers I abstracted from his pocket and have here' – he tapped the breast pocket of his tropical khaki shirt – 'when, I say, he lay dying among the used condoms and orange peel, a prostitute came giggling into the alley with a British soldier and saw with horror a fairhaired man in mufti gurgling his last.'

'Did either of those two recognize you?'

'Believe me, do you, now, sir? Good, no more calling me a bloody liar. The prostitute did, I think. Her name is Conchita.'

'Where's Whitcombe now?'

'He's gone to Detached Mole to give a lecture on the constitution of the Japanese army. Whitcombe will confirm the truth of what I've told you. You wouldn't want to call Whitcombe a liar, sir. He was senior lecturer in Slavonic Studies at the University of Durham.'

Woodruff groaned bitterly. 'I take it there was no sign of the police.'

'No, sir. The *Guardia Civil* was not around. I think they were chasing children with their steel whips. Children who go round howling for *peniques*. They let the side down in some way. You know, advertising Spanish poverty. No, sir, no police. I legged it to the frontier and Whitcombe followed, panting and complaining. We got across without any trouble.'

'And then you went straight to your quarters and said nothing to anybody about this?'

'Well, not quite, sir. I had a couple of beers in the Pay Corps sergeant's mess. Naturally I said what I'd done. The Pay Corps RSM was incredulous just like you, sir, but I showed him the dagger. There was dried blood on it. Then he agreed that it was the job of a British soldier to kill whoever of the enemy he could find. The dagger is in my quarters, still rusty with German blood. You can see it any time you like. Sir.'

The captain rose from his desk as in great pain and went over to his dog's basket. He took the little beast in his arms and hugged it as though it represented sanity. He made various *grasséyé* noises at the extreme back of his throat. They were not sounds he used on the rare occasions he spoke French. He said: 'Murder. It's bloody murder.'

'Murder, yes. But it's also known as total war.'

'You said something about papers.'

'Oh yes, papers.' Reg took the papers from inside his shirt. 'There's nothing in them really, sir. A couple of near nudes cut out of some German magazine, probably to comfort his loneliness. A letter from a girl I take to be his betrothed. Her name's Trudi. She says she's lonely and he too must be lonely, and the bombs have been dropping. Addressed to Wolfgang Trautwein. She calls him Woferl. Mozart was called that by his family and intimates. He too was a Wolfgang. The address on this envelope, see, is the German Consulate in Seville. Poor Woferl seems to have been in the foreign service. I don't know whether you could really call him a civilian. No rank, true, except Herr Doktor. They're all doctors if they've been to a university. Like Doctor Goebbels. I'd be a doctor if I were a German. You, of course, not.'

Captain Woodruff sat again very deliberately at his desk and carefully placed his little dog upon it. 'Give me those papers,' he said.

'You don't read German, sir.'

'I know I don't read bloody German but I don't keep a dog and bark myself.' That was not strictly true. 'I want that knife as well. You say you bought it from a Spaniard. You bought it with the intention of doing this Trautwein character in?'

'Oh no, sir. I bought it earlier on, when I was eating a fried egg and chips. Done in olive oil. Providential, you could say.'

'You talked with this Trautwein, damned silly name. What did you talk about?'

'Not a silly name really. Appetising really, but quite adventitiously. Trout and wine. But *Traut* doesn't mean trout. Trout in German is *Forelle*. In Russian too.'

'It strikes me, Sergeant Jones, that you're a bit lightheaded.'

'Well, yes, sir. The pride of a killer. A legitimate one, of course. Our glorious war leader would approve the pride.'

'Oh Christ Jesus,' Woodruff gritted. 'Answer my bloody question.'

'Could I sit down, sir? I know it's irregular, but I'm a little tired. The killing, you know.'

'You may not sit down. This is not a cosy little bloody chat all rank matily bloody set aside. I am your commanding officer and you are a subordinate and this would be conducted in the proper army way if you weren't so facetious and bloody lightheaded. What did you two talk about?'

'Oh, nothing much. His Spanish was better than his English, by the way. He said the war had gone on too long and it was a great pity that two brotherly nations should have had to wage it, that Hitler had had the right idea in some if not all ways, and now the Bolsheviks were going to take over Europe and it had really been the duty of the British and the Germans to fight the Russians together. He also said that one of Hitler's really bright ideas had been the killing off of the Jews. I told him my wife was Jewish. He then sneered and said they were all right in bed he supposed. Then he spoke certain English words. He said: Fuck them and then cut their throats. It was then that I decided to cut his. But instead, as I told you, I gave it him in the back. Up to the hilt. In a dark alley. Behind the bar known as the Baraja.'

'There's nothing in your, er, dossier,' Woodruff said, 'about your wife being Jewish.'

'That's nobody's business but my own, sir. The British army has not yet become the German army.'

'Nobody's business, eh? You killed this man for a highly personal reason. That's your best defence.'

'Defence? *Defence?* I need a bloody defence? You talk as though I face prosecution for having performed a plain soldier's duty. I did in a German and that's that. I've made my report and that's that. Now I should about turn and off. Having saluted. Sir.' Reg saluted but remained where he was. Then the telephone rang. The little dog started and jumped off the desk for the security of its basket. Captain Woodruff answered the telephone.

'Yes?' Then his voice stood to attention. 'Yes. Ten o'clock. Very good.' He put the receiver back on its hook. 'That,' he said balefully, 'was the Convent.'

'The Governor, sir? About this business, sir? They've been quick.'

'The Governor's ADC. He didn't say what it was about. But we both know bloody well what it's about. Smarten yourself up. Put your cap straight. Take that bloody pen out of your top pocket. If you think you've done a soldier's job try and look like a soldier.'

'Sir.'

Captain Woodruff gave his little dog some crumbled biscuits and some condensed milk from a tin; he told his little dog to be a good little dog in his absence. Then he marched with his sergeant to the Convent on Governor's Parade. It was not far. The summer heat was killing. The great rock growled down. Captain Woodruff wiped the sweat off his face as he waited with his sergeant in the anteroom with its portraits of Rooke and Heathfield and its ill-painted panoramic picture of the capture of the Rock from the Spanish in 1704. Reg lit a cigarette without rebuke. He lit another. It was ten forty-five when the ADC, a roundfaced captain with an ill-clipped moustache, came in to say that HE was now ready for Captain Woodruff. He did not quite understand what this sergeant was doing there, but perhaps Captain Woodruff had his own reasons for bringing him. 'I've got my reasons all right,' Woodruff said grimly, marching in.

In the office of Mason-Macfarlane the Lieutenant Governor of Gibraltar Captain Woodruff threw a smart salute and was asked to sit down. The office was large for so cramped a territory; its size made it cool, but the shutters were drawn for further coolness. There were relics of old Gibraltar – a Saracen in bronze who could have been Tarik ibn Ziad; the plans of the Anglican cathedral in the Moorish style; battle scenes with the huge indifferent tawny lion of marble and limestone at rest beyond; bells of wrecked frigates. There were a stuffed Barbary ape and stuffed partridges, woodcock and pigeons, the Rock's fauna. There were asparagus cacti in pots. Major Willard-Gibbons was present on a chair. The chairs were of uncomfortable eighteenth-century elegance. The Governor said:

'Thank you so much for coming so promptly. You two will

know each other, I think.' They did; they nodded warily. 'We need Willard-Gibbons's advice on what seems to be a matter of civil law. Whether it's also a matter for army intelligence I'm not sure. I received a report from across the border in a somewhat circuitous way. As you know, we entertain the fiction that the Governor of Algeciras is really the Governor of Gibraltar. He's due next month for his triumphal visit, no harm in it, keeps the Spaniards quiet. I received from Algeciras a notification that a German had been found apparently murdered. The La Linea chief of police tried to get through here to the civilian police, but that's highly irregular. This is a military garrison. The notification came from Algeciras but the apparent murder was committed in La Linea. Police inquiries in the town elicited the information that the German, known by name in the town, got the name here somewhere, never mind, was last seen in the company of one of ours. Very awkward, that. A British soldier, in mufti of course, seen with him in one of the bars. The police don't take too much notice of the reports of, ah, ladies of pleasure, but one of these claims to have seen one of ours pulling a dagger or something out of the body. Doesn't know his name but would be able to identify him if she saw him. The point is that the Spanish authorities are claiming that a British soldier, in La Linea for the evening on pass, committed a murder on Spanish territory. As an intelligence officer have you received any, ah, intelligence of this or a similar kind?'

'Oh yes, sir,' Woodruff replied heavily. 'The German's name was Trautwein, in the consular service in Seville, away from his territory, evidently spying. He was indeed knifed by one of ours. One of mine, to be specific. Sergeant Jones. I've got him outside.'

'Oh no,' the Governor said. 'Very awkward. Admitted it, did he?'

'Sir. He formed up this morning to deliver the news. He's proud of it. The job of a soldier, he said, is to kill the enemy. I suppose in a way he's right.'

'Told anybody else, has he?'

'He told the entire Pay Corps sergeants' mess. Give him a chance and he'll have it printed in tomorrow's *Gibraltar Chronicle*. As I say, he's proud of it.'

Major Willard-Gibbons now spoke. He was a fleshy middle-aged officer of the General List, a barrister in civil life, usually at leisure, occasionally called on to give legal judgments in areas where civil and military law uneasily nudged each other. 'Yes,' he said. 'If he'd killed in a recognized theatre of war he'd be a hero – well, hardly that, just a soldier doing his duty. The trouble is that he was on neutral territory. The Spaniards are right to construe this as an act of murder. According to international law they could demand extradition.'

'Very awkward,' the Governor said. 'The question is, though, who at present is, as it were, in charge of international law? I mean, there's nobody who can enforce that kind of demand, is there?'

'Well,' Major Willard-Gibbons said, 'that's not the way one's supposed to approach the matter, really. You have to look at it from the Spanish point of view. A German's been killed on Spanish soil, and the Germans are, from the Spanish angle, really being very decent about not invading Spanish territory in order to take the Rock. Now the Germans are going to be very nasty and Franco's going to be made very uncomfortable.'

'Surely,' the Governor said, 'this business won't get as far as Madrid? Won't they want to hush it up and keep it local?'

'That won't happen, I'm afraid, sir. If, as Woodruff here tells us, this German was in the consular service in – where? Right, Seville – then they'll know where he was and want to know why he didn't come back. And remember that the Germans have a sort of hold over the Spaniards, helped the Falange to win and so on in that civil war of theirs. A murder's a big thing, especially the murder of a German national by a British national on Spanish territory, and it's not going to be kept quiet.'

'What do we do then?' the Governor asked. 'Hand this chap of ours over and let him stand trial for murder?'

'That's what should be done, of course, but we won't do it. It's an interesting case really. You remember that business in London in September 1939? No, it wasn't made public, too dangerous. This chap had a German brother-in-law he detested. Kept his German nationality, had a German passport and so on, a genuine Nazi apparently, working for Lufthansa in London and he'd married this English girl. Well, the girl's brother knifed him shortly after the announcement of the declaration of war.

That wasn't playing the game, of course, you have to give the German Embassy and the consulates and the rest of them time to get out, but this chap's plea was that he'd struck a blow at the enemy.'

'I hadn't heard about this,' the Governor said. 'Did he get away with it?'

'They brought in a verdict of manslaughter, not a jury of course, it was done behind locked doors, but his appeal's still going on.' This story was a total lie, but Major Willard-Gibbons fancied himself somewhat as a teller of tales. He had written an improbable fiction about a man accused of murder in Detroit whose alibi was that he was committing a murder in Chicago at the time. There was ample evidence that he had committed both, but he could not have committed both and he played one murder against the other. 'There is,' the major now said, 'this point about playing the game, you know. Some things simply are not done. I don't think HMG would be too happy about a man in mufti killing another man in mufti on neutral territory, especially when the man who was killed wasn't armed and didn't have a chance to defend himself. It doesn't smell like real war somehow.'

'What do we do then?'

'Well, if what Woodruff tells us is true, he's putting himself in grave danger, this chap I mean, by blowing the gaff about what he's done. At the moment, all that the Spanish police are saying is that a British soldier in civilian dress has murdered a man who has the right to walk unmolested on Spanish ground. I mean, they don't know who he is but they soon will if he brags about it. It'll get into the Gib Spanish language newspaper *El Calpense* before nightfall and they read that over there. What the Spanish police have a right to know, I take it, is what British troops were over there last night eating egg and chips and being picked up by tarts. They have a right to have them over there again to be shoved on an identification parade.' To Captain Woodruff he said: 'Do we have records of who goes over?'

'Well, yes, in a way. A man has to get permission. I mean, there's a kind of quota. We couldn't have the entire garrison traipsing over into Spain just when they felt like it.'

'So there's a record? I mean, we could get everbody who went across the border last night on parade and take them across to let the police have a look at them?'

'We could, I suppose. Less, of course, Sergeant Jones.'

'That's his name, is it?' the Governor said. 'I see. All this is very irregular, of course. What you're suggesting, Captain Woodruff, is that we put up a kind of show of compliance with the request we're, ah, rightly anticipating from the La Linea chief of police and yet protect the man who actually did the job? Not playing the game somehow, is it?'

'Oh, I see all that, sir,' Woodruff said. 'But our job is supposed to be killing Germans – well, in a way, I mean we don't get the chance to do much killing here, what I mean is we're at war with them, when all's said and done. What I mean is that Sergeant Jones has killed one of the enemy and it doesn't seem right to punish him for it. For that matter, even if we sent over the other bods who were there last night the Spanish police would be only too quick to grab one of them and hold him just to please the Germans.'

'From a strictly legal point of view,' Major Willard-Gibbons said, 'we ought to keep the war out of it. Spain is neutral territory. A man sticks a knife into another man. Homicide pure and simple. He shouldn't have done it. I mean, you don't conduct a war in that manner. The enemy's faceless and impersonal, if you see what I mean. And even if Adolf Hitler turned up in La Linea and one of our lot got him HMG would find itself in a very embarrassing position. It's this business of neutral territory, you see.'

'I don't think he would have done it,' Captain Woodruff said. 'If he hadn't said something nasty about the Jews.'

'Who did?' the Governor asked. 'Who said something nasty?'

'This German, sir, Trautwein. He said something very nasty and he said something even nastier when Sergeant Jones told him that he was married to a Jewess.'

'This Sergeant Jones,' the Governor said, 'has a Jewish wife?'

'Yes, sir. My own feeling is that he wouldn't have drawn a knife on him if he hadn't said something nasty about the Jews.'

'Now then,' Major Willard-Gibbons said, 'we're getting somewhat outside the region of killing the enemy because he happens to be the enemy. Your man killed this German for a highly personal reason.'

'Yes,' Woodruff said, 'but the highly personal reason is really tied up with what we're supposed to be fighting the Germans about.'

'Not really,' the Governor said. 'We went to war because of Poland. We didn't declare war on the Germans because they were killing the Jews. I mean, we didn't know they were doing that, did we? Of course, they've got to be stopped from killing the Jews and killing everybody else for that matter. What I mean is, saying something nasty about the Jews is no excuse for getting a dagger out.'

'The Germans have to be killed,' Captain Woodruff said. 'We're killing them right left and centre. Women and babes in arms. That's not supposed to be fair play either.'

'Do you think we ought to have a word with this sergeant of yours?' the Governor asked. 'Tell him at least to keep his mouth shut?'

'I've got him outside,' Woodruff said.

'One moment,' Major Willard-Gibbons said. 'There's an immediate urgency. All trips into Spain banned forthwith. Can that be put into effect at once?'

'Fortress orders go out at midday,' the Governor said. He rang for his ADC. 'That can be done. Have a guard posted at Four Corners just to be on the safe side.'

'The next thing,' Major Willard-Gibbons said, 'is to have this chap off the Rock as quickly as you can. An immediate posting.'

'Oh my God,' Woodruff groaned. 'It's not all that easy to arrange a posting. Where do we post him to? If he's sent back to UK the situation's worse than it is here. I mean, there you have the Spanish Embassy getting at Churchill and enquiries into the conduct of relations between – I beg your pardon, sir,' he said to the Governor. 'This is your pigeon. I beg your pardon for that expression. But things are going to be pretty awkward for all of us.'

'The really awkward thing,' Major Willard-Gibbons said, 'is our being forced into a position of mendacity. Not telling the truth, that is. You lie to the enemy, that's part of the normal procedure of war, but you don't lie to a friendly nation.'

'Is,' Woodruff asked, 'Spain friendly?'

'They've stopped the Germans marching from the French border straight down to Gibraltar. That's friendly enough,' the Governor said.

'I think,' Major Willard-Gibbons said, 'a policy of masterly inactivity in respect of the Spanish police is called for. They can't really do anything. Not so long as you don't have this chap of ours crying his guilt to the heavens.'

'Not really guilt,' Woodruff mumbled. 'Not really from our point of view. But he was a bloody fool. I beg your pardon, sir.'

'I agree,' the Governor said, 'about this immediate posting. It's a horrible thing to say, I suppose, but the only way this thing could be resolved, ah, neatly would be for this sergeant of yours to be sent to a combat zone and die fighting. That would shut everybody up. That would satisfy the Spaniards.'

'Us too,' Major Willard-Gibbons said.

'Pretty beastly when you come to think of it,' Woodruff said.

'Oh, war *is* pretty beastly, you know,' the Governor said comfortably. His ADC came in, 'Ah, there you are, Tony. Something has to go in Fortress orders.' Captain Woodruff said:

'I'll bring the blighter in.'

He went to the anteroom but found it empty. Rooke and Heathfield gazed at him sadly from the wall. Oh Jesus. He went out into the noise and blaze and spoke to one of the two sweltering sentries. He was told that the sergeant in question had gone off in the direction of Main Street. Woodruff, with his intelligence training, guessed where specifically on or off Main Street Sergeant Reginald Morrow Jones might specifically have gone. From the Convent guardroom he telephoned the officer of the *Gibraltar Chronicle*. He spoke to Sergeant Shorter, who, with various corporals, was in charge of that newspaper. Is Sergeant Jones there? He is, sir. Print nothing of what he tells you. That is an order. This is Captain Woodruff of Intelligence speaking. Tell Sergeant Jones to come at once to the telephone. Captain Woodruff groaned in his stomach. His little dog would now be peeing all over the floor.

REG flew into the dying sun that very evening on an aircraft of RAF Transport Command, along with a private soldier who had a skin disease undiagnosable in Gibraltar, a master gunner on highly compassionate leave, a staff officer class two going on a staff officer's course, and large bundles of mail. Reg was very angry. He was entitled to disembarkation leave and he was not to be granted it. A privilege, he had been told, *not* an entitlement. They didn't want him at large blabbing to the *Daily Mirror*, a rag that would publish his story with the front page headline PUNISHED FOR KILLING HUN. He was in a sort of custody. The SO II of the Army Educational Corps had been given orders from the Convent to hand Reg over to the military detachment retained for such and similar purposes that was suffered by the RAF to subsist on the airfield at Northolt for which they were now bound. Reg was very angry. He wanted to see his wife. He had written lovingly every week and she less lovingly when she felt like it. He had, in a sense, killed that German because of his love for his wife. Greater love for his wife hath no man than that he do in a Hun or Boche with a commando dagger for that the blood of his wife had been reviled and envisaged as fit only for the nourishment of German asparagus. Reg was still lightheaded.

Not so lightheaded, though, as he had been. He had been told, and by the Governor of Gibraltar himself, that it was not the done thing to drink with strangers in foreign bars and then knife them in back alleys. Even in total war one played the game. There was a difference, then, was there, between war and murder? There most certainly was. The essence of modern war was that you killed at a distance, anonymously and without immediate animosity. You killed, or ordered killed, in a generous spirit and you sustained the generosity of spirit by not being directly aware of the agony and then annihilation of your victim. The history of war, as of civilization itself, of which war was an aspect, was the history of increasingly distancing and more thorough anonymity. Did he, Sergeant Jones, think that the brave saturation bomber crews who nightly smashed old people's homes and maternity wards would be capable of continuing their heroic missions if they actually witnessed the human as opposed to strategic results of their devastations? The point, anyway, was that according to the law of the nonbelligerent world, a world admittedly in the minority at the moment, he, Sergeant Jones, had committed murder and neutral justice craved a reckoning.

It was out of the same generous spirit already alluded to that he was being permitted to fly beyond the reach of Spanish kidnappers anxious for the fulfilment of Spanish justice and participate, so far as his essentially nonbelligerent specialization permitted, in the conduct of a generous war in a major zone of belligerence. He had put the Rock authorities in an awkward situation vis à vis their neutral neighbours and entailed disruption of a civilized administration process by imposing on those authorities the necessity of organizing a rapid and irregular posting. It was hoped that he was duly appreciative and, for that matter, apologetic. So here he was, flying slowly north. His knees were very cold. The metal bench was hard to his bony bottom.

And then his body was hot all over save for a sensation of freezing in the area of his heraldic, as opposed to anatomical, heart, namely the space behind his left pap. He had killed a man. The man had bought him a cocktail called by Juanito the barman a Spitfire – Spanish gin and sour Seville juice – and had discoursed amiably about the folly of war and less amiably about the destructive canker of Jewry. In the dirty alley in the Andalusian dark he had unbouttoned his fly to piss against a wall, and Lance-corporal Whitcombe had, the term was more appropriate in his scholarly case, micturated against a wall opposite, though mocking Hemingway jocularly by mentioning the declaration of a separate piss. Then he, Reg, had struck the middle seam of the back of that man's blue blazer. The man was astonished but his hands still held his merrily fountaining penis. Strike again, deep. The man had gone over, penis still exposed, coughing and bubbling. Reg had finished him off in his heraldic heart. Then Conchita had appeared at the end of the alley with a stupid soldier in mufti who was saying: 'Big eats, big man.' Reg had run, retching Whitcombe after.

There had been a film once, an early talking film, called *The Man I Killed*, in which a Frenchman who had cut the throat of a German in that other war went, bubbling with remorse, to the village of the slain one to confess his sin to the bereaved family. At the end of the film he had been adopted by that family, a surrogate son. There was forgiveness for everything, then, though he, Reg, had no great desire to be adopted by the Trautwein family, wherever it was or if it still existed. It then dawned on him that he had, though belatedly, fulfilled what he had joined the International Brigade to do, namely kill on Spanish soil. Neutral, indeed. There was no neutrality. The English were a lot of hypocrites. His Welsh and Russian corpuscles sang an instant in the air. His children, if ever his dear wife put down her drumsticks to conceive and bear, would be Jewish and Russian and Welsh. That was fine, that was good, and to hell with the bloody English. He had killed a German for them, and look at the thanks he was getting.

When they landed in a rainy English summer dawn he was driven, along with his kit and the SO II AEC, who said, 'This isn't really my job, you know,' in a jeep to a cluster of Nissen huts on the periphery of the airfield. The SO II presented him to a sleepy lieutenant of the Service Corps, along with an envelope sealed with the seal of the commander of the Rock garrison. The lieutenant came wholly awake when he confronted a sergeant of the Intelligence Corps in crumpled tropical khaki, bare knees and all. It was as if a character from an Errol Flynn film of the Burma campaign had materialized in the wet English dawn. Reg explained that he had only one viable battledress, the other having been soaked in oil and marine filth when he had fallen into the Med from a launch plying between Detached Mole and the mainland. The one viable one had been taken to a tailor to have its loose collar tightened and had not yet come back, not that any hurry had been envisaged in a long Gibraltarian summer. The lieutenant, hungover and in need of a mug of gunfire but the cooks were not yet awake, said that Reg was improperly dressed and could be put on a 252 for it, though distractedly, reading as he was the official letter. He squinted up at Reg and said:

'You seem to have blotted your copybook.'

'All I did was kill a German, sir.'

'Did, did you? Well, it looks as though you've passed a kind of test that qualifies you to kill more Germans. According to this you're to be sent down to Portsmouth to await sea transport for Normandy. You're to report to the OC troops at Arromanches. Know where that is?'

'In Normandy presumably, sir.'

'Very funny. It's where they've set up Mulberry Harbour, a

triumph of British engineering. All right, knock at Hut 2 and wake my sergeant major. Tell him that you can't get on the road dressed like a bloody Chindit. He'll have to find a quartermaster's store somewhere, Christ knows where.'

'Not my fault, sir.'

'It strikes me, sergeant, that you're a bit bloody bloodyminded.'

'Sir.'

Reg was not in fact rekitted out until he arrived under military police escort in a three-ton truck, the only transport available, at a transit depot in Portsmouth. The quartermaster there, a ranker lieutenant with a Bermondsey accent, had a number of cleaned-up battledresses salvaged from the cleanly dead, such as had died from nonbelligerent ailments in military and EMS hospitals of the region. It was now that Reg, finding the battledress of a regimental sergeant major of the Hertfordshire Regiment which was a perfect fit, decided to promote himself to WO I as a reward for killing a German. He decided more. He would get away from the two military police lancecorporals waiting outside the store. Disguised, he would take his disembarkation leave, damning the consequences. The demotic British press, at a pinch, might support him. The Rock authorities should not have mentioned his blabbing to a rag, since he himself would not have conceived the idea. He had wished to keep the matter local, and the *Gibraltar Chronicle*, the oldest newspaper in Europe, was acknowledged to be no rag.

Reg decided to abandon his kit, dumping it in a corner of the quartermaster's store already encumbered with the kit of the presumably discharged dead. But from the bottom of his dirty blue kitbag, crammed with dirty washing, he extricated two keys on a ring: one was for the front door of Zipporah's apartment house; the other was for the apartment itself. These keys he kissed and then stowed in the left blouse pocket of his new battledress. From his khaki backpack he took a little notebook which contained his sister's telephone number. He fancied he would not be able to reach Manchester that evening, as it was already noon; he proposed telephoning his sister in London to see if she was there and to forewarn her of his coming: she might otherwise be caught in bed with somebody. Zip he would not telephone; he would overwhelm her with the surprise of a soldier husband's unexpected return. Here he was showing his usual lack of discretion and acumen.

He exchanged his cap FS for a peaked one with the dulled badge of the Army Veterinary Corps. Among the odds and ends of salvage on a tray he found a pair of steelrimmed respirator spectacles. He was surprised to find that they improved his sight, perhaps excessively. He had not thought himself to be in any state of ocular deficiency but, at his last all-round medical inspection, the MO had said that they were counting eyes these days, not testing them. The quartermaster came back from the office where he had been slurping tea as a kind of preprandial cocktail to find a transformed Reg standing before him. Reg explained that his promotion had come through on Fortress orders the day of his departure from the Rock, signed for his new acquisitions, then got out rapidly. He saw the military police escort sitting on a bench on the landing of this second floor where the store was, the one reading *Blighty*, the other probing a back tooth with a matchstick. They saw incuriously a cheesecuttered RSM with specs on come out. Reg went leisurely down the stairs. In watery sunlight without he was less leisurely. There were two reasons for not taking a train to London: one, he had only Gibraltarian banknotes; two, the rail termini would be full of military policemen looking for him. Him, who had killed a German. He had to get on to the road.

It happened that I was myself in Portsmouth on that day. I was on a week's privilege leave from Aldershot, where I had joined the depot instructional staff, and I was spending the leave with my parents at their rented house, Hanway Villa, on Brunel Avenue. I was due back at Aldershot that evening. Portsmouth was a mess. It had suffered sixty-seven air raids, though the one in May of this year proved to be the last. My father told me about his work on Mulberry Harbour, at which Reg was supposed to land. Six miles of breakwater, and it had been a hell of a lot of trouble for the dry docks round the British coast to build the caissons that had been needed, two hundred feet long and in six heights ranging from sixty feet to twenty-five. I understood little of this. 'Whose side is God on?' my father wanted to know. That storm that sprang up a fortnight after D Day had never been known in any previous June. 'The Yanks got the worst of it, craft breaking their moorings and smashing into the caissons. Thank God the breakwater was nearly finished on our side and the seabed was firmer. Thank God, I say, but we don't have to thank God for anything. Although I'll say thank God I'm ready to retire.' My father, whom his work had kept brown and fit, filled his Dunhill with St Bruno and said to me: 'This war's going to be over in about a year I'd say. What did you think of doing?'

'I didn't. Go back and take my MA perhaps. But I seem to have outgrown philosophy.' Meaning that I had been stuck deep into the phenomenal world, training those paratroopers who had dropped behind the enemy lines before D Day, teaching them how to cut throats. Not Occam's razor but the real sharp phenomenal. My mother was working at the dining table on her rarefied hobby – the transcribing on to vellum of her own epigrammatic verses in Venetian minuscule. She gave these artefacts away as presents, though not to her two children. The verse she was indian-inking now was:

To be or not to be is not the question.
The only thing that matters is digestion.
But if that B means belch from beer or bacon,
Its social implication is well taken.

She was grey, plump, varicose, but still handsome. She said:

'Get in early on the foundation of the Jewish state. That's where your future lies. Learn Hebrew properly, that's what your father and I are doing. Not just the kitchen scraps we used to throw at the servants in Jaffa and Jerusalem.' I was surprised. I said:

'Do you two propose emigrating to Palestine?'

'Israel is or will be the name,' my father puffed, looking very British in his tweeds and with his aromatic St Bruno. 'No gesture of Jewish patriotism on our part, except perhaps historically. We want to go where it's warm and we can pluck oranges in the back garden. We've both had enough of English cold. Listen to your poor mother's chest.' My mother rattled a brief chain of phlegm in illustration. 'And it's all over with England, you know. This war's done for England. Your mother and I want to get to the right side of the Mediterranean. Civilization began in Palestine, and that's where it's going to be remade. But it's your generation your mother and I want to watch remaking it.'

'What do you mean, it began there? How about Egypt? How about Athens?'

'Monotheism,' my father said, 'not that I believe in it, or polytheism for that matter. The Semites invented the art of phonetic writing. They invented the social contract. Make no mistake about it, the new Israel will be nourished by the brains of the Jewish world, united after its long diaspora. Yes, I suppose that does sound like patriotism, but we are, after all, Jews.'

'Atheistical ones.'

'Jewish atheism is different from anybody else's. And even Jewish atheists have spiritual resources cultivated with priestlike fervour. Music, for instance.'

'There was a time when you didn't much care for music.'

'Oh, I've come to see certain structural qualities in it. Like engineering, you know. I heard the Hallé Orchestra on the radio. A work called *Belshazzar's Feast*, baritone and chorus, very Jewish.'

'Written by a Lancashire Christian.'

'Oh, he must be Jewish. I heard Zipporah thumping and clashing away. She could be a founder member of a great Israeli symphony orchestra.'

'And me?'

'You could teach philosophy in the University of Jerusalem. Or you could join the Israeli armed forces and help to train them. Teach them how to smash the bloody Arabs.'

'Language, language,' my mother rebuked, inking with care.

'Under a benign sun,' my father flourished, 'and a sky of deepest cerulean.'

'Sucking oranges.'

'Why not? It's a long time since any of us saw an orange.'

The displaced orangesucker Reg was already in the cab of a civilian truck carrying drainpipes to Hounslow, telling the driver that he had done a Hun in and was therefore on the run. I took a train that was filthy with overflowing lavatories and frowsty with toothsucking troops. A soused petty oficer facing me snored and was suddenly incontinent in his trousers. The little girl next

140

to him said to her mother: 'Mummy, he's wee-weed all over himself.' Hush, darling. When we got to the terminus I was surprised to see more military police than usual. I had to show my leave pass. I could not understand why they spent more time on me, recently promoted to WO I, than on toothsucking privates. Two of these, travelling without leave warrants, were hauled off. I was, after a long examination of my AB 64 Part I, allowed to go. Clearly they were after somebody.

The somebody in question had only Gibraltarian pound notes in his pocket, but he had coins common to the colony and the motherland, and he used two pennies to telephone his sister Beatrix from a box in Hounslow. A male voice answered: 'What then?'

'Miss Beatrix Jones.'

'Piss off.'

'This is her brother calling. It's urgent. Who are you anyway?'

'Sod off.'

'Sod off yourself. This is her brother, I tell you. Put her on the line.'

'All the way from Stalag whatever-it-is, eh? Oh, very clever. Piss off, friend, it's not your night.' And the handset was slammed down. Reg tried again. This time the receiver was taken off the hook and he could hear faint sounds of physical movement more or less rhythmic. He shut them off. Manchester then. He had been dumped near a transport caff where his driver from Portsmouth proposed tea and fried spam for himself before spending the night with a woman whose husband was fighting his way towards the Rhine or perhaps the Rhone. Reg entered this smoky hell to be greeted with the song 'Kiss me goodnight Sergeant-major'. Anybody going north, he wanted to know. There was a man who, when he had finished his reconstituted dried eggs on toast, was to resume the carriage of a cargo of roof tiles to the Newcastle in Staffordshire. That would do. Reg tried to change some of his Gibraltarian pound notes. These were examined with curiosity but there were no takers. He spent his last sixpence on a kind of pork pie most of which he fed to the caff dog, an overfat spotted mongrel, and prepared for the journey by taking a pee in a foul jakes, reading at the same time the inscriptions on the wall at his eye level: Winnie of Warwick is a good fuck; Needs a rebush and rebore; Oh how I wud luv to get it in. Then he got into a new cab and told his new driver that he was on the run because he had killed a German spy. He seemed not to be believed.

He got a lift in an American staff car outside Stoke, where the driver told him he had more chance of picking up something northward. He sat with what looked like an exhausted US general who kept saying 'Surely, surely,' while his chauffeur hummed 'Don't Fence Me In'. At Matlock he hailed a three-ton truck with Western Command flashes on it, empty except for its RASC driver and a blowsy ATS private who said to Reg: 'Did you get them fighting cats for telling lies?' At dawn his heart thwacked his chest (Oh how I wud luv to get it in) as he walked from an army transport depot in Moss Side to his wife's apartment on Wilmslow Road.

There used to be an extensive mythology about the soldier returning without advance warning to his wife. The soldier going into the pub dripping wet and explaining: 'She was in the bath, see.' The soldier with the cricket bat who banged it thrice on the front door and then ran round to the back with it: 'I've never missed the bugger yet.' The soldier who said reproachfully: 'You and me was butties. Worked the same shift together. And now look where you are. Stop doing that while I'm talking to you.' But mostly, and not without reason, the wifesick soldier had a vision of her waiting in a bright kitchen apron, a hot cup of tea in her hand. When Reg had unlocked the front door, tiptoed upstairs in the wan light, and then eased open quietly, his aim being not to disturb sleep overmuch, he entered the comic world of the cuckolded warrior. For there was my sister, naked, her fine plump buttocks working away, on top of a stranger equally naked, procuring an orgasm which she very satisfactorily procured while Reg, unnoticed, gawped at the door. The stranger then thrust upwards three or four times and shuddered, his mouth open like Reg's though in the expression of a sensation very different. The two then kissed slobberingly and Zip collapsed at his side. There was a lot of the heavy beathing of achieved athletes, followed by something like normal respiration, though still profound. Then they saw Reg. Reg had to think of something to say other than 'oh no'. He said: 'What did he do it with? His bloody piccolo?' Then he saw on the floor, with day clothes of both sexes on top of it, the black mock leather case of some far heavier musical instrument. He ran out. There was nothing really to say. Zip did not call after him, since what could she really call? Reg, halfway down the stairs, turned to shout: 'I killed a bloody German for your sake, and this is the bloody thanks I get, bitch and bastard.' The *your* justly worked as a plural, though meant initially as a singular. Reg went out on to the road, where, war or no war, a milk float rattled, and zigzagged up it careless of traffic though there was no traffic, other than the milk float bland and harmless as its burden. He said aloud oh God oh God oh God many times. He was distract-edly surprised to find that literature was, after all, relevant to certain human situations. *La casada infidel*. But that was adultery seen from the adulterer's angle. *Othello*. Put out the light and then put out the light. The French boulevard comedians thought it all a great joke, despite or because of *crime passionel*. Oh God a beast that wants discourse of reason. But that was notional incest and failure to observe the etiquette of widowly mourning. Oh God Oh God oh God had to do for a long time.

And, of course, the emotion that shook him was not simple. Shock, outrage, also lewd excitement. Seeing his wife as a whore, the lineaments of gratified desire, which Blake wanted in a wife. That agitated lovely body and the Teresan ecstasy as her black hair settled. His own face on the body of that stranger, tuba or trombone player. A fake RSM zigzagging with a real erection. Back there, forgiveness, let us do together what you and he were doing then. I know, the war, absence of legitimate lover, only to be expected. But she would not want forgiveness. Women never did, always ready to justify themselves. Slide in on the other fellow's scum, as one lewd sergeant artificer had once leered to him, filthy bastard. Reg tottered and then leaned against the window of a tobacconist advertising no cigarettes, to sob drily. A policeman chewing something, starting his morning beat, surveyed a regimental sergeant major scriking like a baby and said kindly:

'Owt the matter, mate?'

Reg gave him dry eyes of great pain and said: 'My wife.'

The policeman nodded, assuming as was right for the times

the discovery of playing away, not death or mutilation or labour, and said:

'There's a lot of that going on. Can't do nowt about it. It's the war, that's what it is. It's like the war, mate.' And then Reg, seeing the total waste of his desertion and deception, decided to throw everything over and submit to whatever justice lay closest to hand. He said:

'Is the station far?'

'There's Didsbury Station up thurr, but trains is no longer running. Other stations is in town centre.'

'No, no, *your* station.'

'Ah, see what you mean. I'll take you.' Meaning a chance for another drink of tea and a listen to somebody's trouble, less boring than being on bloody beat. He took him. The blue lamp was still on, waste of electricity. Reg spoke to the desk sergeant. He said:

'Before I go any further can I make a phone call to London.'

'This isn't a public convenience,' the sergeant said ambiguously. He wore glasses on a long nose and quizzed Reg over them.

'I'll pay for the call if you can change a Gibraltarian pound note.' And Reg thought: women. His sister and his wife both caught on the job. At this hour his sister would, he thought, just be about ready to get up. If that foulmouthed sod who seemed to be her present lover was still there he would probably be flat out, snoring. Or sent away, as he knew was her custom, in the early hours with preferably a long walk ahead of him. The desk sergeant and the conducting constable both took a long and interested look at the Gibraltarian banknote with its picture of the Rock. The sergeant said:

'Tell you what, give me this and I'll give it to my youngest, collects things like that, and you can make your call.'

'Bloody expensive,' Reg said.

'Well, it's only foreign money, isn't it? Nothing but paper. All right, go on. Personal, is it? Me and him'll get out of your road for a bit.' There was a kettle singing somewhere. Reg asked for Beatrix's number and, after hearing an alien voice cry *No, no, I can't believe it*, got her hello, thorny with static. Reg said much, rapidly and not too coherently. As a Foreign Office official she

144

was interested in the diplomatic problem raised by her brother's knifing the enemy on neutral soil. As a sister she was sufficiently indignant about the way he had been treated, also disturbed about his present situation vis à vis authority. As a single woman given to free love she found Reg's discovery of his cuckoldry in the naked act vaguely amusing, though she kept that to herself. In some other capacity she did not for the moment disclose she was unexpectedly reassuring. Go through with what had to be done, she counselled, then wait. You won't have to wait long. Reg put the receiver down. The sergeant and constable came in with tea mugs in their fists. From a distant cell somebody laughed insincerely. Reg said:

'Right, gentlemen. I'm a deserter.'

The sergeant sipped thoughtfully thrice and said: 'Not our business, is it? That's between you and the army.'

'It's a matter of the law, isn't it?'

'There's law and law,' the sergeant sipped. 'Army law is one thing and the other kind of law is different entirely. What's unlawful in one connection is neither right nor wrong in the other, if you catch my meaning. If you'd robbed a bank or done some old woman in for the pension she'd drawn, well, that would be our pigeon. But if you did in a sleeping comrade like Danny Deever' (Reg was surprised, but the world was full of surprises) 'that would be another kind of crime. Murder, yes, but not our kind of murder.'

'Meaning,' Reg said with some acerbity, 'there's no absolute crime and no absolute justice.'

'Absolutely not,' the sergeant said, though not really understanding.

'We're brought up,' the constable added, 'on Moriarty's Police Law. It's all laid down in a book.'

'What we can do,' the sergeant said, as though conferring a favour, 'is to ring up the military. We do things for each other, so to speak. We pick up the odd swaddy drunk and hand him over. It's got to be admitted they don't do much for us. They're not real police, only in it for the duration. Anyway, you hang on here and I'll get on the blower. Sorry we can't give you any tea, it's rationed.'

'He can have a sup of mine,' the constable said.

Reg had, like other soldiers, seen his fill of military policemen patrolling streets and railway stations, but he had never conceived the notion that the Bastards, as they were popularly called, had holes like foxes or, indeed, the kind of scrubbed and whitewashed barracks he was shortly after marched to by a full corporal and a lance one. He was taken before a captain of excessive smartness who wore a snowy web belt and gleaming anklets and sat in an office adorned, as in a real police station, with photographs of men wanted, mostly gormless-looking privates. There was certainly no one of Reg's rank, real or assumed. Reg told his story and the captain said:

'Yes, I think something came through about you last night. Given yourself up, that's a point in your favour. I'll have to get through to your depot.' Kindly he added: 'If you want to get some breakfast in the sergeants' mess there's nothing to stop you. Yours is a funny sort of case all round. Don't think I've met anything quite like it before. All right, you'll be wheeled in again when you're wanted.' Reg found the sergeants' mess unexpectedly frowsty and cosy, a bolthole from pedantic and starched law and order. In the anteroom Reg saw a warrant officer class two smoking hard and listening to the mess radio. It was serious music and Reg heard a baritone crying: 'Praise ye the gods'. Good single God, it was *Belshazzar's Feast*. The bloody bitch. He was a late breakfaster and there was only an orderly to see him shaking over the fat bacon and fried bread. Not even the orderly could see the bitter erection under the table. He grew flaccid again over his second cup of tea. When he went back to the anteroom the chorus was moaning that the light of a candle would shine no more.

Reg read the *Daily Mirror*, in which the only real news was the latest instalment in the strip, how apposite, cartoon about a virtuous girl named Jane, who was always losing her clothes. The war was going all right and a corporal in Huddersfield had shot his wife, clearly not virtuous. It was time for the morning break, with a tray of doughy wads and a tea urn dripping, when Reg got his summons from a clerkly man of his own, true, rank. The captain looked incredulous about something. He said:

'You're to report to the War Office, the *War Office*, at nineteen hundred hours today. Don't ask me why, that's the order that's

146

come through from your depot. What exactly has been going on?'

'Search me, sir. Does it say who at the War Office?'

'No, it says at the main entrance. There's something here I'm buggered pardon my French if I understand going on. You'll know better than me being in the intelligence lot what it is, but it looks pretty irregular. Anyway, I've to give you a rail warrant and you're to nip down a bit jildy to London Road to get the 11.58 to Euston. As you are, and not under escort.'

'As I am?'

'Yes, you were a bit previous, but the rank you're wearing is the rank you've now got. From midday, anyway.' The captain goggled at Reg then turned his head in order to shake it in continued incredulity at the gallery of gormless privates gone missing. 'All right, Mr Jones, hang on for your warrant, it's being made out now.' *Mister* Jones. Only subalterns and warrant officers got that; other ranks saw it as a summit, commissioned ones as a nadir. Mr Jones got his travel warrant and went for a bus. In the train he was presented, on the seats opposite, with a kind of tableau he thought he might some day be able to interpret: a clergyman read Monsignor Ronald Knox's *High Jinks at Low Mass*; a master gunner of the RA brooded on an inner vision; a blonde ATS of the type known as an adj's at and a disdainful rating of the Women's Royal Naval Service respectively smirked and stonily smoked. None of them had an eye for Mr Jones. But next to him a small boy picked at the cloth coat-of-arms on Reg's sleeve and his blackclad mother feebly smacked him. And so, in the early, late-August evening, Reg got to Euston and took a tube train to Westminster. From there he walked to Whitehall, finding with some difficulty the War Box, as it was called. Outside it his sister Beatrix was waiting, smart in a square-shouldered beige costume but with rings of weariness under her eyes. Reg said:

'Why? Why you?'

'I'll explain at my place. Foreign Office and War Office working together at something, just what you'll find out.'

'You look tired, Trix.'

'It's these flying bombs, Hitler's final secret weapon. One keeps awake listening for them. God knows why. When they get you they get you. Come on, I've got a War Office car to take us.'

'Oh my God.'

The car was waiting in the car park with a lancecorporal driver who put out his cigarette smartly and opened the back door with a flourish. 'Colonel Waggett's car,' Beatrix explained. 'Poor devil, lost a leg and he's neurasthenic.' The car passed odd piles of rubble, the work of V–1s. The driver seemingly knew the way to Beatrix's flat well. There was rubble across the street from it. Beatrix's bed was unmade and there was an extra imprint on it, as well as male underpants.

'I phoned, but there was some bastard here who told me to sod off.'

'Yes, a poet, rather highly regarded. Never mind him. We've important things to talk about.'

'Have you anything to eat? I'm starved. Rushed from pillar to post and only Gib pound notes in my pocket.'

'There's a bit of cheese and a lot of vodka.'

'A lot? Where did that come from?'

'We have a Russian cousin in London. At the Embassy. A nephew of mother's called Yura Petrovich Shulgin. You've heard her speak of him. Lost part of his thumb in 1917, quite the little hero. She's even sent him birthday presents, but none of them ever seem to have got through.'

Reg ate all of the bit of mousetrap with stale bread and downed some neat vodka, going 'ugh' at its rawness. Beatrix drank him in with her lovely eyes, a thin man, bronzed, fighting cats on his forearms. She said: 'The War Office is bigger than Gibraltar. Everybody jumped when Dick Waggett got through. You won't have heard about this, but England is teeming with Russians. Picked up in Normandy, a lot of them in German uniforms, a lot of them slaves of the TLO.'

'Which is what?'

'The Todt Labour Organization. It makes things very awkward for everybody. They're not really prisoners-of-war. They're not really anything but displaced Russians. Ukranians too, even a couple of Tibetan shepherds, they tell me, who followed their sheep on to Soviet territory, got shoved into the Soviet forces and then picked up by the Germans. The War Office decided the

148

best thing to do was to bring them over here and put them into army camps deserted after the Normandy invasion. But they're not really army, not many of them. I mean, there are women and children. Every day a new batch is ferried over. It's a mad situation.'

'Where do I come in?'

'These camps are desperate for interpreters. That's where.'

'And you arranged for my promotion and my posting to one of them?'

'Waggett did. He moved fast despite his wooden leg.'

'But you're not even in the War Office.'

'No, only the Foreign one, but all this is primarily a Foreign Office matter. It has to be, you see that? Displaced Russians and what to do with them. It's us that the Soviet Embassy is dealing with.'

'How dealing with?'

'They're a good deal embarrassed by the disclosure that some of their citizens voluntarily joined the German forces when they were captured. You know, to fight against a regime even worse than Nazis. They want them all back on Soviet soil, guilty or innocent, volunteers, conscripts, slaves of the TLO.'

'The what?'

'Don't you listen? A lot of them don't want to go back. They're scared that Stalin will have them shot because they've been polluted by contact with the outside world and may start spreading the gospel that paradise lies outside the Soviet Union. I say let those who want to stay stay, but the old man thinks differently. Of course, he has a point.'

'Who's the old man?'

'Oh, come off it, Winnie the Pooh, our glorious war leader. The point is that a lot of our prisoners and American ones too are in the eastern part of the Reich which is going to fall to the Russians in due course. Winnie thinks that the Russians will hang on to our prisoners when they get to them and hold them as hostages against the return of their own people. Of course, from our point of view, we have a stake in the old man's policy.'

'Who's we? What stake? Look, I'm still hungry.'

'Stay hungry. We is you, mother and dad. Dan's at a Stalag near Roggen on the river Oder. We got that information from the Swiss Red Cross, though belatedly. Do you want Dan to be a Soviet hostage?'

'He speaks the language. I don't see what difference it would make to him. As long as they gave him a bit of fish occasionally he wouldn't much mind where he was. Plenty of fish in the river Oder.'

'You bloody unbrotherly bastard. Dan's worth ten of you. He was fighting in Italy while you were sucking oranges.'

'That's all anybody thinks we do on the blasted Rock. I'm getting a bit tired of it.'

'All right, you chew bananas as well. I don't know why I should do anything for you, you unfraternal nuisance. But I suppose blood is thicker than. Listen, the camp that's causing the most trouble is the one near Ickton in Suffolk. About twelve miles north of Ipswich. You'd better find your way there at once.'

'How do you know all about this?'

'Northern desk, with special responsibility for Soviet citizens on British soil. Big trouble at Ickton, but we managed to hush things up. The local vicar is a kind of expert on Dostoevsky, whom he reads in the original. He knows the NKGB are around. Beating up decent Soviet citizens who get drunk in local pubs. He was going to spread the news and start an outcry until we brought the bruisers in.'

'Beat him up, you mean? And what's the NKGB when it's at home?'

'Honestly, your ignorance. The *Narodny Komissariat Gosudarstvennoi Bezopasnosti*. I need not, of course, translate. No, he wasn't beaten up, just brutally warned about the Official Secrets Act. You've got a delicate job to do in Ickton. Play along with Stalin for the sake of our POWs in the east. That means your dear brother Dan.'

'All right. I need a delicate job to do, after the way that bitch behaved.'

'You're a bloody fool Reg. You just don't walk in on people, not even your own wife.'

'Wives are supposed to be faithful. It's different for husbands.'

'Yes, of course, they have urgent sexual needs denied to mere women, and if they feel guilty about infidelity they can always say they were pretending they were doing it with their wives. Men make me sick.'

'Make you sick, do they? Even men with neurasthenia and a missing leg? You seem to like being made sick. One of these days you're going to get a nice large shock.'

'What's that meant to mean?'

'You'll see. You'll meet somebody you can't *use*, that's what I mean. Fall heavily. As I fell. Then you'll start to suffer. I'm going to get a divorce.'

'It'll take a long time. There's quite a queue. Get on with your job. Wait. Write her a letter saying you're sorry you dropped in just like that. You'll know better next time. And no nonsense about forgiveness. But don't be astonished if it's she that asks for the divorce.'

'Oh, what nonsense, what screaming unadulterated bloody balderdash.'

'Yes, she may be in love with this tuba player or whatever he is. It's easier to love people when you see them all the time. The husband away, sucking oranges for his country or whatever, he just turns into an abstraction.'

'What do you know about love? You've never loved anybody in your bloody life.'

'I love you, in a way. I love Dan. I find it hard to bring love and sex into the same area. Sex is sex, the nerves excited and then appeased. Look, this is no time for light chat about trivialities. There's a Rail Transport Officer, RTO they call him, waiting with your travel warrant. At St Pancras. As for the document confirming your posting – '

'Trivi-bloody-alities, oh my God. Youre too bloody cold to live. What's that noise?'

'Hitler's secret weapon. Don't worry, it's not coming here. Too cold to live, eh? It's being cold that keeps me living.'

'You wait, that's all, just wait.'

I HAD quite a vivid dream about Beatrix while I was lying in my bunk at Aldershot. If dreams mean anything at all, they mean not just unenacted desires but events to be fulfilled, in their own good time, in real life, though not necessarily by the dreamer. I have never had any doubt that dreams tap the future, which makes me very much a man who grew up in the thirties. The dream began with my buying, with what looked like stage money, several sheets of clothing ration coupons from a shady hermaphrodite with a toothbrush moustache in an Aldershot pub. The motive for my buying these became clear later in the dream, which cut to a huge hotel bedroom of the kind I was to meet only when I visited Rio de Janeiro. The month was January, so a big calendar said, evidently something to do with the name of that city I was predestined to see, and there was snow on the windowsills. I was totally naked and very brown. Beatrix was there, fully clothed, and seeming to sneer at my uncapped phallus. There was no bed in the bedroom, only a great rug and sewn animal furs, striped, spotted, polar white. I began to tear the clothes off Beatrix. She fought back, but the strength of a WO I physical training instructor prevailed. I tore off her smart little jacket, of a design not contemporary with 1944, and ripped the blouse underneath. I bit through the valley between the hills of her brassière, which my dream, invoking Yiddish or German brutality rather than French delicatesse, called a *Brüstenhalter*, and saw it fall away from her superb breasts. My teeth had become scissors which snapped at her silk knickers. She was now near naked, and I took her upright, thrusting at a dryness which was soon irrigated. I took her many times, orally, anally, and in her golden armpits, finally subsiding with her on the massed furs for a slow and almost loving bout. Then I gave her the clothing coupons.

Her response to the gift was a puzzled one. 'The war's over,' she said, 'and nothing's rationed any more.' Then she demanded to be hurt, abased, bitten, lashed, ridden like a beast. 'I'm a slave,' she said, 'a winnow' (I did not know the word and still don't) 'and it's very important for us to remember that nothing's rationed any more. So you can eat me if you want to.' Then I awoke sweating.

Reg, at about that time, or so he told me, dreamt that Zip was performing in *Le Sacre du Printemps*, beating a whole range of timpani from deep bass to piccolo. He appeared at the back of the orchestra and, at a nod from the conductor, who appeared to be Stravinsky himself, wrested from his unfaithful wife the two felted sticks and began to belabour her with them. But she was stronger than he and snatched them back, converting him to a new kind of percussion instrument which gave out a whole metallic scale. The audience laughed, and the dream came to an end. Reg's dream clearly had nothing to do with the future.

PEDWAR

I T is time to get up,' Marya Ivanovna Sokolova said. It was a damp Suffolk dawn in January 1945. She looked at the cheap wristwatch Reg had given her for the English not the Russian Christmas, shook it and satisfied herself that it was going, then shook naked Reg more violently. He responded by trying to take her sleepily in his arms, going mmmm. But she was one of the two camp vratches or medical officers and she had a dawn parade of the sick, meaning the incurably syphilitic, the gonorrheal who needed analgesics for the aftermath of micturition, the genuinely catarrhal or dyspeptic or wounded in fracas, those who believed alcoholic crapula merited serious medical attention. Reg would not let her slim body, with its faint black flue, out of his grasp. Awake now, he told her he loved her. She said she loved him too, though with qualifications there was no time to elucidate. She slapped him hard, calling him lazyarse, and then put on ATS issue slacks and shirt and a driver's leather jacket over. Her shoes were also ATS issue, but they were too big and she had to line them with bits of yesterday's *Daily Mirror*. Russian soldiers always lined their footwear with paper anyway. They mostly used their British army socks, of which they soon lost one of the pair, as noserags, neckrags, mud-removers. Marya's tarblack hair, now shaken back and tamed with a rubber band, disappeared inside a peaked cap of the type issued to women SS officers in female extermination camps. This was the trophy of somebody now dead.

She went off, after a quick loving scolding, to grab a quick mug of black tea with a dollop of apple jam in it at the mess hut for displaced Soviet citizens of her rank, not that rank properly existed here except for the British camp personnel. Reg continued to lie in his narrow bed in the private hut that was the privilege of his rank, smoking a cigarette and caressing the imprint of her body. They had had the same discussion as always, having made love in the foredawn. She was a free woman, he said, and could stay in England if she wished. He would teach her the language, he was teaching her already, not that she was taking it with the right seriousness. Some day they could marry. Nonsense, she said, she was married to Pyotr Lavretyevich Sokolov, power plant engineer in Sverdlovsk, and to him she wished to return. He would no longer be alive, Reg brutally said, but she knew differently, a woman's tenth sense. As for love, there was love of the narrow time and love of the broad one, meaning the love proper to marriage. The narrow time was now. When, the shortage of medical officers in the Red Army being what it was, she had been conscripted with lieutenant's rank, she and Pyotr Lavretyevich recognized that the narrow time was upon them, marriage a bourgeois institution anyway, and that vows of eternal physical fidelity could turn, temporarily, into mere Pushkin stuff. He, Reg, was a nice boy, soberer than Pyotr Lavretyevich and with a nicer smell, but he lacked the Russian heart, despite his mother. But I love you, love you, Reg had kept on protesting, in the very tones of his mother when she had grabbed him roughly as a boy and suffocated him with Russian kisses. Y'a vas lyublyu, with its strenuous vowels delicately iotised, sounded more genuine than the English, the refrain of vapid songs: he meant it, he thought. To hell with Zipporah, let her be violated with her own xylophone hammers. He had not written, and she did not know where he was. It was, he considered, all over.

He read again, as the morning lightened, the airmail letter he had received from Whitcombe, now a full corporal. That Spanish business too was all over. One of the intelligence tasks had been to set up an information room with photographs of concentration camp atrocities, proud SS records recently captured, which had made men vomit and which one of the Rock chaplains protested against. Less talk about fair play, the only good German a dead one. What Reg had done and Whitcombe witnessed could not but be approved. In La Linea a man arrested for knifing his father-in-law had willingly confessed to knifing a German as well and the case was closed. The knifer had apparently been given a light prison sentence, the term *provocación* being used in both the genuine and fictional defence, and the two knifings ingeniously conjoined in the tale of a rampage fuelled by drink. So that was that.

Reg, shaven and in battledress newly pressed by a Russian named Postoev, once a tailor, went to what was called the sergeants' mess, though, besides Reg as RSM, there was only a trio of sergeants, one of them lance, and a WO II quartermaster. The latter went 'Ay ay' in a falling tone as Reg entered, signifying that he knew what happened in the RSM's private quarters and he did not approve. An RSM had his privileges, but cohabiting with one of the three female Russkies was asking for trouble. There would be complaints, unfounded, from some of the displaced about favouritism, meaning more meat, which the British camp staff already called *myahso* and would soon call me arsehole. Moreover, the Russkies could be treacherous bastards, and Reg might wake one morning with a knife in his back. Revenge was a funny thing and worked in a funny way, the Q had said darkly, knowing what Reg had done in that La Linea back alley. What he had done to a foreigner a foreigner would yet do to him. They call the Russkies our glorious allies, but I wouldn't trust one of the bastards, the Q said, and more than once.

Over the tea, porridge, and greasy corned beef rissole, Reg heard from Lance-sergeant Scammell, who ran the provost side of the camp, that a bunch of five unshaven Russkies had broken into the house of a Mrs Levinson, an aged widow of the little town, and taken five pounds ten and an ormolu clock. That should properly be a civilian police matter, but the police had been told to turn a blind eye to the petty crimes of these displaced who were neither army nor real civilians. What the hell were they, anyway, except obstreperous transients waiting for ships to take them back to Mother Russia? You couldn't discipline the bastards. Nearly four hundred of the thousand-odd at the camp near Norwich had scarpered last week and were living off robbery and violence in various parts of Norfolk and Suffolk. Whose job was it to catch the buggers and bash them back to a sense of decency and discipline? The Q said:

'It looks as if they've got their own people on the job seeing about that. It's bloody irregular, but who are these buggers with hats on and raincoats scowling around? I saw three of them in the Crown, asking for vodka, I know that much of the lingo, and playing hell because they didn't get it, then spitting good British beer in the sawdust. I don't like it.'

'They're worried,' Reg said, citing his sister. 'Too many of this lot have seen British capitalism and they like what they see. What we call shortages looks like abundance to them. The Soviet paradise doesn't seem to work too well.' Sergeant Cross, a lean lad lacking energy, shook his head and said sadly:

'We was brought up at home to think different. My dad went to Moscow on a trade union trip and said it was all right. Not much of anything though bags of cheap wallop, but what there was was shared equal. It was the big ideal, he used to say, and before he got seen off in that accident with the lorry he used to say it was what we was all fighting for.'

'Don't kid yourself,' Reg said. 'It's been a negative war, defending the bad against the worse, as the poet put it.' They looked down at their empty plates in embarrassment: they didn't like talk of poets, especially from an RSM. 'On the job,' Reg said, getting up. But, the lance-sergeant muttered, what exactly *is* the bloody job?

It was a bleak morning, and most of the camp inmates were back in their huts after failing to swill their messtins of the incrustations of morning porridge. A dirty lot. There were one or two genuine holy Russians around, notable for spectacular filth. When Reg, his oficer style raincoat collar turned up against the chill, had looked into a few of the grim Nissens to observe men moaning in hangover and others already at raucous card games, he walked through mud to the wooden hut once used for storing ammunition to see how the women were getting on. There were only two of them, though with five children between them, and they were cut off from the eight hundred males by barbed wire and an armed sentry. The armed sentry at the moment was Pte Dawes, an unhappy young man muffled with woollen comforter, balaclava, and a pair of filched despatch rider's leather gloves. Bloody cold, sir, he told his RSM. He had had to poke his bayonet at an early rising Russky who wanted to get in there. Reg found Vera and Yevgenia, he did not know their surnames or patronymics, feeding the stove with bits of an old chair. The children, who had been taught to call him *dyadya*, ran to him yelling for *shokalat*. He gave them a packet of Wrigley's spearmint, a Yank gift from the PX store at Bury St Edmunds. Vera and Yevgenia were unwholesome robust women in outsize ATS skirts and jumpers stolen from a store, and the kids, not all theirs, were the fruit of association with Polish fellow workers in the Todt Organization. What a bloody mess it all was. They wanted to stay in Angliya, they told him yet again, and when where their permits going to come through? Soon, he told them hopelessly. Then he made his way across the parade ground where there were no more parades to the single smoky chimney of the camp headquarters. About forty shaggy and chronically unshaven though not yet bearded inmates were waiting outside, being poked into hopeless order by Lancesergeant Scammell and Lancecorporal Crankshaw. But they did not seem to know what order was. What they needed was a good dose of communism.

Lieutenantcolonel Secker was trying to make sense of a lengthy complaint from a one-eyed redolent ruffian who swore he was a major in an armoured unit, Major Khmelkov, and was demanding privileges, their nature for the moment unclear, in accord with his rank. Captain Murray the adjutant, whose knowledge of Russian was even smaller than his superior officer's, saw with relief the RSM enter saluting but said:

'Late again, sergeant major.'

'Camp inspection, sir. I was delayed by the female contingent.'

'Ah yes, the female contingent,' Lieutenant Colonel Secker said. 'We know all about that, don't we, Murray?' He had a blue-eyed stare of great innocence belied by his record in the Ordnance Corps, a matter of not entirely confirmed irregularities to do with the imprest account. His Russian was derived from a fortnight's crash course. 'You'd better see what this, ah, tovarish thinks he wants.' Reg listened long and at length spoke at length. Then he said in English:

'There's no proof of his alleged rank, but I suggest he show responsibility before he claims privileges. Put him in charge of a cleanup squad. And make that crowd waiting outside the squad in question. Sir.'

'All right, tell him that, will you?'

'I've already told him.' Alleged Major Khmelkov went out declaiming and beating the air with filthy fists. 'Up your arse,' Reg said. And then: 'I'd like to know, sir, precisely what you meant when you leered just then in connection with the female contingent. Sir.'

'Watch your language, sergeant major. You're not indispensable though you may think you are. Quite definite instructions have come down to you about the extent to which fraternization may go. You seem to be going beyond the allowable, ah, extent. For the moment I say no more, do I, Murray?'

The adjutant, who stood, cap on and stick under arm, behind his superior's chair, had an eye-twitch gained in battle. He had been seconded from the Scots Guards. He twitched his eye at Reg and said: 'No, colonel.' Then he twitched his eye at the unwashed window that looked out onto the parade ground and said: 'Christ, they're early.' He went at once to the door and Reg followed. Three Russian army officers and a civilian were getting out of a Humber Snipe in the charge of a Service Corps driver. The civilian seemed vaguely familiar. Familiar was the right word, familial rather. Reg's mother's eyes and a thumb joint missing. Beatrix had told Reg to expect him sometime. Yura Petrovich Shulgin. Reg did not for the moment disclose name or relationship: they seemed irrelevant in the context of the grimness of the three officers. An inmate left out of the cleanup squad, which was genially buffeting the alleged major, gawped and cried: 'Mother of Jesus, the Czar's come back.' He had not previously seen epaulettes blazoning rank, a recent innovation of Stalin's. Inside the office Lieutenantcolonel Secker, on his feet, greeted with a *dobriy dyen* and a held out hand which was ignored. Colonel Bogoleev, Major Limonov and Lieutenant Shargorodsky from the Soviet Military Mission in London. Shulgin from the Embassy, who would interpret. Colonel Bogoleev wanted the whole camp on parade. He was Russian enough to know that would take time. First he would examine the nominal roll and then inspect living quarters, cookhouse, latrines and information room. Lieutenantcolonel Secker spoke. Reg said:

'You have no authority to inspect the camp. As a matter of courtesy you may be permitted to do so, but my colonel wishes

159

to make it clear that this is British military territory, that rations, clothing and pay are administered by the British military authorities, and that, since the Soviet authorities rejected the proposal that Soviet personnel on British soil should be formed, on the analogy of the Free French, the Free Poles and the Free Czechs, into a military organization necessarily armed, Soviet responsbility for these personnel begins only when the act of repatriation has been accomplished.' Colonel Bogoleev was shorter than Reg but very much broader. He frowned at Reg and fingered the insignia on his battledress right forearm, wanting to know what this imperial symbolism signified. Reg said: 'It would be considered proper for an allied army officer to be acquainted with the badges of rank of comrade fighters against the German fascist menace.' Lieutenantcolonel Secker said to Reg:

'I didn't know what you were saying then but it strikes me you're going too far.' Reg said:

'He says he wants to see the nominal roll.'

Sergeant Clarke, who was the sergeant clerk, pencil behind his ear, brought in from the orderly room a four-page list typed in Romic and Cyrillic. Lieutenant Shargorodsky, who had the dapper dress and manners of a Czarist officer and a neat moustache to go with them, spent some time counting the names. Reg said:

'That includes women and children. It is the original nominal roll, but about one hundred and fifty of the Soviet personnel posted here are no longer with us. We cannot use the term desertion since the personnel in question were neither prisoners-of-war nor regular members of an officially organized military formation. This is regarded as a free country, and the personnel in question are free to come and go, subject to the regulations administered by our Ministry of the Interior, which we call the Home Office.' Colonel Bogoleev boiled at some length at that, and Yura Petrovich Shulgin, speaking English precisely but with a heavy accent, told Lieutenantcolonel Secker that Colonel Bogoleev was far from satisfied. It was a supererogatory statement. Colonel Bogoleev stated, with much spitting on the consonantal compounds, that what were truly deserters despite this functionary with the imperial insignia's disclaimer would be

160

captured and brought to book. Reg said: 'We know. SMERSH is already at work in the land.'

Colonel Bogoleev grew very angry with Reg and poked him repeatedly in the stomach with a stubby index finger. Reg told him to stop doing that or, whatever the exaltation of his rank, he would be given a thick ear. Lieutenantcolonel Secker suggested that Pte Watts, a clerk in the orderly room who doubled as a sort of bugler, should be told off to call the camp inmates on to parade. They responded readily enough to his cookhouse call, and they confused other calls with it. Let him then call Fall in B Fall in C Fall in Every Companee and let the NCOs get them into some kind of order on the parade ground, indicating also that the mugs and messtins they would undoubtedly bring with them they would be bringing prematurely. High Russian officers had a word to address to them.

First, though, the representatives of the Soviet Military Mission wanted to see the camp information room. A number of political commissars or polkoms had been captured by the Germans and these, uncorrupted by Nazi ideology, had made themselves known as such to their liberators, so that the Soviet authorities in London could employ them in the camps of the displaced as sources of Marxist refreshment and agents of instruction as to the progress of the war, meaning the war on the Eastern Front, those on the Western and in the Pacific being regarded as effete, capitalist, and largely irrelevant. Reg had regretfully to report that the polkom posted here, Pavel Andreyevich Viktorov, had early availed himself of democratic liberty and was said to be living with an Irishwoman in Bungay. It was Major Limonov who now boiled within the limits of his thinness, which looked like emaciation. He kept on the boil in the information room, which lay behind the headquarters block and was tended by two camp inmates who, from their ingrained dirt, must be very holy Russians. The information room had been partly converted into a chapel, with a blanket-covered table as altar set with paper flowers and wooden ikons, all made on the premises, and a gaudy portrait in crayon on brown paper of the Virgin and young Jesus. Reg spoke with referred pride of the religiosity of a fair number of the inmates. A Russian Orthodox pope came from Lowestoft regularly to hold very well attended services in the local Anglican church. The local Anglican vicar had been very helpful. He had provided a little Russian library for such as could read. Here it was. Major Limonov gloomily surveyed Tolstoy, Dostoevsky, Gogol and Chekov in old Czarist editions and threw angrily on to the floor works by exiled writers like Dubyonkov and Badin. Those books must be burned. 'Who burns books,' Reg quoted, 'will soon be burning men. And these, remember, are the property of the local Anglican vicar.' Major Limonov clawed blindly at British Ministry of Information posters of the beauties of the English countryside.

Groaning, the representatives of the Soviet Military Mission examined the cookhouse, where a British version of borshch was being prepared by a corporal cook and a couple of Russian assistants. This, Reg informed them, was the preferred and invariable diet; borshch twice daily: there were plenty of beet-fields in Suffolk. The bugle wavered its general fall in, and soon the four Russians saw their unclean compatriots fighting to get into the dining hall, wielding messtins clonk clank as weapons. It was a slow and lively business moving them to the parade ground. Some of them, seeing three grim or boiling Red Army officers, shuffled away. It had also started to rain. Under a mewling Suffolk sky Colonel Bogoleev roared at a rough open square of hungry sceptics that Marshal Stalin had not forgotten his comrades in arms and every effort was being made to repatriate them as quickly as possible. The trouble was the dila-ltoriness of capitalist England, torn by workers' strikes and debili-tated by endemic idleness, in providing marine transport. Reg, unseen of this colonel but not of his own, made a sharp pronging gesture with two fingers to indicate that this was a propagandist lie. The restive audience appreciated that and groaned or guffawed. There were many loud cries of disaffection. You bet Marshal Stalin has not forgotten. Wants our bloody heads for the bloody chopper. Up his jaxy and yours too, comrade field marshal or whatever you are. But Angliya land of the free will look after us.

'It will not,' Yura Petrovich Shulgin said later to Reg. 'Your Mr Churchill and Anthony Eden are very anxious to please Marshal Stalin and rid themselves of an embarrassing burden. The world is being reorganized.' He spoke Russian. He was a closecropped blond man going prematurely grey, handsome enough with his squat muscular body, fleshy chin, wideset eyes of Reg's own mother's blue, a little too short in the neck. They stood by the Humber Snipe in lessening rain, while the representatives of the Soviet Military Mission inspected the pay parade in the dining hall: two halfcrowns for every man, his weekly dower, some of whom railed to officially abolished heaven if they were given instead of shillings or florins, the piece of eight possessing a mystical value outlawed by revolutionary decimalization. Yura Petrovich Shulgin had given Reg two bottles of vodka, vodka donor to the entire Jones family except for poor Dan. He said: 'I was fond of your mother. She was good to me the brief time I was with her. She was brave during the abortive revolution. Your sister is very beautiful and clever. She will go far. As for you, you must restrain yourself more. You are making enemies. What do you propose doing when this war is over?'

'Teach Spanish perhaps. I haven't really had time to think about it.'

'Teach Russian instead. It's clearly the language of the future. And you have an affection for it. It's your mother tongue.'

'You believe in the Russian future?' Reg asked, knowing it was a foolish question even while asking it.

'Of course. But I accept the principle of the duoverse. Meaning the impossibility of the Trotskyite dream of world socialism, the need for the Soviet system to define itself positively but also in terms of what it is not. The West exists, and here I am in it. But not for long.'

'Back to Moscow?'

'Yes, to work in the Ministry of Culture. Not just for the promotion of Soviet culture but for the dialectical exchange of cultural diversities. Ballet, music, football.'

'Not literature?'

'Literature is different. Literature mirrors ideology. Ah, here come the military comrades.' He kissed Reg warmly on both cheeks, regardless of Colonel Bogoleev's disapproval. He seemed to have nothing to fear from the Military Mission. Then he got in the car first. Reg saluted. Lieutenantcolonel Secker and Captain Murray saluted, rendering Reg's salute redundant. The representatives of the Soviet Military Mission made quasi-saluting

163

gestures, frowning the while. They were displeased with their visit and were unlikely to be displeased less when they visited Camp 44 outside Ipswich. Some of the camp inmates gave the departing car various allotropes of the soldier's farewell.

That evening, in Reg's hut, Marya Ivanovna was delighted to see two bottles of vodka, one of them of the pepper variety. She had had a hard day, and so had her colleague Dr Nozdrin. Dr Nozdrin's medical orderly had drunk a pint of surgical spirit and had kept coughing out the nozzle of the stomach pump. One of Marya Ivanovna's sickbay patients, recently operated on for a burst appendix in the military hospital at Norwich, had torn open his stitches in a fit of extreme depression. The woman Yevgenia was five months pregnant: you could lock a cat on heat in the woodshed, but it would still kitten. Marya Ivanovna needed her vodka. Soon, naked, she was giving Reg very peppery kisses. 'I love you, I love you,' Reg said. She loved him too, she said, with a love appropriate to the narrow time. She had the most delicious heartshaped face and her tarblack hair should have had an odour of deep woods.

PTE DANIEL TETLOW JONES was a prisoner in Stalag B339 near Roggen or, its Polish name, Żyto, in the Reichskommissariat Ostland, a good way east of the river Oder. Despite the name in both German and Polish, there were no ryefields around. All the prisoners could see in the January of 1945, beyond the barbed wire and the tigerboxes, was snow snow and again snow. *Schnee. Śnieg.* Very white and very flat and stretching a long way. You could just see the church spire of Roggen or Żyto on the eastern horizon. There were twelve hundred prisoners, US, British, and some odds and sods from the French colonies. The senior officer was Colonel Hebblethwaite of the Royal Lancs, Dan's own regiment, though from a different battalion. The German commandant was Colonel Fresser, a decent enough old bastard who still suffered from the gas emitted by his own side on the Somme in the first lot, the wind suddenly deciding to blow the wrong way. Despite his name he was no great eater. Like Dan he was fond of fish. He had several times allowed Dan out of the compound with a couple of armed *Unteroffizieren* to fish for carp in the town pond at Roggen. There was not much point in anybody trying to escape anyway. Wouldn't get far. The mandatory escape committee, under Major Soames, had come up with various harebrained schemes – tunnelling under the wire, feigning grave illnesses to get to Roggen hospital then making a dash for it, stealing *Feldwebel*'s pistol and sticking it in Commandant's back: all dreams, games, schemes to pass the time. They knew the time would not be long, anyway. Colonel Fresser knew it too. He got his news of the progress of the war from old comrades on the telephone, also from the BBC, to which it was death to listen. The prisoners strolled in the snow, played halfhearted football on a snow-cleaned pitch, improved their chess or bridge, learned Rusian. Dan taught Russian but taught it badly. He could not explain the verb forms. It was his mother's milk and he was no hand at lactic analysis.

Dan got up early on 22 January. His eleven hut companions slept, snored, groaned, dream-cried the name of a wife or sister-in-law. He did not turn on the light, forbidden at that hour, but scratched a match and enflamed a candle, one of the thoughtful gifts of the Red Cross. He got the stove going with laths from Red Cross boxes. Then he ate the remains of a tin of pilchards he had opened the night before. Not like the real thing but better than bully. Then he sniffed the close air of the hut and sensed that something unusual had happened. He heard Pte Shawcross behind his back yawn and sigh. Dan lit two fags and took one over to him inn the bunk above his own. Dan said:

'There's something that doesn't feel quite right.'

'Really? Seems the same as usual to me. Dark dark dark. And candid snowglare waiting to greet us when we get the shutters down.'

'There's something that doesn't feel quite right. Listen. Did you hear that kind of bump? A bump a long way away. Then another bump. Do you hear it?'

'Nothing except snores.'

'There's bloody bumps a long way away. I can hear them.'

When he went outside in his greatcoat he could hear them better. The bumps seemed to bounce off the snow all the way from the sun that was just feebly getting up out of its grey blankets. Corporal Chester from the next hut was looking out of the doorway. 'There's something funny going on,' Dan said. He teetered over ice where the snow had been cleared towards the wire perimeter. There was nobody in the tigerbox up above. It was a long walk towards the camp gateway, and he fell four times, bugger it, and when he got there he found that the wide wired five-barred gate was open and unguarded. The sort of guardroom there was untenanted. The buggers had gone in the night, the jerries had hopped it. They had got word the Russians were coming and they had cleared off. The truck Dan had heard starting up about three in the morning he had not thought to be anything out of the ordinary. The Nazis had always been great ones for coming and going in the night. A supply of Polish prostitutes or sides of pork from the army butchery at what was it called Biegunka or somewhere. He had also heard a whistling train from Roggen station three miles away but that too was nothing out of the ordinary. Dan considered it to be his duty to go over to the officers' quarters and report that the jerries had abandoned their charges. When he knocked on the door of the hut where the Yank second in command Major Pilpel slept he got a sleepy grunt in reply so knocked harder. What Dan had to say woke him up all right.

There was no *Appell* that morning, but Colonel Hebblethwaite got the camp on parade in the snow to tell them what they already knew. Dan as always marvelled at what a lot of men twelve hundred added up to. Four battalions really, in a closed square with Colonel Hebblethwaite standing on a box in the middle, turning and turning so that his words carried, smoky breath everywhere but his smokiest because he was speaking. The bumps to the east and the faint fireflushes would be the Red Army on its way. Colonel Fresser had left quietly with no farewell, soldier's or other, his office neat and empty, the files removed, the portrait of the Führer with its face turned to the wall. When the Germans did a thing they did it thoroughly. The ration store had been cleared, the camp pigs led grunting off, the cows with never a moo removed from their byre. The cycles and motorcycles no longer in their white-line demarcated parking place. Not even a goodbye note.

Everybody looked up fearfully as two planes hummed in from the sun and swooped low. Red stars on them. Reconnaissance.

They circled neatly and droped lower still over the town of Roggen, then they were off back to base.

Well, gentlemen, chaps, this looks like the end of our captivity, but God alone knows what we can do with our freedom. We can stay here and wait for the Russians, but the Russians don't know a great deal about prisoner-of-war camps, they prefer to kill Germans rather than cosset them, they're not signatories to any international convention, they've never seen any of their Western allies and won't know what the hell we are. Fortunately we have a Union Jack and an Old Glory, our frog friends or frenchified brown brothers who don't understand a blind bit of what I'm saying will have to accept their doubtful shelter, it was thoughtful of the Red Cross so to attempt to raise our spirits with the emblems of our countries. As for staying here, it will seem strange to be at liberty and yet still in our prison. True, the gate is now open, and we can start walking down the railway line westwards, but there's no doubt that the Red Army will get to wherever we're going a damn sight quicker than us. I propose sending a recce party to Roggen to see what's going on there.

The Krauts may still be around, colonel, Major Pilpel said.

Well, our dear departed camp comedian was kind enough to keep me informed of the situation on this front. The German line of defence is apparently set up a good hundred miles to the east, ready if need be to fall back on the river Oder. It's a pretty thin line of defence, the Hun being rather busy these days on the Western Front. I should imagine that Roggen is ungarrisoned and its population already evacuated by train or lorry, to say nothing of family transport. There may be supplies there. Our Red Cross fodder won't last much longer and there'll be no more deliveries. Could I now request volunteers?

Dan knew Roggen, he had fished in its pond. He might fish there again, the ice once broken, and he would take his home-made rod and line. He volunteered, as did Pte Shawcross, Pte Massinger, Lance-corporal Moxley (who had clung to his stripe though his rank was acting unpaid and no longer valid), Pfc Leonardino, a Yank corporal named Schwarz who knew Yiddish, said to be not unlike the German dialect spoken in these parts, Sgt Cobb of the Royal Engineers, and, officer in charge of party,

Lieut Svenson of the US infantry, Yank leadership here reflective of Yank leadership everywhere.

The other ranks had strong powdered hot coffee before setting off, and Pfc Forkner from South Carolina donated a lacing of deadly liquor from his private still, fermented spudskins mostly. They set off muffled, trailing long codas of curses as they engaged icy wheelruts. The fields of snow stretched to the circular horizon, the landscape was treeless. The day turned into a cloudless one, the sky scoured by the spiteful wind from Siberia that bit at such segments of their faces as showed. The sun was the decorative red bulb of an electric fire whose bars are broken. A quarter of a mile before Roggen there was a crossroads, with a sign down that gave no help as to the direction of either Gorzów or Schwierzyna. In a dead white field an untethered goat gave them sardonic greeting. On the outskirts of Roggen or Żyto there was a garage owned by a departed Schmidt, with a tractor in for repair unrepaired. Then there were houses, brown brick and iced-over red roofs, with shut doors shutting nobody in. A spotted dog lolloped up to the party with desperate pleasure. Nothing for you, mate, get lost. The little town was deserted all right. There were shops on the main street, cleared of snow, icy patches sanded over. Bürger's shop offered *Metzelei*, though not now. Salböl's *Bäckerei* was breadless. A *Spielzeug* shop for kids still had flaxen dolls and little metal heilhitlering SS men in the window, the jerries were great ones for pampering their kids, though not anyone else's. 'Nowt here that's much good,' Sgt Cobb said. There was the town pond, in which carp brooded under ice on what they had brooded on during the Thirty Years' War. Dan told him, though in courtesy keeping his eye on the round bewildered eyes of Lieut Svenson, that he'd been told by the guards who had accompanied him on his fishing trips that that place back of the pond was a litle *Mönchskloster*, which he had taken, after some dumbshow of cowled praying, to be a monks' cloister, though the monks, mostly Poles, had long scarpered, and it had been turned into a *Kriegsvorräte*, which he had gathered was an army store. That little church there attached to it was called the *Kirche* of Saint Benedict and the monks had been monks of Saint Benedict, called Benedictines like the stuff, sweet and strong and a bit herbal, you could drink if you had the money and a mind to. 'Stores,' Sgt Cobb mused. 'I doubt there'll be grub there.' The sharp ears of Corporal Schwarz caught what he said he was sure as hell was clucking. You know, a poultry run. It was coming from down a narrow alley between a *Kurzwarenhandlung*, whatever that was, and a house with a sign that said *Zahntechniker*. That must be like what we call a *tsohn*, Cpl Schwarz said, baring his pegs in illustration. At the bottom of the alley they found a netted henrun at the back of a little house with an empty clothesline. There were five hens and a ruby cockerel preparing to mount one or another. 'We're going to eat those buggers,' Sgt Cobb said, 'if you've nowt against it, sir.' Did anybody know how to wring the necks of the bastards? Cpl Schwarz said he could kill in the kosher manner, a knife in the throat, clear all the blood out. Lieut Svenson suggested that somebody check on what was in the *Kriegsvorräte*. 'Right,' Sgt Cobb said to Dan and Pte Shawcross, 'go and have a look at that there monkeyhouse.'

Pte Shawcross insisted on going into the church first. Dan was surprised to see him dabble his fingers in the dry font just inside the front door, sort of shrug, and then go ace king queen jack with them. An RC then. He followed Pte Shawcross inside, and Pte Shawcross started to bend the knee but then thought better of it, saying there was nothing to bow to, they'd taken it away. The altar was like a bare butcher's chopping block. There were darkish squares on the white walls where holy pictures must have been removed. There was an archshaped stained glass window high above the altar showing a baldheaded monk raising two blessing fingers to every bugger. It was a nice little church, all clean white except for the six eight ten pillars which were goldpainted. Pte Shawcross led the way to what he called the sacristy. 'Cases of communion plonk perhaps. Or perhaps the great monkish firewater itself.' But there was only a family of mice nibbling round white bits of bread. 'Pretty things,' Pte Shawcross said. 'Nature goes on, despite war and consecration.'

He looked round the church with his keen schoolmaster's eyes. At the back, to altar left, was an archshaped door under an arch, just under a gallery meant for a choir, though there were no organ pipes, pure unsentimental Gregorian chant doubtless. He said: 'That will lead to the belfry. Let's get a view of the surrounding countryside and see if our glorious allies, ignorant and impulsive, are perhaps on the road yet. And I must ring the bell. I must. My fingers itch for the handling of a bellrope. I was one of the Youths of St Botolph's, you know. Treble bob majors and so on. But this is a humble little church.' He went first, pushing open the door uncaught by any latch, and led the way up spiral stone steps worn by a century or so of monkish feet. At the top they saw a stout single bell, bronze, of solid German founding, agitated minimally by the winds of heaven. Pte Shaw-cross eagerly grasped the padded bellrope and, with an effort, tolled. Joy misted his respirator spectacles. Great bronze mixed fundamentals excited a whole population of harmonics. The departed population of the town was called to nothing. But, Dan saw, looking down, Sgt Cobb and the rest of the party, rushing out of the alley, some swinging dead hens by their necks. And then the Russians arrived.

'Look what you've done,' Dan said.

A kind of jeep drove up to the pond and halted. After it came a truck of the three-ton variety. The red star was painted on both.

'Better get down there,' Dan said. 'It looks like I might have to do some speaking of Russian.'

Dan could not tell the rank of the officer, who wore a very useful fur cap with a star on it. He had with him in the jeep what Dan took to be a Russian giant who should have been bearded but was not. He surveyed fiercely the chicken-carrying Anglo-American party. The officer had his pistol out. Cpl Schwarz spoke Yiddish, and this did not make the officer the more inclined to stow his gun. A lot of troops with rifles and good grey greatcoats as well as topboots were getting out of the back of the truck. Dan spoke. The officer listened with incredulity. He said: 'You should not be speaking Russian.'

'Who says so?'

'You are an English soldier and you are speaking Russian. There is something wrong there.'

'My mother's a Russian. My dad's a Welshman. Is that not allowed?'

'I have not heard of it before.'

'Well, you're hearing of it now.'

'What are you doing here?'

'I thought this was our war as well as yours,' Dan said. 'We've been in it longer, anyway. We only just got here. We're in the prison camp down the road, but the Germans have gone and left us. British and American, a hell of a lot of us. What do we do now?'

The officer was more interested in poking out possible Germans and German supplies. He ordered a squad to run to that squarish building there behind that *tserkof* and see who or what was in it but to beware of boobytraps. He allowed the others to smash windows with their gunbutts, break down doors, looking the while benignly on. To the giant with him he said: '*Agon. Bolshiyiy agon.*' And then he seemed to be reciting poetry:

'*Shest' desyat ish v vetrozhoge*
Smuglish, spo-veselich lits.
Po mashinam! Po doroge!
Na Evropu! – navalis'!'

'What's all that about when it's at home?' Sgt Cobb asked Dan.

'He says he's got about sixty men with dark skins and blown about by the wind and they're very cheerful but bad buggers really and they've got to get into trucks and move into Europe and smash everything.'

'But they've only just got out of their truck, the silly bugger, and they've been in Europe all the time, if Russia's part of Europe, which is what it is, the silly sod.'

'It's poetry, sarge.'

'Oh, poetry, is it?' Sgt Cobb spat on the ice. The giant bawled for splintered doors and whole counterfittings and a can of *benzin*. Then they all saw what was meant by a bolshy big *agon*. The fire whooshed on the frozen grass near the pond, and Dan saw what the officer meant about *spo-veselich lits*, everybody's face getting blackened by firesmuts. Then the officer said to Dan:

'You go back to your camp.'

'But what do we eat? Each other?'

'Starving for a time will do you no harm. Leningrad starved.'

'We're not bloody Leningrad,' Dan said in English. As if to show they were not, Sgt Cobb, L/Cpl Moxley and Pfc Leonardino

171

began to toast their chickens on the fire, using splinters from splintered doors and windowframes. Then some of the Russian troops, cheerful and wicked, warming bare chapped hands at the blaze, began to sing a song they seemed to have been taught in greeting of their Western allies:

Okeh, Britaniya ant Rossia ant de Yu Ess Eh.

The song was no more than that line repeated. Pte Shawcross noted that it was in a minor key. This seemed to him ominous. It seemed to him curious that these Russians preferred a fire in the open air to one in, say, that kindergarten school they had passed or the apparent town hall which had had a swastika flag flying from it before six hardy Russians climbed up and brought it down. Big boy scouts really, though clearly with reserves of brutality. Dan turned his back on everybody and began fishing in the clear black hole he had dinged with his boot into being on the icelocked pond. He had brought bait, some mushy pilchard in a page of the hut Bible. Some Russians, with loud shouts of triumph, had found more substantial fodder – a pig in a backyard, which they had had the delicacy to riflebutt to death offstage. This they heaved with great cries on to the fire. The giant hefted a case of vodka out of the back of the jeep. All was set for a sort of party. The Western allies were not sure whether they were guests or not. But, damn it, they had got here first. Dan brought from the pond two carp and a pike. These were grabbed without ceremony and chewed raw by the giant, who spat out a multitude of tiny bones. The ransackers of the cloister returned to report, according to Dan, that there was nothing useful left behind by the jerries, only some big wooden cases containing ikons, bits of paper, gewgaws. They had brought a couple of boxes in illustration. They threw top laths on to the fire and straw packing, which the fire ate in an instant, and showed a couple of crucifixes, a chalice, and a rusty sword that the man who held it kept shoving in and out of its crumbling wooden scabbard in a grinning gesture of rutting. The officer looked incuriously at a pile of yellowing paper. Pte Shawcross was more interested. 'Music,' he said. 'Pretty old music. Good God, *Der Hausfreund* – *Singspiel* – Wolfgang Amadeus Mozart.

Give me that.' But the officer kept it to himself. The time for a showdown had arrived. Lieut Svenson said to Dan:

'Tell this officer that any German property in this town is hereby claimed by the party which I am leading. We got here first. On the instructions of the commanding officer of our camp we were to forage and confiscate whatever the enemy left behind.' Dan translated that in his own way. The Russian officer replied at some length. Dan said:

'What he tells me to tell you is that this is their front not ours and that we're prisoners-of-war and not a proper armed whatsit. What he says is that we're out of the war and we'd better stay out. What he says is that he is grabbing anything the Germans left behind and having it sent back to their base or whatever they call it. And he says we'd better get back to the camp and start starving.'

'Thanks a lot, tell him.' Dan told him. The Russian officer acknowledged that with a genteel nod. To Pte Shawcross he did not seem to be the most trustworthy of officers. There was something shifty about him. He did not like the way he was handling the pile of music manuscript. It was as if it was to him a load of Nazi rubbish fit to be thrown in the fire. As the officer shuffled the yellowed sheets Pte Shawcross could swear that he saw Ludwig van Beethoven's name in flowing penmanship and *Skizze eines Klavierkonzerts*. Pte Shawcross said to Lieut Svenson:

'You'll remember those packing cases that travelled with us. I've got a feeling that they're here. They got unloaded with us, you'll remember. Nazi loot, and now it's Soviet loot.'

'We can't do much about it,' Lieut Svenson said. 'That's a matter for the top brass.'

'But, Christ, look what he's doing.'

The Russian officer was preparing to light a papirosa, White Sea Canal brand, with a corner of music manuscript. Pte Shawcross leapt on to him. Rifles pointed. 'Oh Jesus bloody Christ.'

'I reckon we'd better get out of here,' Sgt Cobb said. 'I don't think we're wanted.'

'YES,' Colonel Hebblethwaite said later to the returning recce party, 'I thought something like that would happen. It looks as though we're prisoners of our gallant allies for the moment.

Nobody's stopping us from getting out of here, of course, but where do we get out to? As for supplies, you see this lot, dumped.' There was a small mountain of canned meat on the ice in front of the officers' quarters. 'I couldn't get much sense out of the officers and men who had the goodness to visit us. Vice versa too, of course.' Dan examined one of the cans, clearly American in origin, with a Soviet label clumsily pasted on to the original. Dan said:

'It says here pig meat, sir. My mother always said that no good Russian would eat pig meat without a bayleaf. The Yanks haven't bothered to put them in is what I'd say, so the Russians are dumping it on us. Sir.'

'I see. Not really so charitable, after all. Well, we'd better get back into the warmth, such as it is. Tomorrow, as somebody says, is another day.'

Next morning Dan cooked pig meat rissoles for the twelve of his hut. No change in the bloody weather. The bumps and flashes from the east were coming nearer. Colonel Hebblethwaite convened no parade. About midday, however, all were out of their huts to see a jeep bumping in over the ice with a couple of Russian officers in it. Colonel Hebblethwaite said: 'Pretty fair cheek, I'd say, using American jeeps without acknowledgment of origin. Red stars all over the damned thing, made in Stalingrad or somewhere. Let's see what they want.' The Russian officer who addressed the uncomprehending colonel, with an occasional side-glance at Dan, who had been introduced as interpreter, was a large man with eyes trying to meet over a large nose, his skin purplish; probably, in the Russian manner, an alcoholic. Dan heard him out and said:

'Sir. They've got two thousand German prisoners marching down the road and they want to put them in here. They say we've got to clear out. Sir.'

'Nonsense. We've claimed this Hun property on behalf of our two nations. Let him look at those flags.' The Union Jack and Old Glory had been affixed spread, as if to dry, on a patch of the barbed wire perimeter. Dan told the Russian officer, who seemed amused. To Dan he said:

'As you're presumably a trained infantryman and are Russian in origin you are entitled to a place in the glorious surge westward of the Red Army. I take it you speak American as well as British.'

'Ah no,' Dan said. 'I'm staying with my own lot. But thanks for the invitation.'

Colonel Hebblethwaite said: 'Where exactly does he expect us to go? Does he want us to march north or south or something in the bitter cold while a load of Hun prisoners nestle into our blankets?' Dan translated this and received a long reply. He told his colonel:

'Sir, south is where we're supposed to go. If we go north or west we'll get mixed up in the fighting.'

'How far south, for God's sake?' The Russian answered that without benefit of translation. Dan said:

'The Black Sea, sir, wherever that is.'

The colonel exploded. 'Good God Almighty, is the fellow mad? The Black Sea's the end of the world.'

Dan said: 'Sir, he says he's not arguing. Red Army orders. We're to be out of here first thing tomorrow morning.'

'Good God Almighty, the fellow's loopy. Did you hear that, Pilpel?'

'I guess we'd better take a look at a map, colonel. It seems one hell of a long way to me.'

In Dan's hut all crowded round a map in Pear's Cyclopaedia, one of a dozen books (they included the Bible, a compilation of prayers and hymns for the especial use of POWs, a cookery primer, and a manual – the designation highly suggestive – entitled *Love and the Lonely Man*) sent by some private charitable organization. Pte Shawcross traced a finger along a possible route. 'We're about here, aren't we, yes? Further south than you'd think, in spite of the brass monkey aspect. I mean, look at Latvia and Estonia and whatnot, real scrotum-tighteners.' The crowding men complained: Get your bonce out of the way, let's have a bloody shufti, can't see with your fucking big fat swede in the road. 'Southeast, really. Szestochowa, Lwow, Tarnopol, Podolsk. By the time we get to the Black Sea it'll be green and warm and lovely.' A lot of fucking snow before we get there, it's fucking miles and miles and fucking miles. 'Look at it this way. Imagine walking from Land's End to John O'Groats. It's only that with a few hundred miles added.' Ignorant men were getting the first geography lesson of their lives. Poor men were arguing as with a travel agent. Is the railways running? They'll all have been knocked to buggery. What do we do for bleeding money?

Colonel Hebblethwaite paid an unexpected visit to the hut, accompanied by Major Pilpel. All stood to attention.

'Stand easy, men. Jones, where's Jones, ah, there you are, Jones. Extraordinary thing, isn't it, you a Russian speaker. The only one in the camp, far as I can make out. Well, it's obvious that you have to join the first group, isn't it?'

'What's this about groups, sir?' Pte Shawcross asked boldly.

'Clearly we must travel as an army formation, in platoons under junior officers assisted by NCOs. Headquarters section goes first, under myself. We shall require the services of Jones as interpreter.'

'I'd like to go with my own lot,' Dan said, not yet sullenly.

'Ah no, can't have that, I'm afraid. Your services are too valuable to be ah dissipated.'

'Us lot are going together,' Dan said, sullen now.

'I'm aware,' Colonel Hebblethwaite said, 'that prison camp conditions have tended to induce a relaxation of regular standards of military discipline. From now on, however, the maintenance of such standards will be essential to our survival. You've been given an order, Jones, and I expect it to be obeyed. Everybody parade at first light tomorrow morning as you know, fully equipped but all inessentials left behind. We've a long trek ahead of us.' He marched out, and Major Pilpel gave them all a sardonic mock salute before following.

The men of the hut relaxed into: Fucking old idiot, military fucking discipline up his arse and so on. Pte Shawcross said:

'Well, there's only one thing to do, isn't there? Steal a march, as they say. Tiptoe off at sundown. There was a nearly full moon last night, we can get some way under that. Get ahead. What do we care about military discipline and being put on a charge? The war's as good as over. The Black Sea will be full of ships waiting to get us back to England, home and the other thing. We'd welcome your views on the matter, corporal.'

He meant acting unpaid Lancecorporal Moxley, the only NCO in the group, though in a somewhat theoretical sense. He was a longfaced youth, not overbright but good with internal combustion engines. He had been promoted from driver in the RASC, the lowest rank in the army. He said: 'They'll get you sooner or later. The buggers always do.'

'You propose then to travel with the bigger formation?'

'I'll come with you lot. But I don't want to be in charge. God knows why I kept this fucking stripe on.'

'It was always a lame dog's leg,' Pte Shawcross said. 'Shall we start packing?' He made it sound like a group holiday excursion. Pte Buckley said:

'It looks like it's going to be a hell of a long walk.' He saw inwardly something like a trudge from Manchester to Liverpool. Few of them could think beyond the thirty-mile route march, nice hot mug of char and foot inspection at the end. None had been taught to look at a map as a picture of human pain.

LIEUTENANTCOLONEL SECKER called a meeting of the entire camp staff, except for Pte Dawes, who was ineffectually guarding the women. He said: 'The situation has been made totally clear. You, sergeant major, would probably say abominably clear. None of our inmates may make application for British residence. All must prepare themselves for repatriation. These are orders from the highest level and no exceptions may be made.'

The meeting was being held in the CO's own office. The other ranks stood, except for WO II Brophy the quartermaster, who was permitted to sit because of his gammy left leg. The adjutant too stood, as ever, behind his chief's chair, stick under his arm. The window was partly open to let cigarette smoke out and the precocious spring air in. Reg, the RSM, said: 'If I may say so, sir, this situation is totally irregular. Any alien who finds himself on British soil is entitled to apply for residence and even naturalization. There's no law that makes an exception of Russians.' The adjutant, who had been reading the business up to his own bewilderment, said:

'It all seems to have something to do with this Yalta conference. Something to do with splitting up Europe into two camps. What Stalin wants Stalin gets so long as he keeps to the right side of the great divide I suppose we could call it. Sorry, colonel, you were about to say something.'

'Thank you, Murray. I was merely going to say that as soldiers we are in no position to question enactments which are, ah, enacted at ministerial, I suppose I ought to say prime ministerial level. Winston Churchill, to put it bluntly, says that repatriation must be effected as soon as British ships are available to, ah, repatriate. It seems that British ships are at last available. Some have already taken subjects for repatriation to Murmansk. Our own people here are booked to sail on the *Duchess of Bedford* from Liverpool on – yes, here's the date: March 14. The destination is apparently Odessa.'

'Odessa?' Reg said with incredulity. 'But that's a hell of a long way, longest route possible. Why Odessa?'

'Search me, sergeant major. It's a Russian port, and the Russians don't seem greatly worried about getting their people back in a hurry so long as they don't have to wait on British soil. I think the point is that a large number of British and American prisoners-of-war have been released by the Russians from East German camps and have been concentrated at Odessa. They get their own people and we get ours. And the one thing depends on the other. Quartermaster, I take it the supply of army clothing indented for has already come through?'

'Part of it, sir. It seems a hell of a lot, if you don't mind me saying so, sir. It's more than our lot get – I mean, four pairs of boots, two greatcoats, four underpants long, socks pairs of six–'

'That's the allotment requested by the Soviet authority, quartermaster. They want their people to arrive well kitted out and presumably smart, a credit to the Soviet Union so to speak.'

'Looking like British soldiers, sir?'

'There was some talk about dyeing the khaki grey or blue or something, but then Winston Churchill put his foot down. They're lucky to get what they're getting.'

'Bloody lucky, sir.'

'Sir,' Lancesergeant Scammell said, 'I don't see how we're going to collect all those that have scarpered, run away I mean, sir. I mean, the country's swarming with Russkies, and it's not our job nor is it the job of the civilian police to round them up.'

'I know, sergeant, but the Russians are taking care of that themselves. They've done a fairly efficient job of, ah, rounding up.'

'The position's totally untenable under British law,' Reg said. 'A foreign police force has no right to operate on our territory.'

'Yalta,' the adjutant said.

'I mean, the NKGB are here and SMERSH and–'

'What is this smersh you're always talking about?' Lieutenant-colonel Secker asked.

'*Smert Spionam*, death to spies it means. It appears that anybody's regarded as a spy once he's in a position to be corrupted by capitalist luxury. He's seen off without trial. God knows how it's been kept out of the newspapers – I'm thinking of those five corpses we heard about at the railway crossing near Bungay–'

'Security,' Lieutenantcolonel Secker said. 'There are some things the great British public is not permitted to hear about. After all, we're still at war.'

'And war's being made an excuse for the British government's condonation of bloody murder,' Reg said hotly.

'Got to keep our private feelings private,' the adjutant murmured.

'Well now,' Lieutenantcolonel Secker went on, 'the important thing – and this comes whizzing down from the highest possible level – is that these charges of ours are not to be, ah, apprised of their destination. Not till they actually embark. There must be no word of their enforced repatriation, not even when we get them on the train to Liverpool. They have to be told they're being transferred to another camp, because this one will be needed for a new big batch of German POWs. They'll find out the truth when they get to the docks.' He looked at his little staff and said: 'This is all a very funny business. But we have to play along. All right, dismiss for the moment. Sergeantmajor, stay behind.'

Reg stayed. His commanding oficer looked very sternly at him and said: 'I did not wish to say this in front of your junior, ah, colleagues, sergeantmajor, but your knowledge of Russian and your too well known sentiments about this whole business make you a security risk.'

Reg went very red. 'You mean that I'm likely to disobey orders and tell the truth.'

'Exactly. The Soviet Military Mission has been attacking the War Office about its choice of camp interpreters. They say they're not suficiently in sympathy with the Soviet way and purpose. Just the opposite in some instances, including yours. We got a very bad mark, you know. We're having a couple of genuine Russians posted here. Not Czarist refugees or their descendants but Military Mission people without a word of English but plenty of Russian. You, sergeantmajor, are to be posted. Wef now.'

'Just like that.'

'We're living in strange times, sergeantmajor. Your security riskiness operates as from this instant. Murray, perhaps you'd be good enough to call in those two.' The adjutant went to the orderly room.

'No opportunity to say goodbye to anybody?' Reg asked, tremulous.

'Least of all that. Ah, come in.' The sergeant MP and a lance-corporal colleague, all blancoed webbing and polished cap-badge, saluted with pedantic panache. 'Sergeant Clarke, I take it, has filled out your travel warrants. Good. I'll sign them while you assist RSM Jones here to get his kit together.'

'Where am I going?'

'You're going to No 6 Transit Depot, Marylebone, London. I'm sorry about the need for an escort, Jones, but we're living in strange times.'

'You've said that already, sir.'

'Yes, and I'll go on saying it, with your permission. Thank you for all your help in certain sectors – I think you'd go along with that, Murray, wouldn't you? – and I'm sorry about this. The difference between us two, Jones, rank and experience aside, is that I keep my sentiments to myself. Good luck.'

'Good luck,' the adjutant echoed. Reg saluted, performed a correct about turn and marched off. He did not acknowledge the presence of the escort that followed him to his quarters. It was only when the three of them were together in the train that called at Ickton on its slow way from Ipswich to London that Reg began to curse and blaspheme. The sergeant MP was sympathetic. There was nobody else in the compartment. He said:

'What's it all about then, major?' He spoke in the brotherly tones of the mess. Reg said:

'What do you know about this?'

'Nothing. Me and him were called out in a hurry and told

we'd got this job to do. Take you to this transit depot and hand you over.'

'And make sure I don't run away?'

'Well, that came into it. You're not likely to, are you, major?'

'I'd get caught. Second time unlucky.'

'Got in trouble before, have you, sir?'

'The first time for killing a German. Now for trying to stop a lot of Russians getting themselves killed.'

The sergeant MP perceived that he was in the presence of matters it would imprudent to enquire further into. He offered Reg a ship's Woodbine. He and his lancecorporal kept very close to Reg when they detrained at the terminus. They kept closer still on the underground train to Marylebone. The RSM at No 6 Transit Depot, the same who had exhorted me, your narrator, to be back in at 23.59, informed Reg, in the subdued tones appropriate to the addressing of one of his own rank, that Reg would be conducting a party to Avonmouth the following day, there to take sea transportation to Gibraltar. No pass permitted. A provost sergeant took in Reg's face and general appearance very thoroughly before he was permitted to hump his kit upstairs to the bare room allotted, a single one appropriate to his rank. Reg took off his field service cap, welshcombed his hair, sat on the dirty fawn bed biscuits, leaned an elbow on the pile of four folded blankets, and finished smoking the ship's Woodbine donated by the sergeant MP in farewell and relief. He tried to work out a plan. He was certainly not going back to bloody Gibraltar. He was going to be in Liverpool for the sailing of the *Duchess of Bedford* in one week's time. He was going to prevent Marya Ivanovna Sokolova from getting on that ship. She persisted in her innocent belief that her native country would welcome her back and that Pyotr Lavretyevich Sokolov would be well, waiting and loving in Sverdlovsk. She was unwilling to grant credence to Reg's insistence that, in the view of Marshal Stalin, great suckingpigsharing pal of Winston Churchill, no Soviet citizen who had been tainted by contact with the West could be considered innocent of a sort of treason. The Soviet vision had been impaired by even unwilling temporary exile, and those genuinely guilty of defection to the Nazis were in no different situation from the merely captured and enslaved. For all of them

181

the labour or death camps held wide their gates. Marya could not see this. She had tended the wounded first on one side and then, enforcedly, on the other. She had been loyal to the Hippocratic oath which transcended faction, ideology, even nation. She considered modestly that, in a Russia which was nearly as ready to create heroes as to punish traitors, she might be regarded as having attained a certain lowly degree of heroinism. She would kiss, but she would not listen.

Reg went below. He wished to make a telephone call to the Foreign Office. Regretfully the depot RSM informed him that this was not to be permitted. Reg cursed and blasphemed, though quietly. He was in the same situation as when he had arrived from Gibraltar, though now more warmly clothed and of a more exalted status which, nevertheless, conferred few privileges. He had had no disembarkation leave then; now he was to have no embarkation leave. He had not been well treated by His Majesty's army. And, while he was about it, to hell with His Majesty; to a deeper hell with His Majesty's myrmidons and functionaries, who had learned lies and hypocrisy from the Russians and ruthlessness and efficiency from the Germans. The ruthless efficiency of the day's enactments astonished him. This was not like decent bumbling Britain at all. He felt no more loyalty to either country or king. His allegiances lay elsewhere, but it would take some time to sort out precisely what they were.

He rejected the warm slop of the dining hall and tried to go out for his dinner. But the provost staff smiled sadly. He got up from his insomniac bed at four in the morning, only to meet the changing of the guard. He tried to slip out via the kitchens after breakfast, but the provost sergeant of the day before was not having that. For the time being resigned, he reported to the RSM with his kit at 0800 hours and was introduced to the party assigned to him. It consisted of five sergeants of the Army Educational Corps, all uxorious, for their wives were on the street outside the main entrance waving at them, and there were ten people wet-eyed, though three young children were dry and indifferent. They had had it cushy in the Home Forces. Reg had no compassion for them. The posting of one of the five seemed to him highly eccentric. This sergeant, Burges, was to be sent to the Falkland Islands via Gibraltar, Suez, Aden and Cape Town.

He had three kinds of clothing – temperate, tropical and polar. Apart from Reg's group, there was a bundle of sappers under two subalterns, also a quartet of military police, one of them a warrant officer class two. They kept stern eyes on Reg.

The Gibraltar-bound travelled first to Paddington Station by army truck. Reg held the travel warrants for six. He saw with hope that the train for Avonmouth was not solely for troops: there were rock scorpion dockyard maties going home having visited their evacuated wives; there were ordinary newspaper-reading civilians with civilian business in Bristol and other points west. He went to the toilet before Reading and the WO II CMP accompanied him as far as the door. Egress by window was an impossibility. The sea air at Avonmouth was the close air of a prison. Ship transport officers kept the group awaiting embarkation together. A whole infantry battalion had come west and was first aboard. Mounting the gangway, Reg mentally revised his swimming strokes. The sea would be cold.

I ARRIVED in London on a forty-eight-hour pass the day after Reg left it. This pass was scrutinized by MPs at the terminus, so it seemed that a new errant WO I, or perhaps the same as before, might, despite all precautions, still be at large. My main purpose in coming to London was to attend an interview. I had received a letter from a man who signed himself merely Aleph, the first letter of the Hebrew alphabet, but who identified himself as one of my instructors on that course in South Wales dedicated to torture and murder. He wanted to see me. So did two other men, also formerly my instructors, who called themselves respectively Beth and Ghimel. The interview took place in a house in Goodge Street, ill-patched after bomb damage. The dark emaciation of these men, who were pared down to political bitterness, was a kind of identity in itself, but they had hobbled from anonymity to pseudonymity and would, they threatened or promised, some day soon be known by their names. I was given a long lecture by Aleph on the Balfour Declaration, the treachery of both the British and the Arabs, and the coming dawn of the Zionist state. There was a part for me to play in the formation of a kind of police corps to be known as Massad. About this I say no more.

There was perhaps some irony in the fact that I went straight from this interview to a room in a hostel run by the Young Men's Christian Association. But how Jewish was I, and what did the term really mean? I had a certainly nonkosher horsesteak in Soho and then went to drink in the Fitzroy Tavern. There I saw Beatrix Jones, at home in the smoke, homosexuality, pseudoliterariness, as smart as wartime austerity permitted (as always, as always), sipping a half of bitter beer with a man I thought at first was her brother Dan in the fancy dress of a GI's uniform. But he was too swarthy and large-nosed for Dan, too sharp and literate also. He was a New York Jew introduced to me as Irwin Roth. He was a graduate of Columbia University but had rejected all promotion in order to write the definitive war novel, whose point of view had to be that of the ordinary suffering soldier. Thus he remained a private first class. He was not short of money, however, since his father was a partner in a distinguished New York firm of stockbrokers. This Beatrix was to tell me at another time. I did not see how he could write the definitive war novel when his army experience had so far been limited to camps in the United States and Great Britain, with a trip on the *Queen Mary* in between. But, he said, his outfit was due for posting to the final phase of European liberation in a week or so. 'Have a drink,' he said.

What I noticed, and was shocked to notice, was that Beatrix's attitude to this Jewish private soldier represented a seismic revolution in her sexual life. She, the cool, the user of men, seemed at last to be in what looked very much like physical love. I could read the signs. It was the way she gazed on him, drank in some sort of promise from his eyes, was happy to be pressed rudely against him when drinkers aware of the approach of closing time thrust themselves to the bar. Her watch had stopped, and this excused her taking his wrist, as if feeling for the pulse of passion, to see the time from his own, not that she needed to know the time. How can one explain all this? He was physically acceptable, I supposed: lithe but not muscular, plentifully haired. Not handsome, far from it. His body, his smell, his movements must be giving off sexual signals that had found an eager decodress. And then I thought about Reg and my sister Zip, whose visible betrayal of him I so far knew nothing about. Was there something in that Welsh Russian family that was seeking fulfilment among

184

the Semites? If so, why not myself? Was I not dark and Jewish enough and a good deal physically better formed than this Pfc Roth from New York? Perhaps I was not exotic enough. Perhaps it was enough for women to say, as they often did, 'He's not my type', meaning 'he does not belong to the range that will in time, though I doubt it, be revealed as containing the one and one only with a totally matching set of chemicals'.

I read once a commentary on *The Acts of the Apostles* (God knows why I was reading it: perhaps it was a passing curiosity about how a Jew could become a Christian) that God chose Saul or Paul because he needed his destructive energy. The man was not really converted: he had merely turned on his heel to confront a new set of theological convictions; he otherwise remained the same. Perhaps Beatrix's conversion was similar. The sexual energy remained the same, but the mode of its arousal had become different. Probably overnight on a kind of road to Damascus. She had formerly given the erotic orders but, as they were willingly obeyed, she might have saved herself the trouble. Women need to yield, and to order a sexual partner to force her to yield was an anomalous exertion of the will. This reversal should not perhaps really have suprised me. The important thing was sexual satisfaction. She was proclaiming to the world, or to such drinkers in that bar as might be interested, that she was getting it. She had not done so before: that, of course, occasioned my shock.

I remembered my dream of Aldershot – the January bedroom without a bed and my reduction of this cool girl to a palpitant slave. Had I been, outside time, enacting the role of this man she was yet to meet? I asked the question, and neither understood why: 'How long have you two known each other?' Pfc Roth said:

'Oh, a couple of weeks, isn't that right, Beatie?' She had always been Trix to the rest of us. 'Seems longer. Funny you should ask that question. I was in this ha ha hostlerah in where was it, Gloucester pronounced Gloster, and a guy walked in and I was certain we'd met before. So was he. We tried to work it out. He was British and he'd never visited the US, and this was the first time since I was a very little kid I'd been in Europe. I wondered if I was mixing him up with some British movie actor, but it

185

wasn't that. I don't want to believe in metempsychosis, but this kind of thing happens, I guess. Perhaps we Americans are more deeply bedded in Europe than we want to believe. You know, "that ocean where each kind does straight its own resemblance find". Andrew Marvell. Or if not resemblance the other half of the Platonic creature.' He was literate all right. Beatrix hung on to his every exotic, but not, him being a New Yorker, too exotic phoneme.

And then it was closing time and after, and he had to find a taxi that would take him back to Hounslow. He had no difficulty, being American and ready to quadruple the fare, what the hell. He was going to drop Beatrix at her digs but, being only a pfc, he probably did not have a sleeping-out pass. That was a small comfort but as momentary as the sour belch after my pint of bitter. Deeply bedded in Europe. They would be deeply bedded enough, had been already I had no doubt. I felt pity for Beatrix, that once queenly asker. She was in some kind of thrall. Was I in love with Beatrix, had I been? I suppose yes, even though, being a woman, there was something of the chestnut tree in her. I could now safely say to hell with love, though the world remained full of surprises. I walked to the YMCA hostel.

If Private Roth had proposed spending the night with Beatrix, or had had the allnight pass that enabled him to spend it, he would have been thwarted. For in her room Beatrix, warm I presume from a goodnight kiss while the taximeter ticked and the engine throbbed waiting, found to her shock her brother Reg, naked except for a blanket round him, downing vodka for a cold. He crouched over the little gas-fire and looked up blearily as she entered. Landlady choo had given him the key, sorry for him choo bugger it. Reg's uniform, boots and underwear were drying but not drying well. 'For God's sake,' Beatrix said. 'You again.'

Reg said, between sneezes and coughs, that they'd posted him with uncanny dispatch and efficiency from the camp of sad and furious Russians back to Gibraltar because he was a security risk. The repatriated Soviet citizens were going to be imprisoned or shot or both; he knew it and seemed likely to foment riot. Beatrix sat on her tangled sheets with care and said:

'Who told you about this?' He was impatient to recount his adventures from Avonmouth on but he said:

'Christ, you couldn't miss it. Bloody SMERSH going round seeing off those who escaped. The odd little murder in a dell or wood or outside jakes of a pub quite in order but a bit difficult to exterminate a whole campload, British army staff included. The more articulate of my Russians were very eloquent and very well informed. They knew because they'd been told. Get captured and you become the enemy. Straight to Siberia if you're lucky. If not a season in jail and then a shot in the back. I take it the bloody Foreign Office knows all about it too.'

'We know something about it. But not all. We get reports. They're not really our concern. We've no responsibility for Soviet citizens.'

'Not even choo blast it on British soil?'

'It's Yalta.'

'That bloody place again. Always Yalta, wherever it is. Oh Christ, I feel terrible. I've been in the water, you know, the bloody Bristol Channel. Not swum for years, and there I was overarming through oil and shit and filth.'

'Tell me.'

'I got on board, there was no alternative. They put me in a cabin with a master gunner. I'm always seeing this damned master gunner. Never says a word, perhaps he's bloody God in disguise. The ship didn't sail till midnight. All troops bedded down for the night in their hammocks, poor sods, but senior ranks, meaning me, given the run of the ship. So I was there when they dropped the pilot. I couldn't get down his ladder because they pulled it up too quickly, so I jumped from A deck just as his boat was pulling away. They dragged me aboard and then there was a confab as to whether they should hail the ship and have me taken back on. But they thought it best to settle all that on shore. My business, all said and done. All they'd done was pick up a drowning man, and that was damned near true enough, I'd got cramp with the cold. There was a kind of pilot's office with a fire where they let me dry off a bit. Look at the state of those clothes, all oil and gunge and muck. Chow. Choo. Sod it. I got a lift on a truck going from Bristol to Ealing, but when I told the driver what had been going on he got very shirty

187

about giving comfort and aid to a deserter, so he dropped me outside Swindon. Nobody wanted to pick me up the way I looked so I had to walk a bit. I got to Hammersmith in an army truck driven by a very decent ATS girl. And here I am. Arch. Blast it. Chow.'

'And what now?'

'I've got to get to Liverpool.'

'Right away?'

'No. Not right away. In time for that ship on March 14.'

'I see. You singlehanded are going to prevent the fulfilment of a procedure over which the British and Soviet governments shake hands. You're mad, of course.'

'There's one person who mustn't get on board. I can't do anything about the rest of them.'

'A woman, of course.'

'A woman doctor. Too innocent to live. Oh God, that's a stupid way of putting it. Never mind, it's true. I need civilian clothes.'

'I see. A regimental sergeant major might at least stop armed British troops from firing on recalcitrant Russians. An anonymous civilian with a bad cold won't even get near the docks.'

'You seem to know all about it. Has that sort of thing happened before?'

'There's been some trouble. There've been some suicides too. It's a dirty business, but we have to get our POWs safely back. It's always the same ships.'

'You're thinking of blasted Dan.'

'Of course. The eastern camps have been liberated. So much we do know. We can get them back from whatever ports they reach, with no help from the Russians naturally, in our transports, so long as we fill them with Russian displaced first. Empty ships can't dock.'

'So we obey Joe Stalin.'

'It looks like it. I'll get that unfiorm cleaned up for you tomorrow. There's a Polish drycleaner round the corner. And I'll see about getting you some reach-me-down mufti.'

'You're with me in this, then?'

'No, not really. I merely recognize that you've some mad part to play in the general mess, and I don't see how you can really be stopped. You'd better do the job properly. Travel north as a civilian. Then join the army again. But God help you if you're caught.'

What Reg wore the following afternoon was a pair of grey flannels, a blue shirt with an Old Etonian tie, a cashmere pullover and a fawn sports jacket. They fitted well enough. Beatrix had spun some story to a male colleague at the Foreign Office about her brother coming unexpectedly on leave, falling in the dark into a bomb crater full of dirty rainwater, and needing something to wear until his uniform was cleaned. It was as near to the truth as no matter. The colleague had gone round to his Bayswater flat during the lunch hour and returned with the gear. Beatrix had it sent to her digs by special messenger. As simple as that. Men would do anything for Beatrix. Reg went out and bought himself a razor, though he had difficulty in finding blades. He had, for second time, lost all his kit. He boldly walked into a teashop and had weak tea and a fruit pie with mashed swede in it. In the evening he went alone to a cinema to see an American film with Tyrone Power as a British army deserter in a cap FS not quite the right shape, caught in an overrealized London Blitz and picked up by fancifully dressed MPs at an unidentifiable railway terminus on TRACK 4. Beatrix had made her own arrangements for the evening. He coughed all night on the floor and, the folowing morning, bought a large-sized bottle of Owbridge's Lung Tonic which he drank in its entirety. He slept solidly for two days on Beatrix's bed, proving immovable, so that she had to take his place on the floor. More or less cured of his cold, but thin, haggard, wild-eyed, he travelled, his clean uniform in a brown paper parcel, from Euston to Liverpool.

The *Duchess of Bedford* would be sailing from the North or Prince's stage. Reg, changed back to a WO I in a public lavatory for the price of one penny, his borrowed civvies wrapped and under his arm, assumed that the train carrying the condemned would be a boat train, drawing in not too far from the quay. But you could not be sure what with this new cunning the government and its arms were learning in the treatment of hapless allies. Keep the illusion to the last that the suspicious displaced were being transferred to a new camp, let them arrive at one of the city termini, shove them in shrouded trucks or buses with blackened windows, push them up the gangplank. Reg got on to the docks without trouble, stumbling over wet cobbles and dodging between parked lines of rail goods trucks under a thin rain. He found a passenger platform guarded by an armed platoon of Liverpool Scottish in battledress. He boldly introduced himself to the subaltern in charge as an interpreter – his IC flashes confirmed the possibility of that – and asked what time they expected the train. It was already dusk. Sea wind and gulls, that had once spoken of adventure, blew and quarked in with a different message. The *Duchess of Bedford* was there, dim working lights going on. They expected a train all right but God knew when. Reg nobody had expected, but the subaltern said that somebody had got his finger out at last: there was nobody there who knew a word of the damned language. And so they smoked and waited. The subaltern was uneasy. He sought information from Reg. Surely they were not expected to shoot at the bastards? Were they not all eager to return to Mother Russia? He was a naive young lieutenant with a bad chest. He had never had this sort of job before. He had not yet fired a shot in anger or anything else. Our allies, aren't they? Seeing off the jerries for us at a great rate.

A Salvation Army grubwagon was trundled on with char and wads for the platoon. They were still chewing when the train was signalled. An engine and tender, dying pistons, much steam. Right, lads, we've got to get them out, line them up, march them aboard. Reg was on the train first, with '*Gdye Doktor Sokolova?*' He strode corridors empty of men. They remained huddled in the crammed compartments, all in new greatcoats whose buttons they had neglected to polish, boots, anklets unblancoed, clutching kitbags overflowing with army issue. They were not going to get out. They had smelt the sea air a long time ago, they had been cheated but they had known they were going to be cheated. The subaltern following Reg cried 'Jesus Christ', not answering the full corporal behind him who wanted to know if they had to bayonet the buggers out. The subaltern had never seen Russians before. It was a mockery to turn them into a kind of British soldier, not that in a million years would they ever look British. 'Come on, you lot, out,' he kept saying, but with no tone of authority. They would not come out. Doctor Sokolova was nowhere. Has she then seen the light without Reg's flashing it?

A British sergeant and two men, unarmed, were marching towards Reg from the back of the train. Yes, they'd come with this lot from Ipswich, though Christ knew what they was supposed to do with them except stop them from jumping off and doing theirselves an injury. A doctor? Go down to the guard's van and you'll find a bloody hospital. The lights of the train had been turned off as if to abet the chaos. Reg heard a rifle shot behind him. Didn't mean it, sir, the bloody thing just went off. Some of the Russians were getting out now, wailing high, cursing deep. Reg could see them fisting British privates who were too bewildered to retaliate with threat of bayonet or buttthump.

In the guard's van Reg stumbled over prone and supine bodies. Then dim lights came up again and he saw Marya Ivanovna in shirt and battledress trousers hopeless at being unable to tend the injured. One man had slashed himself with a broken bottle, another was bloodyheaded with having battered himself against a carriage bulkhead. Marya Ivanovna was unequipped for her trade. A man had cut his throat and was leaving life very peacefully. Others groaned and called on their mothers with injuries undefined what with the huddle. She recognized Reg. Where were you, why did you go? You're coming with me, Reg told her. The subaltern and his sergeant arrived. Jesus Christ all bloody mighty. What did they do with this lot, sir, the sergeant wanted to know. Soon they found out. Members of the Soviet Military Mission appeared to help with the embarkation. There were a major, a captain, and a number of men without rank, all in uniform. There were also some civilians, secret bloody Soviet policemen on British soil. Reg began to hit out as screaming injured were dragged by their feet. They heard his foul Russian and hit back without deference. He clutched Marya Ivanovna in protection but she was pulled away.

He breathed open sea air and saw small lights. They were getting them aboard, except for one who had grabbed a bayonet and fallen on it, others frothing and kicking in what looked like self-induced epilepsy, three who ran to the quay's edge and threw themselves in with audible splashes. The moaning injured and even a man who seemed to be already dead were thrust upright into a shoved mass of uninjured and borne by the press

191

up the gangway. Reg cried the tongue of his mother and was shoved with the rest, identified as repatriated Russian by his speech and battledress together, the fighting cats on the forearm unnoticed or interpreted as a bit of capitalistic prettiness. He found himself on deck and still being moved on. The ship's hooter now dominated the noise and even seemed to turn the scene into a piece of classical Eisenstein, all dumb howling gobs and fists. A startled British officer in a cheesecutter seemed aware that he was in the wrong film but was held in place by two scowling Soviet Military Mission men. Reg foresaw with a small but bright-eyed portion of his brain a rerun of the Avonmouth escape coming in a future reel, though with two leaps over the side. This made him accept his enforced embarkation, though he lashed out and cursed in English when an apparent NKGB man asked where his kitbag was and punched him for having lost it, not before grabbing the Old Etonian parcel under Reg's, miraculously still there, arm. He was pushed down a companionway and then down another and saw a frightened ship's steward in a dirty white jacket. There was a *Three Men in a Boat* blast of oil and old vomit and yesterday's fried fish. Then he was below decks in an enclosed space he recognized, sleeping accommodation for troops, though without hammocks waiting to be slung from overhead hooks and murderously overcrowded. In the Russian manner his companions were moving out of their manic phase into one of grim acceptance of man's lot, tears, the telling of invisible beads, the small comfort of reciprocal recognition. Many now recognized Reg, though not all. These men were not all his, though those who had been his moved into a large complication of responses – British betrayer, British betrayed, friend, little father, spy, informer, lickspittle Soviet or capitalist jackal. There were claws out for him as well as beseeching black-mooned fingernails of ancient hopelessness. He cried, ineptly, that he was in the same boat as they. He tried the hatch but they were shut in and there was no getting out.

There was getting out when a hooting colloquy of ships and tugs above drowned moans, howls, prayers to a longbanned *Bog*. Three miles out they were unbattened and allowed up for air. Back there under a cloudy moon were the docks, the Liver Building, the free battered city. Reg fought up a companionway and was met at the top by an officer of the mercantile marine. Can't come up here, comrade. Reg swore. Sorry, wack, thought you were one of them. Reg asked for the cabin of the OC troops. Couldn't tell you, wack. This one would know. Reg found himself face to face with a man of his own rank. They surveyed each other with surprise, as in a somewhat distorting mirror. Reg told all. The ship's RSM as he was, one of the Queen's Own, deeply lined, ready for bowlerhatting, said with a cracking tobacco-tarred rasp:

'None of our business. I've done this trip twice and we've got strict orders to keep out of it. The Russkies aboard look after their own, if you can call it looking after. Never in twenty-one years of service did I think I'd end up like this. Just don't bloody exist on the trip out, doing the job only on the way back when our lot gets aboard. It's for our POWs and the Yanks that we're here. I reckon you've got a bloody case against Joe Stalin, warrant officer class one of His Majesty's army battered about by Russky thugs. Keep that blood on your face, don't wash it off, show it to the old man.' Meaning the OC troops, to whose cabin they were now proceeding. Reg asked if the ship stopped at Gibraltar. To his relief he learned that it did not. First port of call Genoa.

The OC troops, a weary old man with the pallor of one who had served this war only in the Home Forces, had taken his tunic off and sat in natty braces over a bottle of navy rum and a glass already sticky with it. He heard Reg out. 'That's the way they are,' he said. 'We've just to keep our mouths shut. We only come to life on the return voyage. Then the ship becomes British again. Never in my wildest dreams. We feed them, clothe them, tend their wounds and their gonorrhea, all the Russians do is say they're in charge and behave like it. Our punishment for not opening the Second Front quickly enough. No good complaining. Well, you're surplus to ship's establishment but we can find a use for you. Shout back at the comrades in their own lingo when they start shouting at me.'

'What do you do about all these wounded that were dragged aboard?' Reg asked, adding, as the OC troops shakily poured rum for himself, 'Sir.'

'The ship's sawbones looks after them. We're not having Russian brutality in that sphere, at least he's not. But I gather there's a Russian doctor on board. A woman, would you believe it. Not the only woman. We embarked six this morning. Kids as well. And another kid clearly on the way. Never in my life have I seen anything like it. Don't go near the women. You'll get a bayonet in the guts. Don't go near any of our Soviet guests. Find yourself a cabin and stay put. I'll call on you when Major Kissitoff or whatever his name is comes calling on me. Never in my wildest dreams.'

ACTING unpaid Lance-corporal Moxley, titular head of the party, and Privates Addle, Buckley, Cresse, Crossbow, Evans, Gough, Handley, Jones, Knighton, Shawcross and Timpson had not yet left Poland when the *Duchess of Bedford* weighed anchor. They had not realized that Poland was so bloody big a country. What they had certainly expected was nothing but snow and dead cows and human corpses, but they found the place pretty lively with Soviet troops mopping up and meagre strings of jerry prisoners desperately unshaven. It had been Pte Shawcross's idea to take the big Union Jack, a pathetic triple crucifixion on the barbed wire perimeter, and to display it when segments of the Red Army appeared, thoroughly at home in the snow and ready to fire at what was not Red Army and therefore probably enemy, ask questions afterwards. Not many had ever seen a Union Jack before and they admired it even when they had shot at it, though with no apparent intention of killing its bearers, Ptes Buckley and Gough, spreading it out like an airdried bedsheet before the folding. Something like a flag that was. In a Soviet truck the British party was transported from Ziemniak to Kapusta, if those were the right names. It was important to get well ahead of the marching platoons that Colonel Hebblethwaite had threatened, though God knew how they could march down the deep icy ruts and through the virgin drifts that comprised late winter Poland. The Russians even handed over cans of American pork, rejected because of lack of bayleaf by fastidious proletarian palates, and glugged raw vodka down their protesting gullets. What the British party needed was a good hot cup of British tea.

If the Russians were at home in the snow L/Cpl Moxley's party was not. Tramping along a road of it that first night under a gormless staring moon, they had slipped and slithered and gone

194

sod it, but recognized that they had to push on and get well ahead of Colonel Hebblethwaite. By dawn they had covered only three miles, arriving in an abandoned village called Cetkica or some such name. They dossed for an hour or so in a byre that reeked of uncleared cowshit, and then L/Cpl Moxley's sharp nose for internal combustion engines led him to a truck, in some sort of order but empty of fuel, evidently left behind by retreating jerries. The road sloped and they were able to freewheel for a mile or so, and then they came to a singletrack railway line with a ganger's trolley lying idle. They depressed and raised the hefty handle without much energy and got to a ruined country station with some such name as Smutny: here the line gave out in a kind of granny knot of tortured metal. At Ustep they found people, genuine Poles liberated from the Nazi yoke. They could not understand Dan Jones's Russian. They responded well however to the Union Jack and dug out some hens refrigerated in the snow and prepared a soup with tufts of weed and a frozen spud or so as vegetable content. There were an old man and his wife, who had the shakes, and a couple of sons who looked like twins and coveted the British military greatcoats. It was a relief to huddle round a woodfire in a farm kitchen which had lost much of its outer wall and chew tough hen in hot water. Pte Shawcross reckoned they had covered about fifty miles and it was about five hundred to the Ukrainian border. He had torn out all the maps from Pear's Cyclopaedia. They had to keep on a southeasterly route, watching out for places like Glogow and Legnica, though these, by his reckoning, were still a hell of a long way away. They dried their boots and socks by the fire, and L/Cpl Moxley's feet were not roses. The stink, he said, which Pte Shawcross translated to fetor, ran in his family. They had extra socks and another pair of boots in their backpacks and, by God, they would need them. Their beards were already sprouting hard.

When they left Ustep, if that was its name, it started to snow, and there was a soft and treacherous sheet of it over the frozen stuff. We can't bloody do it, we'll never bloody make it, Pte Cresse complained as they trudged and slipped. But Pte Shawcross threatened him with Colonel Hebblethwaite and cockeyed military discipline. They had to make it for at least twenty miles and then they could take it easy for a bit somewhere. Not that the road seemed to lead anywhere. It was all snow and dead trees and an occluded sun. They saw the virtue of trying to keep in step and even sing There were rats rats big as bloody cats in the quartermaster's store, but there was too much stumbling and slithering. When they came to a ruined farm near Poziomka they were nearly too exhausted to use what bits of broken furniture had been left behind by combusting jerries or comrades to make a fire in an outhouse still with its roof on that might have been a dairy. When Pte Crossbow said his left foot had gone all dead, Pte Shawcross woke up and got a blaze going. They had plenty of matches and some packets of fags that would not last long. Something to eat was going to be the trouble. They found an intact can of what was labelled *olej*, meaning oil, different from the Russian *maslo*, Dan said, but perhaps potable or useful for frying in that rusty skillet there. They each took a shallow draught of it heated to moltenness then mostly wished to vomit. Pte Evans's mam had used to make him drink olive oil for his winter cough and that had tasted sickly but fruity, not like this. They ate what was left of the canned Chicago pork with a Russian label, grateful for Illinois foresight and considerateness as they turned the little key the Yanks had embedded in the base of the can. Then they fed the fire anew, finding that the rounded fat leg of an oak table would not let the flame get through its black varnish. They slept. Dan dreamed of another journey, the jolting thirsty one that had taken them from Rome through Firenze and Bologna and Trent into Austria and then into Germany. Getting to prison had been less of an effort than getting away from it.

In the morning Dan collected fishbait – a spider and its web full of flies for later eating, scraps of canned pork. His homemade rod and line stuck out of his backpack like a radio aerial. They slogged along an iced road that ran parallel with an iced river, perhaps a tributary of the one with the smelly name, but the ice was too thick to crack with stamping boots. But they came to a pond in the middle of a deserted village that might have been Kauczuck or Cowmuck or some such bloody name and, while the rest looked for whatever might have been left behind by jerries or Russes or Poles, Dan broke the ice with fair ease and fished, but the pond seemed only to harbour sticklebacks. The rest found no food, but L/Cpl Moxley, with his ready nose, came upon an open farm truck, in bad repair but that would be no problem if only there was some petrol around. He had heard of people in a time of severe fuel shortage hiding cans of the stuff under their beds. To his qualified joy he came across half a square tinful of foul-smelling stuff, not like ours but it was petrol all right, under a load of rubble that might once have been a shed. He poured in and got the thing started with much cranking, howling that it was giving him a hernia. They did about twelve miles, and then the road ran uphill and the truck coughed itself to sleep.

They had forgotten about the war, except as a source of misery unconnected with immediate danger, in the last day or so of slogging south. But now they heard loud explosions and saw yellow flashes on the eastern horizon and gathered that it was still going on. Clearing the jerries out of Skrzypce and Przekro-czenie and other outlandish shitheaps. Then they discovered they were a bit too close to the war when they saw jerry troops under a coughing officer shambling along a hill road. They were in a kind of dip or hollow at the time, getting a bit of shelter from a wind that had recently blown up. Have to be careful, lads, L/Cpl Moxley said unnecessarily. Better stow our Union Jack. Pte Crossbow said his left foot was frozen stiff, he could hardly feel the bugger. Stamp on it, stamp on it, Fred. Pte Crossbow stamped it into snow but could not get the bugger to wake up. He had to be halfcarried by Ptes Addle and Buckley as far as what looked like but couldn't be a sort of bus shelter, and then they got his boot and sock off and didn't like the colour of his toes, all blue and red and purple. Pte Shawcross rubbed the toes till he sweated and seemed to get the circulation back, but the colour did not change to a reasonable pink. They were all dead beat, but they had come no way at all. Eleven of them feared that they would have to find something somewhere that would serve as a stretcher, an old door or something, because Pte Crossbow now said that his other foot felt like it was going to go all dead as well. He said, and the steam of his breath sort of printed it on the air: 'I can see the way you buggers are looking at me you don't think I'm going to make it. It's circulation, that's what it is, and it runs in the family. If I could get them into a bowl of hot water I'd be all right.' They all had a blurred vision of a cosy back kitchen and a big black kettle on the hob. L/Cpl Moxley said:

'You're going to be all right, Fred. You mark my words.'

'Corporal Moxley,' Pte Shawcross announced, 'you're justifying that stripe. You've displayed considerable powers of leadership so far on this fragment of what looks like being an endless journey.' They did not understand him, L/Cpl Moxley least of all. 'I have a feeling that if we follow a scent of spring on the air with sufficient eagerness we'll come to a south without snow more quickly than we think. *Thalassa, thalassa*. This is what the Greeks called an anabasis.' They looked at him as if he were barmy. L/Cpl Moxley said on their way then.

At nightfall they came to a village not quite deserted. It was a single street with humble little houses still in fair nick. In the middle of the street L/Cpl Moxley, with the confidence of Pte Shawcross's expressed confidence, called: 'Anyone at home?' At once three men in what they knew to be German uniforms emerged from a house with their hands up. They gawped at the Union Jack and the twelve unarmed men in British greatcoats and brought their hands down. They brought them down as far as their mouths and made champing gestures with their unshaven jaws. 'We're in the same position as what you are,' L/Cpl Moxley said. 'No grub, no nothing.' Pte Shawcross said: '*Wir auch haben nichts zu essen*, sorry, gentlemen.' Pte Crossbow said: 'Let's get some water boiling.' They joined the jerries in a little house that seemed to be all kitchen. There was a fire in the grate and one jerry too sick to move lay on the earth floor by it. There was a fairsized black pan nearby and Pte Shawcross had a good look inside. 'Jesus,' he said, 'look at these little skeletons. These people have been eating the inedible.' But he took the pan and emptied it on to the snow outside. He came back with scooped snow inside it and set it on the fire. They all sipped hot water from their messtins before allowing Pte Crossbow to set his bare feet in the pan. Pte Shawcross's sharp eyes saw that the jerries had something their own party did not have: knives. A knife was a weapon, and prisoners-of-war were, by definition, weaponless. There was something of a struggle to wrest those knives from their owners, the first hand-to-hand combat with the enemy these British had known. The jerries had dropped their rifles somewhere in the retreat from Klopot or Spodnie or some such bloody place. They wept to lose their knives. Pte Shawcross did not have specifically in mind the lopping of Pte Crossbow's gangrened toes; he was looking ahead to the esculent, a dead horse in the snow, a lively but innocent buck in a green glade.

MAJOR Mashuk addressed words of comfort to his fellow countrymen over the ship's public address system. This was in the Ligurian Sea as they approached Genoa. 'Comrades,' he said, 'fellow-fighters in the struggle against fascism, that exaggerated version of capitalism from which our country has suffered and against which we have stood alone for years too many to compute. You are filled with an unreasonable apprehension which it is my present purpose to liquidate. Some of you fear that you will be punished for crimes you have not committed. It was no crime to be captured in battle. It was no crime to be absorbed unwillingly into the fascist war machine. Perhaps those of you who, in a fit of madness or temporary aberration of spirit, voluntarily joined yourselves to the fascist cause, would seem to have justification for fear. Treason is treason, no light matter. But we have the assurance of our glorious war leader that you are all, innocent and guilty alike, absolved of the past and encouraged to look to the future. The work of reconstruction needs all hands. The building of a new Soviet Union whose achievements will astonish the capitalist world requires the unremitting labour of all. We are calling at the Italian port of Genoa to collect five Soviet citizens who, in the apprehension I have already mentioned, threw themselves overboard on a previous voyage home to the motherland. They were picked up and the Soviet consulate in Genoa looked after them as a mother hen looks after her chicks. At the Turkish port of Istanbul we shall be picking up another seven misguided Soviet citizens who attempted an identical premature disembarkation. They too have received comfort and reassurance from the Soviet authorities. You have already seen how, in spite of the neurotic apprehension some of you still nurse, your country has been looking after you. You have been issued with warm clothing and you have comfortable berths. If the food is not as good as it ought to be, you must blame the British merchant navy. Soon you will be eating borshch and drinking kvass on your native soil. Think of your fighting comrades pushing fast towards Berlin, think of their heroism and their suffering. They would give much to be in your boots, even though those are of capitalist manufacture. It has been a hard struggle. Now we approach the end of the tunnel. *Nye zabudem! Nye prostim! Krov za krov!'*

Reg heard this over the ship's communication system and considered that the peroration was far from reassuring. Do not forget. Do not forgive. Blood for blood. He was confined to his cabin, with RSM Noakes present much of the time on the upper berth, in pain with a duodenal ulcer but willing to escort Reg to the heads and back again. The marine, army and Soviet authorities on board had concurred in having Reg so cribbed. He had been the cause of three men throwing themselves overboard in the Bay of Biscay, rescued with some difficulty by hardy but grumbling sailors, and another trying to sever his windpipe with a table knife. All now ate with spoons and fingers. Major Mashuk's proposal that Reg be posted away from the ship at Genoa was, in the view of the OC troops, reasonable, but he had to stand out against it on principle: the British army was doing enough for the Russians without having to obey them in matters of the disposition of British troops.

Reg had seen Marya Ivanovna once only before his sequestration. That had been in the sickbay to which he had helped to escort the Soviet woman Yevgenia, whom he had met taking a deck walk under the guard of a weedy young Soviet soldier with glasses. Seeing Reg and screaming at him as though he were the father, she cried that her time was upon her. It proved not to be, but a child might be born somewhere in the Sea of Marmora. Then Reg and Marya Ivanovna talked, though briefly. She said to him:

'What you did was very Russian. To put yourself in danger with your own people because of your love for me was like something in Pushkin or Lermontov. It was heroic. We shall write each other letters as good friends, but we shall not see each other again. It was an idyll in a bad time, but now it is over.'

'You don't quite understand,' Reg said. 'It was not a matter of just wanting to take you in my arms again, though that came into it of course. It was a matter of the danger to you. The danger to me is nothing. I will not be shot or even put in a military prison. The war is nearly over, anyway. But the men in the camp and on this ship had a right instinct. They fear the worst. They seem to have reason to. I can't bear to think of you in the Lubianka or somewhere because of a mad whim of Joseph Stalin. I wanted you safe in England.'

'Without Pyotr Lavretyevich? You have a good deal to learn about love. Now please go away, I have that man who tried to put his eye out to look after.'

'Innocence, innocence,' Reg cried to the white walls and the Mediterranean beyond the porthole.

'Besides, I shall be safe whatever happens. I have become the mistress of Major Mashuk.'

'Oh my God. Just for the voyage?'

'For the voyage and such time after as shall be needful.'

'Oh my God, infidelity.'

'In the Soviet Union we recognize only one kind of fidelity. You are an English capitalist and will never understand.'

'Oh my God.'

During the long nights without sleep, ulcerous RSM Noakes groaning in his dreams on the upper bunk, Reg masturbated to an image of naked Marya Ivanovna which, as he ought to have expected, modulated all too easily into an image of my sister, his wife. Sometimes both women got themselves into the old steel engraving of Belshazzar's Feast, but that shed its erotic extravagance and became a page of the family Bible, holy, home. He was adrift, homeless, very much at sea. He saw an empty future, but he comforted himself with the reflection that most men, after six years of war, saw no fuller one. During one of his immediately preorgasmal deliria he saw the Right Honourable Winston Churchill in a bow tie and Edwardian coke, grin bisected by gross Havana, lifting podgy fingers in a sign the troops took to be the old Roman one, up yours mate, but which the ruling class read as V for victory and Dr Goebbels as V for *verloren* and other past participles of defeat. Reg would have liked to shove that cigar, burning coal and all, down the old bastard's gullet. Churchill and Stalin had licked their podgy fingers at a feast of roast suckingpig and chortled over the bloody division of Europe. Reg felt it was his duty to write a letter to the popular press about British complicity in Russian murder, but he knew it would never be published. He had never, anyway, been much of a hand with English prose, though he had made a few verse translations of Lorca. He tried writing verse on some of RSM Noakes's lined thin letter paper to get the bitter hurt out of his soul. He wrote about a devastating sword called Amor and then crumpled up the execrable lines. RSM Noakes knew his full name was Reginald Morrow Jones and had started calling him Veg, short for Vegetable Marrow. RSM Noakes grew giant marrows in the little back garden of his semidetached, to which he hoped soon to retire. He said to Reg as they approached the Straits of Messina:

'It's bloody stupid keeping you shut up in here all the bloody time. You and me's going for a walk on deck.'

'How's the ulcer?'

'Grumbling and then it stabs like a bloody knife. I'll have to have it cut out when we get back. Ought to have a wound stripe for it. It's the war what's caused it.'

They went up on to B deck. The ship was negotiating the gap between Calabria and Sicily. A spring wind blew heartily. 'Scylla and Charybdis,' Reg said.

'Who?'

'Scylla was a monster with six heads and twelve feet and a dog's bark, and she had wolves' heads springing from her body. Charybdis lived on the other side, under a figtree, and swallowed the sea like a medicine three times daily and then spouted it out again. This is the place where they were supposed to be.'

'Where did you get that rubbish from?'

'Homer. Ovid. What they call a classical education. Is that sour expression the ulcer or your attitude to learning?'

'I've had education. In peacetime you have to get army certificates of education before you can get promoted. But I never got taught that rubbish.'

'It's only that rubbish that gives us the right images for the times we're living in. Six-headed monsters sprouting wolves' heads like supernumerary tits.'

'That's what you get after a cheese supper.'

'We're all living in the aftermath of a cheese supper.'

'You've got some barmy ideas, Veg.'

But when they were steaming southeast over the Ionian Sea, RSM Noakes woke screaming with a nightmare. Reg was still awake. 'The pain?' he asked, unhanding his penis.

'Bloody six-headed monsters and a wolf bit straight into my guts. You shouldn't have told me what you did. Give us a match for my fag.'

They sailed through the Kytheran Channel and then dodged between the Cyclades in the Aegean Sea. The Greeks had created the best monsters, leaving their realization to later history. They had also created logic. The two somehow went together. Reg leaned over the taffrail and watched the boiling wake. RSM Noakes, or Charlie, said in wonder that his guts had been a lot better since that wolf bit into them. Then Major Mashuk appeared to order Reg back to his cabin. Reg said that he took no orders from murderous Bolsheviks. Major Mashuk grinned in no good advertisement for Soviet dentistry at the imputation of Bolshevism and then repeated his order, giving Reg a slight push. Reg said:

'These, comrade major, are the isles of Greece where burning Sappho loved and sung. All you have from Greece is a deformed alphabet and a perverted Socratic dialectic and a logic in the service of the proliferation of monsters. You make filthy the Hellenic seascape. Get out of my sight before I spew.' Major Mashuk was very angry and tried to buffet Reg, but RSM Noakes had been too long in the British army to countenance the beating of a British warrant officer by a foreigner whose military commission was of doubtful legitimacy: he was old enough to have seen the Czar on a state visit to London. He said:

'You'd better bloody stop that.' Major Mashuk backed away, as from the Czar's own presence, now smirking and leering in the knowledge of Reg's sexual jealousy, almost mouthing *revnivi revnivi*, recalling bed-talk about British insufficiency in the act or acts, but then waving fists frowning and making threats. He would, he promised, have Reg thrown into the ship's brig, if the soft British merchant navy had such things.

'Six-headed bastard,' Charlie Noakes said. Reg said:

'I'll get him. I'll use him.'

'What barmy idea have you got in mind now?'

'I'm going ashore at Odessa. I'm going to find out what's going on there.'

'What goes on there is that the brass band plays for the poor buggers and they get stripped of their British army issue and go marching off in rags and bits of old bandages wrapped round their toes. Then our lot comes aboard, or so we hope. Could be a nice place, Odessa. They have these steps going to the harbour.'

'I'm going ashore.'

'You won't get ashore. Russky orders.'

'I speak the language, don't I? The world's got a right to know what's going on.'

'What's going on is their own bloody affair. Keep out of it, me old meat and two veg. Don't try anything you'll regret. These are very funny times we're living in.'

'Monstrous.'

'I'd go along with you there.'

IT was spring by the time Reg's brother Dan and a reduced party of trudgers through Poland, or it might have been East Prussia, touching Czechoslovakia, got to the Ukrainian border. They had been held up a long time in Wczoraj or Jutro or some such place because of Pte Crossbow's blood poisoning. Pte Shawcross had been in a hell of indecision as to whether to amputate the dead toes, but his courage collapsed with guts that had tried to digest boiled beechtwigs. They had Pte Crossbow moaning on a filthy old sofa in an old farmhouse that was scratched by scampering rats all the black night long. There was a rat trap in the kitchen but no bait except potentially possibly Pte Crossbow's dead toes, otherwise they might have made a sort of stew of ratmeat. A decaying rat corpse they nosed out under a sideboard served however as fishbait when Dan went wandering off to a rivulet in whose ice a hole had been knocked by a firtree uprooted by the wind. He fished freezing for a long hour and went back with what looked like a dace and a pair of chub. These, guts, fins, scales, head and all, they simmered to make a soup, of which Pte Crossbow would take none. He moaned in delirium about a rockinghorse his carpenter dad had made for him when he was a little kid, but the front leg had come off and his dad was then no longer alive to put it back on. It did not look as though he was going to last long. Pte Evans was having trouble with what looked like dysentery and Pte Timpson had sores all over his face, no bloody beauty to start with.

They feared for a time that the regular formations from the Stalag would catch up with them, and then they hoped that they would. They needed officers' orders about Pte Crossbow; they needed Captain Morley, the MO who would surely be in the vanguard. But the road southeast remained theirs alone, save for old straggles of defeated jerries and the very occasional Russian truck going the wrong way. Perhaps the overwhelmingly main body of the Stalag was still cosily there, fresh arrangements having been made for the jerry prisoners, costively nourished by rejected canned pig. Perhaps they had gone west in a Soviet convoy to join the advancing Anglo-Americans and be shipped or planed home. Perhaps they were all in Moscow under the protection of the embassies, spooning in caviar, hearing news of the war's end. Perhaps they were all dead.

When they woke one morning they found that Pte Crossbow was dead, a rictus of great pain on his face. Burying him would be a bit of a job, you'd need a pneumatic drill to get under the ice, so they left him under a mound of old sacking in the back-yard, first having removed his red identity disc. That would be for records or somebody, to show that he was dead. They ought to have had a burial service over him, but none of them was all that religious. Pte Shawcross made up a kind of prayer that went: 'O God Almighty, if you exist, let him rest in peace. He's had enough of the other commodity. And, if you're alive and list-ening, let those of us who have survived so far push on to the end.' He added:

'He on the day when heaven was falling,
   The hour when earth's foundations fled,
Followed his military calling
   And took his wages and is dead.'

The rest awkwardly said: 'Amen.' Then they got on their way.

Zelazo, Rdza, Stal, Miedz – the names didn't matter much, where names even existed. They must, surely, Pte Shawcross puzzled, tiny crumpled map of Central Europe in chapped fingers, be not far from some great civilized though ruined centre of life like Brzeg or perhaps even Cracow. They had been, he had marked the days off in his Letts' diary, six weeks on the road. They were on to their second pair of boots. Their liquid intake had been more than adequate – a boilup of snowbroth over fires fed by ample wooden ruins – but solidities had eluded them. Dan Jones had fished, but ponds and rivulets had yielded scantily. It was with weak joy that, near Nysa surely, they now remarked a hump in the snow of a field and dug out a refrigerated horse. They hacked feebly with the jerry knives at its rump and took the hard flesh and fat to the barn forlorn on the horizon, a long stumble over blinding white. There they made their fire and scorched their meat. Pte Gough was the saltcarrier: he had found a lump, a cowlick probably, in a byre beyond Kciuk or somewhere, thirty miles back. They chewed the sweet flesh seasoned and drank warm snow. They felt fuller but sickish. Before they drowsed by the strong-smelling woodglow, Pte Shawcross tried to tell them stories by the brothers Grimm, but they were shocked by the undisneyfied ending of the Snow White tale, with the wicked queen forced to dance in redhot iron boots till she dropped dead and the wedding party applauded. Then, to the surprise of all, Pte Dan Tetlow Jones told them about Attila the Hun.

'It might have been in these parts,' he said, 'that he found the sword with its point sticking up from the ground, and whoever got that sword had to win all the battles. And on that sword he had the letter A sort of written or hammered in with a nail, to show it belonged to Attila. And over these parts he came with his men on horseback, just like the Russians are coming now. But he never got to England, which was called Britain in those days. The sword he had was passed on to King Arthur, who was a Welshman, and the A didn't stand for Attila any more. And that's the sword we saw that time when that Russian kept pushing and pulling it into and out of that wooden thing that was sort of keeping it safe. The Russians have got it now, but the A doesn't stand for anything any more.'

Pte Shawcross looked at Dan with great curiosity. 'Where did you learn about Attila the Hun?'

'My dad has this book. It was written by somebody he met in

hospital in the first lot. My brother Reg, the bastard, was named after him. The man that wrote the book. My dad never forgot him. He used to read to us from the book when we were kids.'

'And you say,' grinning, 'you saw that sword?'

'You saw it too. I saw the A on it, but it didn't sort of sink in till afterwards.'

'Swords,' Pte Shawcross said, 'get rusty. They fall to pieces. Swords don't survive.'

'I saw it and you saw it.'

Pte Evans now went out into the snow to vomit, and this encouraged Pte Handley to follow him to the same end. They had eaten too quickly of flesh more scorched than roasted, and the sweetish taste had not been overborne by the salt. When Pte Evans had vomited, the squitters came on to him again, and he had to go and crouch shivering and bare-arsed in the dark cold corner of the barn. He kept going oh God oh bloody God. Pte Shawcross then spoke violent words, so that the others feared for the sanity of one who had seemed all too sane.

'Yes, bloody God is right. I've tolled the bell for you times without number, I've eaten of your substance in the form of bread. I've wondered at your existence, whether we fashioned you or you fashioned us, but now I'm sure enough you exist. Only a divine master could contrive all the pain of the world. We know you by your works, but now we demand a theophany. Show yourself, bloody God, and kill or comfort. You brought us out of the land of Italy to the land of the Hun. Now we go south looking for sun and spring and green fields, but the Hun is everywhere still. Attila is little father, as the cuckolded husband reminds us in his drooling over the romance of words, and Atta is big father. Atta or Abba or old Nobodaddy, come out of the clouds in a glory of levin, why skulk abased in unleavened bread? If we are going to live, give us a sign.' Pte Knighton, a Shropshire lad, said:

'Watch it, Shawky. Don't tempt him up there. I'm not much of a chapelgoer, God knows, but there's limits.'

'If we are going to die, give us another sign, and let that sign be the immediate striking down with the sword of thy bloody wrath of this thy bloody unhumble unservant.' But there was no God in the metal sky. He had hidden in that frozen horse and,

207

throughout the long night, twisted and stabbed and drained their tortured entrails.

A NEW Soviet citizen greeted the world with his tiny combative fists in, as Marya Ivanovna had prophesied, the Sea of Marmora. In the roads of Istanbul the ship lay for a night, and older and more cowable Soviet citizens came aboard from a motor launch. An assembly of a hundred or so seasick Soviet citizens was convened on deck to greet them, which they did with half their hearts, some with fascist salutes. The Sea of Marmora had been choppy, but now they were to enter home waters ever calm and warm, the climate marxly mild and stalinly sunny, passing to port the windborne scents, though faint, of citrus fruits. Midye, Igneada, Akhtopol. Some Czech civilians, secluded for the voyage, landed at Burgas, having downed thimble after thimble of vodka with Major Mashuk and Captain Chepyzin and issued to them a cordial invitation to visit Czechoslovakia on behalf of the government of which they were to be minor functionaries. 'We'll be there without your invitation,' Major Mashuk's bad teeth grinned as the Czechs waved from the quay. Reg heard that. Major Mashuk did not see Reg as Reg looked landward from the deck above.

Reg had visited Major Mashuk's cabin on A deck during one of the now regular genial harangues, full of blood and revenge and the building of future glory, over the public address system. The whitecoated steward Major Mashuk insisted, in an autocratic spirit officially withered away, on having attend to him, make his bed and press his uniform, gladly opened up for Reg, couldn't abide the overbearing bastard. Major Mashuk's fur hat and winter greatcoat, discarded for the spring weather in the bulk-head locker, Reg tried on and found a reasonable fit. He would have those later. He examined with interest other of Major Mashuk's possessions, mostly acquired in London – a box of Durex condoms, some limp and unrolled but undiscarded, ready, with mean economy, for further use; a bottle of Black and White whisky, a rarity for British citizens; a Fairisle pullover; a Dundee cake; a ceramic pot of Keiller's marmalade. There were also lists in duplicate of the poor sods who would soon be disembarking into paradise: they had been divided into groups of twenty, presumably for ease of processing. Reg heard the peroration of Major Mashuk's speech: *'Krov za krov!'* He had better get out and go to his cabin, where what was called the tea meal would soon be brought – black char and a tabnab.

Varna, soon to be named Stalin; Mangalia; Constanta. At Constanta another party of Czechs went ashore, presumably potential members of an alternative government or opposition. They then came to Sulina and the mouths of the Danube, Attila's own river. In a sumptuous dawn they took on a pilot and steamed with oldwomanish care into the bay wherein the Dniester emptied itself. Here, on the curve of the magnet, lay Odessa. Charlie Noakes, in whom the ulcerous pain had renewed itself, moaned but admired, with Reg, the great port the Greeks had founded, the Russian revolutionaries ruined, Stalin's economic foresight restored to life. 'Bloody lovely-looking place, no two ways about it. Funny it should be part of Russia. More like Naples really, vino and knockingshops. Look at them steps going down to the sea. See that woman going down with a pram.' There was a battleship in the harbour and a commercial transport being loaded with what looked like old iron. The *Duchess of Bedford* seemed loath to have her skirt defiled by a proletarian port; she was, with fidgets, forced to the quayside. Hawsers and bollards and dark men with moustaches, Ukrainians, Tartars, something. There was a long line of godowns beyond a tramrail. A smell as of rotten bread was wafted in from the hinterland. 'Right,' Reg said. There were as yet no tremulous passengers ready for disembarking. The gangway was for squat civilian officials and a couple of army officers coming up as if they owned the bloody ship. 'Right,' Reg repeated, and he went to his cabin to dress in Major Mashuk's fur hat and greatcoat. It was a warm morning. The swine had not yet done his packing, but soon he would miss his property. Reg, ill-disguised as a Russian major – the Celtic earnestness of his face showed through between starred fur and greatcoat collar; he wore khaki trousers and blancoed anklets – hid in an open passageway on the deck where the gangway was a swaying ligature between Russia and Britain. He saw that a military band from the Odessa barracks had assembled under a consumptive-looking bandmaster with a heavy baton – piccolo, clarinets, cornets, trombones, bombardon, even belltree, above all two bassdrums. He saw something else which at first puzzled him – a trio of fighter aircraft circling low. Their racket would drown the row of the band. Fairly close he heard what sounded like a sawmill. A very mixed noise of greeting. The band began to play what sounded like the new Soviet national anthem, no more Comintern nonsense of the *Internationale*, and the bassdrums just about made themselves heard under the hum of the aircraft. Then the first twenty repatriates, heavy bundles of British kit under arms, were being impelled down the gangway. Major Mashuk, *slava Bogu,* was not to be seen: he and Captain Chepyzin would be below sorting out the others. The impellers seemed all to be of the shore party. Reg took many deep breaths.

He took many deep breaths and marched to the gangway and then down it after the first twenty, who were being directed by a young armed private soldier with spectacles. The next twenty, he turned to see, were ready for the descent. He caught bearded hopelessness, gaunt, resigned. He marched down. The first lot was being motioned towards the opening of Godown A. He followed and heard shouts from the deck. The bespectacled soldier was doubtful, but Reg shouted at him: 'Do your job, lad,' not knowing what he meant. The authentic officer Russian calmed the boy, who was ready now to direct the second party of twenty to the second godown. Reg found the heavy double doors he approached now slammed in his face. The aircraft circled, the sawmill buzzed, the band was visibly blowing and thumping. In a mystery of upper partials the belltree festively tinkled. Now he knew what was going on. He ran left alongside the long body of the great shed, noting distractedly chalked obscenities – a crude sketch of anal penetration, the word KAL – and came at the back to what he had expected: a truck being loaded with British battledresses and boots, grey bundles of woollen underwear, even rattling knives, forks and spoons, by a fatigue party under a blustering NCO. The back doors of the godown let out smoke in lazy drifts. There were twenty naked bodies, not all dead; a couple staggered. The killing was in the hands of what looked like boys of not more than fourteen, their uniforms too big for them. They were being directed by a subaltern who stiffened at the sight of Reg. He gave an order for the recharging of the hot rifles and started an apology: not right for the young, he knew, but they would have to start learning sometime, not yet adept at the clean shot. An unarmed party of babyfaces began to drag the corpses out. One corpse came back to life and they dropped it. It was seen off finally with a couple of close shots. Reg, preparing to scream at the Ukrainian heavens, found himself grasped from the back by Major Mashuk, raging at the theft of his clobber, and a couple of unknown other ranks who obeyed a brisk order and thumped Reg with a riflebutt or two on his now bare head. He left the scene and was admitted to blessed universal blackness.

It was disclosed to him when he came to with a blinding headache and tender bulbs sprouting from his scalp that the mercantile marine transport had more than a brig: it had a padded cell. Foresight on somebody's part: foreknowledge that he would scream and hammer. A tiny sane segment of his brain, no more than a matchglow in the wind, told him that he was going mad.

If this were a novel and not a record of historical fact, it would have been pleasant to have Reg's brother Dan aboard, having waited long on the Odessa steps, footsoles worn away, bearded like a patriarch, now welcomed aboard though with no Soviet band, ready for the long voyage home. But at this time Dan and his reduced party were only just into the Ukraine, where an early spring burgeoned and men and women spoke a language that Dan could just about understand. It would be a long time before Dan and his companions, and the thousand-odd they joined, Colonel Hebblethwaite not among them, puzzled over circling low aircraft and a distant belltree, seeing an undoubtedly British ship curiously slow at having them aboard.

CAPTAIN EISENAUG, of the psychiatric branch of the Royal Army Medical Corps, took Reg, in his hospital blue, on a little walk among the pale narcissi in the grounds of Cranford Lodge near Salisbury in Wiltshire. 'You will see,' he said, 'that not all is horror and murder in the outside world. Listen to the birds, how sweet they sing.' His eyes belied his name: they were not ironhard but of a dreamy violet. His accent had a sweet Teutonic lilt, the lateral consonants a clarity apt for high *Heldentenor* notes.

211

He had left Vienna at about the same time as Sigmund Freud. He was not Jewish, but he was an opponent of Field-marshal Goering's brother's Aryan psychiatry; this made him also an opponent of Jung. He did not believe that Freud had all the answers, but it was Freud himself who had vouched for his professional integrity and apoliticality when Eisenaug sought British naturalization. He had joined the RAMC as a lieutenant general practitioner but, with the reluctant admission of the medical military that the soul might after all exist in a sense unacknowledged by the Corps of Chaplains, he had been able to concentrate on an eclectic kind of psychiatry. Reg's troubles, for instance, had no etiology in some primal Oedipal scene. Reg might wish to kill Winston Churchill and Anthony Eden, but they were not father surrogates. Nor was Joseph Stalin, far from it. He called Reg Reginald. He did not address him by his reduced rank of sergeant. He asked to be termed doctor not sir. He said now: 'So it was the same dream, only sharper and clearer?'

'Less a dream than a dramatized presentation of intent.'

'You would never get away with it, Reginald.'

'I present myself at the door as a representative of Winsor and Newton. I have watercolours to deliver. I find the old swine in his garden crooning at his goldfish. I stick a knife through his fat.'

'This is revenge.'

'This is revenge.'

'Revenge should always be a dream. It is not good for real life. Christianity has the right idea, though you may not think so. Vengeance is mine, says the Lord. This means a hell spent eternally brooding on wrongs done and realizing they were wrong. There is no such place as hell, of course, but it is a good image of retribution. The wrongdoer must know he has done wrong. If he will not come to that realization there is no doing anything with him. To annihilate him does no good. The state takes its revenge. Revenge goes on and it loses its meaning. You hate, Reginald.'

'I hate and I go on hating.'

'I would ask you to consider if it is possible to hate or to love for that matter something that belongs to the past. Is love of a

212

dead woman possible, for instance? Can you justifiably hate Attila the Hun?'

'Justifiably in one of his living impersonations. Stalin, for example. I hate Stalin.'

'And therefore you would wish to kill him?'

'Of course. But I'd never get at him. I could get at Winston Churchill or Anthony Eden.'

'It would do no good. You could publicize what you think to be their crimes, but the crimes could be distorted into acts of benevolence. As it turns out, they were wrong to believe that the sending home of Russian expatriates to probable murder was a condition of repatriating allied prisoners-of-war. But it could be considered no crime to have the welfare and safety of these as a motive for handing over displaced Russians to their own government. That government is in alliance with our own. Stalin is a friend.'

'The just man has no friends.'

'You honestly believe that to be true? You think yourself to be a solitary voice of justice? Can you not yet see that that is a kind of paranoia?'

'I know. I'm here because I'm mad.'

'Deranged through none of your fault. Remediably deranged. You no longer have to be tied down or forcibly fed. You are getting better. You are eating now and you are sleeping well.'

'Long, not well. Too many nightmares.'

'A nightmare is a safety valve. We all have nightmares. The war is over in Europe, but there are plenty of nightmares still to come. In German we call nightmare *Alpdrücken*. I dream of alps pressing down on me. I wake sweating and wonder at the ingenuity of what we call the *Traumsystem* in so torturing us when we are asleep and defenceless. But it is nature and nature cannot be fought. Dogs and cats twist and shake in their nightmares. Nightmares we must accept.'

'You counsel acceptance of the wicked world? Normality consists in not worrying about it?'

'Oh, we have to worry and we have to change it. But not through acts of revenge. A more sensible way of overcoming the vengeful impulse is to convert it into something else. We have in German the word *Demütigung*. You would say humiliation. To humiliate we call *erniedrigen*, which means to bring low. If you think of Marshal Stalin stripped of his uniform and showing to the whole of Red Square against his will a pot belly and shrivelled penis, then you have *Demütigung*. If you steal from him something he values highly then you *ihn erniedrigen*. The Allies have been right to turn Adolf Hitler into a figure of fun.'

'The better to close their eyes to his infamy.'

'Have they closed their eyes? Is not the infamy now being shown to the world?'

'Belatedly. When it's already been enacted.' Reg moaned. 'When are you going to let me out of here?'

'If we let you out, where do you go?' Reg had no answer to that. 'Do you go back to your wife? Do you perform your first vengeful act on her?'

'She did nothing except humiliate myself to myself. I should have not seen, that's all. It's better not to see.'

'That is the only answer to living. Not to see too much. Your Edmund Burke said we must try to live pleasant.'

'Not my Edmund Burke. An Anglo-Irishman.'

'Is it important to you to be what you racially are? Has not race caused us all a great deal of trouble?'

'I thank God I'm not English.'

'Oh, come, we are both speaking English. It is a good language and nearly as expressive as German. I am becoming English enough. I lust for tea with my *Jause*. There are worse countries and worse people. It is a country that must now take a back seat in the affairs of the world, but it has taught good customs. Tolerance, for instance.'

'Tolerance of the wrong bloody things.'

'That is a chance you must take when you are tolerant. You have this capacity for tolerance in you. You are prepared to be reconciled to your wife, I think. That is good.'

Reg saw highstepping over the lawn a woman lieutenant of the RAMC. She wore a white coat over her khaki slacks and shirt and her long black hair waved behind her like a flag in the early summer breeze. Hair was in fact the flag of feminity. She was aware of that loosened hair as a symbol of the end of war; she knew too its probable therapeutic value in wards full of depressed men. 'Let us sit down,' Captain Eisenaug said. He was in battledress and cap and even carried a stick. Playing at soldiers. He took off his cap, short, fattish, prematurely bald, violet eyes behind respirator spectacles. They sat on a wooden bench beside a waterbutt. 'Your wife has written to me,' Captain Eisenaug said. Reg said:

'I mean, the whole thing is made more evil by the lack of information. Were they all shot? She? The women and children, including the newborn one? I'm scared of writing to her. If I get no reply how shall I interpret the silence?'

'Forget it. You have to write it all off as part of the war. She has joined the others, it is best to be in no doubt about that. And she was merely a surrogate for your wife. Your wife,' he repeated, 'has written to me.'

'Meaning you wrote to her first.'

'Naturally. She is your next of kin. She has a right to know what has happened to you and where you are. She proposes a visit. What do you say to that?'

'I must start by apologizing. *She* won't apologize.'

'Why should she apologize for what you permitted yourself to see? It is the seeing that was out of order.'

'We start the new era blind.'

'That is one way of putting it. Should we not say wilfully myopic? We all have to live, or try to. *Il faut tenter de vivre*, as the French poet says. Perhaps you should write her a letter.'

'I've already tried. I tore it up. I seem to have difficulty in managing English. I wrote a letter in Russian. In the cursive script my mother taught me. And then I was scared of sending it. The address isn't exactly a pinpoint on the Russian map. Care of a husband in Sverdlovsk. I tore that up too. No, I won't write. Tell her to come.'

'I have already done so.'

It was a week before Zipporah, my sister, arrived at Cranford Lodge. It was a wet day and the greenery lisped in the wet wind. Women are so absolutely pitched that they have to make a point of external change. Zip was thinner, her Mediterranean round-ness apparently inflected, now she had come to maturity, by English angularity. She had let her black smoky hair grow long, as Reg saw when she removed the rain hat that matched her bold red waterproof. He gulped at that. The hands that grasped the bag Reg had given her two years before were the powerful instruments of a beater of drums, but the fingers crawled with a sort of diffidence over the wet surface of the plastic. 'Here I am,' she said. The voice was no longer girlish. Reg, on his feet in hospital blue and a drab issue dressing gown, kissed her wet cheek. It was the sort of kiss I would have given.

'Here I am too,' he said ineptly. 'If we go into the dayroom there we can have some tea.'

It was not a good idea. There were four fellow patients who sat at the table by the window, gloomily watching the rain. The dayroom radio played 'There I go, leading with my heart again'. One of the four had a severe tremor; a fellow held his mug for him while he drank tea. They were all what an outworn orthodoxy called shellshocked; Captain Eisenaug knew that the roots of the ailment were infantile and sexual. Zip said: 'Oh no. I don't want any tea anyway.' So they went back to the empty four-bed ward, and there Reg embraced her. 'Better,' she said.

'They tell us there's a future just beginning. Japan will be knocked out of the war before the year's out. I do love you, you know.'

She grinned and said: 'I don't quite see the connection.'

'Oh, you and me, real marriage. The world's supposed to be getting over its adolescence. There's nobody else, is there?' She noted his tremor.

'There's been a fair number, if you want the truth. All in the family, in a way. All in the orchestra. I'm thinking of resigning. Give my wrists a rest.'

'It's been the war, hasn't it?'

'You could say that, I suppose.'

'I'm in a fairly early release group. I leave the army in November.'

'When do you leave here?'

'It won't be long. I'm cured, I think.' Then he wept bitterly. 'Sorry, sorry, sorry.' He wiped his nose on his dressing gown sleeve.

'It was a bad time.'

'Oh yes yes, it was. And now it's all over.' He howled to the ceiling. She patted him. Then she took him in her arms. Her

216

waterproof rustled. 'Why don't you take that damned thing off?' he sobbed.

'I didn't want to make myself too much at home. Didn't want to presume too much.'

'Presume all you like. I've been the presumptive one. I do love you, you know.'

'As you said. You'll have to start looking for a job, won't you? But I suppose they give you paid leave so you can start looking.'

'They do, yes. I can teach Spanish somewhere. You're not really giving up banging and crashing, are you?'

'Not for ever. Too big an investment. But it's an aggressive sort of activity. I thought we might have a baby or something.'

He grinned through his tears. 'Or something?'

'Settle down for a bit. That's the something. And a baby.'

'Russo-Hebreo-Welsh. An interesting combination. United Nations.' And then: 'I do love you, you know.'

'That's all right, then. Love, I mean. That's all right. I think I could drink some tea now.'

'It'll be cold.'

'Make them give it you hot. Presume. Assert. It's been a bad time.'

'Oh, it has, it has.' Then she took off her blaring red raincoat.

PUMP

'PERHAPS that's what it's all for really,' Reg said to his brother. They sat together in the rare bus that went from Gilwern to Abergavenny, the bag with the week's takings on Dan's knees. They were going to pay it into the District Bank on the High Street. It was Saturday morning in high June. 'I mean, what can you do with it except turn it into nightmares?'

'I don't have them,' Dan said. 'Never have had. Except when I was a very young kid. And then it was screaming women with a lot of teeth and the odd snake that talked.'

'What I mean is that he's turning it into a kind of entertainment.' Dan didn't understand. 'Making a book of it isn't a bad thing to do. Neither you nor I could do it.'

'Wouldn't want to if I could. He took it all down then he said he was going to turn it into all Yanks. Being a Yank himself. She's all over him. She thinks the bloody world of him.' He glowered.

'It's time she settled down.' But Beatrix was still working for the Foreign Office, and her New York Jew, Irwin Roth, was at Cambridge at the feet of F. R. Leavis, writing the great American war novel in his ample spare time. GIs set free from a Polish camp. Pfc Stein, hard as stone, tramps from Lwow to Tarnopol to Podolsk to Kishinev to Odessa, shedding his companions on the way like moss. Macaulay dies in delirium after the jackknife amputation of four frozen fingers; Bergman and Hanks, foraging in a farm, are battered to death by outraged Ukrainians who hate all foreigners; all left are jailed at Podolsk but only Stein escapes. Fantasy full of dreams of past fucking set out in the style of John Dos Passos. Irwin Roth had not set foot outside England: a

218

dose of pneumonia had saved him from Normandy, and then a
Lieutenant General Hoffmann, friend of his father, had secured
him a propaganda post, turning a load of photographs of the
farce of Theresienstadt into a book with prose commentary. Dan's
war was no good to Dan, but it was very useful to Roth. Even
his Russian was.

'He won't get over it,' Dan said. He meant his and Reg's
father, coughing his life out in his bed above the public bar. The
customers heard the coughing and nodded over their rationed
pints. Poor bugger, coughing better he is. Art it will be, the art
can't stand it. Weak art after twenty days in an open boat. The
Titanic it was. We've come through some bad times. That was
true, anyway. 'What's going to happen to mother?'

'I've a mind,' Reg said, 'to look after the pub for a bit. All I'm
fit for really. Country air in my shirtsleeves and not thinking
much. I don't want to think.' Cured, he still shook, or it might
have been the shaking of the bus.

'Thinking,' Dan said, 'never did anybody any good.'

'The bastards,' Reg shook. 'The bloody bastards.'

'They were bloody bastards all right. We get off here.' They
had passed through green and birdsong sustaining the cycle to
which war had been an irrelevance, and now they were in the
town where the butcher's shops had only sliced corned beef in
the window and the tobacconists announced no cigarettes. But
in the bank there was money being paid in and paid out, though
nothing to buy with it. It was soothing to Reg to hear the double
vowels which were the Welsh version of diphthongs. The Welsh
girls had delectable white necks. Reg and Dan waited behind a
man in a grocer's surgical coat who was paying in much copper.
Then a very Welsh voice said:

'Sorry about this I am, but hands up everybody.' Some
laughed. 'Look, I bloody mean it, so get them up in the air, you
too, missis.' Reg and Dan saw a couple of men with masks on,
the kind of thing kids bought to play bandits or outlawed saints.
They both had Lee-Enfield rifles, not handed in on demob (they
dropped overboard, sir. Ah, well, never mind, the war's over).
One man waved his, the other fingered the trigger. 'Won't take
long. You, miss, just hand it over.' Dan at once began to claw
the fifty quid in notes from the bag into his demob suit outer

right-hand pocket. 'Ah no, not having that we're not. Hand it over, like I said to her.' The plump girl teller at Dan and Reg's part of the counter went '*Duw Duw*' and, with wide grey eyes, offered cylinders of grocer's copper. 'Keep that, it's the big stuff we're after.' The manager, in a suit not demob, appeared at his office door and looked sternly through his glasses. 'You in charge here, is it? This is what they call a raid. Give us all you've got and there'll be no bother.' The twelve customers still could not believe it; films about this kind of thing did not help its attachment to the real world of an Abergavenny summer Saturday. A swimsuited girl on a calendar offered clean teeth to the robbers, affirming their unreality. The one who had not spoken now spoke, finger temporarily off trigger, in a bass that would have been useful to a chapel choir:

'All for your own good this is, if you could only be made to see it. Mean no harm we don't, money only it is we want.' The manager said:

'This is a place of serious business. I've no time for your little games.'

'Games, is it?' the bass sang, and he aimed the rifle at the girl on the calendar. She loudly lost her teeth, her nose, and her left eye. 'Marksman I was and still am. So hand it over.' There was smoke and the smell of a frying breakfast. A little girl with her mother began to cry. Dan's right ear rang with the explosion and he called:

'We've had a bloody nough, six years of it, you buggers. Get out before I get bloody nasty.'

'Language,' the first robber said, 'and before ladies and a little *plentyn* too. You're not in the army now, you're in at the beginning of Welsh independence.' The equal stresses playacted the word to Reg's ear. Reg said:

'So that's what it is. I never thought you meant business. Take what you want and get it over. You'll get caught, the notes will be traced, he and I are going out now to scream blue murder in the street and you're not going to stop us.'

'Look now,' the masked bass intoned, 'I won't kill, wouldn't be right, but I'll maim. You wouldn't want to be maimed now, would you, be sensible.'

'Oh, for God's sake, get it over with,' Reg said, and he made a show of vomiting.

'We'll want a bag too,' the other said to the manager as he piled a couple of hundred pound notes on the counter, best get it over, insurance will pay. 'Forgot to bring one, new at the job, fair play.'

'Have this,' Dan said, and he threw the old scuffed gladstone. It caught the bass on the left *clust* or lug but caused no pain. The bass chanted loud and threatening:

'We'll have our eye on you from now on, make no mistake. Enemy of the liberty of the Welsh people, watching you we will be.' And then, when all that was going into the gladstone had gone, not much really, millions it would be in one of those films about bank robbers, 'Off now we are and *diolch* to one and all. Wales for ever.' Then they left and the bemused customers looked at each other blinking as from the cinema. The woman with the child said that there ought to be a law, and the bank manager said there is, Mrs Evans. Reg and Dan went out to the sun and saw the men, rifles slung, take off on a motor cycle, the pillioned one waving the gladstone to the Abergavenny air as in a triumph an admiring public would acknowledge. A policeman taking from a United Dairies shop a gill bottle of rationed milk for the station tea watched the blue farting exhaust amiably. Reg said to Dan:

'A good thing I did what I did.' He pulled two pound notes from his trouser pocket. 'And don't start talking about robbery after we've seen what we've seen.'

'Pinched those from the bag did you when I wasn't looking?'

'From the till, actually. This is buckshee money. We can have a pint or two at the Angel. Two hours till the bus back.'

'You thieving bastard. You'd rob dad of his last breath if he'd let you.'

'Don't talk about his last breath. It's indecent.'

The news of the bank robbery had already reached the public bar of the Angel. Well, you can't expect a return to normal times overnight. Taught young lads the crime of killing and the sin of scrounging as they do call it. Good luck to them if they can get away with it, the banks is rolling in the stuff, all insured anyway. Dan and Reg had arrived in time for the dregs of the barrel of bitter, no more deliveries if you could call them that till next Wednesday. But Gwen behind the bar said: 'Try this, mead it is called.' Reg admired the pure long high front vowel. Sack mead and sack metheglin. A scholarly man, tall and in leggings, his face a map of purple rivery veins, said:

'Well, it's the Welsh national drink, or was. Should properly be *meddyglyn*, liquor being *llyn* and *meddyg* from *medicus*, the healer.'

'Is that a fact now?'

'What it heals the Lord only knows. That it doesn't get you drunk is a truth long acknowledged. A dry table wine, no more.' Dan said suddenly with passion:

'Land fit for bloody heroes, they said. Fish banging their heads on the seashore to be caught and the coal crying to come up from the ground, and the grates empty and the fish shops shut.' Reg admired this new eloquence.

'Blame the labour government you put in,' a man coming back from the dartboard, stowing his darts in a mock leather case, stowing that in his breast pocket, said.

'Me and him,' Dan said, 'didn't put any bloody government in,' jerking his head roughly towards his brother. 'Too busy fighting the bloody war. Which some was not doing.'

'Are you accusing me of bloody scrimshanking?'

'No politics here,' the landlord said. 'And no bad language neither.' He was in his waistcoat. 'Let's all keep our respectability, even though times is bad.' Dan and Reg had two more thimbles of sack metheglin. They then spoke Russian to each other. The legginged man listened with care, nodding occasionally. The landlord said: 'That doesn't sound like any Welsh I ever heard. And I don't hold with people speaking foreign languages about other people.'

'We were discussing private matters,' Reg said. 'No politics, no swearing, no beer either, and now no Russian. Nice sort of pub you've got here.'

'You two Russians then?' an old man with no upper denture asked. 'Well, there's a lot around. There's one that keeps a pub not far from here, and a fine figure of a woman she was till she took to fat.'

'Be careful,' Reg said. 'You're talking of the woman we love.'

222

'Ah, that would be your mother then? Explains it then, fair play. Well, that's where the future lies, so they keep saying.'

'A future,' Reg said hotly, 'of tyranny and murder.'

'Organization,' the legginged man said, after sipping sweet bottled lemonade with a sour face. 'Omelettes and the necessary smashing of eggs. What we lack here is organization. Do we not all laugh at the law?'

'Hitler had organization,' Reg said, more hotly. 'He tried to organize a whole race out of existence. The founding fathers and mothers of the faith of every tinpot Beulah chapel.'

'No politics and no religion either.' The landlord stabbed a back tooth with a pointed matchstick and registered the surprise of pain. 'Bugger,' he said, against his own rules.

'A bit too clever the Jews are,' the man with the stowed darts said. 'Fought a war for them and you'll find their houses running with gin and whisky. Not that I've anything against the Jews.'

'You'd better not have,' Reg said.

'What's that supposed to mean then? Every man's entitled to his own opinion.'

'I could kill, I could bloody kill,' Reg said, showing all his teeth. Dan took the mead glass from Reg's hand before he could crush it. He said:

'*Balnoy*. You still are. Let's start to walk back.'

'It's the war,' the old man said. 'It'll be a long time before we get over it.'

'It'll be a long time before it's bloody finished,' Reg cried.

'Get him out of here,' the landlord said to Dan. 'That stuff's stronger than you'd think. Get him a cup of coffee at Aunt Megan's Tea Rooms if you can call it coffee.'

Dan did not understand much of what his brother said as they walked towards Gilwern. 'Easy for that Kraut psychiatrist to say what he said. The birds are singing and the daffodils sprouting and life's bloody lovely. The past is the past and you're supposed to settle down to a nice lovely future, bygones bygones. And what you've gone through is for the great American war novel written by that bastard who sat on his arse, and what I saw others going through is politics and the bloody government we've got now sing "The Red Flag" and long live Joe Stalin. What are we going to do, what are we bloody well going to bloody well do?'

Reg wailed to the bus that Dan flagged. This was Wales, and a bus stop was where someone waved to the driver.

'What I'm going to do,' Dan said, as they sat behind a woman nursing a parrot cage whose inmate squawked and looked with a wicked eye, 'is to get my own fish shop. When there's fish to be got. It's no good shutting your eyes to it. Dad's going to die. There'll be money when he's gone. And what you have to do is to get back to your book learning and being a teacher.'

'Hahahaha,' the parrot went, and 'Hush, Polly,' its mistress.

'I'll take over the pub,' Reg said in gloom, 'and Zip and I will have a child born in the Breconshire air. If we can. Either I'm sterile or she is. I suppose we ought to see a doctor.'

'I don't see,' Dan said, 'why people want to have children. I don't want to have them. I don't see the point of them. Nor getting married neither.'

'You're short on libido. You shouldn't be. Fish is a great promoter of sexuality. Religion is fertility, and Jesus Christ was a fish.' The woman with the parrot looked round, shocked. Dan let his brother's madness fly out of the half-open window to be lost in the elms and the hedgerows. The parrot cocked its wicked eye. 'We get off here,' Reg said, rising.

'We're not there yet.'

'I want to see the Arthurian remains. There,' pointing. And he called to the driver to stop.

'But it's a hell of a long walk then. We'll be late.'

'They'll keep it hot for us.'

The lane was a narrow one in which summer foliage had scraped and stroked the windows of the bus. The gate that led into the field uncultivated, more of a paddock, had lost two of its bars and was unhinged. An old grey horse tore at a tussock. Dan grumbled at the stumbling walk over the grass. The wind from the east was freshening and a cloud like Africa was blotting out the sun. 'Don't see the use of it,' he said. 'Who does it belong to, anyway?'

'To nobody. To anybody. Like a dolmen. Like Stonehenge.' There was not now much to see: old stone, the curious slit in the buttress of a ruined wall, Reg's own name after GLAD ART.

'There was a Naafi girl named Glad,' Dan said. 'And some people are called Art. Three names, and yours is one of them.'

The ruins were in a deep hollow, suitable for lovers on a summer night, and the spears of the grass clumps shook in a wind that did not seem like a summer afternoon.

'That's sex too,' Reg said. 'That vagina waiting for a sword. You couldn't have seen what you said you saw,' he said. 'The force of imagination or something. But what puzzles me, with all respect to a loved brother, is that you don't have much of that commodity.'

'I saw this thing with an A on it, like in dad's book,' Dan said fiercely. 'It flashed in the fire these Reds built in the town whose name I've forgot, and Shawcross who was educated but that didn't save him from getting in the way of somebody's gun, Shawcross said we'd gone with it nearly all the way from that place in Italy where the real fighting was, we were just playing at it they said, to the monks' place where the Reds dragged it out. And now they've got it and nobody knows where it is because,' he informed Reg as of a new truth, 'Russia's a hell of a bloody big place.'

'He meant Monte Cassino,' Reg mused, 'and that ought to make sense according to the other book. The Benedictines and the British royal house. It gets into one godless set of paws and then another. A tool for barbarous slashing cleansed by a Christian king who fought new barbarians who are now the English, and then it gets back to the barbarians once more. And it might have been here in that stone there, if it's genuine. Only he, the once and future, could pull it out. But this may be a fake.'

'There's a light comes off it,' Dan said, 'in the dark. Like one of these watches.'

'Eh?'

'I saw the light come off it the other night when I was passing in the bus. Like off fish.'

'You're still not well, Dan. Any more than I am, and I don't expect to see any light.'

'I'm well in my brain,' Dan said truculently. 'It's only in my side where I got the bayonet jab that I hurt. And only when it's going to rain. Like now. I knew it was going to rain when I got up this morning. I can feel the rain like other people can smell it.'

'I can't smell,' Reg said. 'That's one thing I've lost. The olfactory nerve damaged in bloody Spain. Cabbages and roses all one. We've all got our wounds. Funny how wounds respond to the weather,' he said, his eyes on the immovable scabbard. 'Living things, like crows wheeling and cows lying down. But this bloody nose responds to nothing. Zip can have chronic bad breath for all I'll ever know about it.'

'You shouldn't talk of your wife that way. She's a nice girl, and she's worth ten of you, you thieving sod.' But the truculence was factitious, more of a memory of old brotherly enmity, and even then more mythical than historical. 'And,' he added, 'there's such a thing as a cabbage rose.'

'Stopped-up drains, then.' The sky, now all grey, began to blubber gently.

'Told you it would. I had the pain this morning. Now we have to walk all through it, bastard.' The horse, part of nature, was unmoved by the rain. Only men, not part of nature, responded with drama to weather changes. The horse chomped and watched Reg and Dan hurrying in their demob suits to the gate. On the narrow road they were lucky. Dr Lewis, in the little Morris for which the state allotted ample petrol, a priority profession his, was on his way to see his patient, their father. He said:

'Hop in. That windscreen wiper's stopped working. You, Dan, give the wet a wipe with a dirty handkerchief, if you've got one.' Dan used his demob tie. 'Couldn't get in earlier as I promised. Mrs Pritchard's youngest again. That child's an encyclopaedia of infantile ailments. Thrives nevertheless, with a monstrous appetite. Not been getting much sleep, either of you, from the dead fish look of those eyes. Well, the cough's hurting him more than you. He ought to be moved, you know that.'

'You know him,' Reg said from the back. 'He doesn't like hospitals. How long do you give him?'

'Not much more than a week or ten days. He'll be glad to go, I should think. Coughing up a thing that won't be coughed up. It's the strain on the heart that'll do for him. I'm going to give him something that'll make him sleep.'

'For ever?' Dan asked.

'Not quite that. I believe in euthanasia in theory. In practice my Wesleyan Calvinst background gets in the way. Thou shalt not kill and so forth.'

'What does that big word mean?'

'Euthanasia? Good death, I suppose. Greek.'

'We didn't see Greeks,' Dan said, 'except for one of these Yanks who said he was a Greek called Poppadopolous, which is no sort of name. But the Greeks are liars if they say death is good. It's not good, nor never will be.'

'How's that thing in your side?' Dr Lewis asked.

'The stitches have sort of melted away and I think it's healed up now except for the little hole that water keeps coming out of. The bastards said we were Germans. That bastard stuck it well in, a big grin on his mug. I must be a German they said if I spoke Russian so good, the Germans being a cunning lot that learned Russian to turn the Russians against Russia.'

'Not again, Dan,' Reg sighed. 'We've all heard this too often.'

'And you'll hear it again and again, you thieving sod,' Dan said with truculence. 'There's too many that wants to forget what that lot was like. They'll hear it till they're sick of it. Missed all those boats at that place because the bloody thing wouldn't heal, and even in that hospital they kept saying I was a German. No AB 64 to show them,' he explained to Dr Lewis. 'And they said I might have pinched the uniform I'd got on.'

'Yes yes,' Dr Lewis soothed. 'It's been a terrible business. Here,' he added in some relief, 'we are.' There was an old man with a cap and raincoat on sitting outside the pub with his pint in the now easing rain. Elm leaves dripped into his beer. He doubtless preferred the wet to the dry coughing inside. As the three got out of the car they heard it however, though faint from the open upper window. In the bar Zip was putting a towel over the beerpumps. She said as the three entered: 'Closing now, gents.' The only two customers there were leering farm lads. Zip's beauty was only too leerable at. The cough now was loud from above. 'I'll give him something,' Dr Lewis said. Zip boldly went over to the farm lads and waited till they downed the last drops. They leered at Zip, and one said: 'How about a little kiss then for the road?' Reg was quick to get in there. Reg said:

'Out, you bloody scrimshankers. Pretending to work on the bloody land while better men than you were lying under it.'

'Reserved occupation it was, keep your hair on, boyo.' But they left, mocking the cough.

In the kitchen Ludmila Jones, thickening and greying but still beautiful with her Baltic green eyes and firm chin, greeted the doctor but looked fiercely at her two sons. 'You are late,' she said, 'and everything gone dry.'

'We were robbed,' Reg explained. 'We were held up in the bank. At gunpoint.' Dr Lewis smiled with his mouth at the heavy joke.

'It's true,' Dan said, 'but this thieving bastard here took two quid from the till.'

'I will not have the word bastard,' Ludmila Jones said.

'Hold-up, eh?' Dr Lewis said. 'You mean it?' Zip came in, saying:

'I never realised that *petrushka* was parsley. *Petrushka* to me was always a heavy drum part. And now I know that *petrushka* grows in the garden here.'

'He says,' said Ludmila Jones to Dr Lewis, 'that he will lie in the garden. He will no more stay in the bed. He speaks of his father dying in the bed and making everything dirty. He says he will lie on an army groundsheet he calls it in the garden with old coats over him. He says he will die in the air.'

'Let's not talk of dying just yet,' Dr Lewis said. 'Have your lunch. I'll go up and give him a little injection. Did the milk stay on his stomach?'

'On his stomach nothing will stay. He throws the blanket off it and tries to get up to go and lie in the garden.'

'Let him,' Reg said. 'He cries out for air.'

A respiratory depressant, Dr Lewis kept saying to himself, liking, as always, these expressions of his trade which made abstract the nasty realities of human machines grinding to the stopping point. He gave David Jones, grey and wasted under the harlequin coverlet, a single grain of diacetylmorphine hydrochloride. He would come in again in the late evening to repeat the dose. David Jones, dyspnoeal, dysphonic, nodded. 'You'll feel better soon,' Dr Lewis said. But a single grain, as he knew, could be fatal. David Jones croaked: *Outside*. Dr Lewis nodded in his turn. Why not? Irregular, but the weather was warm.

So David Jones lay under the sheltering wall of the garden, hidden from the outdoor men's urinal by an old roller and a hedge of empty lemonade crates, on a groundsheet and covered by a couple of blankets and the harlequin coverlet. It would rain, of course, hardly a day passed but it rained in South Wales, but Reg and Dan brought from the cellar the two table umbrellas given free in the thirties by a firm, now gone, that was trying to promote a soft drink called Limorange, which sounded like a place in France. The spines of these umbrellas were of metal and they had spikes which could be stuck into the ground. He did not want company, he wished to be alone to digest his past. The survivor from the *Titanic* and a great war, but survivor for what? To make a strange marriage with a Russian beauty in the borough of Brooklyn, to beget three strange children he would never understand, to run a restaurant in Manchester which never made as much money as it should. He had fed people well, and that was something, and not people of the common sort either. There had once been an article on the restaurant in *Picture Post*, with himself raising a glass to a glamorous actress, now dead of being unable to breathe, named Tallulah Bankhead, Noël Coward crushing a cigarette into an uneaten dessert, Charles B. Cochran whom they called Cocky embracing Evelyn Laye and Jessie Matthews over plates moderately well cleaned. Mark Hambourg, a fat pianist who loved his food, had taught him to cook lobster pernod flambé with a sauce cardinale. There had also been ham en croûte, as it was called, a favourite of the violinist Szigeti if that was his name. Cook a medium-sized tenderized ham in chicken stock and marsala and slice to the bone and spread each slice with canned chestnut purée and ground almonds and cover ham with puff pastry. He had never mastered the French pronunciations, calling croûte 'Kraut' until he was laughed at. The Russian dishes had been the best. What was the sweet called that had black cherries and mandarin oranges and strawberries and beaten egg whites on vanilla ice cream? A favourite of the Czar and Czarina or Rasputin or somebody.

The brownstone house in Brooklyn had been sold, but the money was all hers. Those gold sovereigns from the cockloft had been forced by the thieving government to be turned into paper. But he still had his Australian gold, and what would it be worth now? It was illegal to have it, so he was told, and he wondered why illegal. It had been in the family a long time and he wanted to have it with him now under the bedclothes. It was a thing that throve though to what end if it could not be converted into goods or land? Something to kiss and embrace as a thing precious but useless, a symbol of the unchanging, like the God who did not exist. He would ask to have it with him like an unresponsive wife under the bedclothes, clutching it in the final spasm he foresaw. The cough was coming back along with a clarity of thought that the injection had numbed. He coughed, and the birds would be listening, heads cocked, as to a strange animal perhaps dangerous.

IT was not too far away from the village of Gilwern that Aled Rhys, Ben Griffiths and a former private soldier named Tom Probert sat in conclave in a decaying farmhouse for which they paid a derisory rent. It was the temporary headquarters of their flank of the movement, which, more or less firm in its object, was unsure in its strategy. That was why they sat around a kitchen table in their demob suits and listened to Terence MacMahon. MacMahon, unusually for an Irishman, had married a Welsh girl in Liverpool while working in a bicycle shop. He had committed a crime in Carlow of which he would not talk and had escaped from justice in a boat sailing from Rosslare. That had been in the early thirties. He had worked for the cause of a united Ireland but now lived calm in Llanelly, where he ran a bicycle shop of his own. He was at least fifty but had kept much of his red hair. This and the pale untannable skin that went with it spoke of high temper more than his words. He rememberd the Irish language but now only read in it, and it sometimes angered him that the Cymric tongue and it had branched away from their common origin. Welsh he could hardly at all understand. He said now:

'History shows it and always will, that liberation is not a thing you can go on your bended knees and ask for. Sure enough, there's plenty of grand talk about human rights from them who are least willing to grant them. To ask for a peaceful transference of rule is to talk through the hats none of you have. You start in violence and you go on the same way. For freedom is a thing you wrest, not ask for, and you're going the wrong way about it all. For have you not already committed violence and in consequence are committed to it?'

'Violence?' Tom Probert asked. He smoked a pipe, more suit-able to a contemplative than a revolutionary. 'Oh, you mean doing violence to property, if money in a bank can be called that. The movement has to be financed, and this way of financing does no harm to anyone. The money we draw from the well is replaced at once from the springs of insurance companies. People may be frightened, but nobody really suffers.'

'But you, Rhys,' MacMahon said, 'said something about an old lady dropping dead of a heart attack in the bank raid in Coleford was it? You're showing guns, which is the means of death, and that's violence too, and there, whether you like it or not, you have a kind of murder on your hands.'

Aled Rhys, who still kept something of his Mediterranean tan, though not on the bald head formerly covered by an army cap, said: 'Our aims have to be known, and that means getting irregular finance to print the pamphlet that Tom here has written and for putting advertisements in the papers. The Irish Republic-ans have done that too in their time. We're an honourable move-ment and we don't like dishonourable tactics, but once the aims are known we'll be honourable enough. Remember that we call ourselves the Sons of Arthur, which is a better title than any the Irish have, and we're resuming the fighting of the battle he never won. We can't kick the Saxons out of England, not yet, not in our time, but we can have a bloody good shot at kicking them out of Cymru.'

'You're mad, you know,' MacMahon said, 'with all your fine talk of honour and dishonour, which are words without meaning. If I was you I'd get back to doing the jobs you have and living the gentle life. For nothing will come of what you dream about. Who wants the English out of Wales? There's been marrying and intermarrying and the Welsh that were on the English throne, the dishonourable Tudors, were as Welsh as you are but they called themselves Saxons. Forget all about it is the good advice of one who knows all about the great struggle against those cunning sons of bitches.'

'But what in God's name,' Ben Griffiths said, 'has been the point of spending millions of money and millions of lives on the business that's just over if it isn't self-determination and the rights of the small nations? There's been revolutions before and a lot of them succeeded.' He was still lean, dark, flashing. 'The French, the Russian, *big* revolutions. We're talking more of devolution. And if that's a dream, then so is the whole of human history.'

'It was always violence,' MacMahon said, headshaking. 'You've got to frighten the occupying power or else just weary it. If you frighten it too much by killing the king or a popular princess it turns against you in a big way. Bombs in post offices and cinemas, the seeing off of a minor statesman – a few years of that and you become a force to be reckoned with at some kind of negotiating table. But what the hell do you Taffs really want? A frontier with passport control from Cardiff up to Rhyl or whatever, sealing the bloody place off while you forge a constitution and elect a president? Welshification of industries which are all international anyway? Get rid of English and install compulsory Welsh?'

'Cymraeg we call it,' Aled Rhys said, 'the other name means foreign. Wales, land of the foreigner. It's the Saxons who are the foreigners.' His sharp Cymric consonants were knives to the dumdum bullets of the Irishman's. 'And speaking the tongue is not all that important, any more than it is in Ireland. Sealing the country off doesn't mean breaking communications. Today's big language is American, which it's permissible to speak with a Cymric accent.'

'The Republic of Cymru speaking Yank,' MacMahon sneered.

'Well now, as for that,' Tom Probert said, 'how can the Sons of Arthur think in terms of a republic? Arthur was a Roman *dux* but also a *rex*. ART REG – you've seen it on those ruins the Luftwaffe kindly revealed not ten miles from here. We think of a Christian king, not a secular president.'

'Oh, bloody nonsense,' MacMahon cried. 'You mean an established United Board, with one kind of Calvinist sticking the knife into another? Talk sense. Government's nothing to do with religion. They tried that in Geneva, and all their predestination meant was clocks and watches. King Arthur, if he existed at all, fought for Roman Christianity against heathen invaders. You want to turn the Welsh into Catholics? You've left it too late, you can't suck the poison of Harry Tudor's Reformation out now.'

'Christian principles, no more,' Tom Probert said. 'Meaning

that we're not Godless communists or equally Godless fascists. And we know it's going to be a long fight. And we think we know that means blood spilt, though not too much.'

'Not any,' Aled Rhys said. 'Or, if any, only in defence of rights. We present the Saxon with what do the French call it a *fait accompli*, and then we see what happens. We say publicly, in press and pamphlet, what we're going to do. Then we do it.'

'And what precisely do you do?' MacMahon asked, grinning. It was the Welsh or Cymric voice he could not take seriously, singing when it was meant to be aggressive, a land of bloody singers, that was what it was, a country of bloody *Eisteddfodau*.

It was Ben Griffiths who answered, taking a deep breath before doing so. 'We have a Prince of Wales already waiting for us. All right, laugh, but it's true.'

'You mean,' MacMahon got in quickly, 'that the king and queen of Great Britain and Northern Ireland have done what Ann and Joachim did in the bloody bible – produced a son against all the laws of genetic bloody possibility? Because that's the only Prince of Wales that's possible, man, eldest son of the British monarch.'

'Listen to me a minute,' Ben Griffiths said, 'and stop that Irish scoffing which is indecent and unnecessary. You can define our Prince of Wales, not theirs that doesn't exist, as the man willing to be elected and crowned. Of pure Cymric stock, so let's talk about the Prince of Cymru, independent and with his own land–'

'And putting money into the organization?' MacMahon grinned. 'So. Where did you find him?'

'He found us,' Aled Rhys said. 'Have you heard of the Cadwallader Steel Mill?'

'All steel's nationalized now,' MacMahon said. 'Or at least a bill's going through when they can decide about compensation. I see. This Cadwallader character gets his money from the socialist state and puts it into Welsh, sorry Cymric, nationalism. Some barmy old bastard who wants a harmless hobby.'

'Not old, not barmy, not a bastard,' Ben Griffiths said. 'The old one died last year. His son inherits. Fully legitimate and only twenty. He missed the war. He wants adventure. Graduate of the University of Wales, Cymru, honours Welsh, Cymric, language and literature. And his first name's Arthur.'

233

'Quite a coincidence.'

'Not really. There's always been a strong strain of devotion to the Cymric past in that family,' Aled Rhys said. 'There had to be, with a name like Cadwallader. I met him on disembarkation leave, if you want to know. In a pub, if you want to know, in Newport. We got talking.'

'I don't doubt,' MacMahon said. 'It's all bloody talk, as you'd be the first to admit if you'd stop dreaming. What do you do – crown him at Carnarvon Castle and say that Wales, Cymru, is now an independent principality like Monaco where Monte Carlo is? I thought you were burbling about something bigger.'

'A principality can be a monarchy,' Tom Probert said. 'The original Arthur was really a duke. A duchy can be a monarchy. In Lancashire they drink to the Duke of Lancaster, who's also the king. The title king would seem pretentious. But he can rightly claim the title, once and future, when he draws the sword from the stone.'

'What sword? What bloody stone? Look, I'm getting out of here,' MacMahon said, though as yet making no move. 'I've met some mad bastards in my time, not excepting in the IRA, one reason why I got out was the frothing at the mouth and there was one occasion when a kid was posting a letter – but never mind. Take up making life miserable for the British, the bastards deserve it, but stop this nonsense about crowning a bloody prince and making him preside over some bloody round table or other. Jesus.'

'We,' Aled Rhys pronounced, 'are the British. The Brythonic Celts. The enemy is the Saxons. You don't know the Cymric language, do you, but the first line of Cymric poetry that's survived is *Gwyr a aeth Gatraeth gan wawr* – the men at arms went to Catterick at dawn – and you know where Catterick is. We propose nothing extravagant. We've no men at arms to attack the Saxons, but we have the right to a free kingdom which for the moment we will call a principality – its true name even to the Saxon swine – and the restoration of the whole island to its rightful possessors can come even in a thousand years. The first Cymric song we know by name is *Unkeynyaet Prydyn*, which is about the monarchy of Britain. That will come again, and perhaps these mad Sons of Arthur you deride will be remembered in some future song that will resound over the Cymric hills and what are now the fat fields of the Saxon.'

'Meanwhile,' MacMahon grinned again, 'you give old women heart attacks when they go to draw out their miserable bits of money.'

'You pluralize unfairly,' Aled Rhys said.

'Orders are not given for any specific mode of appropriation,' Tom Probert said pedantically. 'We have an executive officer, situated where I will not say, who is in charge of an activity admittedly regrettable but certainly necessary. The young men he sends on these missions are not always of the highest moral calibre, but they are under stringent control. They fear the consequences of disobedience or greed. They have their fair cut. They get money before we do. We are not yet even able to pay for the printing of a thousand pamphlets.'

'Which you wrote.'

'Which I wrote.'

'Well,' MacMahon said, looking round at the evidence of minimal finance – the old kitchen with its dusty broken floorboards, the stone sink with its dry tap, a prewar calendar from Jones the Garage, the wobbly filthy table, the Welshmen in their demob suits, 'you've committed yourselves to what the state will call crime, despite your high words and your stern resolve and the rest of the bloody nonsense. And that's Excalibur, is it?' He referred to the crude wooden sword that sat like a mace on the table.

'The *cleddyf*,' Tom Probert said. 'The real *cleddyf* will come. We hear rumours that it is around in the world, though where none knows. But it will come again, like Arthur himself, and will be raised in the cause of righteousness.'

'A load of balls, if I may say so,' MacMahon said.

'You may say so.'

COAT the steak on both sides with salt and pepper. Put butter and oil into heavy iron pan and sear the meat quickly on both sides. Drain fat carefully. Pour cognac over meat and set steak alight. The fire of hell, that was, but there was no hell. Brandy and benedictine soufflé was a favourite of the contralto with the huge bosom, and the benedictine burned merrily, not fair on the

235

Benedictines. They would not burn, they had been great ones for carting things away from the burning. The fillet was a whole one, about two pounds and a half, and it was basted with beef stock and red wine with a teaspoon of sauce diable as they called it, Lea and Perrins really. A Waldorf salad was chopped celery and apples and walnuts in a mayonnaise. None of these fiddling things were on the table at Belshazzar's feast, loaded with roasted Israelites, bare Babylonian concubines sprawling around the feet of the king, thou O king art king of kings O king live for ever. But in that same hour as they feasted. What David Jones held in both weak hands was not an engorged penis he ran away with to Cardiff docks but the family gold. There were a lot of people round him now, some crouching, some upright that he might see up their noseholes. Not all family. Some customers stood with their pints to see the poor bugger snuffing it. No more cough anyway. He called for Beatrix.

'I'm here, dad.'

She was there with him she had married, another Jew, a swarthy Yank with a New York accent, David Jones knew New York accents. The Welsh blood had been mixed with Russian and now would be further mixed with Jewish. Well, there was no harm in it, there might even be good in it, for all mankind was one flesh and all flesh was grass, grass to grass, he could smell the summer grass about him. A thrush sang over and over: *Die nice*. That was funny. There had been a man in Blackwood, a David like himself, but from England, and he had been told he had to be given a nickname and he said he did not mind so long as it was a nice un. And he had been called Dai Niceun.

'Why are you laughing, dad?'

'Dai dies.'

But he did not die yet. He went into a peaceful sleep that the afternoon's heavy rain did not disturb. When Dr Lewis came to see him his hands were quite firm about the gold, but it was not rigor mortis. Dr Lewis felt that it might as well be now as later, so he injected two grains of diacetylmorphine hydrochloride in the wasted left arm. That ought to do for him.

There was quite a crowd round the kitchen table while Mrs Bowen upstairs saw to the laying out. Reg and Dan had carried the corpse to the bed it had not died on. It had defiled nothing except the old army groundsheet. He had gone like a soldier, under easing rain and resumed birdsong. They sat round the table drinking strong tea, all except Irwin Roth, who had just become Beatrix's husband. He asked for coffee and was told sternly by the widow to make it himself out of the bottle of Camp coffee and chicory mixture. He settled for a glass of tepid gin. In the middle of the table sat the gold with all its impurities, not yet, in all those years, refined into an ingot. 'It was a bit of a struggle,' Reg said. 'It was as though he wanted to take it with him into the next world.' Dan said:

'You're not taking it into any bloody world, you thieving sod.'

'This language,' Ludmila Jones said, both hands round her warm tea mug, 'is not good. It is not good at any time, but now is very much not good with your dead father upstairs.' But her eyes were looking at nothing. Irwin Roth said:

'You ought to get that assayed. You have quite a bit of solid cash there.'

'Getting solider and solider all the time,' Beatrix said, 'and not ever to be liquefied if I have anything to do with it.'

'Your mother,' her mother said, 'will decide.' Then she looked from her Jewish son-in-law to her Jewish daughter-in-law and back again.

'That depends on what he says in his will, doesn't it?' Irwin Roth said. 'He may have left instructions about it.'

'You are Jewish,' Ludmila Jones said, 'and you think of money all the time.'

'That's a filthy insult, mother,' Beatrix said. 'You have some very stereotyped ideas about Jews.'

'Let it pass,' Irwin Roth said. 'Money's the last thing I think of.'

'Except by way of the Great American War Novel,' Reg said.

'That's different. If it sold nothing I'd still have to write it.'

'This bastard my brother here had to suffer it first.'

'Who're you calling a bastard, you bastard?'

'We will not have it,' Ludmila Jones said. 'Bastard and bloody and sod. It was your father's last words – what sort of family is it we have brought up, he said.'

'Those were not his last words,' Reg said.

'It was what he was always saying, first and last and always.

If they were not his last words, that was because he was too weak to say last words. Poor man. My poor husband.' Her eyes were dry however and she drank the last of her strong tea like a toast to continued living. Zip then boldly said:

'Why are we all sitting here?' Ludmila Jones said:

'You are Jewish and you do not know why? You are all sitting here to know what my poor husband has left. It is his money you are all after.' There were loud protests, except from Reg, who said:

'Well, my brother here for one would like to know if there's anything for him. He's talked enough about wanting to set up his own fish shop. The rest of us don't care much.'

'Bastard,' Dan blustered, caught out.

'We've done our mourning already,' Reg went on. 'Now's the time for what's called the panegyric, which I take it will not be delivered at the funeral service. Our father used to say that he was a lucky man. He was a survivor. He passed his luck on to us, which he always considered not possible, expecting rather the opposite, but we've all survived. The question is, I suppose, whether we've survived for any special purpose. He died young, but it is not growing like a tree in bulk doth make man better be. What is young, what is old? Can life properly be quantified? He was a good man who did no harm to anyone and his memory will long be honoured. Is there any more I can say? I think not. Amen.'

'The money,' Ludmila Jones said. 'You will want to know so I will tell you. Everything is left to me, whom he called in the will he wrote his dear wife. There will be what Mr Owen the lawyer calls death duties, and these are to be paid to the government. When you die you must pay for dying. That is the law. What is left is for me. Your father said you were *da i ddim*–'

'What?' Irwin Roth asked.

'It means good for nothing,' Beatrix said.

'But he said that Dan must be looked after. So Dan will have his fish shop. Beatrix is married to a Jew, so she needs nothing. Reginald is married to a Jew also but he must work. He has had a good education in Spanish, but he says he will not teach Spanish. Very well, he must do what his father did, which he says he is willing to do. It is a matter of passing the thing on, I have forgotten the word.'

'The licence,' Reg said. 'But the licence passes to the widow.'

'Ah no,' his mother said. 'I will not stay. I am going to Petersburg. My aunt is dead and my uncle Boris is very old. I have done my duty here and here I am not needed. In Petersburg I am.'

There were noises of astonishment. Beatrix's clear voice rose over the babble, saying: 'But it's not St Petersburg any more, mother. It's Leningrad now. There was a revolution, damn it all you were in it, or at least the rehearsal for it. Russia's communist now, it's not a free country. You'll hate it there, nothing to eat, secret police and brutality and death camps.'

'I go just the same. Russia is Russia. But sometimes I will come back to see my children.'

'Once you get in there,' Beatrix said emphatically, 'you'll never get out. They don't like people advertising to the free world what a mess Soviet Russia is. That's what the slaughter of the Yalta victims was all about. The gates are locked and barred.'

'I have my passport. I am British subject.' Reg meanwhile ground his teeth. Then he said:

'Stay out of the bloody place, do you hear? I'm head of the family now, and I'm giving you an order. I'm not allowing my mother to go to hell.'

'Russia is Russia. I am British subject but only because of your father. Now your father is gone and I am Russian again. But I keep my passport.'

'You'll lose it.' Beatrix shook her head fiercely. 'They'll take it away from you. They'll say that you're a Soviet citizen and have no right to a foreign passport. Damn it, I work at the Russian desk. I know what goes on.'

'We bury your poor father and then I go to Cardiff to the Russian consul.' She looked at Reg with her sharp Baltic eyes. 'You do not tell your mother what she will do. I am free woman.'

'You won't be a bloody free woman in the Stalinist utopia.'

'Reginald, I say again that I will not have this bloody and to you, Dan, that I will not have this bastard.'

'What will you do with this precious metal?' Irwin Roth wanted to know. 'You'll get it confiscated when you cross borders.

Nobody's allowed to have gold any more except governments. Lord Byron would go from here to there with gold in a chest, real international currency, but those good days are over. Not only Lord Byron, of course,' he added.

'Yes, that's what the Jews did. Goldberg and Goldstein, I remember such names when I was little in Petersburg. And the same names were in Brooklyn. I do not know what to do with it.' She then began to speak rapidly in Russian. Irwin Roth and Zip were out of it. They kept hearing the word *zolato* and her children kept echoing *zolato*, so they assumed this was gold. Dan then said ferociously:

'What I say is curses on the stuff. Bloody curse the thing that's brought nothing but quarrels and thieving. Throw it in the Usk is what I say.' Irwin Roth, a musical man, listened with interest. That was Alberich cursing the Rhinegold. All myths were fulfilled sooner or later in everyday life. Irwin Roth said:

'I have my contacts still with the US Air Force. We could get it flown over to Europe and converted to cash. Though the best place is Tangiers. They say gold prices are the highest in the world there. Or there's Bombay, but that's too far I guess.'

'And then,' Beatrix said, 'what do you do with the dirhams or rupees or whatever they are? You buy gold with them. What I say is do what was done before. Wrap it up neatly and safely and shove it in a safe deposit.'

'You don't seem to understand money,' her husband said. 'What good is dead metal? It's been sitting on its ass, pardon me, ever since it was mined, or so you told me, and it's done nothing. Gold's the only real money. Spend it.'

'Meaning convert it into unreal money,' Beatrix said.

'Excuse me,' Zip said, whitefaced and getting up quickly.

'What is it?' Reg asked anxiously. 'Is it something we said?'

'The Lady of Shalott,' Zip said at the door leading to the stairs.

'Oh God.' Beatrix also knew what she meant. She made a face at her ohgodding brother.

'Takes time,' she consoled. 'Sometimes a lot of time.'

'Opening time,' her mother said, looking at the clock on the wall. 'People die and yet drinking must go on. It is a law of life.'

'Irwin and I will get to Abergavenny,' Beatrix said, 'and catch the first train in the morning. Then we meet again at the ancestral burial ground. Poor dad. Do what I say with that thing.' She kissed her family. Irwin Roth made gestures of farewell. Dan said to his sister:

'Come out here in the garden.' He grabbed her bare arm fiercely.

'Dear dear, such fraternal urgency.'

Out in the garden near a dead rosebush Dan said: 'What did you go and marry that bugger for?'

'Because I love him, Dan. Because he and I are going to be happy together in the next world, I mean the New World. No hurry about that at the moment. I'm with the Foreign Office for another year or so and he's at Cambridge. But then we go to live in New York and I settle down. Time I settled down.'

'He's no bloody good to you.'

'Jealousy, is it? Unworthy of you, Dan. Not a day will pass without my thinking of you selling fish and knowing that you're my dear brother who I love more than anything in the world.'

'But you said it's that bugger you love.'

'Well, there's love and love, isn't there? Brotherly love and wifely love.'

'And he's such an ugly bugger.'

'Not really. The eye of the beholder and all that nonsense. Don't worry, Dan. I'll always be there when you need me. Not that you'll need me much. You got through the war all right on your own and now you're going to sell fish. If there's any fish to sell. And now we have to get the bus.'

'I don't like you marrying that bugger.'

'There are some things we have to make our own minds up about, Dan. Like you being a fishmonger. Let go of my arm.'

I WENT back to Manchester University in October 1946 to work for my master's degree. I was given grudging permission by my tutor, F. D. Ashley, to write a thesis on an ethical subject – the grounds for supposing that human life was sacrosanct in a world dedicated to taking it. This was disguised as a critique of Schopenhauer's *Ueber die vierfache Wurzel des Satzes vom Zureichenden Gründe* (The Fourfold Root of the Principle of Sufficient Reason), which I pretended to have read in its impossible German. My theme was oldfashioned, I supposed. Philosophy had become less speculation about reality than wrangling about meaning and, especially at Cambridge, metaphysics had been devalued and even derided as profitless idea-spinning. About morality few teachers of philosophy were prepared either to discuss existing systems or proffer new. But at Manchester University the ghost of Samuel Alexander still walked, and his Epstein bust in the Arts Building spoke dumbly, to the lovers who fixed their trysts by it, of point-instants and values. My thesis, as Ashley refused to recognize, had more pertinence to the era of the atom bomb and the disclosure of the truth about the Jewish holocaust than anything that most professional philosophers and, for that matter, theologians were able or willing to present. This was an epoch of evasion, and logical positivism was masterly evasion. What I suggested in my hundred-odd pages was that the sacredness of human life, as opposed to life in general, was derived from the narrowing of idealism to solipsism. The life-preserving mechanism built into the individual (really Schopenhauer's *Wille*) generated so powerful a *Vorstellung* of the importance of his own survival that he was prepared to extrapolate it on to human life in general. But at the same time he was ready, either individually or collectively, to justify manslaughter or war in terms of survival. The intellect worked against the instincts, but the intellect was called upon to justify them. Solipsistically speaking, we know that the only evidence of the existence of the external world is to be found in our experience of it. Transfer that conviction to a world of solipsists, and murder is, in a sense, the snuffing out of oceans and galaxies. The value of human life is the supposed value of the universe, or *Vorstellung*, it experiences. But human life is all too easily brought into being, the irrelevant-seeming offshoot of a spasm that is powered by unconscious engines. Nature is careless both in the spending of seed and the snuffing out of life, and we are children of nature. I recognized even at the time of writing that there was a lot of the Marquis de Sade in my argument. Nature made earthquakes and made men capable of making bombs and gas chambers. The value of life was a kind of Schopenhauerian illusion fostered by the survival mechanism. If we had to live in a world of murder we had to modify our neuroses about it. Experience was what it was and not what it ought to be. There was more of Wittgenstein in that conclusion than I realized.

I read with some amusement one morning in my Rusholme lodgings (over my fortnightly breakfast egg: there was a plethora of people in the world, all murderable, but not yet much food) about the crowning of the Prince of Wales on the Arthurian site in Gilwern. The ceremony was taken as a harmless joke by both the *Times* and the *Daily Mail*. There was in the latter a photograph of the prince, Arthur Cadwallader, grinning rather stupidly under a stage coronet. Not many had turned up for the event, which had taken place under rain, as was to be expected in South Wales. Words had been spoken in both Welsh and English about an independent Cymru, and every good Cymro and Cymraes, making up the totality of the nation known as the Cymry, was to help to initiate the resurgence of an ancient patriotism by disobeying the laws of the English. This, I thought, would not be difficult: the Welsh had never been good at understanding, much less obeying, the enactments of government either local or national. Taxes, the prince said, must not be paid. Cymric reservoirs must not be permitted to feed water to Gloucestershire. The *Daily Mirror* thought it a fine joke that a Welsh patriotic poem had been recited by the Russian landlady of a local pub. I fancied I saw, in the background of the photograph of the crowned prince, Reg Jones hunched in a raincoat. The Jones family then, including my sister Zip, were, if not involved, at least in contact with the Sons of Arthur. I finished my breakfast and was ready for the delivery of the mail. My mind moved to the independence of another territory. My father wrote from Tel Aviv:

The Hill of the Spring, or of Spring, I'm not sure which, this being what Tel Aviv means, has come on surprisingly since we last saw it – you, of course, wouldn't remember. Jaffa still looks like the Middle East, but Tel Aviv is very much modern Europe, no doubt about it. Your mother and I are busily nuzzling all the oranges that aren't exported and are nicely situated in this apartment, part of the annexe to the King Solomon Hotel, overlooking the kaduregel field (football to you), while we look around for a little place of our own in the garden suburb part of the town. Rents are damnably high, as we expected. It looks as though I shan't be retiring after all. The Tel Aviv Lighter Port, built as you know because of now historic trouble about the use of the port facilities at Jaffa, is to be expanded and I am to be in on the costing report, thanks to a Mr Weingartner whom you may remember – he was at Trafford Park and came to tea once or twice. I can't say the life is altogether peaceful, what with the Stern Gang that hates the British more than the Arabs and, of course, the Arabs themselves, who are scared of the forthcoming Jewish home-land and are throwing bombs and cutting throats as an earnest of what they will do when the state of Israel officially exists. Your mother and I don't go out much at night and are circum-spect during the day. We think more about our British-based loved ones than ourselves. Perhaps when you've got your MA you might consider trying for whatever vacancy may exist in the university here. The Israelis will need to be philosophical and I take back all I used to say about the uselessness of pure thought. We not only think a good deal about your sister but worry about her. I don't think that marriage is working, but I'm not going to be stupid about it and say she shouldn't have married a goy. I know that Reg had a bad time in the war, two wars to be accurate, and that excuses his erratic behaviour and occasional nastiness, but the whole way of life he's imposing on poor Zipporah isn't what we could approve. She's trained as a musician and has a very expensive lot of musical instruments gathering dust and rust in a Manchester depository, and that costs money, but she's being made to live the life of a sort of barmaid in a godforsaken part of Wales. And there seem to be rows about his or her fertility, as though the begetting of a child were a test of something or other. Israel is going to need babies, but Britain, what with the break-up of the Empire and the liberated colonials preferring to emigrate to the home of the old oppressor rather than face the threat of independent oppression, is not likely to be a demographical desert in the future we all face. Your mother sends fondest love. Her bronchs are much better in this warm dry air. And I send mine. Do write sometime soon. Dad.

That was in the April of 1947. In May I had to argue over my thesis with visiting examiners – Dr Schwarzkopf, Professor Ridgway, Mr Stockwell, an Arab whose name I never caught, and an undoubted Welsh Kantian called Griffith-Jones. They did not like the thesis. It was less of a critique of Schopenhauer than a sly attempt to preach subversive and highly inhumane doctrine. There, of course, I agreed, but this did me little good. My written papers, it seemed, were satisfactory, though Dr Griffith-Jones said that I had an imperfect grasp of the Kantian categories. The Arab was surprised that I knew nothing of Islamic Aristotelianism. Dr Schwarzkopf, whose blackheaded nose the May sun suddenly shone on, droned something about Hegel's *Gründlinien der Philosophie des Rechts*, and then Dr Griffith-Jones began to distinguish between Hegel and Hegelianism, meaning Kant, Fichte and Schelling, and I was out of a hot argument conducted in German German and Welsh German. I might as well have crept off, unnoticed. When Dr Schwarzkopf, very good-humoured after his defeat of Dr Griffith-Jones on a point of interpretation of something in the *Phänomenologie des Geistes*, beamed on me as a sort of nodding ally, I knew that I had probably got my MA. It was time to start looking at the hind pages of the *Times Educational Supplement*.

These pages contained notices of vacancies in schools and colleges, some of them in Wales, where the heading NO CANVASSING meant the opposite of what it said. Though I had no local influence, I applied for the post of junior lecturer in philosophy at the Coleg or College of St Asaaf (really Asaph, though it could also have been Assa or Asa) in Aberdare. It was a theological college but my being a Jew would not, I thought, in South Wales go against me. I applied for other posts as well, but the only interview that came up was at Aberdare. It was pretty clear to me that the vacancy had already been filled and that the applications of non-canvassing candidates were being considered only in a spirit of fair play, meaning its opposite. My interviewers wre the principal of the college, a local councillor, a housewife with a shopping bag, and the bishop of the see of Llanelwy (appropriately, since St Asaph had been its first incumbent). The councillor asked me if I had my matric, and I told him I had gone much further than that. The bishop wanted to know what I meant by philosophy and was satisfied when I said the love of wisdom. The principal showed off his knowledge of the categories of logic, which he said was very important in theological studies. Then I was asked what I knew of theological studies. Nothing, I replied, being an agnostic Jew. My people had suffered, the housewife said, and then I was permitted to leave. A Mr Davies, who was not present, got the job.

At least the College of St Asaaf had paid my return fare from Manchester, thus subsidizing a trip to Gilwern to see my sister. I got there after afternoon closing time on a foul June day, found the back door open and saw Reg and Zip at the kitchen table gloomily picking at a pie. They looked up at me without surprise. It was as though I had just walked in from a lecture to take coffee in the university cafeteria. Zip even asked me if I wanted coffee. I was offered nothing to eat. I said I had come from Aberdare. 'Staying, are you?' Reg said, with no overtone of welcome. He was in shirtsleeves, quite the publican. Zip, in a stained flowery working frock, already had the rosy look of a countrywoman, though the faint frown lines above her eyes bespoke no country contentment. Reg's eyes were curiously unfocused.

'So you're running this on your own,' I said. 'Sorry about your father, a good bewildered man. And your mother's departure, Zip wrote about it, seems to say the least of it eccentric.'

'Nostalgia,' Reg said. '*Hiraith*. But she's keeping a hold on her capitalist shekels. The Gosbank welcomes her sterling.' He looked at me without pleasure. 'An academic,' he said. 'Heartiest congratulations.'

'An innkeeper,' I said. 'Reciprocal felicitations. It's a noble trade. You ever read Fothergill? His publican's diary was a bestseller. An innkeeper's wife,' I added, trying the term out on Zip like a hairstyle. It didn't fit. She said:

'A musician. I'm going back to it. Nature never intended me to be a – ' I thought she was going to say wife. 'Mother,' she said.

'Banging and tinkling,' Reg near-snarled. 'Coming home when she feels like it. I never thought it would be like that.'

'Tell me,' I said to Zip.

'Nothing to do with when I feel like it. When I'm not working. I'm entitled to practise my art.'

'Crashing and thumping and. An art, yes, an art.'

'Its the Orchestra of the South West,' Zip told me. 'Full of refugees and prisoners-of-war who decided to stay on. Grants from what they now call the Arts Council. Potatoes and bread are rationed, but the nation can always fill up on music. Etheridge asked me to be the percussion section.'

'Etheridge?'

'Jack Etheridge, second oboe of the Hallé. When he had the accident to his lip he set up as a conductor. A Bristol man, I thought you'd met him.'

'Well,' I said. 'I suppose this is good news. Although Reg doesn't seem to think so.'

'Nothing goes right,' Reg said. 'I thought we could settle down. The days when people could settle down seem to be over.'

'Meaning we're all DPs?' I said.

'Displaced persons, you could say that.'

'Reg's heart is in holy Russia,' Zip said.

'Shut up about holy Russia,' Reg said loudly. 'She's dead anyway.'

'Your mother?' I said, shocked, stupidly.

'No,' Zip said. 'The girlfriend he took on when I was supposed to have let him down. A letter from the bereaved husband sent care of the Foreign Ministry thanking him for his kindness.'

'I'll get the bastard yet.' Reg jabbed his fork into the unclothed kitchen table.

'The husband?' I asked.

'The lot of them. The filthy murdering swine.'

'Oh my God,' I said. 'It's all over.'

'Ah, no, it's not. It's not bloody well all over by a long bloody chalk.'

'If you'd like me to help serve in the bar or tap barrels or something,' I said, 'I'm ready. For a bit, anyway. I'm still applying for jobs. I take it I can get the *Times Educational Supplement* in Abergavenny. How's the rest of the family?'

'Dan,' Zip said, 'has his own little fish shop in Netherbury.'

'Where's that?'

'Somewhere or other. It sounds a vague sort of place. And the beauteous Beatrix is still in the Foreign Office sleeping with her literary husband at weekends. What you might call placed persons.'

'Beatrix,' I said somewhat bitterly.

'I know, I know,' Zip said quickly. Then: 'I'm going to Cardiff tomorrow. The orchestra gets together. My thumping and tinkling instruments should be arriving in a plain van. Reg objects to shelling out. To hell with Reg, I say,' but not unsweetly.

'We're living off practically nothing,' Reg complained plaintively. 'I thought I'd get something out of dad's death, but all I get is the licence and the premises of a free house, meaning,' he said to me as to one who knew nothing of pubs, 'untied to a brewery. And there's hardly any beer coming from the breweries, and the allotments of spirits are ridiculous, and the only profit lies in the sandwiches.'

'Which I make,' Zip said, 'though not for much longer. But there are plenty of would-be drinkers and fulfillable sandwich munchers coming in after viewing the Arthurian site. Americans too. Americans mostly.'

'For this,' Reg said, 'I studied Spanish and Catalan.'

'It's up to you,' I said. 'Nobody's forcing you.'

'The desire to be out of it all forced me. The desire for a return to innocence. And now my mother writes to say she's seen the sword.' The connection was unclear. 'In the Ermitage in Leningrad. On exhibition there with other loot they got out of East Germany. Dan was right and dad's encyclopeadia was right and that book by my namesake was right. Somebody in Leningrad says it's the sword of Attila, with an A on it to prove it, miraculously – no, not miraculously, they don't believe in miracles any more, the godless bastards, preserved anyway. Deconsecrated. The sword of the Hun.'

'This sounds like madness,' I said.

'You can talk of madness after all we've been through? If the world comes to an end tomorrow with their godless atom blasting will you still talk about madness? It's all bloody madness which is taken as sanity.'

'How,' I asked, 'is your mother finding things in godless Russia?'

'She daren't say too much. Letters are censored. Look,' he said to Zip, 'I'm going upstairs to lie down. Unburden your suffering soul to your dear brother here.' And he shuffled out in carpet slippers like an old man. Then I kissed my sister almost guiltily in belated greeting.

'It's not been good then.'

'We tried to have a baby,' Zip said, 'but it didn't work. I sort of eject. Then he says that my kettledrums and tubular bells are my babies. He's right in a way. You can't have it both ways, not really. I feel a bit unhappy about leaving him alone. But I don't think he'll be here much longer. There's a grammar school in Bridgend that wants a Spanish teacher. The Welsh seem to like Spanish.'

'So he won't be here and you won't be here. Does that mean you're splitting up?'

'I don't know, I honestly don't know. I don't think so somehow. We've got to make a go of it, haven't we? He went through a lot of pain, you know, over me. I didn't do any suffering. And know I'm going to have sticks in my hands again and start counting two hundred bars rest.'

'You know, I've never really understood the difference in status between a timpanist and a percussion player. Won't it be a bit of a comedown?'

'Well, the timpanist is there all the time, and Jack Etheridge got hold of a very good refugee Jew, Apfelbaum, who got out of Dresden when they started aryanizing German music, bloody fools and criminals. You only have percussion for modern stuff. Which means I'll be back on the circuit – called on by other outfits when they decide to do *Ein Heldenleben* or Benjamin Britten or something, but there'll be a kind of contract with this South West lot and I'll be substitute timpanist when this Apfelbaum character's doing something else. It's the way things work nowadays. There's not much money in it.'

'A way of augmenting the family income.'

'You could call it that. Reg will start getting on about this gold that's sitting in the bank under his mother's name before the evening's out. It's become a kind of obsession with him. Every morning he looks at the gold prices in the newspaper and does calculations. A packet, he says, and it's doing nothing.'

'Poor Reg.'

'Well, yes, that's the way I feel about him.'

That evening I drew beer and counted change. There were not many customers. It was a dull life for Reg and Zip, I could see that. Old men drank a single pint apiece, making it last. Local farmboys played darts. How dull people were, really. Spatter them out of existence with a brengun and they wouldn't be missed. And yet the law of nature seemed to be that the dull should survive and the talented be starved or slaughtered. I thought of the talent liquidated at Auschwitz. The desire of the dull to go on being dull was confirmed when a couple, strangers to the landlord and landlady, came in and asked, with the expectation of not getting them because none here knew what they were, dry martinis. They were a pair, man and wife or man and mistress, who looked as though they might have done well out of the war, city-dwellers travelling from somewhere to somewhere and amused to be calling in at a pub in a village whose name they did not know and did not care to know, they would not be calling again, where the landlord knew what a dry martini was. They had a prosperous smell, and the man was plump and purplish around the nose, the woman was pale and asthenic. When they asked for more martinis, Reg had to tell them that there was no more gin. The man said:

'One of the things that those with long noses have a corner in.'

'Meaning the Jews?' Reg said politely. 'Well, here are three Jews who have a corner in nothing. But if you're not out and round the corner in three seconds flat, sir and madam, your delicate Aryan noses will be flat, and that's flat. Go on, bugger off.' This, perhaps, was no way to run a pub. The regular customers heard a voice raised against antisemitism and welcomed the small excitement, but they also looked reproachfully at Reg. No way to run a pub. I said at closing time, while we were washing glasses:

'Three of us, eh?' Reg said:

'Solidarity. I might as well be a Jew as anything else. I know I don't qualify, being prepuced and unbarmitzvahed, but what are the Jews anyway? A people driven into diaspora as the Welsh were driven into the mountains, deprived of a homeland. Suffering and put upon.'

'The Jews will be getting their homeland soon,' I said, 'not

that I want any part of it. I don't define myself by race or nation.'
Then I remembered. 'Was that your picture I saw in the newspaper photograph when they had this nonsense about crowning
a bogus Prince of Wales?'

'Mother and I put up a kind of refreshment stall for the
occasion. Bottled beer against the law, not that the law matters
much here anyway, and fishpaste sandwiches and welshcakes
baked by Mrs Evans. You call it nonsense, but you wouldn't call
the Jewish homeland nonsense. If the English are those sods
who were in this evening, get the bloody English out.'

'You mean that? You've joined the party?'

'The party?' Reg was amused, meaning he sneered. 'Look at
that.' There was a copy of that day's *Western Mail* behind the
counter, very wet, and opened at a quarter-page advertisement
which said, under the prancing dragon, 'CYMRU is our country.
A comely country, Cymru. It is not Wales, which means the land
of the foreigner in the Saxon tongue. Fight for a free Cymru,
under its own rulers. Refuse to obey English laws or pay English
taxes. Strike against the invader. Fight for the rights of Cymru.'
It was signed Arthur, Prince of Cyrmu. I said:

'Oh my God. This is comic.'

'Well,' Reg said, with a new thoughtfulness, sightlessly wiping
a pint glass, 'I suppose the claims of small nations like the Welsh
and the Basques and the Catalonians must always seem comic
to the founders of empires. But it's hopeless. They can't prevail.
The only good thing about Welsh, sorry Cymric, nationalism is
that it gives the English the odd kick in the pants. Complacent
lot of bastards. Murderers too.'

'If you're thinking of the victims of Yalta – '

'I am, among other things.'

'The common people weren't to blame. They never are. If the
Welsh nationalists want to burn an English fish and chip shop –
yes, I read about that in the *Daily Mirror* – they're missing the
whole point. The big enemy's always government. And if you
ever got self-government here, which you won't, it would have
the same face as the louts in Westminster.'

'It would have a Cymric face.'

'So you *are* on their side.'

'I'm on nobody's side.' He wiped the lady's martini glass,

having had some trouble with a kind of veronica of lipstick, spat in it viciously, then washed it again. 'I just feel there's something I have to do.' I thought he meant kill, so I said:

'You've done your killing.'

'Yes, and it was surprisingly easy.'

'And it did no good.'

'Oh yes, it did a lot of good. And you know who I did it for.' He looked in the direction of Zip, who had helped with the wiping, but she had already gone silently to bed.

I stayed for not much more than a week, sleeping in the bed which had formerly been Beatrix's. There still seemed to be a faint odour of her undressed presence in the room and this produced one or two painful engorgements. I saw little of my sister. She had gone to Cardiff to assist at the rehearsals for the first concert to be held in the City Hall there by the new orchestra, staying, so she said, with a second violinist who had a flat just outside Cathays Park. The orchestra, so I gathered, had already given concerts and even some broadcasts in its primary or classical form – that is to say, apt for Mozart and Beethoven and Brahms, but not yet ready for works which called for cymbals and glockenspiels. A concert without a chorus would never draw the Welsh, so the Glamorgan Choral Society was to sing Vaughan Williams's *Towards the Unknown Region* and Parry's *Blest Pair of Sirens*. It was an orchestra raised in the South West, but it proclaimed the new internationalism of refugee Europeans. It was to be at home in Kodaly's *Hary Janos* suite (plenty of percussion there) but puzzled by Sir Edward German's *Welsh Rhapsody*.

Reg was not easy to stay with. I paid for my keep by helping in the bar and cutting doorstep sandwiches of spam and snoek, the latter heavily parsleyed and seasoned with malt vinegar. But I wandered the fields and country roads outside opening hours, marvelling at the useless leafy wealth of the sycamores, sick of fecundity like Roquentin. I visited the Arthurian site and one day was overwhelmed by a party of Americans snapping away at the stone scabbard plinth, doing their touristic duty. They were not happy with Britain: too much rain and everything rationed; they looked forward to getting to Paris. Dull, dull, *überall* dull. And then a little Welshman appeared, it seemed, from nowhere, leaped down lightly to the hollow where the Celto-Roman ruins lay and addressed the Americans, saying:

'I speak for free Cymru, which you would call Wales, and call on America to help us in our struggle to be liberated from the English. You struggled too and won in your war for independence.' The four syllables carried equal stress, in the Welsh manner, and sounded like something ill-learnt from a lexicon, carrying no harmonies of real life liberty. 'It is your money we want and also your carrying of the word of our struggle among the sons of the free. Daughters too, of course. Every little will help and earn our thanks with the fine old words *diolch yn fawr*. And I am asked to tell you that the very name of your country is a Welsh name, for the name America comes from the Welsh ap Meuric, which means the son of Maurice, and Richard Amerik was the heaviest investor in John Cabot's second voyage to the New World in 1498.' That was news to me as to the Americans, some of whom muttered, 'Well, what do you know,' meaning no question. What sounded like a hard fact, date and all, impelled some of them to dig into their hip pockets and unpeel the stage money of pound notes, which the eager little Welshman collected. I asked him, putting in my own two halfcrowns, where he had got that historical information from, and he said 'That would be telling.' I did not for one moment think that he represented the Arthurian brotherhood: a university student probably gathering easy cash for highly material ends. Who could take the nationalist movement seriously?

The men who did take it seriously I met the night before leaving. Reg had locked the door of the public bar, and he and I were starting to wash glasses when there came a great thundering and shouting, as of someone very tight. Reg swore, 'Christ Jesus, them again,' and opened to men he knew well from his dour nodding. They were, as I found out, his old army comrades from Gibraltar, and with them was a mad-eyed young man who was quick to introduce himself. He was quite drunk. He cried: 'Bow to your lawful prince and to bloody hell with the licensing laws of the Saeson. I spy strangers,' meaning myself. 'Out, friend, for this is a lawful congregation or synod of the sons of the soil, and you clearly are no Cymro.' Then he cried: '*Rhyfel, rhyfel,*' going behind the bar without Reg's invitation and shakily drawing himself a pint of weak Welsh bitter ale. His three companions were sober enough. *Rhyfel*, I learned later, is Welsh for war. Reg said:

'This is my brother-in-law, and these are my premises. If there is ordering out to be done, then I do it. Drink up that pint, your bloody highness, put your English money on the counter, and then be kind enough to bugger off.'

The bald man of the three old comrades sat heavily to the left of the dartboard and said: 'We are on our way to Tredegar, and this is meant to be a friendly visit. You are being very frivolous, but then you always were. There is a thing that only you can do, and we ask you again to do it.'

'Bloody nonsense,' Reg said and, to me: 'You'd better go off to bed. As his bloody highness says, this is Welsh business.'

'Less of the bloody,' the Prince of Cymru said. He raised his pint and cried: 'Death to the stranger in our midst and the dragon flag flying over our lovely land.' Then he drank thirstily, spilling half. I went out of the bar and up to bed, whence I heard loud undistinguishable words below and the undoubted smashing of glass. Welsh nonsense. Next morning, our breakfast of tea and fried bread was a silent meal until I asked Reg what it had all been about. He affirmed that it was Welsh nonsense. He then said:

'Alone alone alone. I shall call on little Megan.'

'Who's little Megan, besides being evidently a Welsh girl of small size?

'She's in the village, looking after her *modryb* or aunt. I can't pay her much, but I'll only need her in the evenings.' I said:

'I wasn't greatly impressed by your Prince of Cymru.'

'Part of the nonsense. A figurehead and easily disposable. I get the idea that he's going to be a fabricated martyr when they get his money from him. It's a bloody big game for the lad. Remember our assassinated *dux* and arraign the dirty murdering English in the court of the world. That's the part that isn't in his game. If you don't drink that tea a bit jildy you'll miss the bus.'

And so I went back to Manchester for the posting of my achieved MA and the resumption of looking for work. I found it as a physical training instructor in one of the new emergency colleges which, owing to Britain's expanding population and a shortage of teachers in the primary schools, were training men and women released from the armed forces who considered that they had a teaching vocation. I was permitted to run also a subsidiary course in the history of Western philosophy, not that the authorities considered it to be more than a cultural frippery. What was the good of Aristotle in a primary school? In my interview with the principal and a couple from His Majesty's Inspectorate, I suggested that the puzzlement of children at the great unfolding world was a philosophical puzzlement and that, anyway, the educators should themselves be educated. That I had no civilian qualifications in physical training at first was against me, but my MA mysteriously put that right. I would, when not wearing a tracksuit, be wearing a master's gown, while most of my colleagues would be enrobed by courtesy of a five-pound fee to a teachers' organization. So there it was.

I lived in a tiny flat attached to a students' sleeping block and ate my meals free in the dining hall. The college, formerly an American army camp, was not far from Bolton and Bolton was thirty miles from Netherbury. There Daniel Tetlow Jones had his fish shop. I took a rugger team to play against a works fifteen from near Preston and, after our game on the Netherbury ground, we all went sweatily to a pub to down pints and be rough males together. There alone at the bar stood Dan. The other customers kept their distance from him, and I could smell why. Dan reeked of old fish. Fish was sewn into his skin as well as into a striped apron stained with thin blood and exiguous guts. Dan did not recognize me, and painfully and slowly I had to relate our previous meetings and even our marital relationship. I asked how his sister was. He said:

'She married this ugly Yank and he's in one place and she's in another. Working for the Russians or against the Russians because she knows Russian. I talk Russian too.'

'That I knew and know.' A thin grinning man in a dirty raincoat came in, greeting and greeted as the pub clown, and he performed a brief comic turn of being asphyxiated by the smell of Dan. Dan muttered something about his being a bloody *shoot*. I addressed my student team and the nearer customers as well, saying: 'The smell of fish is good and holy. It was a stinking fish that Tobias in the Apocrypha used to drive out the demon

Asmodaeus. Jesus Christ is a fish.' The landlord muttered something about no talk of religion in *his* pub. Dan finished the pint
I had bought him and left with no valediction. Not all there, not
at all all there. A toad that worshipped a princess, vision from
the upper atmosphere. A weird family all round.

For six years British citizens had been shipped out to the far
places of the world against their will. The time had returned for
seeking permission to travel, which meant paying the government for permission to flash its own property, namely a passport
from Petty France. A dark moustached Jew looked with no
pleasure at the immigration officials from the proffered tough-
bound document at Boulogne. A dark moustached Jew, all too
lifesized and three-dimensional, smiled at the prospect of wine,
Gauloises, *coq au vin*, a temporary refugee from British austerity.
Returning, slightly fatter, having spent the meagre foreign allowance permitted, I was glad I had that passport. A cable had
arrived at the college the day after the start of my holiday:
MOTHERS CONDITION GRAVE COME FATHER. Exchange
control would not come into it: I would still be in the sterling
area. I had to wangle a cash advance from the bursar, dash down
to London, and see how most quickly to get to Tel Aviv.

ONE way was by BOAC to Cairo, then by train to Haifa, but my
travel informants in London were unsure about this last segment
of the journey, since the line had been mined, with heavy loss
of lives among the departing British garrison, by terrorists north
of Rehovoth. I was advised to fly to Cyprus, via Paris, Rome and
Athens, and see what sea transport was available from Larnaca
or Famagusta. The turboprop, of modified bomber design, had
both Turkish and Greek Cypriots aboard, the latter in the
majority. One lot sang wearisomely and defiantly at the other,
keravnos bouncing against *gök gürlemesi*, and lightnings of
contempt and hate jagging from black eyes in that clear upper
air. But a Turkish Romeo and a Greek Juliet, in each other's arms
when not smoking or eating, gave silent witness to the stupidity
of cultural hate. My mother, my mother. Well now, how well
did I know, how much had I seen of, what was the extent of my
love for, my mother? I drank thirstily of the tepid tea offered,
but I could not eat the shives of dead meat on a skewer. The

stewardess, a decent Home Counties girl with an accent to match, was unhappy among these clucking and whistling brownskins, but her protective rooster, a thicknecked chief steward with a naval air, hit out at dirty fingers offering to engage the girl's skirt or bosom. My mother, my mother. I hammered feeling into my heart with the masturbatory rhythm of the word. What condition and how grave? While the aircraft, three times refuelled, was flying over the Bay of Antalya, after a journey that had begun at dawn and was ending after a blinding sunset, most passengers slept noisily, but they came alive and boisterous when the descent began over the whelkshaped island. There was frank punching as they retrieved their parcels and cardboard suitcases from the racks, and there was even a genuine fight on the tarmac. It was a moonless night, and airport police shone torches at the belligerents. War war war, *Harb. Polemos.* Also *rhyfel*, to say nothing of *milchamah.* Unfortunate Hebrew word, suggesting a nurse and nursling. There was war in Palestine.

I stayed the night in a filthy hotel in Nicosia, though its smells were modified by the breeze that stirred the lemon trees in a garden yowling with cats. I could not sleep because of nightlong song, dance and the smashing of plates below. In the cool dawn, the day already rubbing its hands at the prospect of generating terrifying heat, after thick sweet Greek or Turkish coffee and a chunk of unleavened bread with apricot jam, I caught a bus for Famagusta. This was full of bitter blackshawled women and ancient men who spat brown juice, also caged poultry and a magisterial grey gander that patrolled the aisle. A Greek steamer called the *Avrio* was loading pig iron and grain for Beirut. I was welcome, for an excessive fare in sterling, to a place on the deck among dark and dirty people who dug pale dirty *gögüs* or *stithos* or possibly *tsadye* out of foodbags and slit it to accommodate a kind of anchovy paste that was highly redolent even in the sea breeze. I had melting chocolate and two oranges. When I showed my passport at Beirut the immigration officer spat and pointed vaguely towards where the railway station might be. I took an unwashed train to Acre and then Haifa. Among these dirty brown people the only true civilization had developed among local gods; these were then forsaken and the abstract ones took over to the shame of the Middle Sea. The bus to Tel Aviv was civilized though very hot. Some of the passengers were in decent Western suits and read Hebrew newspapers. A young man puzzled over a little German book. One woman spoke to her daughter in Yiddish and promised her a *gefroirenes* or *glidah* when they got to Tel Aviv. But the girl wailed when she saw no ice-cream stall near the bus stop.

My father's apartment was in the commercial sector of the town, far from citrus groves. It was on the third floor of a new and ugly block with uncarpeted concrete stairs and it was damnably stuffy. The furniture was what I remembered from England – apt for the chill north but not for the eastern Mediterranean in late July. That was one of the bizarre aspects of the new homeland – too many Ashkenazim importing plush comfort, unaware that Israel was a climate and not just an idea. In this land the Bedouin were at home, while the Jews went *oy oy* at the heat. My father wore heavy serge trousers that were loose at the waist but otherwise only a striped dirty shirt that hung out at the back. Then to my shock I saw he wore also a *yarmulke*, all the way from *yagmurluk*, a Turkish raincoat, through a Ukrainian and Polish secular cap. It seemed, as I spoke the first words about my mother, to sum up all the wretched wandering of our century. 'She was already dead,' he said, 'when I sent that cable. One blow at a time. You took long enough about getting here.' I explained. 'No,' he said. 'It wasn't an illness. It was a bloody bomb. She was a daughter of Israel, and she had a right to visit the Holy City. Violation of the truce and where were the famous forces of the United bloody Nations?'

'Did you send a cable to Zipporah?'

'No, I did not. I didn't want her miscarrying again. And I don't want her here, no place for a woman. As far as she's concerned her mother's still alive, and swear now on your dead mother's head that you won't disabuse her. When I think it's time for her mother to be dead I'll let her know. It's one way of keeping her alive even though she's not. Poor bloody victim.'

'All over then,' I said. 'The funeral and everything?'

'Of course it's all over. Done according to the rites of the orthodoxy that rules this secular state. *Kaddish* and all. Hear ye, bloody Israel. You want to see her grave? Tomorrow. The heat here is malignant to corpses. She was already far gone in decay when they identified her from her handbag, clutched so tight they could hardly loosen it. Of course, it's all over. And the president himself present at the burial, remembering an old Manchester friendship with your grandfather. So you'll think it's been a journey in vain. You'll know different.'

I did not understand. 'You don't look well, and no wonder. Have you been eating at all?'

'Eating? In a country where we're bloody eaten? And eaten alive too. I'm drinking, though. Not whisky, nobody can afford that. *Arak*, a word you can find in the bloody Koran which forbids it. The bastards will get me sooner or later, but I'll get one of them first. *Araq* means sweat. They'll sweat all right, they'll sweat bloody blood.'

I had been standing on the ridiculous thick carpet. I sat now at the round polished table. My mother had been working at one of her ornamental inscriptions: the letters of one of her facetious little poems had been lightly pencilled in on the parchment, a spirit for the incarnation of indian ink. It must, I thought, dry up quickly in this climate, but then I accepted that in her regard it had dried up for ever. I wished, for my father's sake, my eyes were not dry. I read the faintness:

The orange hangs for our delight,
A golden lamp in a green night,
Adam's china apple. Eve
Knows bitterness you'd not believe
In Jaffa and in Tel Aviv.

'Poor poor mother,' I said. 'The poor damned doomed Jews.'

'We're not doomed and we're not damned. This is the land that was promised.'

'In exchange for a new method of blowing up innocents. There's nothing for you here, dad. You'd better come home with me.'

'You might at least weep, damn you, and beat your skull against the wall as I did. She was your mother, she brought you into the world, nurtured you and loved you, and you sit there being bloody cynical.'

'Yes,' I said, and I lighted a Gold Flake. 'She brought me into the world and nurtured me, and then we were left like orphans. Not your fault, I know, you went where the work was. But if I weep it's for you I'll weep. You'd better come home with me.'

'This is home. And I don't want your bloody tears. I'll make out.'

'We'd better go out and eat something somewhere.'

'You come here and you hear the worst news in the world, and all you want to do is eat.'

'The Homeric heroes wept for their dead comrades, then they ate, then they wept again.'

'Don't give me that bloody schoolroom nonsense.'

'You can say that here? This is classical country.'

'A modern country being born in bloodshed. No heroes, only victims. But there'll be heroes yet. Give me one of those.' He meant a Gold Flake. He puffed heavily, sighed, looked at me. 'You did well in the war, didn't you?'

'Well, in the sense that I emerged unscathed. Badly, in the sense that I was no hero. But I helped to train the heroes.'

'Have you tried this bloody stuff?' He meant the arak he brought out of the cupboard of mahogany I well remembered.

'No, and I don't want to.'

'Very well.' He sipped straight from the bottle. The label was in English, Hebrew and Arabic. He shuddered. 'Bloody awful stuff, you're right.' He looked at me with more affection. 'Well, I've brought you all the way here. You're looking well, lad. The glowing fitness of one who's never struck a blow in anger or otherwise. There's some men who want to have a word with you.'

'Impossible. I know nobody here.'

'What kind of a contract do you have at that place where you are?'

'Why do you ask?'

'What kind of a contract?'

'It's an emergency college, meaning the contract runs out with the emergency scheme. No permanency. It's a place where you read the *Times Ed Supp* in the staffroom and look for permanencies. Why, is somebody offering me the post of professor of philosophy somewhere?'

'I said that in a letter, didn't I? The Jews needing philosophy or something of the sort. No, it's not philosophy that anybody has in mind. You're right. We'd better eat something. No sense in bloody starving. I hope you won't mind eating kosher.'

'No blood in a land of blood. That thing you're wearing, *yarmulke* or something, does it mean what I think it means?'

'Pronounce the r more. Yes, it means precisely that. How do you define a Jew except by his religion? We've been corrupted. Diaspora, scattering our seed abroad.'

'That sounds like the sin of Onan.'

'You can say that too. Come on, there's this little place round the corner. It's not much good, but it's kosher.'

Windows of groundfloor apartments were open for the sunset heat, and music from Kol Israel fought urgent Hebrew news from Kol Hierushalayim. It was a noisy street in a noisy city. The restaurant was called the Dvorah, and a huge smiling multi-coloured bee had been painted on to the otherwise whitewashed shop-style window. Inside there was a rage of noise, and little children howled at being force-fed. Well, it was life going on, which was what my father needed. He greeted the proprietor, a man who looked like an unfrocked Jesuit, with a sad *schalom*. Then we ate black olives and bland overboiled chicken with watery spinach, finishing with sugared orange slices and coffee obligatory black. 'I've never understood the dietary laws,' I said. 'Why can't I have my coffee white?'

'It's to do with seething a calf in its mother's milk,' my father said.

'I've never seen that.'

'It all makes sense in time. You'll learn that when you've been here a month or two.'

'But I'm not staying.'

'Tomorrow you talk with these people. They're waiting for you. They know all about you.'

'How, for God or Jehovah's sake?'

'*El*, we say *El* here for God. I'll tell you. There was a man to do with security who turned up with Chaim Weizmann at the funeral –' He paused to drink down sad mucus. 'We got talking about where the family was from and your name came up. This man thought he knew you but he'd make sure by looking at the files. You'd be amazed what they have on the files here. Do

261

you remember doing some training during the war under some civilians?'

'Oh God, it's them. Was there talk of Aleph and Beth and Ghimel?'

'The Hebrew alphabet never came into it. I'm to give them a call now you're here. I'll do that first thing tomorrow. Do you know what they, we, call tomorrow here? Well, it's *machar*. That's a good strong word for you. It sounds like a call to arms and a tough future.'

'Am I being called to arms? Because it's not a call I'm inclined to listen to. I've had enough war. You get on with it on your own. I won't see them.'

'You'll see them all right. A matter of courtesy apart from anything else. No obligation, true, but you'd better think of your poor mother. Poor little girl. Let's have some more coffee.'

'I don't like it black. Is there some kosher arrangement which turns it white without offending the Book of Leviticus or whatever it is?'

'No jokes, please. You can have it white in the morning. I'll make it for you. I've become used to getting my own *aruchat boker*.' Then he cried to the ceiling, or to *El*: 'Curse the bastards,' and, to the orange skins on his plate: 'Poor lass. She did no harm to anybody.' There was no embarrassment in the Dvorah either at his malediction or at his sobs: this was a place of public lamentation where there was even a book about it. We went back to what my father called home. I leaped up the concrete stairs and he limped sadly up after me, using the iron banister as a crutch. Panting, he showed me to a room as small and airless as a broom closet. There was a truckle bed and a single thin blanket, like an earnest of military austerity to come. I opened the window to its limit and heard from across the street the unintelligible harangues of Kol Hierushalayim. I slept soundly, as though protected by belligerent Jehovah.

The following morning, after the promised white coffee and a stale honey cake, my father took me to see my mother's grave. It was in a very small cemetery within the noise of the city, not far from the Tel Aviv bureau of the *Palestine Post*. I was not surprised to see the inscription in Hebrew. Beloved wife of was buried beneath the curved strokes, lettering of the lamb's fleece.

A dried bunch of sweet william rested on the stone, from yesterday my father said. He sobbed and then said briskly: 'Your appointment's now. I phoned while you were still snoring, do you have adenoids, we start work early here.'

'Where?'

'At home. They can have some of my arak or coffee or something. I want to sit in.'

'Providing the odd moral exhortation from a grieved widower?'

'That's not funny and it's not nice. I have a father's rights.'

The three men who came on the stroke of ten were recognizably Aleph, Beth and Ghimel, but they had become Mediterraneanized since my last sight of them. In England they had been gloomy Kafka figures in cheap black; here they were in flannel slacks, sandals, and snowy shirts open to show black hair bristling on the sternum. Aleph, or it may have been Ghimel, greeted me with '*Schalom*, sergeant major.'

'Good morning, gentlemen. You behold a civilian and a master of arts.'

'Congratulations,' Beth said. The accent had changed from Central European to a kind of Israeli posh. I seemed to remember bad teeth on this one, but he was now fully dentured. Palestine, I knew, produced dentures in great grinning numbers, along with tombac and heisheh, whatever they were. 'Tell us what you think you know.'

'Of what?'

'Of the brief history of your country.'

'England's my country.' My father shook his head sadly and produced the arak bottle. All shook their heads, though not sadly. My father shuffled off to make coffee. 'All right. Of Israel I know little. I know that it is a secular Zionist state that was officially born the day after the end of the British mandate in 1948. May the something. Then the United Nations said that Palestine was to be divided into eight or nine segments, was it? But the Jews started infiltrating everywhere they shouldn't. All Galilee, all the Negeb – '

'Not quite all,' Aleph drawled like a don. 'East as far as the Gulf of Akaba.'

'I do know,' I said boldly. 'that there's well over half a million Arab refugees. They ran away in panic after the massacre of

263

somewhere or other by some organization or other helped by the Stern Gang. And that Arab villages have been forcibly cleared to make room for Zionist immigrants.'

'Not bad,' Beth said. 'Six hundred thousand is nearer the true figure. The massacre was at Deir Yasin near Jerusalem, and the organization you refer to is the Irgun Zwi Leumi.'

This was a little too much like my *viva voce* at Manchester. 'I'm not here to get a degree or a job,' I said. 'Like everybody else in England I pick up what I can from the newspapers.'

'Which are mostly antizionist,' Beth said. Aleph said:

'I detect a note of pity in your voice for the Arabs. The Arabs killed your mother, remember that. The Arabs never accepted the Balfour Declaration and no Arab country has so far accepted the *de jure* or *de facto* establishment of the state of Israel. But, illogical as always, they do accept that the Jews living in their territories are now foreigners, to be thrown out and their property confiscated, or even to be more brutally persecuted. Make no mistake about it, the Arabs are the enemy.'

'That's already been made very clear,' I said. 'Small farmers and their families are the enemy. An Arab kid tumbling in the dust of Israel is the enemy. I suppose it's a little too soon to expect the setting up of extermination camps.' My father, coming in with a coffee pot and cups, wailed and shook his head as if to dislodge it from its scrawny stem. Beth said:

'Don't go too far. Israel is doing all it can for its native Arabic population. In Jaffa you'll even find an Arabic daily newspaper published by Jews. *El Yom*. Arabic is to be taught in our schools. But the Arab states have vowed destruction of the state of Israel and we have our answer to that. Or will have.' They all looked at me, as though I were the answer. Aleph said:

'You have studied philosophy, or so your father says.'

'I'm still studying it.'

'There are two German philosophers whom I have studied closely. One is Kant, who distinguished between the phenomenon and the noumenon. The noumenon, or *Ding an Sich*, or thing in itself, is the reality, but we can approach reality only through phenomena.'

'I know all about that. What's it to do with killing Arabs? I get uneasy when philosophy is made to smell of gunsmoke.'

'Good. Think now of Hegel, who taught that reality, even divinity, rested in the state. The phenomena we pursue in affirming the state are nothing like the noumena, or so we assume. The killing of a child playing in the dust is a phenomenon qualitatively different from the preservation of the state, but state preservation deals in such phenomena.'

'That's pure Hitlerism,' I said.

'We take it that Hitler read no philosophy, nor did he have the kind of brain capable of understanding it. He had other qualities, though.' Surely that faint smirk was not one of grudging admiration? 'Some of his intellectual followers dealt in such metaphysical justifications, however, for the extermination of our people. The great thing is, if possible, not to see what is done. What I am trying to say is that we must be philosophical and not sentimental.'

My father now nodded, pouring coffee, and said: 'I told him that. Israel needs philosophy.'

'True, true, very true,' Ghimel sang, then said: 'But she needs a well-trained fighting force first.' The labiodentals spat on to the dusty air of the little salon. He turned eagerly to me and said: 'You don't know the Israeli military strength. Men, women too, about a hundred thousand all told with more to come. East European trained, Hungarian chiefly. If you can call it training. Still, trained well enough to drive the Egyptians out. I refer to El Haganah, equipped mostly from Czechoslovakia. But we don't look to Eastern Europe any more, how could we when it's in the grip of a godless and antisemitic empire? Antisemitism goes back a long way. It wasn't invented by the Nazis.'

'I always suspected that,' I said. They all looked sadly at my sarcasm, sipping *kavah* to which a little *chalav* had been added. Aleph put down his cup, good English bone china, and said:

'The name has been mentioned already, but I mention it again. The Irgun Zwi Leumi. Add to that the Stern Gang and you have a kind of preemptive strike force. The Stern Gang will soon be proscribed, however, genuinely a lot of gangsters who will kill anyone, anyone. What you learned when we were involved in your training was that battles are wasteful. Israel can't afford waste. You have to decapitate the millipede, not pull off its feet one by one. Strike behind the lines. Terrorize the enemy in the

265

person of its leaders. Assassinate. Don't laugh at the slaying of the Egyptian firstborn or the plagues or the snipping off of the power supply.' I was not inclined to laugh. 'The bible is not a bad military manual.'

'This is merely a nationalist expansion of what you said when the other war was on.'

'Yes, when you were being trained to train others in ungentlemanly killing techniques. You have a chance to resume that training, after having been first retrained yourself, to the same end of the survival of our people.'

'More than your, our, people were involved in the old days.'

'Very true,' Beth said. 'The issue is much cleaner now. The survival of one nation. We have good boys, good girls, prickly pears as well as pale-skinned immigrants.'

'I don't understand the prickly pear bit.'

My father was glad to explain that. '*Sabra* means a Jew born here. It comes from *saber*, correct me if I'm wrong, gentlemen, meaning the thing in question.' Unimpeachable Hebrew etymology, Beth's nod said. I said:

'You want me to be concerned with terrorism?' They smiled: the term had not yet gained a totally bad name. 'Filling the enemy with terror, throwing Molotov cocktails into Cairo cafés, sending letter bombs to Islamic leaders, that sort of thing.'

'Oh, we're not so simple-minded as we were,' Aleph said comfortably, also ambiguously. 'The post offered, I'm in order in saying I think, carries the rank of full captaincy with the possibility of rapid promotion to major on the basis of a renewable three-year contract. You can sign today if you wish.'

'I'm signing nothing,' I said. 'You've been trying to trap me into the spirit of vendetta,' I told my father. 'I want a bit of peace in my life.' Aleph, Beth and Ghimel made the *moues* proper to an obscene word. My father wailed to a small brown scorpion that had just emerged from behind the heavy mahogany bookcase.

CHWECH

NOW, I think, we come at last to it. The scene, anyway, is Leningrad, where Ludmila Jones was very surprised to open the door of the apartment at 32 Ulitsa Mizinchikova to her son Reginald. She said: *'Ya nye ponimaiu.'*

'But I wrote,' Reg said, 'from home, and I sent a postcard from Moscow.'

'I got nothing.' Her English had almost disappeared.

'Soviet Russia is efficient only in its techniques of liquidation.'

'Be careful what you say,' his mother said. 'You do not know who may be listening.' There was an old bent man on the landing a floor below in a collarless shirt and a near buttonless waistcoat. He bore a widenecked jug and he gawped up toothlessly at the smart stranger. Reg went in and his mother closed the door. So this was it. This was domestic Soviet Russia. A small square sitting room with a window looking on the Fontanka Canal, not at this season of the year frozen. A rocking chair from the prerevolutionary time. A table of more recent manufacture with flimsy legs and a coarse flowery runner. On the floor two rugs of a sick pink colour. A door led to a miniature corridor off which a doorless kitchen gave and two closed, presumably, bedroom doors. Reg, smellless, sadly thought that there must be here the immemorial reek of old cabbage, aniseed, and stale papirosi. But not for him, not any more. It was like reading Russian in translation. An old man's hopeless cough rang loud, and Ludmila Jones called for dyadya Boris. A door opened and the owner of the cough shambled out in worn English pyjamas covered by a raincoat serving as a dressing gown. So this was great-uncle Boris, who said:

'Bore da. Ydych chi wedi codi eto? Ydw.'

'Oh my God,' Reg said.

'I teach uncle Boris Welsh. It is something for him to do.'

'Oh my God.' Great-uncle Boris was as old as God and looked like him, all dirty grey staring hair and patriarchal filthy beard, though stained with a human artefact, Soviet tobacco tar. He sat in the rocking chair and rocked, looking benignly on his great-nephew. He said:

'*Rydw i'n edrych yn well, on'd ydw i?*'

'*Ydych, yn wir,*' his niece said. 'Reginald does not speak Welsh. You must speak Russian to him.'

'He is like his photograph,' the old man said. 'Where are the other children?'

'How,' Ludmila asked, 'are the other children?'

'Dan,' Reg said, 'is busy trying to sell fish, and Beatrix is still with the Foreign Office. You do not ask how it is I happen to be here.' Then he kissed his mother, her surprise at seeing him not having previously permitted the gesture.

'Sit, sit,' Ludmila said. 'What did you bring?'

'Twining's English Breakfast,' and Reg pulled the square tin out of a pocket of the raincoat he had put down on one of the table chairs.

'Good English tea, uncle. We shall have some good English tea.'

'He wears,' the old man said, 'good English clothes.'

'Very moderate,' Reg said. 'Off the peg at Marks and Spencer's.'

'Marx? What is this of Marx?' Reg sat and said:

'I am here on what is known as a cultural exchange. We have had the Moscow Dynamos showing us how to play football and the Bolshoi showing us how to dance. Now I come with the Orchestra of the South West and a choral society from Glamorganshire. They are not considered to be of the highest artistic standard, which is in order, since Soviet Russia's sense of its artistic superiority to the West must not be impaired. I come as husband of one of the instrumentalists and also as interpreter. There was a performance in the Grand Hall of the Moscow Conservatory, at which Comrade Stalin was present. Here there is to be a performance in the Leningrad Concert Hall.'

'Comrade Stalin,' the old man said reverently. 'Comrade Stalin spoke to you?'

'He spoke to all of us. He said *Muzika massam* and turned down the thumb of his left hand. Meaning that he did not consider our music to be music for the masses. He said however that the chief percussionist was very pretty and banged the bells in *Kartinki s Vistavki* very nicely. You know, of course, mother, to whom he referred.'

'The Jew girl your wife. Where is she now?'

'She is sleeping in our room in the Astoria Hotel. It was a rather tiring journey from Moscow.'

'And how is Beatrix with her Jew man?'

'I don't like this antisemitism, mother. Your coming back to your native land seems to have exacerbated it. And how do you like being back in your native land?'

Ludmila was about to go into the kitchen to make tea. She stood, as plump as in wellfed Wales but maturely beautiful, her shapely feet in old slippers, her greygold hair sloppily back-knotted, her body in a loose sack of faded royal or revolutionary blue with a pattern of little daisies, holding aloft the tin of tea from Mincing Lane. She said: 'You will not understand. It is home.'

'Enough to eat?'

'It will be better. There was never enough to eat.'

'You don't miss us?'

'I hope that Dan is all right. You other two are *da i ddim* as your poor father used to say.'

'We miss you.'

'I must look after uncle Boris.' She went into the kitchen. The old man said:

'Ah well, she is a good girl. I have not long to go now.'

'Those papirosi will do you no good.' The old man had taken a crumpled pack of Troika from the raincoat pocket and lit up with a kitchen match struck off a horny thumbnail. He coughed and said:

'They bring up the phlegm. Better up than down, as they say.'

'We hear rumours that cigarettes are killing our king,'

'It is a slower way than the revolutionary way. If they are

killing me too it is no matter. I have lived through history. We
ate black beetles during the siege. I have survived.'

'Too many have not survived,'

'They gave their blood. She will remarry.'

'I beg your pardon?'

'Your mother will remarry. She is not old. She sees this man
Gregor. He is a widower as she is a widow. He is the head cook
at the Metropol.'

'Another cook. Very lowly. Most unambitious. And yet you
have a great man in the family.'

'There are no great men any more. That was what the revolution was about, getting rid of the great men. You mean Yurochka. We do not see much of Yurochka. He is a very busy man
in Moscow.' Reg did not tell him that Yura Petrovich Shulgin
was at that moment in Leningrad but would not be there much
longer, nor, for that matter, in the Soviet Union much longer.
There were things going on that he would not confide to his
mother either, who now came in with the samovar and a plate
of stony zephyrs of her own baking. Glasses in tarnished *zarfim*
were already on the table. 'God bless you, little flower,' the old
man said.

When Beatrix Jones went to Gilwern to see her brother Reg,
she was wearing dark glasses, though the sun was a rare visitant
in South Wales, especially in late winter. She was also limping
slightly. Otherwise she was shapely, upright and elegant in a
powder-blue suit with bronze stockings and a white mink coat
that had been bought with a substantial money gift from her
father-in-law to her husband, the father-in-law believing that his
son had married not a *shiksa* but a daughter of the elected race.
It was three-thirty in the afternoon, and she found Reg at the
kitchen table reading *Don Quixote* in the original Castilian. A girl
was washing the lunch dishes and singing 'Jealous heart, O
jealous heart stop beating'. Reg said to his sister: 'Has he been
at it again?'

'He got as good as he gave, better really. The swelling's nearly
gone.' She took off her dark glasses to show, then put them
back on again. 'He's very tense and nervy and aggressive. He's
finished his novel and he's not sure if it's any good. I told him
to send it off anyway.'

270

'The bastard. *Is* it any good?'

'It's certainly long. One thousand two hundred pages of type-
script. We had a fight over the title. I tried to convince him that
Crying to Heaven was too pretentious. I succeeded after he'd
broken the coffee pot. Coffee doesn't do him any good, makes
him very jumpy. The final title, mine really, is *Baptize the
Innocents*.'

'Not very Jewish.'

'Call it the semifinal title. American publishers are fussy about
titles. I insisted on a dedication to Daniel Tetlow Jones.'

'That's only right, the thieving swine.'

The girl, plump and streaky blonde, swayed her hips as she
hummed 'If I'd have known you were coming I'd have baked a
cake'. She was taking it all in. She even, in her pert Welsh way,
made a comment: 'It's the way some men are.'

'Thank you, Megan,' Reg said. 'I'm sure your aunt's crying
out for you. See you at five.'

She ogled Reg, saying: 'Two's company. Okay, be seeing you
then.'

'This, Megan, is my sister, Mrs Roth.'

'Oh, sister, is it?' She appraised Beatrix's clothes and said:
'There's posh that coat is. A pretty penny it must have cost then.'

'Thank you, Megan.' And Megan, hipswinging, left, reprising
'Jealous Heart'.

'Any funny business going on there?' Beatrix asked.

'Zip is kind or discreet enough to telephone to say when she's
coming home. A kind of reminder of what I should have done
that time. No, no real funny business.'

'This,' Beatrix said, 'is not altogether, what's the term, a sororal
visit. Would your whisky ration run to a small one? No soda.'

'Rationed only by price now,' Reg said, rising. He came back
from the bar with a bottle of Johnnie Walker and two glasses,
saying: 'I don't know why you go on living with him, I suppose
he brings out a latent masochism' while she was saying: 'At least
Zip is doing the kind of thing she wants to do, it must be pretty
dull for a woman living here.' Then they said sorry to each other
and Reg allowed Beatrix to state why this was not really a sororal
call. Reg said:

'Are you implying that the Orchestra of the South West is one of Britain's mediocrities?'

'Ah, you want to defend it because you're married to its percussion. Let's say that it's new and raw and has an undistinguished conductor. That's not my opinion, I know nothing about music, but it's the view of Mallory of the Arts Council. A rather complicated chain of government departments is involved in this cultural exchange, but the Foreign Office has to be in on it. You're to go along as interpreter. They won't want to let you interpret, but they have to be shown that they're not the only ones who know Russian.'

'Me?' Reg said. 'Impossible. I'll be thrown out as soon as I arrive. I won't even be able to get a visa. Besides, I've this pub to run.'

'You thought of giving it up.'

'I did, yes. But one look at the interviewing boards was enough. Well, three looks. And I could foresee myself clouting kids and being sued for assault. Everybody's equal nowadays, including kids. I'm better off as I am. Landlord is a proud title when you come to think of it. As for Russia, I might start clouting Russians. My customers are used to my bad temper now. They even like it. It makes their evening.'

'You have to go,' Beatrix said. 'You remember Yura Shulgin? The patronymic is Petrovich.'

'Our sort of cousin. Ah, it comes clear now. He's in the Soviet Ministry of Culture. His idea is it, this cultural nonsense?'

'Naturally. But not primarily for cultural reasons.' She said more. Reg said:

'How do you know he does? And if he does why does he?'

'I know he does because of the code. It started as a joke, during the war. I said to him, sort of laughingly, that if ever he wanted to get out all he had to do was write a friendly letter with the word *petrushka* in it three times. When I got his first letter going on about parsley I thought he was just reviving a silly joke. Then I got another letter with parsley in it four times. Something about I didn't take seriously the importance of parsley, but parsley was not just a good garnishing herb but was actually good for the health. It grows well in the Moscow area because of the rich moist loam. Try parsley with fish, we swear by it here. Try parsley in vodka. And he even ended up by mentioning *carum petroselinum.*'

'What's the Latin name for parsley?' Reg quoted. 'Now I know.'

'What's the Greek name for swine's snout?'

'All this is absurd.'

'*Petrushka,*' Reg's mother said, pouring strong black Twining's from the samovar. 'The silly girl thought it was a piece of music.'

Reg started. He had not been mentioning parsley, only thinking it.

'His chief retires next year,' Beatrix had said. 'A certain Marya Ivanovna Shvernika. A formidable lady, I gather, sister of Shvernik in the Politburo. When she leaves she leaves him unprotected. He's scared of Stalin, and no wonder. He committed the gross error of being posted to the wicked West. It ought to be easy to absorb him into a Welsh choir.'

Reg's mother sipped strong black tea with a spoonful of gooseberry jam in it. Her Russian lips were strong and shapely. The old man slurped and coughed. Reg said: 'Shall I bring her to see you then?'

'Your Jew girl? She speaks no Russian. I do not understand English much any more. Nor Hebrew.'

'She speaks no Hebrew. You haven't approved of either of our marriages, have you?'

'You will always do what you wish to do. I say nothing and I do nothing. I am at home now, looking after uncle Boris.'

'You're to come to the concert tomorrow night. Both of you.'

'Uncle Boris does not go out in the evenings. The night air is not good for his chest. And who is looking after the place now that you are here?'

'Why should you worry? A girl called Megan and a lady named Gwen who used to work in the Angel in Abergavenny but gave up her job after fighting off the advances of the landlord. Everything will be all right there, not that you care any more.'

'It is all over. But your father was a good man.'

'Did I ever deny it? When may I have the privilege of hearing about a Russian stepfather?'

'I told him of Gregor,' the old man wheezed.

'He does not cook as well as your father did. But he cooks for the people. I have uncle Boris to look after.'

273

'Not for long, little rose of the world. You must go tomorrow to hear the music that has come all the way from Angliya. And Gregor can go with you.'

Reg looked at his wristwatch. Three-thirty of a Leningrad spring afternoon. 'I'm glad to see you well and happy, mother,' he said. 'I have things to do here. It is no holiday for me.'

'Thank you for the English tea,' his mother said.

Reg had an appointment with Yura Petrovich Shulgin on Nevsky Prospect under the third of the *yabloki elektricheskikh svetov* from the north end. Light apples, the work of Pavel Nikolaevich Yablochkov, *yablochko* being a little apple. He found Yura Petrovich pacing away from him; when he turned, in a grey suit well-worn but well-cut, made in London, he was not sure whether he recognized Reg until Reg gave him a jaunty mock salute which could not have been Russian. Reg knew him; he also had his photograph in his pocket. Yura Petrovich's cheeks were redder, more applelike than back in 1945; it was as though the Ministry of Culture in Moscow was a collective farm. He did not look harassed. The hat he wore, of Russian manufacture, was well down and almost touching his ears, a badge, so the spy films taught, of powerful officialdom. His blue eyes, the eyes of Reg's mother, drank deep of the Neva. He shook hands with Reg very firmly, saying 'There are a lot of people here, but it will not matter.' True, Leningraders, men in dowdy suits with dirty shirts open at the neck, girls in skimpy frocks and frizzed hair, were taking the spring afternoon air by their river. 'We too will walk up and down.'

'Tit for tat,' Reg said as they began their patrol. 'Have you seen anything of our defecting diplomats?'

'It has nothing to do with my department.'

'When Beatrix told me everything,' Reg said, 'I was surprised that you were able to wait so long. I got the impression that you were in some kind of immediate danger.'

'Do not talk so loud. You were told everything of the situation?'

'About the protective power of Madame Shvernika, yes. You'll forgive me if I display a certain scepticism.'

Yura Petrovich stopped his patrol and looked Reg full in the eyes. 'I don't think I well understand.'

'This isn't my business, and frankly I don't give a damn, but

I should think that even the British Foreign Office has to consider the possibility of this being a put-up job. You know, disinformation and so on.'

'I'm not in the espionage business, if that's what you mean.'

'Never mind. I have here in my pocket a British passport made out in the name of B. R. Lawrence. That's a private joke between my sister and me. A poem by Browning called 'Soliloquy of the Spanish Cloister'. Never mind. There was already a passport-sized photograph at the Foreign Office. Dating from the war. You haven't changed much.'

'You're thinner.'

'It's your bloody Stalinist tyranny that's made me thinner. I saw what happened at Odessa.'

'It's been a bad time for a long time. He's getting old. He won't last much longer. He'll collapse with a heart attack cracking his whip. He'd kill the whole world if he could.'

'Not that, surely. He needs his angels of destruction.'

'Can you give me the passport now?'

'Wouldn't that be dangerous? Surely we're both being watched? See that keen-eyed man there in the filthy raincoat?'

'Perhaps you're right. I'm showing my innocence.'

'Forgive me again for exhibiting scepticism. You couldn't have arranged this better. An orchestra and choir takes over the whole of the MS *Saltykov*. A member of the choir, forgetting the Continental rule of the road, got knocked over by an official Zis in Moscow. If anybody's counting at Leningrad docks there'll be a perfect tally. You're going to get to Tilbury with no trouble at all.'

'I'm leaving the ship at Helsinki. I'll ask for asylum at the British Embassy there. Remember it's a Soviet ship.'

'Speak softer.'

'Nobody's listening.'

'Now then,' Reg said, 'I'm doing something for you, so you have to do something for me. I want a certain object removed from the Ermitage and delivered into my hands.'

Yura Petrovich looked for at least ten seconds, eyes very blue and mouth showing Soviet dentistry, at the evident seriousness of Reg. A young strolling couple giggled. A sophisticated-looking elderly man with an hidalgo look nodded gravely, divining that an unacceptable sexual proposal had been made. 'You can't mean this.'

'Oh can't I just. The Soviet state has on exhibition an object of immense historical value which it filched from the dying Third Reich, the Third Reich in its turn having wrested it from the custodianship of the order of the Benedictines. That object belongs to Britain.'

'You have been asked by your government to commit a crime against the Soviet Union?'

'It's you who'll be committing the crime, am I not right? The Britain I refer to is a country that no longer exists. This is a perhaps romantic act of restitution I'm performing off my own bat.'

'You're mad. Theft of state property means instant death.'

'What do you or I care about the state? There's such a thing as a justice which transcends the trivial expediencies of politics. You and I will be leaving the Soviet Union with the object in question safely stowed among a bundle of percussion instruments. Naive inspectors might even be persuaded that it is itself a percussion instrument. It once struck down enemies.'

'I could do with a drink,' Yura Petrovich muttered. 'You're referring to the sword of Attila.'

'A sword with an A on it, certainly. With a wooden scabbard. It's still on exhibition, as you must know as well as I. I saw it this morning, quite early. As soon as I'd stiffly detrained. You have to tramp three or four versts to get to the exhibition of war loot, past the Fabergé eggs and the Impressionists. But there it is. You, as an official of the Ministry of Culture, boldly present your card and a typed letter on Ministry paper and announce to the curator that there are certain objects which have to be transferred to Moscow. Because of an urgency which you're not at liberty to explain, you are taking something with you now. Giving a receipt, naturally.'

'I think I have to sit down.'

'Generalissimo Stalin and the great and villainous Lavrenti Pavlovich Beria will be very angry, of course. But only angry with me. For back in England I shall take on all the responsibility, leaving you out of it. We don't want issues to be confused. You're not a thief, you're only a traitor. Sorry, I mean a defector.'

'I refuse to help.'

'Interesting. Loyalty? Fear? Both? This makes your proposed defection look highly suspect, doesn't it? Not that I give a damn. All I do is throw this forged passport into the Neva.'

'When?'

'Better. The day we depart. The *Saltykov* leaves at eighteen hundred hours. After lunch should give us time enough.'

'I had not expected that things would be this way.'

'No, I'm sure not. Everything has to be paid for, though. Freedom is the least free thing in the world. This was sometime a paradox, but the times give it proof.'

'*Ya nye ponimaiu.*'

REG AND ZIP had a large comfortless room in the Astoria, with wall lamps that could be turned off only by loosening the bulbs in their sockets, a telephone that discoursed what sounded like a manic diatribe but would not otherwise function, and a lumpy double bed with thin pillows and thread naked sheets. The white nights of St Petersburg were beginning and the window had no blind or shutters. They slept ill, and the brief sleep that Reg had was broken by his wife's thumping his ribs. 'You were speaking Russian,' she said. 'You were calling somebody's name too. It sounded like Maria.'

'Was I? Did I? I didn't know.'

'I can't sleep. Give me a cigarette. I feel, you know, surrounded by foreigners, hostile ones.'

'That's not really true, is it? Yaawwww. Warthog. War. Warsaw. Three hundred members of a Welsh choir and a ninety-piece orchestra. You're blanketed by friends.'

'I could do with a real blanket. It gets cold here at night. You were calling the name of that girl. Will the war ever really be over?'

Reg had given her a cigarette and taken one himself. He puffed out of a foultasting mouth. 'I've got heartburn. Four hours waiting for dinner and then it's uneatable.' And then 'I met a man in Moscow named Pyotr Lavretyevich Sokolov. Once of Sverdlovsk. Now in the electrical works of the capital. He came to see me after the concert.'

'Well?'

'He said that Marya Ivanovna had died of natural causes in the hard winter of 1947. That's probably why she was on my sleeping mind. He said she'd been directed to work as a medical officer in a prison camp near Yarensk. She died of influenza. He said he saw the medical report and the certificate of death.'

'Well?'

'I don't believe him. Or rather I don't believe what he believes. A thin little man with mended spectacles. I wonder what she ever saw in him.'

'How did he know you were who you are?'

'My name on the programme – but of course you can't read Cyrillic. Here we are bringing culture to the swine. They got her all right.'

'It's not the people, it's never the people. It's time you forgot about her.'

'I did and I will again. It's just that someone I knew, was fond of – it was never infidelity to you really, being fond of a person. That they could do that, are still doing it. Are we just nothing, are we just all wipable out?'

'Harry sees no reason why we're not. He wrote his thesis about it. And now he's teaching Israelis to wipe out Arabs.'

'I dreamed one night that it was you. We can't be blamed for dreaming what we dream. It's another self that does the dreaming. We have too many selves. No wonder we're scared of sleep sometimes. Another self taking over. History is all about the other selves. Not the selves that eat and make love and play music. Oh God kindly deliver us from our other selves.'

Zip knew him well by now. She forgave him a good deal. She went: 'War. Warthog. We're rehearsing at ten. The Russians have very tinny brass. Brass bands to left and right of the orchestra. We should have brought our own.'

'We filled up four BOAC Britannias as it was. I'm going to say a few words.'

'I know. That's what you're here for.' And then: 'Oh God, you mean more than just saying who we are and what we're playing? Don't. They'll put you in the Lubianka or somewhere.'

'They ought to know what the music's really about. The writing on the wall.' He cheered up, blindly doused his cigarette on the floor, then took her in his arms. He paused to quote: ' "And in that same hour as they feasted".'

'Stop it. I must get some sleep. I'll look like all hell in the morning.'

'No you won't. You never do. I think this is the moment.'

'What do you mean?'

'One just has a feeling sometimes when the moment comes.'

They were sleeping too heavily when the knocks came at the door. Reg woke to a dream meaning and grasped his naked wife protectively; she opened wide dark brown eyes to the morning, puzzled as to where she was. 'They won't get either of us,' he said. 'Lie still. Say nothing. Pretend we're not here.' But a very Glamorgan voice, that of one of the sopranos, called for Mr Jones. He zigzagged to the door with the one sheet round him and put out his relieved head. There were three girls there, angry at a bad breakfast of weak tea and stale blood sausage. They wanted Reg to complain to the management.

LENINGRAD had fine architecture. They had hoped to be performing in what was still called the building of the Assembly of the Nobility, with a façade by Rossi, but the Leningrad Concert Hall, home of the Philharmonic, held more and had better acoustics. Reg waited at the head of the entrance steps as the audience, in its bits and pieces, came out of the spring drizzle. These Leningraders were atrociously dressed but they seemed eager, harmless, even amiable. It was, as she had said, never the people, but the people were disposable. Reg's mother arrived, smarter than the other women because she had been dressed by the West, along with a squat middle-aged man in a tout's cap. He embraced Reg as a proleptic stepson, and Reg felt no remorse for what he proposed to do while the orchestra was playing *Kartinki s Vistavki* or *Pictures from an Exhibition*, a piano suite by Mussorgsky orchestrated by Ravel. 'He hopes,' his mother said, 'that they will play sweet tunes.'

'*Muzika massam.*' This head cook, Gregor, was pleased to hear that. There was nothing of Reg's father about him save the smell of tired oil, the anxious eyes of one who watches many pots, and the small imperiousness of a man in charge. Reg let them find their seats and then strode with his own small imperiousness

279

down the central aisle. The chorus would not appear until after the interval, but the orchestra was already in place, skirling and blasting and waiting for its A. Reg mounted the side steps and waved cheerily up over the fiddles and wind at Zip, lovely in deepcut black; she answered his greeting with a rimshot on the sidedrum. Orchestra of the South West indeed: displaced Ashkenazim mostly with the odd unsuffering guiltless Anglo-Saxon, rosy farmers' lads among the tragic, haunted and bumptious. Reg took a seat by the conductor's rostrum, feeling, in his not new lounge suit, like a workers's representative among all these tailcoats, many of them rusty. The timpani far behind him gave out G G G E flat, a promise of victory, and the bass trombone, played by a Pomeranian dwarf, farted a pedal note. Soviet Russia sat all before him, filling the hall to its corners. He knew his RSM voice would carry. A slung microphone high above him would carry his words even further, for the concert was being broadcast. Meir Gillon, the principal first violin, came on to no applause and, to the oboe's A, sawed fifths which the other fiddles echoed. Then Jack Etheridge marched smiling uncertainly to his dais, clapped with the reservations of suspicious Russians who would crack the nut of appreciation between their horny palms only when they had heard what he could do. And now Reg stood and spoke. 'Comrades, fellow citizens of a world both free and unfree, this is an orchestra built in Great Britain out of the orphans of the Hitlerian storm and others born in a kind of liberty. They begin with a tribute to a London long dead, that of an era when that great city was the centre of a capitalist empire recently dismantled by our ruling socialists. It is called the *Cockaigne* Overture, Cockaigne being an imaginary land of idleness and luxury. *Kokenje* is the Middle Low German for a small cake. Out of small cakes the houses of the land were feigned to be built. The term is close to *cockney* but is not cognate. Cockney is the name given to the London working class, but cockney means a cock's egg, implying mysteriously a certain scorn of the capital's proletariat.' Etheridge looked doubtfully down through his spectacles that drank of the platform's light: Reg had not in Moscow spoken at such length. 'The *Cockaigne* Overture, by Sir Edward Elgar.' Then Etheridge poised his baton, jerked an upbeat, and made the violins speak the low G and A of their

280

anacrusis. The audience meanwhile wondered audibly what a cock's egg was. After that they listened patiently to royal splendour, a distant Salvation Army band with that pretty whitearmed girl up there's tambourine, and the clashing glory of the city. They applauded doubtfully, wondering perhaps why capitalistic music should seem appropriate enough for some triumph in Red Square. Then Reg stood and said: 'The quiet section in the middle represents Karl Marx brooding over surplus value in the British Museum.' Then he told them that here was Mussorgsky orchestrated by Ravel. He got off the platform before the first trumpet, in B flat major, started the *Promenade*.

There was a taxi rank at the front of the Concert Hall, but he had to join a queue in continuing drizzle. It was a good fifteen minutes before he was able to order the driver, who was in deep depression, to take him to 32 Ulitsa Mizinchikova. Heavily smoking and wreathed in blue melancholia, the driver said he was willing to wait five minutes. But it took a good three minutes for great-uncle Boris to come to the door. He had a novel of Gorky's in his hand; he had been reading it in bed. A matter of some urgency, Reg explained, also a secret: he was leaving an object of some value in his mother's bedroom but she was not to know of it until he, Reg, left tomorrow. He would put it in a drawer if she had a drawer. The old man coughnodded and said something of the greatness of Gorky. Reg's mother's bedroom was pitiably small and functional: her little chest of drawers was a structure of unseasoned wood and nails. The top drawer contained relics of Manchester and South Wales, photographs and documents tied with knitting wool. Reg found what he wanted, embraced great-uncle Boris, who smelt dreadfully, in goodbye, and found the driver still waiting though complaining that he had come to the end of his papirosi. Back at the hall he found the chorus in place, men in black, ladies in white under a gold hammer and sickle on red, and the orchestra assembling. The borrowed Leningrad brass players frowned over their parts. Reg was soon able to say:

'The text of this work is taken from the Old Testament, which is the first and most massive part of a book you have ceased officially to know. But you may take in its secular meaning and ignore the references to God and the gods. The Jews are slaves in ancient Babylon under a tyrant named Belshazzar. There are slaves in countries less ancient at the present time, under tyrants both cleanshaven and moustached. But the time of reckoning for the tyrants cannot be delayed for ever. The writing on the wall says that the tyrants have been weighed in the balance and found wanting. This is not the music of a Jew, the more antisemitic among you will be glad to know, but of an agnostic who comes from my part of the world. The message is universal. The message is freedom. Let the world rise against its oppressors and strike for liberty.' He had expected a dreadful silence followed by snarls and murmurs, but the audience started to clap. Some even cheered. Oh my God, here were the oppressed who did not know they were oppressed. Hitler was the moustached tyrant, though long dead in a Berlin bunker; the striking for liberty was to take place elsewhere than in Soviet Russia. Reg now proposed shouting, 'Curse Stalin, who killed the woman I loved,' but certain things got in the way – an image of beaming Churchill and sleek Anthony Eden, his wife behind him in the kitchen department momentarily granted a knowledge of Russian, the melodramatic nature of the malediction. He got down from the platform, cheered and clapped, and walked, head down, down the buffwalled corridor that led to the dressing rooms. He locked himself in an *ubornaya* and tried to be sick. He was aware of an impertinent engorgement. The first trombone, not all that distant, gave a B flat to the tenors and baritones, who sang in cunning discord: 'Thus spake Isaiah: the sons that thou shalt beget, they shall be taken away and be eunuchs in the house of the kings of Babylon. Howl ye, howl ye, therefore, for the day of the Lord is at hand.'

There was, he decided, sitting on the seat and wiping a wet brow, nothing in the world that was not ambiguous. The Babylonians, who were also the Jews, were praising the gods of gold, wood, brass, though the Leningrad players seemed to be cheapening the god of brass to tin, and there was great joy in the blasphemy. That percussion instrument which he would filch tomorrow afternoon was stamped with an ambiguous A. The A given out by the oboe for the tuning up was unambiguous in that it was no more than itself, but sounds organized discoursed both a thesis and an antithesis. He was not sure that he wanted that damned sword after all.

He did not appear on the platform to announce the unaccompanied singing of Welsh and English folksongs followed by, full orchestra blasting beneath in patriotic defiance of a necessarily referred kind, the *Anthem Genedlaethol Cymru*. His mother, he thought, ought to be having a good nostalgic weep at that. He would not, he thought, be seeing his mother again.

THE DEFECTION of Yura Petrovich Shulgin seemed genuine enough, though the nature of the trouble that had been feeding his apprehension remained for a long time unsure. What he had tasted of the rationed fleshpots of the decadent West was not really a sufficient reason, since he had served in the Soviet Embassy under direction. That he had been commanded to spy on the lesbian activities of Marya Ivanovna Shvernika, who was overfriendly with the wife of the Chinese ambassador (she, being a Chinese woman, was lesbian by culture) and had been passing on to her odd items of Soviet Far Eastern policy learned from her brother Shvernik, a member of the Politburo and due eventually for a shot in the back of the neck, and that he was already being mistrusted for the simple reason that he had been trusted, did not seem plausible. It was true, however, that his post in the Ministry of Culture was a cover for the surveillance of the defected British diplomat Potts, who was in charge of *Soviet News*, a periodical circulated in the Anglophone world, and suspected of passing on coded messages in free translations of Pushkin. It was possibly true that a show of homosexuality was interpreted as the real thing by his superiors or reported as the real thing by his juniors. Whatever the writing on the wall was, Shulgin read it. He had intelligence to impart to the West about the Soviet Union's intentions for the West Berlin island. He was considered too good for declining Britain and was soon claimed by Washington. A congratulatory message, very discreetly worded, was conveyed to Reg by Reg's sister from the head of M16: Reg's part in the transference of Shulgin to the West had been performed in an exemplary fashion. Actually there had been nothing in it. It was only in spy stories that defectors were shot as they marched up gangplanks. The message from Beatrix was her last act before leaving the Foreign Office and flying with her husband to settle in New York.

As for the theft from the Ermitage, effortlessly accomplished because it was assumed that only a suicidal idiot would attempt it, both Reg and the Soviet Union held their peace about it for several months. Reg had his own reasons; the Soviet Union apparently did not want to lose face. Reg told not even his wife what he had: Zip, seeing an old wooden scabbard with a bare metal tongue emerging from it released from its covering of brown paper, accepted what Reg said: this was a relic of Czarist Russia bought for much needed sterling from one of the Soviet state's antique emporia. Like, you know, an ikon. When Zip went with her orchestra on a northern tour, it was then, after evening closing time on his first day alone, he handled with reverence and a certain fear the sword Caledvwlch, if it was that. It had come a long way in time and space. King Arthur, if he had ever existed, had raised this weapon against the Saxon invader on behalf of a Christian empire threatened by Teutonic barbarism. Now Reg had it and he only. He felt, caressing it, a surge of lust appropriate enough to a picture of Belshazzar's feast in a family Bible but hardly to an artefact that was not representational art, was indeed hardly art at all.

It was nearly half as tall as himself. Its cutting edge was no longer operative but its point was sharp. Its brightness had been dimmed by age and the application of oil, and Reg wondered whether it would be right to restore its shine with Bluebell and a rag. For that matter filing might make it look less like a long spit of land with sea inlets, but the antiquity of an antique had to be respected. The A or aleph, serifed with stylized leaves and a leafy flourish, was clear in a certain light, but the sword seemed to wince with a kind of photophobia when he shone an electric torch on to it. What he had to avoid was being superstitious about the sword, seeing it as a living thing, imagining that a charge of tangible power came off it when touched. It was, after all, only an ancient chunk of forged metal. The wooden scabbard seemed to be no more than a gouged piece of elm wood, unmarked and certainly not the sheath of its original protection. Reg slept with the naked blade under his pillow; it did not induce bad dreams. It did not induce any dreams at all except the memory of seeing an old Hollywood film about the Knights of the Round Table. Having repatriated Caledvwlch after his long exile (the sexed possessive seemed fitting), Reg could do nothing with him except gloat at an easy victory over two lots of barbarian thieves. Wait, though – there was the question of the other sheath, the stone scabbard in the dig. An act of penetration of great mythical import had to be effected. And then Reg felt a kind of religious awe. Was what men called coincidence really part of a divine or diabolic plan? Collocation, collocation. Was this more than a mere chunk of rusteaten ancient steel?

He chose a night of full moon to borrow Megan's brother's bicycle. Caledvwlch rode along the handlebars without protest and, when he leaned the bicycle against the broken field gate, Reg had a feeling that the sword in his right hand yearned towards the bright light in the sky unseen for so many centuries. Reg pierced the orb thrice and then, point raised to the stars, marched and sometimes stumbled over the pitted field towards the dip where the diggings lay. An owl called and the church clock gave out midnight. Eldritch, what did eldritch mean? Reg jumped into the hollow and confronted GLAD ART REG on the stone plinth. It seemed to him that he ought to say a prayer or cry a cantrip, but then he ordered superstition to get behind him. He inserted the sword's point into the sheath, and the only connotations were sexual. It went in easily and to the limit, the metal cross that had housed the ornaments of the hilt bestriding the opening. The fit was astonishingly tight: there was no doubt that one had been made for the other. And then to Reg's fear and wonder he found that he could not draw the sword out. Only one man, *rex quondam et futurus*, was granted the power. This was absurd. Reg tugged, but the sword rested snug and immovable. He sat on the ground, sweating under the sinking moon, and took many deep breaths. Then he tried again. He discovered that by a slight wrenching of the crosspiece to the right the sword came out sweetly and easily. There was always an explanation, there were no real mysteries, but, seeing a bat fly low over his head, Reg had a pang of fear about a living Merlin. Merlin, if he ever existed, was perhaps a great artificer. There must be a gripping device in the depths of the stone sheath. (Eldritch – kingdom of the elves?) The grip could be loosened only by a slight sideways wrench. This did not seem possible: it was overingenious technology unsuitable for the start of the dark ages. Reg trembled as he held Caledvwlch in both hands. Did moonlight show a minute perforation very close to the point? A metal tooth of needle sharpness might enter there and hold. It was possible enough, no eldritch magic.

He rode home somewhat unsteadily with Caledvwlch and, having locked the back door by which he entered, placed him upright on a kitchen chair. The sword immediately fell to the floor with a dull clatter and Reg, raising him tenderly, spoke words of apology. If this was to be a household pet it must be of a superior order, like a Burmese cat. But it was no pet; it was an adjunct of royalty. The masculinity was not in doubt: it was as if the lost system of Anglo-Saxon genders had gone under in order to sexualize one class of inanimate objects, ships, and this that or whom history and mythology had raised above class. If Siegfried had called Nothung he it was because of grammatical gender, *Degen* being masculine, though *Schwert* neuter. Was Caledvwlch, like Nothung, in need of something? Reg read aloud to him from the Catalan book that Don Quixote had idolized, *Tirant Lo Blanc*, beginning 'To the honour, praise and glory of Our Lord Jesus Christ and His glorious and holy mother, Our Lady the Virgin Mary.' The kitchen clock tocked loudly, and the whole of protestant South Wales seemed to shudder at the papist exordium. Caledvwlch was a lifeless antique, but he seemed to drink in the words like oil. Reg was reminded of his own instability, kept under by the dull and pedestrian trade he had inherited. He refused to consider himself mad. But when Zip came home from her tour she reverted to her wartime doubts about his total sanity. For he told her the whole story.

'Look,' she said, 'you ought to see somebody, really you ought.'

'Who? An archaeologist? Does only the present time exist? Was St Helena mad because she discovered the true cross? This is what it is, he is. You are,' he said to Caledvwlch, 'what you are, are you not?'

'Get the damned thing out of the house. Give it to a museum.'

'He's been in a museum in a godless land. He slept too long in a monkish cellar. Now he consecrates our marriage bed.'

'What in God's name are you talking about?'

'He goes under the pillow.'

'Oh no he doesn't, it I mean. Look, you stole it, it's theft, they might have shoved the whole damned lot of us in jail.'

'Theft? The Russians were the thieves. They've got a lot of German booty, and they can call it legitimate reparations, but this is different. The Benedictines held it in trust for the British people and then they forgot about it. Now I hold it in trust for the same people, conscious of what it is. He, him, I mean.' He lowered his head to Caledvwlch in apology.

'If it belongs to the British people give it to them. To the king or prime minister or somebody in charge.'

'And then they'd give him back to the Russians with humble apologies. Besides, it's not the same British people. For the Anglo-Romans to call themselves the British is an insult to the Romanic Celts.'

'Give it to the Welsh, then.'

'The Welsh got themselves absorbed into the Anglo-Normans. The Welsh are not a nation any more.'

'Well, you have this group of madmen shouting the odds and robbing banks and killing old women with heart attacks. Give it to them.'

'Ah no. Ah no. Who are they to say that they represent the Britain that was the western outpost of Roman Christianity? An arbitrary gang of hotheads that started this business to keep what they call their minds occupied in Gibraltar. Ah no. Caledvwlch stays with me, symbol of a faith and chivalry that will revive when the world recovers its sanity.'

'Bloody Heinrich Himmler talked about chivalry. That meant killing the Jews. I hope you two will be very happy together.'

'Happy? What do you mean, happy? What is there to be happy about?'

'Take that bloody motheaten thing to bed with you. Sodomize yourself with it. Either it goes or I go.'

'You go anyway. Clashing your cymbals and tinkling your triangle with a lot of expatriate sheenies.'

Zip had been standing and banging the kitchen table to emphasize certain words. Now she sat and looked him in the eye. 'Sheenies, eh? Say it in Russian and you'll sound like your mother.'

'I didn't mean that,' Reg said, hangdog now. 'Something got into me. I'll hang him on the wall. I'll put him in that cupboard with the family bible. I'm sorry I said what I said.'

'We have another concert in Cardiff next week. I'm going to take it to the Russian Consulate.'

'You do that and I'll slash you with it.' Reg saw a contradiction there so said: 'No, I won't. No, you won't. I'll put it in the cellar with the barrels and cobwebs. I'll keep it out of your sight. It, I say, it. It's nothing anyway,' he lied.

Justly she said: 'You're a liar, and when you're not lying you keep things from me. And you're also a bloody antisemite.'

'I'm not, I'm not, I love you so much, I miss you so much when you're not here.' He held out his arms, though with no apparent desire to enfold her in them. 'I do hope it's true what I said that time in bed in Leningrad.'

'What's true? What did you say?'

'You have to be careful about being specific because the gods hear and start thwarting you. When I said it was the moment.' Zip sighed deeply and hit Caledvwlch, who lay on the kitchen table, with her fist. The flat metal hit back, though not hard. 'When I read notes and count rests it's all solid and I know where I am. Sometimes I think I know where I am with you. And then I know I'm not.'

'All you have to know about me is that I worship you. Let's go to bed. It's an hour before opening time.'

'And that's a horrid thing to say too.'

'I'll take him down to the cellar, it I mean. You won't have to see it again.'

When Zip went to Cardiff to rehearse and then perform in Benjamin Britten's *Young Person's Guide to the Orchestra* and (triangle only in the third movement) Brahms's Fourth Symphony, Reg was quick to retrieve Caledvwlch from the cellar, apologize for that debasement, and give him a massage with liquid paraffin. He read aloud from *Le Morte D'Arthur*. It was strange that a property of that history should be sitting in an armchair before him. It was like the Emperor Constantine reading the gospels on horseback, with one of the nails of the crucifixion hammered into the snaffle. There was definitely a minute hole pierced in the blade an inch or so from the point. He knew something that Malory didn't. More, much more. He held demythicized truth, waiting for him at closing time twice a day. Hip-swinging Megan was not impressed, saying, after singing 'Shrimp Boats Is Acomin'', 'What use is it then?' There was no real answer to that.

Two months after the return from Leningrad, Zip knew she was pregnant. Amenorrhea and morning sickness. She had better get clinical confirmation; still, she was sure. There was the sense of her body's having become a ship whose crew was responding to the order to sail; in a back room of her mind that had not previously been opened a sort of office staff was installed with a calendar on the wall. She told Reg over the softboiled breakfast egg she retched at, and Reg danced. 'That's what I meant,' he cried, 'when I said it was the moment. Paternity has a pregnancy of its own. It must have been the Leningrad air or the pepper vodka. Or something.' Something that lay quietly resentful next to the beer barrels. 'Do you want to lie down, dear? I'll make you fresh coffee. Cancel all engagements, do you hear? No more banging drums.'

'Don't be silly. According to that encyclopaedia of yours it takes two hundred and seventy-four days or thereabouts.'

'That's no time at all. The child's already there. Banging drums will traumatize him.'

'You're sure its a him? Was that another Leningrad revelation?'

'Common gender. The old dream of a cleansed generation inheriting none of our sins.'

'A kind of Israeli.' She sat up straight, saying: 'A Jewish child, you realize that? The father doesn't count. I'd better write to my mother even though she doesn't write to me. This will be a big thing for them.'

'Give up the banging and crashing. Now. Write a letter. Resign.'

'Nonsense. We're playing at the Albert Hall in two weeks. The big noisy stuff. *Petrushka*. Ravel's *Boléro* with twenty minutes of sidedrumming nonstop. I'll be all right.'

'I forbid you.'

'Rubbish.'

I heard my sister banging and crashing and triplesemiquavering. I was in London on terrorist business, a captain in mufti with a British passport, supervising the arrangements for the planting of a timebomb in the Iraqi Embassy. I took Zip back to my hotel off Grosvenor Square, one favoured by El Al crews and already ineffectually hand-grenaded by Palestinian Arabs. She ate a bloody steak ordered from room service. I remarked that it was not kosher. She stared at me.

'I see. You've gone all orthodox. Is horse forbidden by Leviticus or whatever it is? For this is certainly horse.'

'Come to sunny Israel where we don't have to feed the starving Germans. Seriously, though. Dad will want to see his grandchild. Dad would be even more overjoyed if you could produce a prickly pear.'

'I know. He wrote. But it was mother I wrote to. Why didn't he tell me about mother?' Here it was; women were undeceivable. 'She's left him hasn't she?'

'She's left us all, I'm afraid.'

'Oh my God.' She pushed the horsemeat aside. 'When? What happened?'

'Heart,' I lied. 'It was dad's idea not to upset you, not just yet. He didn't want you dashing over there as I did.'

'So that was why you went. It wasn't a sudden Reglike revelation.' Her eyes did not fill. Like me she hadn't known our mother all that well. Absence was not so much a kind of death as a kind of nonexistence. 'So dad's on his own. Shuffling about the kitchen making his own sad coffee.' That was very accurate. 'Are you living with him?'

'I see him often enough. But I have to live in barracks.'

'I wish I could feel something. Still, it's a shock. They were never apart. He must be taking it badly.'

'He feels better at the thought of a grandchild. He'd feel better still if you were there. But you have your own life to live. And you have Reg.'

'Reg is mad.'

'You've always said that.'

'No, he's really mad. He talks to that damned sword of his as if it's a mixture of offspring and holy trinity.'

'Sword? Tell me.' She told me. 'He never lacked courage,' I said. 'Why the hell did he do it?'

'I looked up *baby* in that family encyclopaedia of theirs. Of course it wasn't there. But the volume practically fell open at *Benedictine*. The British royal house and Monte Cassino. Reg burbled at great length about a family mission. Talking about solidities when he's the least solid thing I've ever seen. Down in the cellar making sure it's all right.'

'It all began with Spain, didn't it? Fighting for something clean and holy but not knowing quite what it was. Solidity. Absolute pitch. If he's mad it's a Don Quixote kind of madness. He's really a Jew, I suppose.'

'Reg? A Jew? Don't make me laugh.' That was a highly inappropriate trope. 'Christian chivalry and kicking out the barbarians and the pagans.'

'Meaning the Saracens and the defilers of the holy places. It was a Christian poet who wrote *Jerusalem Liberated*.'

'Poor mother. Poor dad.' She had made the Jerusalem connection through women's magic. 'I could have been told. Are you telling me the truth when you say it was heart? We have newspapers here, you know. People killed by Arab bombs in Tel Aviv. Was it that?'

'She died in Jerusalem. All death is caused by cardiac arrest. She was very severely frightened. Dad felt guilty. A war zone's no place for a woman. Another reason for his not wanting you to dash over as I did.'

'And you're on leave from the war, are you?'

'Oh no. Not really. And in any case I'm not really fighting in it. I teach others how to do that. Commando tactics. Homemade explosives, that sort of thing. Though I have led one or two misisons. The landing at Ras Burun didn't get into the papers. Here there's a little job to attend to at Number 21 Queensgate. It's called terrorism, which means scaring hell out of the enemy. Ask me no more.'

'I didn't intend to. Have you heard of Chaim and Deborah Kishon?'

'They're not Arabs from the sound of it.'

'Correct. They play on two pianos. There's a Bartok thing for pianos and percussion. There's also the arrangement of Ravel's concerto for solo piano and orchestra, Chaim did it for the two of them with percussion. They're commissioning other things, it's not a bad combination. Britten's doing something.'

'Not a bad idea for you either. Are you contemplating a new career at the wrong time? Just when nature's taking over?'

'Oh, there's time. Time to do an Israeli tour. That's what they propose.'

'There's a war on.'

'There was one here too, you know. Bombs dropping, that sort of thing.'

'Dad would be pleased. How about Reg?'

'Reg doesn't come into this. Now it's just me and what's inside. Reg has his blessed Excalibur to talk to. He'll have it in bed with him now. He keeps saying that *he* has his percussion instrument too. Mad, like I said. I'm going to throw this horsemeat out of the window. Do they have dogs in Grosvenor Square?'

WHAT happened was bound to happen, as Aled Rhys made clear to Reg one night after closing time. 'Who told you? How did you know?' Reg asked in agitation. Aled Rhys was not with his former associates. There was a dark man whose name Reg did not catch, a halfbreed from Tiger Bay, and there was a young man called Terry MacMahon after his father. Despite his name he spoke with a Welsh accent. Aled Rhys said:

'You told Megan Pritchard all about it. She thought it was a joke. Her brother Tom didn't. Tom's one of us. As you are.'

'Idiot that I was, am. No, I'm not one of you.'

'Every good Welshman has to be,' said the Tiger Bay quadroon or octoroon.

'I prayed it would happen,' Aled Rhys said. 'It was the thing you were ordained to do for us. Your brother knew where it was. You can get a lot of information from the innocent.'

'Where are the others?' Reg asked. He stood behind the bar as behind a rampart, a halfwashed pint glass in his hand. 'Where's that bloody fool you called the Prince of Cymru?'

'Never mind about him,' Aled Rhys said. 'The other two dropped out. Big ones for words but not for action. It's on the march.'

292

'Meaning a few more bank robberies and a blown up postbox in Llanfynydd.'

'You read the papers, I see. Let's have a look at it.'

'Why? Why should it mean anything to you?'

'Don't talk daft,' Terry MacMahon said.

'It's not what you think it is,' Reg said. 'It's a chunk of old iron I bought in Leningrad for a couple of quid. And even if it was the thing you think he is, it is, what right do you have to come barging in here asking to have a look?'

'It's more than a look we want,' Aled Rhys said. 'Where is it?' He got up from the settle under the window at which a redcurrant bush tapped in the night wind.

Reg held the halfwashed glass out as a weapon. 'You're not coming behind this bar if that's what you think. I'll have you for bloody trespass.'

'We don't want a fight,' the Tiger Bay man said, also on his feet. 'There's enough enemies to fight without going for a fellow Welshman.'

'You don't look much like a Welshman to me,' Reg said. 'You look more like a bloody Arab.'

'Racism, is it? My mother brought some Arab blood over from East Africa, but my dad was a pure Celt and taught me the wrongs done to the pure Celts.'

'Listen,' Terry MacMahon said, still seated on a chalky chair under the dartboard. 'The public has to see something, right? It's no good going on about a free Cymru when they've nothing to look at. A flag's all right, but Aled here says you've got the sword of King Arthur. I laughed when he said that, but there's things that last, like Stonehenge. Raise that sword at a public meeting, get it in the papers, show the Sais we mean business, isn't it? It's a big thing, one of the biggest things ever, and you're hugging it to yourself.'

'Get him, it, made public,' Reg said, 'and the Russians will get it back again. I appoint myself protector.'

'So you admit it then,' Aled Rhys said. 'It was all a lie you saying it was a chunk of old iron. You've got Caledvwlch desecrated by drinking in the fumes of beer in your back kitchen or wherever it is. The people of Cymru have a right to it. What you're doing's unhealthy, like masturbation. Hand it over to the rightful representatives of a free Cymru.'

'And who says you're that?' Reg said. The mention of the true name struck him to the heart, like the pet name of a loved one heard in a public urinal. 'Who says you stand for a free Wales? *Plaid Cymru* claims that too and the Welsh MPs the people vote in at Westminster are the Welsh democratic voices. It strikes me you're a lot of thugs who like violence for its own sake. You no more stand for the Welsh people than my arse does.'

'Vulgarity.' Aled Rhys shook his sad head. 'Cynicism and scepticism. The small nations of the world are rising up against their oppressors and all you can do is talk of your arse. Put that glass down, you're not drawing any blood while I'm around. Take it from him, Terry.' Reg smashed the mouth of the glass against the bar counter and presented dangerous jags to the three. 'Naughty, naughty. Go on, Terry.' Terry rose from his chair and picked it up; its seat sprinkled fine chalk to the floor. He raised the chair against Reg and cracked his right wrist with a rear leg. There was no contest. The broken glass fell and Reg cursed. Reg picked up with his left hand a metal ventpeg that lay in the sink. That went down with the other rear leg. 'No good, is it?' Aled Rhys said. 'We're coming behind there. If you'd be reasonable none of this would be necessary. We don't like violence any more than you do.'

Reg tried to bar the way to the kitchen, which was in darkness. He was thumped in. 'Switch must be by here somewhere,' Terry MacMahon said, fumbling on the wall. 'There.' Light flooded kitchen clutter. 'There.' In the middle of the table, nesting in his wooden scabbard, Caledvwlch lay. The table was all his, except for an open copy of Malory. Reg stumbled to grab, protect, but the Tiger Bay man got him first. Aled Rhys, with the caution proper to one who approaches a dog sleeping but rabid, advanced to the table, delicately picked up the scabbard and drew the sword, which glowered with a matt oily sheen under the light bulb. Reg cursed, but the three, which was proper, drew in reverent breath. Aled Rhys raised the swordpoint towards the ceiling. He said:

'If this is what I have no reason not to believe it is, then here is the most sacred of the relics of the people of Cymru. With this he slashed at the invading Saxon in defence of Roman Christianity.'

'And how were you brought up?' Reg sneered. 'Calvinistic bloody Methodist?'

'I am in the Church,' Terry MacMahon said. 'My mother converted when she married my dad. But it is not the point. The point is a free nation.'

'The point is,' Reg snarled, 'that you've got a priceless object there and you'll sell it to the highest bidder. What's ever been in this nationalist business for you except money?'

'Cynicism again,' Aled Rhys said, lunging playfully at Reg. 'Yes, money comes into it and the movement is still poor, but never would we think, never would we dream – '

'If it is what you think it is,' the Tiger Bay man said, 'it's worth a packet and no mistake.'

'This,' Aled Rhys said, pointing Caledvwlch towards the window and the rising halfmoon, 'is too precious to think of in those terms. This is a miracle. Lying in the dark for fifteen hundred years, preserved by a kind of magic. Can you see a kind of glow coming off it?'

'No,' Terry MacMahon said promptly. 'It's a bit of old iron but it's also what you think it is. A sword's for killing, isn't it? The enemy's going to scream. People will take notice now.'

BEATRIX was sitting in the apartment on West 69th Street, tenth floor, reading the magazine called *Time*. Her husband had torn up the copy he had himself bought: he did not wish her to read the review of his novel, finally entitled by his publisher *Blood on the Snow*, which made it sound like a weary thriller, not an epic of the war. It came, the waspish reviewer of *Time* said, as an anticlimax after Norman Mailer's *The Naked and the Dead*. It lacked conviction. Author Roth beat the big drum of an overliterary prose to drown the unreality of the narrative. That Roth had spent the war chairborne, leaving unliterary men to do the fighting, was not perhaps a pertinent point to raise, but the secondhand nature of the experiences recounted was all too evident. Roth's Polish and Ukrainian geography bore no relation to any known maps, his Nazis and Russians were straight out of comic strips, his American characters were stereotypes. The book stumbled in the snow of Faulknerian verbiage. The wrath of Roth at the agony of serving men was all too factitious. Mailer's Dos Passos pastiches served an artistic end; Roth's were there just to make up the weight. The book was heavy in two senses, indigestible but innutritive. Mailer's mailed fist had knocked Roth into the drifts. The snow was all shredded paper. Author Roth had better wait for the next war.

Beatrix was not surprised by the review. She had broken into her husband's desk to read the clippings sent by his publisher. Only the notices which were straight lifts from the blurb dealt praise. She saw also how his new novel was getting on. It was about a chunk of gold that had got into a family and became a kind of family curse. Beatrix was quite sure that Irwin had missed his vocation. It ought not to matter. His father was kindly granting him a year's ample subsistence to try to make the literary grade, but it was on condition that, not making it, he would take a post in his father's office. Irwin was proving very difficult to live with. Beatrix had nothing to do except superintend the housework of the *schwarze* who came in daily and sang tunelessly over the kitchen sink. The apartment was a good and spacious one, and it resounded to nightly quarrels. Beatrix was the punch-ball on which Irwin worked out his literary frustration. Then, appeased, he gnawed her in the big double bed with its blood-red sheets. Then he demanded that he in turn be gnawed. She shifted sorely now in the Bach-Bentz sliding armchair and looked at the earlier pages of *Time*. The rounded screen of the television set was showing Ray Milland in *The Lost Weekend*. Irwin was doing his nightly round of the bars. She did not think she would be tolerating Irwin for very much longer.

A paragraph in the Foreign Affairs section told of Welsh nationalism and mentioned the comic opera drawing-out of a sword from a stone. The sword had emerged with some difficulty, King Arthur not being present to give it a straight successful tug. The drunken Welshman who announced himself in English as King Arthur's lawful successor had fallen flat on his face. It was a hilarious ceremony appropriate to a stillborn cry for Welsh independence. Wales had long been part of Great Britain (a footnote pedantically told how long) and had confirmed this by giving the Tudors to the British throne. It was all a feeble parody, romanticized in typical Welsh fashion, of the probably legitimate claims of the IRA for a united Ireland.

Irwin came in late and drunk. He mumbled something, said hi, then stumbled to the toilet where he vomited in a long auditory show of agony. He came back to the sitting room with vomit on his rolltop turquoise sweater and tried to put Brahms on the record player. He perked up as the Variations on a Theme of Haydn began on puddingy wind fighting disc scratches and demanded supper. There was, Beatrix said, cold chicken in the icebox. Why couldn't she learn to cook, he wanted to know. Chickenshit. He demanded, in an accent and idiom not his, that she get her goysy ass to bed and be ready to be fucked but good. Then he passed out on the floor while the needle ground round and round on a crack and gave out ad infinitum the same meaningless iamb. Beatrix covered him with a light blanket and went to bed.

Why had she done it? Nature had grown tired, perhaps, of her queenly approach to sex and sent out the odours of submission. Irwin had excited her and still did when he was sober. But her economics course had taught her about diminishing returns. Americans seemed to believe that sexual rapport was enough in marriage; fresh sexual excitement justified divorce. She could get a divorce easily enough, but it all seemed too easy, not quite playing the game. Till death did them part had been her father and mother's inherited and unquestioned view of the matter, and now her mother was prepared to make the same promise in a country where divorce was an aspect of Marxist cynicism towards a bourgeois institution. Beatrix looked an English rose, but her Russian side was asserting itself more in this city which had Russian Jewish newspapers. She needed occupation, and she had received intimations from Washington, probably set afoot by Yura Petrovich Shulgin, that she could be used. But there had been a more attractive proposal from Professor Namier at the University of Manchester – a junior lectureship on her own soil, specializing in Soviet history. The point about her Russian side was that it was not Jewish; it contained nothing of the wail of exile. Her frustration as the wife of a failed novelist was an imposed one: there was no frustration in herself. She had tasted marriage, and she did not much care for it. She had tasted New York, which was not quite America, and found it more provincial than Manchester. She needed independence, but she lacked money. She heard a groaning Irwin staggering to bed. He fumbled for the light switch and then scattered his clothing on the floor. Naked and hairy, he showed her with pride an engorged phallus. He tried to dig it into her from the rear and she hit out. She was not having much more of this.

I read the same issue of *Time* much later in the officers' mess at Tel Aviv. I naturally thought of Beatrix. Then I read the airmail edition of the London *Times* which had an article about the ethics of stealing from the Ermitage in Leningrad. This whole question of theft of national treasures was a subtle one. Whether the filched sword and scabbard were of genuine historical value was not really the issue, though laboratory tests had proved that the scabbard at least was of ancient provenance. The article mentioned in passing the ethical position vis à vis the Elgin Marbles. Was theft from a sovereign state of the same order as common or garden burglary? The Welsh nationalists were proud to proclaim publicly that an ancient treasure of the Romanized Britons had been recovered from a Russia that claimed it only as the spoils of war. The Soviet government spoke harshly of Western hooliganism, demanded of the British government that the thief or thieves be brought to book, and meanwhile held as hostages certain treasures of the National Gallery sent to Moscow on an amicable cultural exchange scheme which had proved nothing more than the bad faith of the West. It seemed to the writer of the article, a certain P.J. Trevelyan, that the British government ought to accede to the Soviet demand, while naturally denying collective responsibility for the theft. The act of an irresponsible individual was not to be considered in political terms, but theft was theft the world over, and the British forces of law and order must be invoked to recover, by force if necessary, property belonging to a friendly state with whose potential enmity no sane government would wish to deal.

The *Daily Mail* felt differently. It, and other popular papers, made a great matter out of the restoration of Excalibur to British soil, though they all seemed to think, especially the *Daily Mail*, that King Arthur had ruled the English. The sword ought to be placed on exhibition in Westminster Abbey for the homage of the British people. This did not mean the Welsh people. The whole business struck me as absurd. And yet what would the continuing existence of the Ark of the Covenant mean to the Israeli people? The sacred chest of shittim or acacia wood, with the two tablets of the law within, had been borne by the Levites at the taking of Jericho. It had been captured by Philistines and set up on the altar of Ashdod. It had been recovered and became the sacred nut of the shell of Solomon's temple. But it was the outward sign of the inward grace of an embattled people of great religious fervour. Could one say the same of the sword Caledvwlch?

The sword Caledvwlch struck in the suburbs of Newport. Edward Golightly, an undoubted Englishman and the head of a shipbreaker's yard, was taken by four masked men with local accents as he got out of his car on St Woolos Avenue. He thought at first it was a joke. He had holidayed in Italy, where kidnapping was an immemorial trade, but he had not thought that trade was practised in peaceful South Wales. He was laid blindfolded in the back of a station wagon he had incuriously noticed parked near his house, and driven many miles. He was pushed out blind and was then allowed to blink in a dirty kitchen where a naked light bulb swung in the breeze from a cracked window. The four men kept their masks on. 'Have to do this, see,' one of them said. 'Don't want you to know who we are, fair play. Might start screaming blue murder about what we look like when you get out.'

'When *do* I get out?'

'Won't be long, we hope. A matter of your missis paying up. All in a good cause. Wales for the Welsh is our motto.'

'How much?'

'Him at the top says ten thousand. But he expects humming and hawing about it. Every little helps the cause.'

'She won't pay,' Mr Golightly said. He was a wheezing man of about fifty. 'There's no guarantee if she pays. I've heard of this sort of thing before, but not here.'

'Not here, no. In on it at the beginning we are. She'll pay all right. How about a nice cup of tea? Sorry we can't give you dinner at night, which is what your class of people has. A few biscuits there are, see.'

'You'd better know something,' Mr Golightly said. 'I'm diabetic.'

'Meaning you can't take sugar in it?'

'Meaning I've got to have insulin, if you know what that is.'

'Heard of that, Jack, have you?'

'There's the youngest of the Robertses has that complaint. They said something about injections. Get the stuff at the chemist's, can you?'

'Only on prescription,' Mr Golightly said.

'There's pity. Can't bring a doctor in, can we? Give the whole show away.'

'You're going to have a corpse on your hands,' Mr Golightly said.

'Don't want that, do we? Fair play. Mind, we only have your word for it.'

'You'll find out it's the truth soon enough.'

'Made a bad choice then we did. What do you say, Jack?'

'Blindfold the bugger again and take him back where we picked him up. Made a bad start then we did. Still, you cannot win all the time.'

This seemed to show that the Welsh had no real gift for violence, but they were learning fast. Dr Lewis, the sole lunchtime drinker in Reg's pub one weekday, remarked on a report in the *Western Mail* about the ransacking of a Jewish pawnbroker's shop in Tredegar and the owner's hitting out with a stuffed alligator only to collapse of an infarctus. He said then to Reg:

'You're not looking all that well. I suppose I ought to prescribe a tonic.'

'I'm all right.'

'No, you're not all right. Nobody's all right. We don't know where the hell we are, any of us. We can't see the future and we're romanticizing the past. We're in the atomic age and none of us knows what that means. We're having a lot of little wars because we're too damned scared of the prospect of a big one. Too many little nations demanding independence in an age when only two big nations count. That gesture of yours was too stupidly romantic to be taken seriously. Who cares about King

Arthur, if he ever existed? You've got this vision of a kind of
Michelangelesco giant slashing the pagan invader with his sword
on behalf of a Christianized Roman Empire. It was a cynical
Christianity anyway, all quarrelling bishops and emperors
believing that Christ was really the sungod. And it was an empire
collapsing from inside with inflation and effeminacy and slaves'
revolts. It had to go. The barbarians had to take over, it was
ordained by history. They became Christianized anyway, so King
Arthur was slashing away for nothing. The Celts had only one
job in history and that was to teach the word to the Teutons.
The British Celts couldn't govern themselves, nor could the Scots
and the Irish, ordained to be a subject people the lot of them,
misty, romantic, effete, a lot of preachers and warblers plucking
untuned harps. And King Arthur, who probably didn't exist
anyway, was without doubt a syphilitic wreck who had to be
lifted on his bloody old nag, coughing his way into battles he
knew he was going to lose. Ugh.'

'Syphilis didn't exist in those days,' Reg said.

'Diseased anyway, and certainly a cuckold. And looking for
the holy grail and the sacred spear because they thought it might
cure impotence and make the crops grow.'

'Quite a speech.'

'Oh, I can gleek on occasion. Who do you think forged the
sword of Attila or Arthur or any other of the swordwaving swine?
The Celts stole the land and booted their predecessors out so
that all they could do was smelt iron for their agricultural masters.
They're still there, small and swarthy, forging bicycles in the
Black Country. The Huns were worse than the Celts, living on
spoils and stallion's blood and mare's milk, not able to do a
hand's turn for themselves, waving the sword of Mars and raping
and looting. And now the Sons of Arthur, as they call themselves, are raising a motheaten weapon in the name of a cause
that's just playacting in an age when the only real contest is
between the Yanks and the Russians. What the hell did you do
it for?'

'There have to be romantics.'

'Oh yes, just as there have to be bronchitics and syphilitics.
Justify tuberculosis because it produced Keats's last poems and
syphilis because it bred the Ninth Symphony. You mark my

words, romanticism is always frustrated and always turns to violence. Terrorism for the sake of terrorism. The IRA go on for ever, it's got a long history behind it, and it runs all the taxis in Belfast. But Wales – God help us. What do the Welsh want – the imposition of a language good only for eisteddfodau and an opting out of the major struggle of the age? Because, whether you like it or not, the big issue now is between the individual and the collective. And by the collective I don't mean just the omnipotent state, I mean the international cartels and the murdering swine who send me free pharmaceutical samples.' Dr Lewis was on his third whisky. He pushed his glass forward for another.

'You're in a bad way,' Reg said, pouring with the optic measure.

'Me in a bad way? I'm at least curing the sick or trying to. I'm tending bodies that house individual souls. Bodies are much of a muchness, but souls aren't. Now souls are going to be hammered into copies of an archetype decreed by the great collectives. America and Russia are the same man with two different hats on. The contest is about what kind of stereotypical soul we're all going to be issued with, souls to be fed to one collective Moloch or another.' Dr Lewis then said: 'Is your wife still banging drums and clashing cymbals?'

'I don't see the connection. Between her and Moloch and whatnot.'

'There's no connection. Well, there's a connection between everything and everything, if we can only find it. She's going to keep that baby. She can go on to the limit, so long as she doesn't mistake her swollen belly for a kettledrum.'

'Even if she goes to Israel?'

'Why shouldn't she go to Israel? The sunshine and the oranges will do her all the good in the world. There's no reason why she shouldn't have the child in Israel.' He looked somewhat blearily at Reg. 'You could do with a bit of sun yourself. Why don't you give up this pub and hand it over to someone who really cares about the trade? It's time you went back into the world again.'

'Doing what? Teaching Spanish?'

'Why not? Or Ladino or Judezmo. The world's bigger than a Welsh pub. I suppose you'd think it a very funny thing if I was to have the tending of your wife's parturition among the orange groves.'

'I don't understand. You mean you're thinking of practising over there? The place is full of Jewish doctors. What would they want with a Welsh one?'

'Me Welsh? Oh, I've absorbed the patois and tramped the damp soil in my wellingtons as though as it was native. My father's name was Levi. Lewis seemed close enough with the kind of w he was brought up on. All right, there's no need to show me your back fillings. I'm a GP not a dentist.'

THE sword Caledvwlch went on public exhibition for the first and last time in the Glendower Hall in Sussex Gardens off the Edgware Road. This was a commodious meeting place for the London Welsh, holding two thousand and equipped with a stage big enough for a London Welsh choir. Gilt organ pipes thrust up at the back of this stage, and dusty banners of the Welsh regiments hung from the flies. The Dedication of the Sword Excalibur had been sufficiently advertised on posters and yellow throwaways, and it was made clear that this was not to be an exclusively Welsh occasion. There was no charge for admission, and hence the attendance was rather smaller than it should have been, there always being a catch in things free. When, to the tune of *Mae hen wlad fy nhadau*, which nobody sang, a party of ten or so took the chairs ranged at the front of the stage, Reg was surprised to see that he knew none of them. They were all, he assumed, of the inner circle of the Sons of Arthur, the hitherto invisible controlling body of which men like Aled Rhys were mere limbs. One of them wore Arab robes and dark glasses. The sword itself was not yet in evidence, a reserved treat dramatically held off. The Welsh members of the audience prepared happily for eloquence when an ancient man in a loose grey suit rose with difficulty from his chair and approached the speaker's desk with its microphones. None knew who he was, but press photographers conscientiously flashed at him. The old man announced himself as Professor Griffiths of the University College of Cardiff and spoke in an accent with no Welsh lilt, saying:

'What I have to say has no political import. I am not concerned with the claim of certain sectors of the Welsh people that the

303

principality of Wales or Cymru should revert to a position of ancient independence under its own rulers. The amalgamation of Wales and England, in my view, is of such long standing that no such reversion could ever be considered practicable. I personally regard the claim, like the cognate claim of the Scottish nationalists, as a cry from the Celtic heart – a demand that the Celtic contribution to Western civilization be given the consideration it deserves, that the Celtic past of these islands be honoured, as indeed should the Celtic past of the continent of which we are a part. The point I would make is that the past is a living current which continually nourishes the present, and that any tangible fragment of the past must be cherished as a symbol of that nourishment. The sword Caledvwlch or Excalibur has, so it appears, at last emerged out of the mists, no longer a myth but a tangible substance, a solidity which affirms the reality of the past as a force which works on the present and, indeed, the future. That the sword you are shortly to see with your own eyes is truly the sword Excalibur we have, naturally, no means of knowing. It seems to be an artefact forged in the fifth century after the birth of Christ. Archaeologists of the Soviet Union are prepared to speculate that it is the sword of Mars discovered preserved in the peat of the Danubian marshes by Attila the Hun, but this is as much romantic guesswork as the ancient legend that the sword was passed on to the Roman general Aetius, thence to Ambrosius, finally to the Celto-Roman *dux* of the Britons. We have, I say, no means of knowing the truth of the matter, but any means of confirming that the past is more than a written record or a deformed dream is to be welcomed.'

There were murmurs in the audience: scientific caution was not good oratory and therefore not good entertainment. A voice behind Reg muttered: 'Let's see the bloody thing, boyo, and make up our own bloody minds.' Professor Griffiths said:

'We are living in an age in which two great nations are committed to the destruction of the past. Both the United States and the Soviet Union dream of a radiant future into which the past can uncoil no qualifying tentacles. The past may be permitted to subsist as the material for museums and cinematic entertainments, but only to be wondered at, derided, mocked, accepted as the garishly coloured matter, ignorant, unscientific, unhygienic, which the radiant future is to supersede. But note this well: the present is a mere uncomputable line between the known and the unknown. The future, however radiant, does not yet exist, and the present is a line without thickness. What we can, perhaps paradoxically, expect with hope from the future is a more comprehensive knowledge of the past. A great war, only recently ended, pushed with inordinate impatience and speed, as wars will, into the future, producing weapons which peace indolently would prefer to reserve to a merely mythical time ahead. Out of that war much of the past hitherto unknown has been literally unearthed – such as those archaeological remains in Breconshire confirmed to be of a Celto-Roman fort, though the Arthurian inscriptions seem to be anachronistic, as well as the Mithraic temples and Roman baths disclosed, with the unpurposing help of the Luftwaffe, in this city where we are assembled. The sword itself has emerged out of the smoke and fire of that war. I say no more for the moment. Maintain scepticism when you see what you have come to see, but honour the past which it symbolizes. Those Celts among you will be encouraged, it is hoped, to learn more of your inheritance and the better be able to compute the extent of the contribution it has made, and continues to make, to the amorphous civilization which surrounds you.'

He sat down to little applause and some hamshifting from the audience. The seats were wooden and not grateful to the wiry shanks of Welsh milkmen. From his seat in the third row Reg turned to look at the assembly – a thousand or so men and women in cheap decent clothes, long-suffering under governmental ineptitude and unconvinced by the tawdry treat of the Festival of Britain, survivors of a long war that had brought a spurious egalitarianism in which there was little to share, eager for anything that rang with an absolute pitch, though what could Arthur's sword mean to them except the faintest superstition that, if nobody of the present was doing it, perhaps someone of the past was looking after them? But now a fat man with glasses that drank deeply of the house lights went to the microphones to feed them politics. He did not announce his name; his voice was demagogic Welsh; he placed hands on his hips inside his open jacket; a waistcoat pocket was full of pens. He said:

'*Diolch yn fawr* to Professor Griffiths for his discourse, which will give us all food for thought sometime in the future when there is leisure for the luxury of it. But at the moment we are more concerned with action and we precede a vigorous programme of action with an act of dedication. Make no mistake about it, we Sons of Arthur, a family that is growing fast both at home and overseas, mean to restore the independence of Cymru, handing back the mineral wealth of the land, hardly as yet explored, to those whose birthright it is, placing its green fields in the horny hands of our native yeomen, allowing its waters to flow in Cymric channels and not be diverted to the benefit of the foreign neighbour with whom we take up our just quarrel. If there are English ears listening tonight, into them we pour a promise, no more empty threat, of harassment which will continue until our dream is realized. Fair words are not enough. The farce of parliamentary democracy avails nothing. We pledge ourselves on the sword of the once and future king, as he was called, to force the foreigner out and to compel him to leave by acts of just aggression performed on his own soil. No one in England will be safe, this we promise, for it is war that we are declaring. Not a war of massed armies, of battleships and of bombing planes, but of knives between the ribs in the dark, of high explosives in lowly places, the implantation of fear until the common people of England cry enough enough to their elected rulers, let there be a free Wales.'

A voice from near the back cried in an Irish accent: 'Bloody nonsense. Brits out of Ulster first.'

'The Celtic cause is a common cause,' the fat man said. 'We have a struggle in common with the overweening English. We appreciate Irish help as we appreciate the help of those of our sundered brethren in America North and South. The freeing of the small enslaved nations is the theme of our age.'

'What's that bloody nignog doing up there?' a Welsh voice called.

'Please, let us have none of this racial abuse. It is very much in order that the justness of our cause has carried even as far as the Middle East. I invite Mr Ibrahim ibn Mohamed Saud to speak a few words to you.'

Ibrahim ibn Mohamed Saud kept on his dark glasses as he

addressed the microphones. He said little in a very refined English, but that little was coloured by no romantic nonsense. 'The curse of colonialism is less the curse of oppression,' he said, 'than the curse of waste. Welsh coal has fired British trains and British ships, but Wales is more than its coal deposits. The exploitation of new minerals, in which the mountains of Wales are rich, is more appropriate to the nuclear age that is upon us than the scraping at coal seams that are approaching exhaustion. If I may allow folk mythology to intrude for a moment, we of the Arab nations have always regarded the Welsh people as that lost tribe of the Ishmaelites or Kahtanites which migrated north and settled in a land which the word of the Prophet could not reach. This may be unhistorical fantasy, but such fantasies are not to be despised. Certainly, the struggle of the Palestinian Arabs finds a parallel in the struggle of the Welsh. The scimitar and the sword are forged from the same metal. Long live a free and prosperous Wales.'

This brief speech was applauded with a kind of condescending vigour. The man who now strode to the speaker's desk did so clapping. He remained as anonymous as his Welsh predecessor but his well-cut grey suit, his springy slimness, the distinction of his middle-aged face, and the abundance of his iron-grey hair, carefully coiffed, spoke authority of a kind that seemed to Reg suprapolitical. 'Do not be disappointed,' he said, 'in the appearance of the sword Caledvwlch. It is old, it has weathered centuries of natural attrition, it looks like what it is – a weapon that has swung at the enemy and been hacked in its turn. It would have been easy to contrive some such purely ornamental device as that which, on the orders of the English king, graced the defenders of Stalingrad. But this is a sword that has been carried into battle. The courage which it symbolizes characterized the act of its recent redemption. Our Cymric brothers who took it from under the very gaze of its Russian captors did so in no spirit of enmity. Against neither the Russian people nor their government does the spirit of the new Cymru blaze in unworthy hostility. The Russians made a mistake in not recognizing the historical worth of what to them was no more than one of the spoils of the war against their foe and ours. They are a stubborn

307

people who are often slow to be taught. But they will learn in time and they will forgive in time. Let me say this – '

'Let *me* say *this*,' Reg cried standing, his RSM voice needing no amplification.'The sword was taken from the grasp of the Russians by one Welshman only, and that Welshman is myself. It was taken from my charge brutally by an old army comrade who called himself one of the founder Sons of Arthur. I yield now to what I recognize as the justice of the expropriation, seeing clearly where Caledvwlch properly belongs, but I claim another justice, a very small one – the justice of the attachment of courage not to some vague Cymric brothers but to the man who did the deed. I am coming up there.'

During this speech Reg had looked down on open mouths in the nearer rows, expressive of doubt and wonder. Some of these mouths now opened wider in applause, others went tight with scepticism. Some hands clapped. Without invitation Reg moved to the flight of four steps to the right of the stage and mounted. 'Your name?' the interrupted speaker asked.

'Reginald Morrow Jones. The name is on the passport in my pocket, as well as a recent visa for the Soviet Union. The defector Yura Petrovich Shulgin will, if you call him in Washington DC, be happy to attest that I am the man who abstracted with him the sword Caledvwlch from the Ermitage in Leningrad. I think I have a right to participate in your ceremony of dedication. Let us all see what we have come to see.' At this the bulk of the audience clapped loudly. The lights of the auditorium now dimmed, at a shrugging signal from the interrupted speaker, and some noble chords, not specifically Cymric, sounded from the organ. A trapdoor in the centre of the stage opened, and a young man in decent brown mounted from the cellarage, bearing a long object covered in black cloth. Reg could see a man in shirtsleeves working dimmers in the wings. Stage light concentrated on the young man as he reverently brought his burden to downstage centre. He whipped the black covering off and held aloft Caledvwlch or Excalibur. Despite the warning of the interrupted speaker, many of the audience were audibly disappointed and some laughed. A long chunk of bitten metal naked in the bright lamp. The past was always smaller than you imagined. The interrupted speaker called on the audience to stand, as for the Hallelujah Chorus, and many did. He cried:

'The sword of Arthur asks us with its dumb steel to pledge ourselves to the rebuilding of a country once great and free, now declining and in bondage. With our friends we will do it.' Then a bomb exploded at the back of the hall and women screamed. Reg wrestled very briefly with the swordbearer, who was stronger than he looked. He raised his left foot and aimed for the testicles. The young man went into a *moue* of pain and was glad to let his charge go. Another bomb gave off noise, light and smoke near one of the emergency exits in the hall. People turned their backs on absconding Reg and stage confusion. An Irish voice yelled, 'Brits out.' Reg was rugger-tackled by somebody and began to use Caledvwlch as a weapon. He got round a dusty upright piano and a pile of folding chairs and found a door marked EXIT obligingly open. In the corridor a couple of police constables were being told by a police sergeant to stay where they were, and Reg was convinced that one of the hatted dark-suited civilians there was Major Mashuk of bitter memory. The sergeant told Reg to hand over what he had there in the manner of one not too happy with his orders, but Reg bared his teeth and lunged. He was firmly embraced from the back by a constable but cried in Russian, still lunging, that he was under direct orders from Moscow and these Embassy underlings had best clear the way. Caledvwlch was, it appeared, to be another victim of Yalta. Reg discomfited the embracing constable by falling flat on his face in the unswept corridor and rolling sideways. A big black civilian boot went down on his ribs, but he lunged. Caledvwlch pierced dark grey trousering and a shin beneath. There were now kicks at Reg's fists that held on to the bare hilt. The sergeant said something about there being a limit to what they was supposed to do by way of effecting a quiet transfer of property. They wanted no violence. Reg was allowed to get dustily up and told to put into the hands of these gentlemen here on orders of the Home Office what was claimed to be their property and no more nonsense. Another bomb sounded off somewhere but the sergeant said to take no notice, that was being taken care of by them at the front. Reg said he gave in, made as, with a sort of bow even, to convey into the charge of the one who had looked like Major Mashuk but perhaps was merely a brother or cousin the weapon that had good Russian blood dripping from its point, then changed his mind, lunged at a waistcoat that drew back, regretfully menaced the sergeant, then saw that the corridor was filling with Sons of Arthur the police could not hold off. There was a great deal of violent speech which Reg did not have leisure nor inclination to follow. He was sure that one of the Embassy men was now drawing a gun. Not having that sir, not here. Reg stumbled towards the fresh air that he could feel on his burning face, then on the back of his neck as he backed, stumbling and lunging. There was an open street door round that corridor bend, voices of people passing. He ran away from confusion and a constable prepared for a flying tackle, kicked a damnably full rubbish bin in the path of pursuit, then met night, air, some broken steps, the waiting car.

A car with a doctor's sticker on its windshield had the privilege of unchecked speed and the flouting of traffic signal pedantry. As they turned right on to Marylebone Road and sped towards Euston Station, Dr Lewis or Levi said; 'Romantic to the last. Settle down now. Enjoy life if you can, not that there's much to enjoy. I hope the Russkies are enjoying Van der Weyden the Elder's Entombment of Christ and Van der Weyden the Younger's Magdalene and Dierick Bouts's Exhumation of St Hubert. They're going to be able to enjoy them in perpetuity now, I suppose. Well, they always were an antisemitic lot of bastards.' Reg did not see the connection.

CHAIM WEIZMANN, first president of Israel, was in his late seventies, not well, ready for death in a year or so. He had things to say to the General Assembly of the United Nations, to the Congress in Washington, and to his old University of Manchester, so he had better say them soon. That I was invited to accompany him as head of a personal bodyguard was less a tribute to my devotion and efficiency than a memento of his old friendship with my grandfather. He was prepared to travel first class on a commercial aircraft of El Al, but it was considered proper to the dignity of a new sovereign nation that he be provided with a personal plane with presidential insignia on the fuselage. So I and my four men, one of whom was an immigrant out of Llanelly, flew in comfort at the rear of the aircraft, dozing, flipping through *Time* and *Newsweek*, brooding on the dirty whipped cream of the clouds, accepting kosher snacks and London gin from the *sabra* stewardess. She was one of the new pared breed of Israeli women, not an ounce of voluptuousness on her, no chestnut tree to oppress Roquentin. I had trained girls like her, very serious girls not given to flirtation, and admired them without loving them. I had not had much of a love life in Israel. Sex was a supererogatory treat, like Kant or Hegel. I sometimes yearned for the philosopher's lecture room as I yearned for suburban peace, unhurried love in a lawful bed, a wife's morning singing and the smell of coffee as I shaved. I did not think, despite the field officer's pay and the sufficient comfort of the mess and single quarters, that I would be renewing my contract.

Weizmann had stressed that this was not a state visit and that his entry into the United States should be unobtrusive as possible. Israel had enemies who might welcome the slowmoving targets of a formal parade on the tarmac, and US security ought not to be gratuitously burdened. So we were met at Idlewild only by an official of the State Department and, naturally, the Israeli ambassador. We were whisked through the entrance formalities, led to automobiles whose regality diminished with rank, and escorted by police motorcyclists through Queens to Manhattan. We were accommodated in the Plaza Hotel on Central Park, where in my room a door or two down from the president's suite, the armourer of the Israeli Embassy, or so I took him to be, issued me with five .45 Baraks and holsters for myself and my team. Officially, the Americans being sensitive about foreign nationals bearing guns, we were to do our duty unarmed.

Actually, the American visit was a fairly placid one. An Arab hothead at the United Nations building cried something about a *jihad* before attempting to fire on Weizmann, but it was US security that winged him. In Washington there was a great welcome for Weizmann and no trouble. He proposed spending the weekend in Connecticut with his old friend Aaron Rapaport, the historian of science, and on the Monday morning we were to fly not first to Heathrow but directly to Ringway. Weizmann had more affection for Manchester than for London, which he

311

associated with antizionism and false promises, and the talk he was to give at the university was to be a nostalgic gesture of affection. It was considered that it would be cumbersome as well as indiscreet to take an Israeli guard to Connecticut, and a couple of quiet Americans in the woods would take care of security. This meant a free weekend for my team and myself. I patted the wad of dollars in my hip pocket and went out into the spring Manhattan evening, ready for any adventure within reason.

In a dark bar on West 57th Street I met Irwin Roth. I had met him only once before, in wartime London, but I had seen his photograph – one of the brooding genius type – on the back of his big bad novel, and Irwin Roth was telling drinking strangers that he was Irwin Roth. He was also telling them that the work of Norman Mailer was shit, and the barman was saying to cut it out. 'Irwin Roth,' I said. 'Permit me to stand you a drink. The very least I can do to show my appreciation of an overwhelming literary experience.' He turned to me with the childlike gratitude of a failed author and said he would have a scotch on the rocks. 'As a matter of fact,' I said, after a 'Cheers' that rang Britishly and was mocked in a dark corner, 'we met once in London. You were with a fellow student of mine. You eventually married her.'

'Fellow student,' he jeered in an inept imitation ofmy accent. 'One of the army that screwed her or was screwed by her. I know all about her distinguished student career. Screwdent, more like it.' You can always tell a bad author by the way he laughs at one of his own bad puns. I kept my temper. I said:

'That is unworthy. She was a very beautiful girl and undoubtedly still is. I once had very honourable aspirations in her regard. I congratulate you on winning where I failed.'

'Look,' he said, in a voice of low would-be menace, 'there's no need to give me that literary bullshit. Honourable aspirations. Fuck you, my friend, and all that rot. She's run out. I know England. Nice little ladylike fucks under the appletrees and behind the chintz curtains. That was wonderful darling over the tinkling teacups. No no no to the hairy dark gods. Not English. Not genteel. Leave my ladylike ass, I do so beg your pardon, *arse*, leave it alone. And don't talk to me about blood and ancestry and all that rot, because it's culture finally tells. A low grade

312

ladylike culture, Miss Mitford and the vicar coming to tea under the fucking appletrees.'

'You watch that, feller,' the bartender said.

'Well, isn't it, isn't it? You're anaemic, the lot of you. Charming decadence, let the big dark hairy wind blow and you crumple.'

'Speaking,' I said temperately, 'as a Jew and an officer in the Israeli army – '

'Importing the rot there too, speckles of rot on the Jaffa oranges. Don't give me that shit. I'll have another of those.'

'This time you pay. Out of your fat royalties. Blockbusting epic of American heroism and true grit.'

He searched my eyes, the same colour as his, for glints of sarcasm. 'I could buy and sell your ass,' he said. 'She's blown, I tell you. Couldn't take it. The realities of passion, too too terrible my dear. Taking her dinky underwear and her Pushkin in the original. Let us read passionate Pushkin together, my dear. So Byronic, so civilized. She'll be back. And when she's back she'll be screwed out of her tiny ladylike mind, fucked to her delicate eyebrows before she's set more than one ladylike little tootsie through the doorway.'

'Where,' I asked, 'has she blown to?'

'How the stinking hell would I know where? Talked about working her ladylike passage, I'll fucking work it for her.'

'Mr Roth,' the bartender said with quiet intensity, 'I said more than once for you to watch that. This is a respectable bar and folks that come here don't want that kinda language.'

'All right, Jack, I'll be ladylike. I'll smell of appleblossom and all that shit.'

'Where?' I asked again.

'Want to recall old days of screwdentship. Ha ha sex under the mulberries or sycamores. This is a great big city, my little friend. She said her old Welsh dad did it so she will too. Shipwrecked marriage, she said, oh very poetical, foundering Titan of literature. Make her way without my lousy help.'

'I want to know where.'

'I want another of those.'

'You've had enough, Mr Roth,' the bartender said earnestly. 'If I was you I'd get some chow inside of you. No good on an empty stummick.'

'Join the chowline, yes. Line up in the messhall. *Maachol*. Or is it *pishcha?*'

'One's Hebrew, the other's Russian,' I said. Then I thought I saw a kind of light. 'Working as a waitress, is she?' I asked. 'In some restaurant or other?'

'Screw in the stink of hot grease,' Roth said, mumbling rather. 'Make the pots and pans rattle. Go on, fuck off,' he then said, 'go on with your building of the new Jerusalem, kosher sex and skin the Arabs. Hi, Ralph,' he said to a bald bearded spectacled dwarf who had just come in in a dirty shirt and an old velveteen jacket. 'Little lamb, who made thee?' The newcomer said not to knock Blake. Here was evidently a writer not ashamed to wear failure as a badge; Roth was dressed ready for any literary photographer who wanted a successful brooding genius. I paid and left, ignored. New York, I was reminded, as I stood undecided on the high hot street, was one hell of a big city.

I went back to the Plaza to look up the names of Russian restaurants. I knew only the Russian Tea Rooms near Carnegie Hall. Then I remembered that my warrant officer, Jascha Grossman, had proposed for himself a lone leisurely meal in the hotel restaurant at Israeli government expense, and that he was a native New Yorker. I found him on a second course of Jerusalem artichokes with a vinaigrette dressing. Grossman was an apt enough name: sweat and vinegary oil clung to the stubble that advertised that he was off duty. But his eyes were the mournful ones of exile, as yet unsettled into the calm indifference of one to whom the new Israel was a home. 'Russian restaurants?' he said in his Brooklyn accent. 'There used to be plenty in Brooklyn. In Manhattan they're not run by Russians. It's all fancy dress and balalaikas. Wait a second.' The ravaged artichokes were removed. 'The best thing is to look in the yellow pages. If you wanted to do a taxi tour I'd go with you myself, major, but I'm kind of committed here.'

Back in my room I looked. There had once been a Nevsky Prospect, but no longer. There was a Bifshtyeka, a Pchela, a Svyokla and one called Ivan's. I telephoned them all, at Israeli government expense, and spoke of an urgency – a waitress named Beatrix or Beatie or Trixie whose brother had just landed in New York with an important message. A pretty girl, blonde.

I got no courteous replies, mostly Look, mister, we're busy; Some has one name some has another, I can't know them all; if you don't want to book a table don't waste my time. I rang the Kukhnya and the voice said did I mean the cook? Perhaps I did. I got a cab and was driven over the bridge to Flatbush.

The point about the name of the restaurant was that the kitchen or *kukhnya* was on full view. It was a kind of altar with an officiating priestess and a boy acolyte. You saw your borshch come out of the pan and the sour cream slapped on to your *aguryets* with a wooden spoon. It was Beatrix all right, in white, hair capped, face and arms rosy at the fire, busy. It was best not to disrupt service, so I sat and ordered. The restaurant was full and I had to share a table with a fat man of the insurance broker type and his little son, into whom he shovelled beetrooty soup the boy did not like. I could afford to wait: I had found her. I ordered chicken *à la Kiev* and a bottle of beer. The chicken *à la Kiev*, which tried, on cutting, to spurt butter on to my university tie, was authentic. Food was a sort of temporal language, a link between the generations with no Great Vowel Shift. It was she who had cooked it who now made contact. She was at my table, leaving some Russian dessert or other to her acolyte. 'It can't be you,' she said, 'but it is.'

'It can be very much me. Very much is. Sit.'

'No, I don't sit with the customers. Quite a coincidence.' She smelled faintly of cooking fat.

'No coincidence at all. I've been looking for you.'

'How did you know?'

'You can always find who you're looking for if you use your imagination a little. Your husband talked about a shipwreck. That was the chance part of the thing. A bar.'

'Of course a bar. Drunk, was he?'

'Drunk. He hinted something about earning enough for a ticket homeward bound. But he said you'd be back penitent and copulated with but good on the doormat.'

'I'm not going back, penitent or otherwise. I've already saved a hundred dollars.' Something flared on the altar kitchen. 'We close in an hour. See you then.' And her exquisite legs hurried her to the flare. The little boy at my table followed the *borshch* which he did not like with *marozhenoye* which he did. It was only vanilla ice cream with an invisible *schlyapa* on.

Beatrix came out of the restaurant in a simple orange shift dress when it closed. I had been smoking up and down the sidewalk: smoke made the little boy cough. There was still a faint whiff of fat about her. She said she shared an apartment with a girl underlibrarian at Long Island University. She would be in tonight, having quarrelled with her boyfriend; perhaps we ought to go to a bar somewhere and talk. I said:

'You're coming back to the Plaza with me. No funny business. No sexstarved advances. You can sleep in the president's bed if you like. He's away for the weekend.'

'President?' I told her all. I ended by saying:

'Keep your hundred dollars. There's plenty of room on the presidential plane. Old Chaim likes pretty girls who speak Russian.'

'This is madness. What do I go as?'

'My betrothed perhaps. Who, by the way, is going to divorce whom?'

'I thought there might be a catch in it.'

'A temporary fiction only. But saying this is my betrothed and your not contradicting it may help put the nonfictional idea into your head. Which, if I may say so, is a very lovely one.'

'The idea or the head?'

'Both.'

I flagged a taxi. The driver, whose displayed certificate gave the name of the author of *I Promessi Sposi*, was overtalkative. Hearing our accents, he asked if we was in show business. He'd been good with the puppets – he took his paws off the wheel to demonstrate as we went over the bridge – but folks didn't want puppets no more. Beatrix and I pretended to listen; she would not allow me to take her hand. In the Plaza lobby she was clearly admired, and a hotbreathing neckless Armenian inched closer to her in the elevator. In my room I removed my tie and rang for large gins and tonic water. I asked why she had done it.

'I thought it was possible to base a rational contract on irrational chemistry. I had to be punished. Sex isn't love.'

'Nobody ever said it was. But sex can be a poem of affection. The routine of marriage dissolving into a glimpse of the absolute.'

'You still talk like an undergraduate.'

'Thank God or El for my innocence. But not for yours. Admit it, you fell for him because he was a Jew. There's something in the genes of your family, thirsting for miscegenation. Well, here's another Jew who made a proposal long before he did.'

'I want to go back to work. That's what I was saving up for. Not just to go home when there's no home.' Her eyes were tired; I imagined how lovely they would be one morning waking, me waking first to watch her wake. She looked, a little unfocused, at my eyes, which probably sparked predatorily but cleanly. She said: 'What gets into them all? He kept saying the hell with Mosaic sex, we don't want to populate the wilderness.'

'There's still a wilderness to be populated.'

'Can you see me as a Jewish mother? Can you see me as a mother at all? I just don't have the instinct. I want to go back to work.'

'I shan't be staying there, you know. I want to teach philosophy somewhere where bombs don't go off. I want a bit of peace.'

'You won't get it. Nobody will get it, not anywhere.' She yawned as it were intimately, that is to say without covering the back of the hand and without apology. 'It's the heat more than the work that gets you.' She then pulled herself together and looked concerned. 'I can't just walk out on them. I ought to give them notice or something.'

'Telephone now. Or in the morning. The presidential bed awaits. I'll ring down for the key.'

'Here will do.' And she flopped on to my bed, still dressed though not dressed in much, kicking off her shoes as she did so. It was an act as intimate as her yawn, but there was no invitation in it. I had been promoted or demoted to a brother. So it was I who sought the presidential bed. In my notebook I found the Connecticut telephone number and got a somewhat wineflown Chaim Weizmann on the line. This is sudden, he said. No, not really. An estrangement, a reconciliation, an affiancement. A graduate of Manchester, a *shiksa* yes, but a half-Russian, speaker of one of the tongues of Jewish exile. Felicitations from the president, and no objection.

Beatrix's luggage was as spare as her dress. We went to

Brooklyn together to get it. Her roommate Janice, who was wet-eyed over something, a quarrel with her boyfriend perhaps, went my my at the suddenness of it and, while Beatrix was packing her books, pushed me fiercely into a corner of the little sitting room with a bullfight poster on the wall and said I gotta be good to her. I was a kind of brother, I said. Don't give me that, brother (a neutral address, not ironic), I know men. I wish to God I did, I said, I wish to God I knew anything.

I wish to God I had kept my eye on my function on that trip. I was being paid by the Israeli government to protect its president, but what could be safer than a trip home? Beatrix sat next to Weizmann in the forward cabin while I and my yawning team lounged at the rear near the toilet or *beth kavod*. Weizmann came up four times on the flight to use it (an old man's bladder, he said jocularly the fourth time) and on each occasion paused to congratulate me. Her Russian was better than his, her economic good sense remarkable, what an acquisition, *shiksa* or not, to the infant republic.

We put down at Ringway in spring civil twilight. Civil twilight occurs when the sun is more than six degrees below the horizon and the light is not good enough for outdoor work. The deeper twilight is termed astronomical. Weizmann, Beatrix and myself had come home. The president had insisted on informality: he needed no official welcome to a city he knew better than either its consular or civic functionaries. The university vice-chancellor had arranged for three hired limousines to take his party to the Midland Hotel, and a sort of hostess for important arrivals conducted us towards them through customs and immigration. Her high heels clicked impressively and seemed to snip a way through the knots of people with handbaggage. We passed through the elegant concourse hall with its chandeliers in procession, Beatrix with Weizmann behind our conductress, an upswept blonde in what looked like chic mourning, the rest of us unalert though armed by favour of the Embassy in Washington. We did not see the dark man with the pistol pointed in two hands pushed forward in a parody of prayer, near to the entrance for his quick tennis-shoed getaway. Beatrix did. She pushed Weizmann, and Weizmann fell heavily. She got three successive bullets and danced back elegantly in three quick

318

successive movements to the percussion, three rimshots of my sister, three-four time in a moderate allegro tempo. There were screams, though none of hers. Then she fell on to Weizmann.

'SO it's to be a republic now,' Reg grinned. 'And you don't need the regal emblem you've evidently come to get. This, by the way, is the new landlord. Llewelyn Price, meet Aled Rhys and two of his associates. They're different from last time, so I'm afraid I don't know their names. Sons of Arthur, if you've heard of the organization. *Not* good customers. They always come at closing time.' Llewelyn Price turned from checking the contents of the spirits shelf and nodded. He was a small stern man with blue jaws and the manner of a clergyman. He had played a grimly efficient game of darts with one of the regulars that evening, winning easily so as to show who was in charge. and his score on the blackboard had the neat regularity of hymn numbers. Aled Rhys said:

'We'd better go outside.'

'You propose beating me up in the dark?'

'Don't be silly.' The two men with Aled Rhys could have been anything – Turks perhaps, They did not open their mouths for some time, so there was no Welsh culture to print evanescently on the damp spring moonlit air. They all stood under the talkative leaves of the great tree, well illuminated by the harsh bulbs of the bar, and one of the two associates gloomily picked at the bark. Reg lit his pipe. 'That's new,' Aled Rhys said. 'You were always a cigarette man.'

'The king is dying of cigarettes. One of the usurping Hanoverians. Call this a kind of wry loyalty.'

'Yes, you're right about the republic. It'll be a long time before we see it, but the work has to go on.'

'Meaning robbing old ladies and blowing up letterboxes just at the moment some little kid or other posts a message to Santa Claus.'

'It has to go on.'

'And who will Wales be in the hands of? The people who get the mining concessions? I've been reading an article by a geologist in the *Times*. Uranium deposits in Colorado, the Belgian

Congo, Joachimsthal, and, believe it or not, the Brecknock Beacons.'

'We want that thing back.'

'Thing, is it? Why – to hand over to the Russians?'

'Have you had a visit from the Russians? Or from the police?'

'A plainclothes man came to talk to me earnestly. His accent seemed strange. I think it was Ulster.'

'We want it back. The new Cymru needs all the friends it can get. Where is it?'

'If you and your pals want to beat me up to get that information we'd better get out of the hearing of the new landlord. The Romano-Celtic diggings would be appropriate.'

'We don't like violence, but we can use it if need be.'

'As I expected. I'll tell you one thing, it's not leaving the country with me. It'll stay where it belongs. In the Lloegr where Arthur used to rule.'

'Duff him up, is it?' one of the Turks or Macedonians said.

'Not necessary, Ianto. There's only one place it could be.'

'Tell me,' Reg said.

'You know and I know. We'll get it.' And then: 'So. Leaving the country then. Dissatisfied with postwar Britain and no bloody wonder. The States, is it? The diminishing colonial empire?'

'Joining my wife. All packed and ready and the luggage sent on in advance. Not much. Amazing how little I've accumulated. All except one thing. Not what you think. A family more than a national heirloom. Though how could it be national when that nation no longer exists?'

'You've never made such sense.'

'Nation,' the other Turk or Albanian said. 'A national conscience. National assets. National culture.' The accent could be Eurasian. 'An aggregation of people or peoples bound together into a state. I have studied these things.'

'Evidently,' Reg said, impressed. 'Embattled nation is a good phrase too.'

'I have heard all about your cynicism. So I think it would be right that you should be punched a little to teach you a lesson. If you have no objection.' He seemed to bow slightly towards Aled Rhys. Aled Rhys shrugged. Then the new landlord appeared at the door to tell Reg he was wanted on the telephone.

Urgent. Long distance. 'When you have come back from your telephoning,' the student of nations said, 'do not bring any heavy instrument to defend yourself with. You are an educated man though a cynic and will recognize the ritual justice of what has to be done.' Reg went in.

'WERE you beaten up?' I asked.

'They were only trying to frighten me. When you called I was scared enough.' We were walking before breakfast among the Roman ruins that surrounded the kibbutz near Caesarea. I had been sent to supervise elementary arms training for the kibbutz-niks. The coast was not far away, and terrorists had already effected a landing, undetectable by radar, in rubber dinghies. 'Embattled nations,' Reg said, kicking a bit of Roman potsherd. 'I want to show you something. That Yank author who's staying here, he showed it me first. His first name's Saul. No Acts of the Apostles resonance. The man David played the harp to. We've got to find a name for our little *sabra*. That was a miracle if you like. A bloody bomb in a bloody radio studio. She was behind her tubular bells at the time.'

'I was away.'

'I know you were away. Planting bombs in Syria or some-where. It's all bombs nowadays, isn't it? But it's the real thing here. The embattled Celts are only playing games. Ah, here it is.' He kicked at jagged chunk of sandstone. A kind of rough hollow had been chiselled into it, and clearly to be seen was the chiselled inscription REG ART. 'Does that mean he was here too? It doesn't seem possible.'

'That probably means REGULUS ARTIFEX or something. A surviving slave name. There aren't many. Pathetic, really, a kind of desire to be noticed by posterity. A name may be the only kind of immortality we have.'

'What do we call him? For that matter, what do I call myself? Is there a Hebrew equivalent for Reginald? I suppose Jones would be ben Yokanan or something.'

'You can't turn yourself into a Jew, you know that. It's enough that Zipporah is.'

'No more Zip, I see. Irreverent, I see that. We're in Mosaic territory.'

'Ah no, we're not. God never allowed him to see the promised land.'

'Bit of a bugger, God.' Reg then looked at the clear sky as if to see whether a punitive fist would streak out of it, and then at the orange groves. 'The roots get tangled in Roman ruins,' he said. 'The tangerines are good. The bananas too. Saul whatsisname pointed out the equine connection – flowers like stallions' pizzles, leaves like horses' manes.'

'How long will you stay?'

'Till Zip, sorry Zipporah, has had enough rest. I'd rather like the idea of being an orange farmer, but the big city calls. I'm learning to read Spanish in Hebrew script. Funny, this nostalgia of the Sephardim for their Iberian exile.'

'We all have to have a nostalgia for something. George Herbert said something about weariness tossing us to God's breast. God who is our home, says Wordsworth. I wish I believed in God.' Reg looked up again at the intensely clean sky, but God apparently was not interested in the denial of his existence: he knew he existed, and that was enough. Hope and charity, of course, were a different matter. 'Still, philosophers have to be sceptics. Or prospective teachers of philosophy.'

'Isn't your father going to be disappointed? Giving up the vendetta, I mean.'

'My father's going to marry a nice plump widow from Cracow. He'll be all right.' Reg sniffed the odorous air, but no odour came through. His loss of the olfactory sense was shutting him off from a great deal of the aesthetic pleasure of the Israeli land. The very grass was fragrant with orange zest. But there was the rankness of cordite somewhere to the north. He said:

'She's teaching now. You'll be together. Your departments overlap.'

'I never really had much chance there, you know. We'd better go to breakfast.' We stumbled through the remains of Caesarea, the broken limbs of superseded godlings, a great scowling stone mask of tragedy, past a whole fallen Corinthian pediment towards the dining hall. Reg asked:

'What would *you* call him?'

'I don't know. I thought that was one of the exquisite agonies of parenthood. Name this child. Be careful – he has to carry it through life.' Or, I thought, till the enemy bullets see him off. For breakfast there was strong tea in glasses with *zarfim*, there were fried eggs, pieces of goat's cheese, sweet onions, black olives and very firm tomatoes, salty sardines. An intellectual discussion was going on between Saul why has the name forsaken me and a Swedish gentile with a dark wife like Zipporah. Zipporah was not present at the communal meal. She was busy being a young mother in the married quarters. One of these days she was going to teach percussion at the conservatory in Jerusalem. We were all ending up as teachers. With two academic incomes Reg and Zipporah would be able to afford a nurse. There was no shortage of nurses in Israel: the young prickly pears had to be as well tended as the oranges. 'So what happened to it?' I asked Reg. He told me.

SAITH

IN the middle of the street three cats, one of them spotted, chewed growling at the fishheads and fishguts Dan had thrown. The Good Friday sunset was obscured by the smoke of a warehouse fire some blocks away. In that warehouse there was said to be an unexploded bomb. The firemen were on strike. Every bugger seemed to be on strike. The power had failed and half a halibut glowered towards putrescence in Dan's little fridge. But, power or no power, the trade was decaying. The small shops could not compete with chain stores. The pubs were doing all right, though, and today they had been open all day, as for the weekly Thursday market, for Netherbury guarded jealously an ancient blasphemous charter that permitted carousal and vomiting to celebrate the death of Christ. Dan went to the dark stockroom with a candle and brought out the howling half halibut. Buggers might as well have it. He chopped it into three chunks on his slimy counter and hurled these at the yowlers for more. Pussypieces the chain fishmongers called cat-stuff. On Dan's counter kippers lordlily defied nature and putrefaction. But nobody wanted his kippers. Dan's brother Reg arrived slipping on the cobbles, wearing a raincoat and carrying a heavy gladstone. 'Thirst,' he said. 'Dying of it. Like Dives howling for the cooling finger of Lazarus.'

'How did you do it what with trains on strike and all?'

'A very curious chance. In Newport I met an old army comrade, RSM on that bloody deathship carrying human meat on the hoof to Odessa. Me old Vegetable Marrow. Me old meat and two veg. Driving his son's car with his two grandkids. At Cheltenham I found the last bus travelling north. I got a lift in a lorry at Stoke. I've walked five miles. Hence the thirst. Take this, the weight's become murderous. Lock up. I'm parched.'

In the public bar of the Crown some candles stuck in their own grease went out on their windy entrance. The entrants were cursed. Certain blinkers, befuddled but their noses still sharp, made melodramatic gestures of disgust at Dan's ancient fishiness. Reg paid for their pints and they stumbled over a floored drunk unnoticeable in the dark to a settle in a dark corner. 'Better,' Reg panted, having sunk half.

'What's in it?'

'You know damned well what's in it.'

'You're a bloody thief and always were.'

'Not this time,' Reg, bloody thief, lied. 'Mother gave me the key in Leningrad. It has to go to you and Trix. Worth a packet now.'

'How is she?' Dan did not mean their mother.

'You got my second telegram?'

'Just before the post office went on strike. How is she?'

'The bullet wounds were all peripheral, meaning that they didn't touch anything vital. Elbow, wrist, shoulder. She was lucky. She was also in all the papers. Did you see the papers?'

'I don't read papers. A lot of lies.'

'But the shock was intense and she's still under sedatives. She kept asking for someone called Dan, so they said on the telephone. That may have been her delirium. So I take you.'

'Where is she?'

'In a very posh nursing home in Didsbury. All at the expense of the Israeli government. Why does that fat bastard there keep looking at us and holding his fat podgy snout?'

'You keep forgetting that you can't smell.'

'That's right. A kind of war wound. We're a terribly wounded lot. How's the hole?'

'Keeps dripping.'

'Look at the futile bastards. Ennobled by the candleflames, sort of.' Redjowled topers downed laughing pints at the bar. 'Dealers in plastic.'

'That thin one there keeps a toyshop. He's got the shakes, see.'

'Christ, that looks like the one. How the hell did he – '

325

'What? Who?'

'No, it's not. I've had the feeling I've been followed. They swore they'd get it. What's that light?'

'That's the fire round the corner. Letting it burn out. Every bugger's on strike. How do we get there?'

'Take the road. Plenty of God's light if he made it. A Good Friday moon. Pick up the odd lift. Your shout.'

'The till's near empty. Have to be yours again.'

Reg went back to the bar, where an ill-made man in a ludicrously well-cut suit asked him how he could stand the bloody reek. Stand anything within reason from a brother. There's chlorophyll, why doesn't he take chlorophyll? You're lucky to be able to smell, paying. Dan said:

'Why is it called Good Friday?'

'Because they stuck a Jew up on a cross and giggled while they watched him die.'

'And that's why it's good?'

'Sup that lot up and let's get out of here. Should be Black Friday really, but the epithet's reserved to Monday. Every Monday. In a well run state Monday would be the Sabbath. But then there'd be Black Tuesday. You can't really win.' Reg then quoted: ' "The whole world is our hospital, endowed by the ruined millionaire." Eliot stole that from a Bach cantata – *Die ganze Welt ist ein Krankenhaus.*'

'Who's Eliot? Who's the other bastard?'

'Never mind. Let's be on our way.'

They left the pub by way of the outdoor urinal. The moon, two days off the full, had risen. A man in the one small unlockable jakes strained and groaned. A stone sink in the open air had a dripping tap lunarly illuminated. Somebody had chalked on the brick above it ALL SOAP ABANDON. Reg and Dan stumbled under the moon back to the little shop on the row of little shops. Cats, full-fed on bad halibut, lay on the cobbles washing furry drumsticks, digesting before the night's business. An old woman was chuntering at the door. Shut up, missis, all shut at this hour. Dan unlocked. She wanted a couple of pair of kippers for her son-in-law's tea. Dan served and then rattled coins in his filthy scaly gutty trousers pocket.

'You can't come like that. Put something decent on.'

326

'I've got my demob suit.' Dan mounted dark stairs that led to what Reg knew must be the horror of his bedroom. 'And I'm to bring that bloody thing down too you said.'

'That too. He too takes the road.'

'Be glad to be rid of the bloody thing. Shines like a bad herring all through the night. And then it talks.'

'Talks, does it, does he?'

'When it swings from the string it's hanging from. It says *tad bach* or summat.'

'Interesting. Get a move on.' Dan brought Caledvwlch down wrapped in his gutty scaly striped filthy apron. 'That'll do.' Dan locked up. Taking the road meant first taking a couple of miles of what Netherbury called its High Street. Dan groused at the heavy bag. Reg's burden was light.

'And what'll you do with it?'

'He's mine. He's in my charge. I'll dispose of him as I think fit.'

'Yours, is it? So you're bloody Attila or Arthur or whoever it was. What did you do with dad's books?'

'The encyclopaedia's full of false information. It has a threepage article on anthropophagy with recipes from New Guinea. It says that two lost plays of Shakespeare, called respectively *If You Know Not Me You Know Nobody* and *Take It Or Leave It*, are deposited in a bank in Austin, Texas. It says Beethoven wrote a tenth symphony with a solo piano in the last movement.'

'And he didn't?'

'I gave it to Dr Lewis, as he calls himself. The family Bible has gone on ahead. It may be a useful crib when I get down to the Hebrew. Do you think those two men are following us?'

'Better nip down this alleyway.' The alleyway lay between a newsagent's shop with nude magazines in the window and a barber's pole, a stylized wrapped bloody wound in the moonlight. The moonlight was filthy with smoke. They nipped down. At its end was the bank of the Stanley Canal, a vista of dead factory chimneys beyond. The filthy moon showed an old man at the tiller of a boat loaded with human manure. It neared the lock, and the two young men aboard it began making distorted dance movements. Dan said:

'There was what's called a ferry on that big river when we got into the Ukraine. That old bugger there looks a bit like that one. He thought we were Germans. He handed us over. That was when we started to try to run away.'

'Forget it, Dan, for God's sake forget it. Think back to the old days. They weren't bad really. Distinguished eaters, but you never knew that. Jack Troy the female impersonator and Julie Falcon the soprano and the Greek jugglers and Lavinia Ennis who danced with pasties and a *cache-sexe*. And the great Zeno who sawed women in half and made the audience faint with the artificial blood. And dad as serious as all hell over the pots and pans. And Sir Oliver Ardgour the hanging judge. We had them all.'

'They weren't too bad of times,' Dan said.

Behind them was the hoot and thud of an explosion. The flagstones beneath them shook. 'Jesus,' Reg said.

'It's gone off. They always said it would. Look, it's all filth and mud here. We'd best get back to the road.' At the entrance of the alleyway between a decayed tripe depot and a ruined corset factory they looked cautiously for possible followers. There were none. They proceeded along the endless black street where failed businesses had yielded their premises to departments of state – Ministry of Foodlessness, of Misinformation, of Unemployment, of Disposal of the Useless. A great sandy dog leapt from the open dark door of a dwelling-place and barred their way with zigzag barking. Reg proffered bare Caledvwlch, but the dog snarled as if cheated with a metal bone. Dan swung the heavy gladstone to little avail. Reg picked up a compounded mess of fagpackets and crispbags and threw it. The dog's owner waddled out, a stained bib round his neck, chewing. He said:

'Come on in, Bruce, you don't own whole bloody road.' He fixed sharp eyes, fatbedded, on the travelling brothers. 'Seen the paper?' he said. 'No, you won't have, there being no papers today, today being Bad Friday as my dad used to call it, six feet under now he is. But it's all scandal and adultery when it's not politics. Little girls with their knickers torn off in dark woods, boys with knives and the police all criminals. As for politics, one side as bad as the other, the way I see it. I stick to football, not meaning I play it, got too fat for the running about when I was no more than fifteen. Down, Bruce. It's feeding him that's the trouble, neither of the parties giving a damn about poor starving brute beasts. Trouble ahead, I can tell you. Pocketing their unlawful gains. Well, you mustn't keep me here gassing. The damned pie's nearly all crust, but a man's got to eat.' He dragged in the dog, which rere regardant snarled at the brothers, by its worn collar. It began to rain.

'God Almighty,' Reg said, as they watched the filthy slanting water arrow out of a boiling sky now moonless. They stood in a shop doorway.

'What's those things in the window?' Dan asked.

'Those, dear brother, are condoms. They frustrate human seed that the world be not overpopulated and they enable ordinary people to buy television sets and motor cars. Ah, here comes one.' It did not respond to Dan's raised fishy thumb, nor did the one that followed. This, to their astonishment, was a Rolls Silver Ghost. It glided by in speed and silence.

'There's money somewhere,' Dan growled. 'Some made money while others was doing the fighting. You saw that couple in the back there, snogging away? Somebody's wife with some-body's husband. When the ashtrays get loaded they buy a new one. Where the bloody hell have we gone wrong?'

'You've got that there.'

'Yes, and a bloody ton weight it is. Not like real money, which weighs nothing.'

'It's easing off a bit.' It was. Soon the polluted moon made a shy peep over a cloud continent. They went on through the defiled town and teetered over a water splash. To their left was an overlarge graveyard, and to their surprise a night burial was in progress. 'Torches, for God's sake,' Reg said, 'flares. What body has sinned so much against the light that it has to go down in darkness?'

'You remember when we was kids,' Dan said, 'we lit a fire on one of the graves in Southern Cemetery. A penny box of matches and all that fire inside it. You could burn up the whole world with a penny box of matches. But the wind was always like blowing wrong.' Violently he said: 'Why do they do it? What's in it for them? Killing the bloody innocent.'

'*Malitia* in Latin,' Reg mumbled. 'You end up with *malus*, meaning evil. I wonder if there's any connection with *malum* meaning an apple? Evil tasting good like an apple.'

'Those two, can't remember their names, did themselves in because they couldn't go on. They'd had enough, poor bastards.'

'Forget it, Dan, please try to forget it. The moon looks cleaner now.' He stripped Caledvwlch of its stripes to raise it that it might take fire, but the metal was dull. Still, the flourish conjured an old Ford car and, without benefit of raised thumb, it stopped for them. Dan looked gravely at the moonlit whitehaired driver in steelrimmed glasses and dirty raincoat, a silly thin-lipped smile saying something about a corporal work of mercy.

'I know you,' Dan said. 'It was in Flaxfield Street Elementary.'

'Taught you, did I? It must be a long way back. Hop in, both. Can't take you far. Turton any good to you?'

'Thanks,' Reg said. 'It's on our way.'

'You gave me the strap once,' Dan said without malice from the back. 'It hurt like bloody hell.'

'Was meant to. You were an unruly lot. Didn't strap you, did I?' he said to Reg.

'I wasn't there. I went to a mixed school.'

'Yes, I know the sort of thing. Little girls wetting their knickers. Halfpenny feels in the back row. Small boys were always my line. Too much my line the authorities eventually decided. It takes all sorts to make a world.'

'It bloody well hurt,' Dan said, still without malice.

'All in the interests of discipline. I was never a sadist. I took my pleasures circumspectly and, yes, lovingly. That your line at all?' he asked Reg. Reg shook his head. 'What's that long phallic thing in your lap?'

'A weapon.'

'I see. Well, with all the charity that Good Friday night can bestow I feel I have to set you down here. I've a weak stomach. I can't stand that smell your friend is powerfully raying out from the back.'

'Fish,' Reg said. 'My brother.'

'Splendid. Here then. Sorry it hurt like bloody hell.'

They still had not arrived at open country, though the shops and terraced dwellings were giving out here. Three tarnished brass balls and a window full of horrid gewgaws proclaimed a pawnbroker's shop. A cinema poster with torn shreds flapping in the rainy wind showed a naked giant with kettledrum pectoral muscles and a gorilla's head shoving halfnaked screamers down a ravine. Yelling heads bobbed on a bloody river. 'God God God,' Reg went. They came to a Wesleyan chapel deconsecrated into a bingo hall. A brick wall with broken glass on top stretched far, a county loony bin. The wall was heavily plastered with electioneering posters showing men untrustworthily smiling. There was an advertisement for Madam Zelda, who told fortunes. Reg raised the sword against mad screams coming from a barred open window but could not exorcise them. On the road was a tarred stretch which to Dan smelt fresh and wholesome. The roller stood cold and the spades unprotected: the workers had downed tools on Maundy Thursday. A croaking of frogs rose from an unseen but putrid-smelling ditch somewhere. They were coming into country. A pub or inn stood alone with bare trees by it. The spring was late here, the leaves slow. The rain started again. 'I could do with a pint,' Dan said. 'How much money do you have?'

'Enough. Enough to get us on a Manchester train when the strike stops and me further south. Enough for a couple of pints and perhaps a wrapped industrial pie with wormy minced guts inside it.' They went in.

'Let's have them glasses,' the scrawny landlady said without conviction. 'There's a new police sergeant and he's a right bastard. I don't want to lose my licence, do I?' She served Reg and Dan willingly with a pair of flat bitter pints or near. There were some jellied eels in a jar. A London delicacy, and a London woman by her accent. Reg and Dan shared a pork pie that tasted of old newspaper. An old merchant sailor from his cap and grizzled beard sat by the dying fire and held the floor. Dan said quietly, nodding towards one of the sailor's audience:

'See that one with the black patch on his gob? Cancer of the jaw, that is. I know the bastard. He's a bluey man. Steals lead from on top of churches. See that little sod with him? Pickpocket on market days. Drunk farmers. Wads of cash on them through selling pigs already dying with worms in the belly. A terrible bloody world.' The sailor was saying:

'Gib it was. Coming out of Gib and making for Ceuta. Don't suppose any of you lot here knows Gib.'

'I was there,' Reg said.

'Right, then you'll know. Got them aboard pissed as newts and all poxy from the knockingshops.'

'No knockingshops in or on Gib.'

'Who's telling the story? The skipper says right, you've had a bloody bad time what with the war and the cruel sea, reading man he was, but remember what you are, you besotted buggers. British and ought to be proud of it. And there you go behaving like animals and brute beasts of the field. Use your bonces, learn a bit, read the Bible. Mad on the Bible he was, used to yell chunks of it out to the wind in the rigging. Well, when we bought it with one of those magnetic mines, he yelled out that it was the judgment come upon us, read Matthew six, fifteen. That was on the North Atlantic run. He could be seen in the water crying out about the Book of Revelations. Then he went under. My point being that the Bible is all a mockery.'

'Let's have them glasses.'

'Proper pong in here,' the bluey man said, peering at Dan. 'Seen you around, haven't I?'

'Not on top of churches.'

'You too,' he said to Reg.

'Not reciprocated.'

'Who are you with your jawbreakers?' The door opened and a police constable entered. He was a tall thin youngish man with a gangster's tash. He said:

'I'll have a pint, missis, seeing as I'm on duty. All right, don't get scared,' he said to the company, 'there's big crimes and little crimes and drinking after hours is not one of them. At least, not when three stripes is not in the offing. In bed with a cold.'

'Not one of what?' Reg asked.

'Who are you?' the constable asked. 'What's that you're carrying? And what's that him there has got in that bag?'

'Private property,' Reg said. 'Travellers in the night. Toothbrush and pyjamas and a change of underwear. Nice to have met you. Must be on our way.'

'Looks a heavy bloody change of underwear to me. A dead weight from the look of it. Come on, you, stinker, open up.'

'Ah no,' Reg said, and bared Caledvwlch. 'Keep your distance.'

'Don't put yourself in the wrong, sonny. Resisting the law's against the law. I'm calling you lot in as witnesses.'

'Not me,' the bluey man said. 'I seen nothing.'

'Now they're going to be after us,' Dan said, leading the way out. The constable barred their exit in three long blue strides. Reg lunged in threat. Dan swung bag to balls. 'Shouldn't have done that,' he then admitted. 'All we want's to get out of here.' The constable mooed in pain, hands on blue stinging crotch. 'Right,' opening the door, 'that's all we wanted.'

They ran a little way under a greasy rain. 'This means that we are, in a manner, on the run,' Reg said. 'Technically, I mean. He's not likely to do much about it.' He stopped running, panting, and rerobed wet Caledvwlch in stripes. There was no sign of a whistling enraged constable at the pub door. 'I think we'll have to doss down for the night somewhere.' Open wet wretched country yielded to a village with no inn but, to its south, a considerable mansion taken over by the Ministry of Pensions. 'Ah, possible transport?' But the roaring bus was coming from the wrong direction, and its blaze caught Reg and Dan full in the eyes as it screeched and stopped by the mansion gate. Out of it monsters, kindly helped by two bluecaped nurses with the extravagant caps of Hope Hospital, tottered or fumbled. 'Oh my God. Look what we missed.' War–mutilated, half-faced, burnt, blind, armless, passed through the gateway. Reg and Dan hid behind a broad elm. The bus roared off. The rain did not ease. Soaked and silent they squelched south until they came to what looked like a barn but turned out to be a shelter for two farm tractors, open to the night. 'This will do,' Reg said. Behind the tractors were oily tarpaulins, empty five-gallon jerry cans, a rusty old jack. 'Dry anyway,' Reg said. Dan said nothing. They sat on gritty concrete, backs against concrete walls. They could not sleep. Dan said at length:

'They called that road the french letter. The weather was just like this. The noise was bloody murder.'

'Forget it, Dan, forget it.' A distant church clock chimed twelve. 'Good Friday's over. Holy Saturday's here.' His wet shoe met something light and mobile. His fingers told him it was of wood.

They later told him it was a discarded child's toy, a little horse on wheels.

'And that big frozen lake and the man and his four kids starved to death. That was in the Ukraine.'

'Forget it, Dan.' Reg willed himself into an uneasy doze.

He woke from a vague dream of Russian giants to find a bright moon, half an inch off the full, ensilvering the dull matt of the tractors. He heard splashing outside. Dan was not here, must be there. He got up groaning to find Dan naked under the moon, tubbing himself in a leaky waterbutt. 'For Jesus Christ's sake.'

'Getting the fish off, aren't I? They won't be able to talk of a pong no more.'

'You'll catch your bloody death.' But it was Reg who sneezed.

'Why don't you get a fire lit in that corner there?' He meant a square yard or so between wall and tractor righthand wheel. 'Dry me. Dry you.'

It was a reasonable notion, but the trouble was finding kindling. Twigs and straw had been blown into the corner. There was a torn old page or two from the *Daily Mirror* with oily fingermarks on it. Reg did his best with these, firing them again and again with his Zippo lighter. He remembered the child's toy horse, brought it, dismembered it, fed. It was not much of a blaze. An oily bit of sacking smouldered long. Reg squelched out to a hedgerow and found more substantial firing – twigs that had sheltered from the rain and what looked like an old thrush's nest. The fire was enough to dry their shoes. Dan tried to scour off his wet with his jacket turned inside out, with Reg's pocket handkerchief, Dan not having one of his own. Reg looked at his wristwatch – nearly four in the morning. His belly rumbled and so did Dan's in echo. They had better push on. The fire died with no need of Dan's crushing boot. Whether Dan smelt less fishy Reg was debarred from knowing.

They came at length to a house abandoned but repossessed. Most of the slates had blown away and slats showed. The windows were broken and the door gone. The house nested in overgrown weeds and straggly bushes. But from within came a guitar twang and out of one of the glassless windows blue smoke issued under the moon. Dan and Reg waded through couchgrass and darnel and entered. In a fireplace newspaper and what looked like fragments of a chair bravely worked at enflaming. On the floor by the fireplace filthy young people sat, two males and a female. One of the males twanged a sixstring E major chord over and over. He, the three of them, looked up vaguely with neither fear nor welcome at the entering pair. But a bearded older man in corduroys, a bare hairy chest and a battledress jacket came through a doorless doorway out of the gloom. He nodded at Reg and Dan and said, without force: 'Repent.'

'Repent of what?' Reg asked. 'Look, do you mind if we get nearer that fire to dry off a bit? It's been a long wet night.'

'But the dawn will come and the sun shine on the repentant. We all carry the sins of the world on our backs.' The girl, who seemed to have dirty strawy hair, yawned very thoroughly. She wore old ATS slacks and a rather becoming furry jacket buttoned up to the chin. Purloined doubtless. 'Drop out of the world. Cultivate humility. Live like the birds.'

'Do I smell?' Dan asked.

'There's a certain fishiness,' sniffing hard. 'Is there food in that bag?'

'Alas,' Reg said.

'Well then. Give us a song, Geoffrey.' The guitarist thrummed his E major chord and intoned in a near monotone:

What we made out of light
The light would not have
So we hollowed out a grave
Where light has forever set.

Caught unawares in breach
Of faith or out of shrift
Or what of festering speech
Upon the air was left.

Like the spent hornblende numb
The eternity eternally to come
Over dead brains we bear
As once we bore the weight of the infinite air.

'But that,' Reg said, 'is hell.'

'Why, this is hell, nor am I out of it,' the singer said. He was

335

not so much bearded and longhaired as long unshaven and uncut.

'Your education has brought you to this?' Reg said. 'What, by the way, is hornblende?'

'Formula $CaNa(Mg,Fe)_4$ $(Al,Fe,Ti)_3Si_6$ $O_{22}(OH)_2$,' the other young man said. 'A mineral of the amphibole group. Such as asbestos, from the negative of the Greek *sbennunai*, meaning to extinguish.'

'Oh no,' Reg shuddered. 'Has it all come to this?'

'Not hell,' the older man said. 'We've all been through that. We seek the way through the refining fire.'

'It's not much of a fire,' Dan said.

'How do you live?' Reg asked.

'We beg. The Benedictines down the road help a little. They give us the first of the morning's milk and a loaf from the bakery. We stew edible weeds in a pipkin.'

'That's what we had to do,' Dan said, 'when we walked away from the prison camp in Poland. We had to do it, and you buggers *want* to do it. It doesn't make much sense.'

'Prison camp? Oh, I see, a soldier. We abjure violence.'

'So,' Reg said, 'there's nothing to protect?'

'Protection entails a willingness to attack. Dilys, it's time for your morning prophecy.'

'Prophesy about the end of the rail strike,' Reg sardonically said.

'Listen.' And the girl held up a dirty finger with a quickbitten nail. A distant whistle seemed to mean a milk train. 'I'll prophesy when I've eaten and not before.'

'I'm getting out of here,' Dan said. 'It smells bad.'

'Listen who's talking,' the guitarist sneered.

'Benedictines, you say?' Reg asked. He gripped Caledvwlch.

'Anglican Benedictines. Three miles down the road,' the older man said. 'Don't beg there. Don't queer our pitch.'

Dan and Reg left. 'According to the map, as I remember from once examining it before a schoolboy excursion, there should be a lake somewhere.'

'These Benny dictines,' Dan said. 'Are they the ones in dad's book?'

'Not quite the ones. I don't know if they connect with Monte

Cassino. I don't think they have any right to him. No. From the vast deep to the vast deep he goes.'

'Barmy,' Dan said.

The Holy Saturday dawn was hinting at the possibility of climbing out of the vast deep when they came to their last village. The moon was setting. The tiny railway station at the village end had lights on in the stationmaster's office, and a yawning porter trundled milk cans towards a lorry. A train had been and gone, but there would be other trains. Dan and Reg felt cold, and Dan shivered. Outside the village was a thickly wooded declivity. There was a smell, though not for Reg, of wet earth and fungoid growths. The birds were not yet stirring. 'It's down there,' Reg said, leading the way, Dan grumbling after. They stumbled through lumpy grass and over fallen branches. Soon they came to the edge of dark cold waters with the setting moon shivering in them. Dan said, thinking of the waters of a long East European trek:

'It's not much of a lake. More like a pond really.'

'Don't quantify. You said you could set the world alight with a penny box of matches. It will do. Now a few words. ''Then Sir Bedivere departed, and went to the sword, and lightly took it up, and went to the water side, and there he bound the girdle about the hilts, and then – '' Arthur spoke of his rich sword, but look at it now,' taking it from the fishmonger's apron. 'Look at the poor dull rusty bastard. In with him.' But he hesitated. Dan did not. He said:

'Right.' He took from the gladstone bag, freeing it from a shirt and the filthy shaving holdall of his army days, the lump of yellow metal that had never been liberated from its grosser matrix. He disclosed a knowledge of cricket that Reg had not suspected, for then he underarmed with vigour and sent the lump plumb to the water, a third of a chain's distance from shore. It sank like lead, or gold.

Reg could hardly speak. 'Why in the holy name of God and all the damnable angels – ' he tried at length.

'Listen,' Dan said fiercely. 'It's like a joke and a bloody heavy one. If that's money I don't want it. Because it's not money at all, it's always going to be money but not just yet. Wait till I die and even then it won't be bloody money. It's always going to be

money but it never is money. Do I carry the thing around for
ever waiting for it to turn into money? That's what *she'd* want
and she's supposed to know all about it. But I say to hell with
it.'

Reg pondered that as birdsong started. 'We've always under-
estimated you, Dan,' he said.

'Did you see that?' Dan said, almost excited. 'It was a fish. If
I'd brought my rod we could have had a bloody good breakfast.
All right,' he then said, as if giving an order, 'let it go. And then
we catch the train.'

Reg gripped Caledvwlch by the middle and hurled.
Caledvwlch span thrice in the moist air and then plummeted flat
to the waters, entering then without raising a bubble. 'Jesus,'
Dan gasped. 'It screamed.'

'Oh no it didn't. Oh no it bloody well did nothing of the
sort. Any more than it bloody well shone like a high herring or
whispered little father in bloody Welsh. Merlin's long gone under
and there's no magic any more. Let's go and see about trains to
Manchester.'

'SO,' I said, as we walked after breakfast, both smoking pipes,
among the oranges and tangerines that Reg could not smell, 'no
arm clothed in white samite, mystic, wonderful.'

'A girl in a white nightgown was drowning herself for love,
and her arm came up for the last time under the fading stars
and grasped at a solidity that was no solidity. Galeblown aspen
branches took and upheld an instant. None of that. It went down
like what it was. Over and out. Amen. Finished. *Consummatum
est.*'

'It was a poor sort of revenge on the hordes of murder.'

'That trick cyclist was right. You can't take revenge on the
past. Law is no good. Justice is no good. The punishment is
always qualitatively different from the crime. Moreover, the
crime's in the past and the punishment in the present. Between
the two runs a timeless river. Lethe is the water of forgiveness.'

'I don't understand.'

'I had to grasp a chunk of the romantic past and find it rusty.
I had to fit myself for the modern age.'

'This is very much the modern age.' I did not add: *Because it's embedded in the past.* Rattles came from the firing range to the north, and then the boom of a bazooka. ' "So all day long the noise of battle rolled," ' I quoted ineptly. 'It goes on. Did you see that little paragraph in the *Jerusalem Post* about your Welsh nationalists?'

'Yes, the idiots. A foiled plot to kidnap Prince Charles. Except for here it's all playacting. And yet you're getting out.'

'You can't be fighting all the time. You ought to be able to take a few deep peaceable breaths now, Reg. You've killed your enemy in cold blood, you've witnessed evil, you've touched the hand of a king who never existed, you've served ale, you've begotten a Jewish son. What more do you want?'

He shrugged. He didn't know. What he wanted, I think, was negative: not to have been reserved for the life of this century. Or he wanted, as we all do, reality transcending time, the kind of thing I was going to teach, changing back to the mufti of drab Manchester. The Roman ruins we stumbled through told us all about injustice that could never be avenged. The citrus fruits outlived them as they would outlive the law of Moses. It was a pity that Reg had lost his sense of smell.

Lugano,
July 1987